Confronting the Bomb

Confronting the Bomb

Pakistani and Indian Scientists Speak Out

Edited by

PERVEZ HOODBHOY

Preface by

JOHN POLYANI

Nobel Prize in Chemistry, 1986

OXFORD

UNIVERSITY PRESS

OXFORD
UNIVERSITY PRESS

Oxford University Press is a department of the University of Oxford.
It furthers the University's objective of excellence in research, scholarship,
and education by publishing worldwide in

Oxford New York

Auckland Cape Town Dar es Salaam Hong Kong Karachi
Kuala Lumpur Madrid Melbourne Mexico City Nairobi
New Delhi Shanghai Taipei Toronto

With offices in

Argentina Austria Brazil Chile Czech Republic France Greece
Guatemala Hungary Italy Japan Poland Portugal Singapore
South Korea Switzerland Turkey Ukraine Vietnam

Oxford is a registered trademark of Oxford University Press
in the UK and in certain other countries

Published in Pakistan by Oxford University Press

ISBN 978-0-19-906833-3

Second Impression 2013

Typeset in ITC Clearface
Printed in Pakistan by
Mas Printers, Karachi.
Published by
Ameena Saiyid, Oxford University Press
No. 38, Sector 15, Korangi Industrial Area, PO Box 8214,
Karachi-74900, Pakistan.

CONTENTS

Contributors

Pervez Hoodbhoy
Matthew McKinzie
Zia Mian
Abdul Hameed Nayyar
R. Rajaraman
Suvrat Raju
M.V. Ramana

Explode, explode, explode the bomb,
The bomb makes Bharat great;
Nor hunger, nor thirst shall then survive,
And hailed shall be the Hindu state.

At which bespoke a roadside wag-
'But didn't Kalam set up the bomb?'
Ah yes, but you do not seem to know
That Kamal was his Vedic name.

Then did Pokharan shudder anew,
Death rolled beneath the sand;
Blessed be the radio-active earth,
Where a temple deserves to stand.

Meanwhile, the world misreads the Buddha,
Who forbade not deterrence, war;
Go write clearly the Dhammapada,
With ink from the Sangh Parivar.

Just then from across the 'enemy' lines
A thunderous noise was heard;
Chagai six mocked the Pokharan five,
The mouse the big cat dared.

Pricked was the pompous balloon of pride,
Saffron thinned out to the pale;
Voices rose from everywhere,
Cut short this bloody tale.

The toiling 'commons', here and there,
The macho sparring cursed;
What fraud this Hindu–Muslim card,
Will either bomb slake our thirst?

Know that the bomb no religion knows,
No nation, no border, no line,
It incinerates with equal heat
The Hindu and Muslim Divine.

The bomb begets no security,
Security is in trust alone,
In peace, awareness, brotherhood,
And a fair life for everyone.

Let go this blasted madness then,
Unite all bordered land;
If security indeed is what you seek,
Go shake the so-called enemy's hand.

— Badri Raina

'Modest Proposal And Other Rhymes' for the Times

AUTHOR BIOGRAPHIES

- **Pervez Amirali Hoodbhoy** has taught at the department of physics at Quaid-e-Azam University since 1973, and now also teaches at the School of Science and Engineering (LUMS). He received a PhD in nuclear physics from Massachusetts Institute of Technology (MIT), as well as degrees in mathematics, electrical engineering, and physics from MIT. He was awarded the Abdus Salam Prize for Mathematics; the Baker Award for Electronics; and the UNESCO Kalinga Prize for the popularization of science. His research interests lie in theoretical high-energy physics. He was a Council member of Pugwash, and is a sponsor of the *Bulletin of the Atomic Scientists*. A strong advocate of the scientific method, he authored: *Islam and Science: Religious Orthodoxy and the Battle for Rationality*. As producer and presenter, he made several documentary series for Pakistan Television aimed at popularizing science as well as for analyzing the Pakistani education system. Hoodbhoy heads Mashal, a book publishing organization in Lahore focusing on modern thought and human rights.

- **Mathew McKinzie** is a senior scientist at the Natural Resources Defense Council (NRDC) in Washington, D.C. He works in its nuclear program which seeks elimination of nuclear weapons left over from the Cold War era. In addition, he works in the NRDC's lands and wildlife program on wilderness and renewable energy issues. McKinzie earned his bachelor's degree in physics from Bard College, and doctorate in experimental nuclear physics from the University of Pennsylvania.

- **Zia Mian** directs the Project on Peace and Security in South Asia at Princeton University's Program on Science and Global Security. His research interests include nuclear weapons and nuclear energy policy in South Asia, and issues of nuclear disarmament and peace. Earlier, he taught at the Yale University and the Quaid-e-Azam University, Islamabad. He worked at the Union of Concerned Scientists, Cambridge (Mass.) and was a Fellow at the Sustainable Development Policy Institute, Islamabad. Mian is Editor of *Science & Global Security*, an international journal for peer-reviewed scientific and technical studies relating to arms control, disarmament and non-proliferation policy. In addition to his scholarly articles, he is the editor of several books and has helped make two documentary films on peace and security in South Asia. He holds a PhD in physics from the University of Newcastle upon Tyne.

- **Abdul Hameed Nayyar** is visiting professor at the School of Science and Engineering (LUMS), Lahore. He received his PhD in solid state physics from Imperial College London in 1973 and served on the faculty of the Quaid-e-Azam University, Islamabad, from 1973 until 2005. Subsequently, he worked as senior research fellow at Sustainable Development Policy Institute, Islamabad, as executive director of Developments in Literacy, and headed the Ali Institute for Education, Lahore. Since 1998, he has been associated with Princeton University's Program on Science and Global Security as a visiting research scientist, and is a member of the International Panel on Fissile Materials. In 2010, he was awarded the Joseph A. Burton Forum Award by the American Physical Society for contributions to society.

- **John Charles Polyani**, won the Nobel Prize in Chemistry in 1986. He has received numerous other prestigious professional awards in chemistry, including the Wolf Prize in Chemistry and the Gerhard Herzberg Canada Gold Medal for Science and Engineering. A Canadian citizen, he teaches at the University of Toronto and remains an active researcher in his field. Polyani was pictured on a Canada Post first class postage stamp on 3 October 2011, issued to salute the International Year of Chemistry. Since the 1950s, he has been involved in matters concerning nuclear weapons. Polyani founded Canada's Pugwash group in 1960, and served as its chairman until 1978.

- **M.V. Ramana** has a joint appointment with the Nuclear Futures Laboratory and the Program on Science and Global Security at Princeton University, U.S.A. After obtaining his PhD in Physics from Boston University in 1994, he worked as a post-doctoral fellow at the Department of Physics, University of Toronto, and the Centre for International Studies, Massachusetts Institute of Technology. He is the author of *The Power of Promise: Examining Nuclear Energy in India* (forthcoming from Viking Penguin). Before moving to Princeton University, he was a senior fellow at the Centre for Inter-disciplinary Studies in Environment and Development in Bangalore. He is also on the national Coordinating Committee of the Coalition for Nuclear Disarmament and Peace (India); a member of the International Panel on Fissile Materials; and serves on the board of the *Bulletin of the Atomic Scientists*.

- **R. Rajaraman** is Emeritus Professor at the Jawaharlal Nehru University; Vice President of the Indian National Science Academy; and Co-Chair of the International Panel on Fissile Materials. After his PhD in 1963 from Cornell University, U.S.A, he was appointed as a member of its faculty and later, at the University of S. California and the Institute for Advanced Study at Princeton. He then returned to India to work at Delhi University, the Indian Institute of Science and finally the J.N.U. Rajaraman has also been a visiting scientist at the Massachusetts Institute of Technology, Stanford, Princeton, Harvard, and CERN. His physics research spans nuclear theory, particle physics, quantum field theory, solitons and Hall systems. His work on nuclear policy issues deals with minimal deterrence, capping nuclear arsenals, fissile material production, nuclear civil defense, and the Indo–U.S. Nuclear Deal.

- Suvrat Raju is a physicist and an activist based in Allahabad, India. He received his PhD in theoretical high energy physics from Harvard University in 2008, and now works at the Harish-Chandra Research Institute. He is active with the Coalition for Nuclear Disarmament and Peace. Suvrat has worked with the peace movement both in India and the United States, on the issues of land rights and democratic rights in India, and has also been associated with the solidarity movements for Venezuela, Cuba and Nepal.

ACKNOWLEDGEMENTS

The book was initially conceived to be a compilation of already published articles relevant to the Pakistan–India situation. But this idea was abandoned and most of the material in the book is new. Those articles included in this volume and published in their original form elsewhere have been revised and updated. Permission from publishers and organizations is gratefully acknowledged for the following:

1. 'Scientists and India's Nuclear Bomb' by M.V. Ramana was first published in *Prisoners of the Nuclear Dream*, M.V. Ramana and C. Rammanohar Reddy (eds.), (New Delhi: Orient Longman, 2003).

2. 'For India Nuclear Electricity is not the Answer' by Suvrat Raju is an updated version of an article that appeared in *Aspects of India's Economy*, No. 48, (2010).

3. 'What Nuclear War Could do to South Asia', by Matthew McKinzie, Zia Mian, A.H. Nayyar, and M.V. Ramana. This was first published in *Out of the Nuclear Shadow*, Zia Mian and Smitu Kothari (eds.), Zed Press (London), Lokayan and Rainbow Press (New Delhi, 2001). Revised and updated second edition, Oxford University Press (Karachi, 2003).

4. 'Pakistan's Nuclear Diplomacy and the Fissile Materials Cut-off Treaty', by Zia Mian and A.H. Nayyar is an updated version of the article first published as 'Playing the Nuclear Game: Pakistan and the Fissile Material Cut-off Treaty', by Zia Mian and A.H. Nayyar, *Arms Control Today*, April 2010.

5. 'The Coming of the Atomic Age to Pakistan', by Zia Mian was first published as 'Fevered with Dreams of the Future: The Coming of the Atomic Age to Pakistan', in *South Asian Cultures of the Bomb: Atomic Publics and the State in India*

and Pakistan, edited by Itty Abraham (Indiana University Press, 2009). This is a revised version of that chapter.

6. 'The Infeasibility of Early Warning', by Zia Mian, R. Rajaraman, and M.V. Ramana is an updated version of the original article published in *Economic and Political Weekly*, Vol. 39, No. 3, 1723, Jan. 2004.

I am grateful to all contributors to this volume, most of whom are associated with the Program on Science and Global Security at Princeton University, USA, where I spent two months during the summers of 2011, 2012.

My greatest debt is to my life-long friend and collaborator, Zia Mian, for his help. His contribution to the volume is not only spread over the many chapters authored or co-authored by him, but also in his criticism of my writings. Although withering at times, it helped me think through issues with greater clarity.

I thank the Heinrich Boll Stiftung which supported the publication of this book. In particular, I am grateful to Britta Petersen for her encouragement and suggestions.

Pervez Hoodbhoy

PREFACE
John Polyani

Nuclear weapons are a plague on the earth, differing from earlier plagues in that they are visited upon us not by God but by man. A plague that is man-made has its origins in a mix of fear, pride and folly.

At the outset of the nuclear age fear dominated. The fear was that Hitler's Germany might secretly arm itself with these ultimate weapons: deadly and indiscriminate. When Hitler's deputy, Rudolf Hess, parachuted into England on 10 May 1941, it was with a message to the King George VI that 'new bombs with stronger explosives'[1] would make inevitable the destruction of Britain. Hess was regarded as mad, and was imprisoned. Meanwhile, the few people who understood the importance of the discovery by Otto Hahn and Fritz Strassmann, made at the Kaiser Wilhelm Institute in Berlin in 1938, that they could split uranium atoms with neutrons, were seriously considering the possibility of a devastating new form of explosive.

Within months of Hess's warning, Leo Szilard and Enrico Fermi, European refugees working at Columbia University in New York, demonstrated the practicability of a nuclear chain-reaction. This demonstration led to the Manhattan Project and thereafter to the two atomic bombs that destroyed Hiroshima and Nagasaki in 1945.

As for Rudolf Hess, whose predictions weren't too far off the mark, he was still considered to be a lunatic and was transferred to a German prison where, forty-two years later, he succeeded in hanging himself at the age of ninety-three. The future comes slowly if, like Hess, you are at the mercy of the bureaucracy, but with the speed of an express train if, like Szilard, you are a free spirit. When things change fast it is because there is a willingness to challenge accepted thinking.

Accepted thinking when Szilard turned his attention to the possibilities of a nuclear chain reaction, was emphatically discouraging. Lord Rutherford, pre-eminent among the founders of nuclear physics, had just stated (*London Times*, 1933) that obtaining energy from atomic fission 'was a very poor and inefficient way of producing energy, and anyone who looked for a source of power in the transformation of atoms was talking moonshine.'

For Szilard, the contrarian, this was a call to action. There had to be a way. He knew enough chemistry to introduce the concept of a branched nuclear chain-reaction, in which every nuclear parent gave rise to two energetic offspring—with Malthusian consequences. At that moment the atomic express train left the station. It will require a similar feat of imagination to stop it.

I was with Leo Szilard in Moscow at an earlier Pugwash Conference in December of 1960, when he described his preferred terminus for the nuclear express, to a Soviet and American elite. He could not resist a Delphic utterance. What was needed, he declared, in order to end the Cold War, was an atomic bomb beneath Moscow wired to an actuator under Washington, and, reciprocally, a second such bomb in Washington wired to a trigger in Moscow. At that level, armament could stop. I was young and callow enough to ask him whether he was serious. What I got in return was an impish grin.

Following World War II the nuclear contagion spread quickly from the United States to the USSR, then on to the UK, France and China. It moved more slowly to India, Pakistan, Israel and North Korea. Nine nations in all—less than had been feared. But the disease remains contagious. With Iran added to the list, expect Turkey, Saudi Arabia and Egypt, which, with Israel, would comprise five nuclear weapons states in, arguably, the most turbulent area of the world.

It is not just fear that renders nuclear weapons contagious. There is pride of possession, ironically most prominent among those within the Nuclear Club, attempting at the same time to limit its membership.

I spoke at the outset of three driving forces: fear, pride and folly, of which folly remains. It resides in the fact that nuclear weapons, though acquired for 'security', heighten insecurity.

In German composer Wagner's Ring Cycle the possessors of gold are similarly cursed by their fear of losing their treasure. Day and night, underground, the Nibelung toil to increase the precious stocks. Fortunately, this folly is no longer entirely unconstrained: the United States and Russia, which together possess 95 per cent of the world's nuclear weapons, have reduced their armory from 70,000 in the 1980s, to 23,000 nuclear weapons today.

Why such a stupendous number, one asks? That was Szilard's question in Moscow. Today, sixty years into the nuclear age, there is serious talk of reducing U.S.–Russian stockpile to a few hundred weapons on either side. What feat of imagination will be required in order to make this a reality? It is no new thought to the military that, with the advent of nuclear weapons, we have left behind the age of Clausewitz. War is no longer diplomacy pursued by other means, since suicide lies outside the domain of the diplomatic. Between nuclear armed powers there is no longer any alternative to diplomacy.

Keeping thousands of nuclear weapons a few minutes away from firing—as is currently being done in the U.S. and Russia—is folly. It does not represent in any sane person's view an alternative to negotiation. Nor is keeping thousands of ballistic missiles aimed at opposing ICBM's (Inter-Continental Ballistic Missiles) in the hope of 'winning' a nuclear war, an alternative to diplomacy. This too we presently do, though the dream of victory is rendered totally fanciful by the destructive power aloft in aircraft, and sheltered from view beneath the sea.

It is an extraordinary failure of the democratic process that these fantasies of winning nuclear wars have been, till now, so ineffectively challenged. Perhaps the time has finally come when the voices of reason and responsibility can contain the nuclear express.

In this remarkable book, the result of a most civilized Pakistan–India collaboration, we have the opportunity to see Wagner's story of the lure of nuclear gold played out on a smaller stage. The story is, if possible, even more terrifying than the posturing between the greater powers. First there are the clearly visible patriotic impulses, heralding the mythical nirvana of 'security'. Then comes the realization of the appalling power of these weapons (this part of the book, hair-raising as it is, was written prior to discovery of the dreadful environmental consequences of a dust-cloud from a limited nuclear war—though one would prefer not to think of the eventuality, the authors of this book confront it unblinkingly). One source of nuclear folly that the present account brings out in the India–Pakistan context—but it is endemic—is the investment of great influence in a few people. There is a deficiency, oftentimes an absence, of public debate where matters relating to a nation's 'secret' arsenals are concerned. Thus, India appears to have committed itself to the nuclear path before there was any consideration of the likely Pakistani response.

As a Canadian, I am well aware that my country's record for foresight is less than stellar. Canada, along with the U.S., equipped India with a research reactor under the Eisenhower 'Atoms for Peace Program'. Contrary to the agreement, this provided the plutonium for India's first nuclear weapon. This bomb was tested in 1974. In a pathetic bow to the country's historic contribution to pacifism, it was officially designated a 'Peaceful Nuclear Explosion'. The decisions that underlay this test were made secretly at the prime ministerial level. In similar secrecy Pakistan rushed to match India's feat, exploding its first nuclear weapons in 1998 just after India's second nuclear test.

All this is by way of introduction to the present far-sighted volume, in which Pakistani and Indian scientists join together to illustrate the predicament of their two countries. Here we find a superb and well-informed catalyst for the debate that has till now been largely lacking.

REFERENCES

1. *Camp Z*, Stephen McGinty, Harper Collins, 2011; p. 84.

INTRODUCTION

Pervez Hoodbhoy

Scientists made the first atomic bomb. These men of exceptional brilliance discovered the physics of subatomic particles, and found just how a few atomic nuclei could be coaxed and cajoled into releasing their enormous energy, and then explicitly calculated everything down to the last detail. Their forbiddingly difficult mathematical formulae were based upon the newly created disciplines of relativity and quantum mechanics. The scribbled symbols seemed utterly abstract, but the deadly fireballs over Hiroshima and Nagasaki in Japan showed just how real they were.

All those who created the bomb and its physics are now dead. Some, like Edward Teller, never regretted their role. Avidly sought after by military generals and national leaders, they happily kept on inventing ever more terrible weapons. But some were appalled, realizing that they had brought humankind to the brink. Robert J. Oppenheimer, the Manhattan Project's scientific leader, famously quoting the lines, 'I have become Death, the Destroyer of Worlds', turned against the bomb and fell under suspicion of being disloyal to America. His security clearance was revoked and he was accused of being a communist, a serious matter in those hysterically anti-communist times. Albert Einstein, whose mass-energy equivalence formula lies at the very foundation of the bomb, became convinced that desperate danger lurked around the corner. Einstein teamed up with Bertrand Russell, the twentieth century's pre-eminent philosopher and mathematician, to write the Einstein-Russell Manifesto. This became the basis of a post-World War II movement for eliminating nuclear weapons.

The opposition to the bomb by some of twentieth century's greatest scientists caused many around the world to reflect and ponder upon the social responsibility of scientists. The authors of this book are among them. Hailing from both sides of the Pakistan–India border (with the exception of one, who comes from far away!), they are scientists who reject nuclear patriotism; that misplaced belief which says hurting an adversary country is somehow equivalent to loving your own.

What prompted these scientist-authors to venture into the world of nuclear weapons, war, strategy, and politics? This, after all, is not their job and can only be distantly connected to the work that they actually do as scientists. In fact, the monopoly of scientists over nuclear weapons evaporated some decades ago. To kill millions in minutes, it is now no longer necessary to have a nuclear physicist in residence. In modern times, nuclear weapon design and construction has steadily descended from high-brow theoretical physics towards mundane issues of engineering, management, and logistics. Seventy years ago the detailed physics of nuclear explosions was a matter of the highest conceptual difficulty. But today, a graduate student with a solid grounding in physics, and access to internet literature, could, as a PhD thesis, design a crude but workable nuclear explosive. Computer codes allow accurate simulations of nuclear explosions, eliminating the earlier need for the intricate numerical procedures used by the early atomic scientists.

And yet, in dealing with thorny issues of war and peace, scientists possibly still have some residual advantage. In part this comes from knowing the physical principles behind modern weaponry. But it comes still more from the nature of scientific education. Scientists are trained to recognize and analyze a wide variety of problems of the physical world. Of course, this does not mean that they are always right when they work outside their own domains. It also does not guarantee that scientists always behave rationally or humanely in their personal lives. But the cultivation of scientific habits is undeniably an asset that allows one to think through various issues of war and peace plainly and logically; identify that which are rooted in fact; and propose ways out of difficult situations. It is this hope that brings the present authors out into a domain which, in reality, does not belong to any single discipline.

DOWN THE STEEP SLIPPERY SLOPE

Once the first bomb was ready, the scientists who conceived and built it became peripheral. They were no longer courted by the political and military leaders who now 'owned' it. These leaders would decide how and when it would be used, and against whom. They now had a calculated strategy for putting terror into the hearts of men.

The decision to incinerate Hiroshima and Nagasaki was not taken in anger. White men in grey business suits and military uniforms, after much deliberation, decided the U.S. 'could not give the Japanese any warning; that we could not concentrate on a civilian area but that we should seek to make a profound psychological impression on as many of the inhabitants as possible . . . [and] the most desirable target would be a vital war plant employing a large number of workers and closely surrounded by workers' houses.'[1] They argued it would be cheaper in American lives to release the nuclear genie. Besides, it was such a marvellous device to show to the Soviet leader Josef Stalin.

And so one fine morning, banner headlines such as 'Jap City No More' brought the news from across the ocean. Joyous crowds gathered in Manhattan's Times Square in New York to celebrate. There was less of the enemy left. Rarely are victors encumbered by remorse. President Harry Truman declared: 'When you have to deal with a beast you have to treat him as a beast. It is most regrettable but nevertheless true.'[2] It is a disappointing truth that six decades later even American liberals remain ambivalent about the morality of nuking the two Japanese cities. The late Hans Bethe of the Manhattan Project fame, and Nobel Prize winner in physics, became a leading exponent of arms control some decades later. Yet, in a speech at the Cornell University, he declared that, 'the atom bomb was the greatest gift we could have given to the Japanese.'[3]

Even as the United States dusted off its hands and moved on, elsewhere the radioactive rubble of the dead cities spawned not only a sense of dread, but also an obsessive desire for nuclear weapons. Stalin raced ahead with his program, while Charles de Gaulle

conceived his 'force de frappe'. Mao Tse-Tung quietly decided that
he too wanted the bomb even as he derided it as 'a paper tiger'. In
newly independent Israel, Prime Minister David Ben Gurion
apparently 'had no qualms about Israel's need for weapons of mass
destruction', writes Avner Cohen, the historian of Israel's nuclear
bomb. Ben Gurion ordered his agents to seek out East European
Jewish scientists who could 'either increase the capacity to kill
masses or to cure masses.'[4]

The wind blew the poisonous clouds of fear and envy over other
third world countries as well: In 1948, while arguing to create
India's Department of Atomic Energy, Prime Minister Jawaharlal
Nehru told parliament, 'I think we must develop [nuclear science]
for peaceful purposes.' But, he added, 'of course, if we are compelled
as a nation to use it for other purposes, possibly no pious sentiments
of any of us will stop the nation from using it that way.'[5] Just three
years after Hiroshima and Nagasaki, those 'other purposes' were all
too clear.

Days after Pakistan's nuclear tests in May 1998, Japan invited the
country's foreign minister to visit Hiroshima's peace museum. The
minister was visibly moved after seeing the gruesome evidence of
mass devastation. His reaction: 'we made our nukes precisely so that
this could never happen to Pakistan.'

The world is awash with terrible inventions, now in the control
of generals and politicians, very few of whom can be trusted with
public funds or keeping solemn promises. Can they be trusted with
the instruments of mass annihilation? And, if not them, then just
who should one trust?

SOME PERSONAL ENCOUNTERS

Logically, those in charge of a nation's nuclear affairs should be
selected from amongst the wisest, most capable, and best informed
people who also have a calm temperament and capacity to withstand
extreme pressure. But in reality these conditions remain unfulfilled.
In India and Pakistan, leaders have rarely weighed the consequences

of their actions. Instead, they have simply reacted to events and circumstances.

India started the nuclear race, so let me start with India, from *circa* 1974. After it chose to test a supposedly 'peaceful nuclear device', there was little care or concern about how Pakistan would respond. The Indian leadership under Indira Gandhi was naive in its nuclear thinking. It could not imagine that Pakistan too could develop nuclear bombs and, ostrich-like, chose to remain ill-informed of Pakistan's capabilities or ponder upon the different options it had at that time. With eyes fixed towards China, perhaps it did not even care. Having dismissed Pakistani technical capability as inconsequential, the thought that India's military advantage could be eventually nullified by a nuclear Pakistan probably never crossed the minds of those Indians who mattered at the time. As it turned out, Indira Gandhi's successors proved as unenlightened as her.

A personal experience: Two months before the May 1998 nuclear tests conducted by India and Pakistan, a delegation from the Pugwash Movement met in Delhi with Prime Minister Inderjit Kumar Gujral. I was one of the delegates. As we sat around a table in the Prime Minister's House, I expressed my worry about a possible nuclear catastrophe befalling the subcontinent. To my surprise, Mr Gujral twice assured me—first in public and later in private—that there was no cause for concern. As we prepared to depart, he came by and, upon learning that I was from Karachi, grew nostalgic about the city he had grown up in. Putting his arm around me he confidently and earnestly told me, speaking in Urdu/Hindi, that Pakistan lacked the competence to make atomic bombs. For quite a while, I felt very confused . . . could he be right?

The Prime Minister was scarcely alone in being mistaken. Senior Indian defense analysts like P.R. Chari had also published articles before May 1998 arguing this point, as had the former head of the Indian Atomic Energy Agency, Dr Raja Ramanna. The Indian intelligence agency RAW, which Pakistanis generally believe to be ubiquitous and infinitely cunning, was also confused and gave contradictory reports. In fact the confusion went all the way up to the top. This became apparent at the time when India was in a state of euphoria in the days after the Pokharan tests. Mass celebrations were still in progress when, brimming with hubris, Home Minister L.K. Advani advised Pakistan to give up its claim on Kashmir because the 'geostrategic' context had decisively changed in India's favour.[6] At a time when Pakistan was supposed to be just a 'screwdriver turn away from the bomb',[7] Indian newspapers taunted Pakistanis: had the Chinese forgotten to send the screwdriver over with the bomb? Or were the instructions written in Chinese? Most Indians firmly believed that Pakistan did not possess the bomb.

But they could not have been more wrong. Pakistan's bomb-makers had long been craving for an opportunity to show their own prowess. Six months after the tests, one of their leaders gave a public speech expressing his delight at the Indian test:

> We had spent our lifetime on the project and still there was no chance of a hot test. And on the morning of the eleventh of May this year, one of our friends in the armed services phoned me and he said, 'Have you heard the news today?' I said. 'What?' He said, 'The Indians have conducted the explosion in Pokharan.' So I said, 'Congratulations.' I was genuinely happy. He said, 'You are congratulating us on the Indian tests?' I said, 'Yes, because now we would get a chance to do our own tests.'[8]

The confidence was well-placed. Only seventeen days later, with a thunderous roar, the mountains of Chagai shook and then turned white as five nuclear devices were simultaneously detonated inside a deeply drilled tunnel prepared years earlier. Two days later, for good measure, one more device was set off under the Ras-Koh hills. India's good cheer was suddenly shattered. Instead, recriminations and excuses started flying.

Mistaken notions extended into the Indian military as well. India's late 'nuclear visionary' and army chief, General K. Sunderji, had preached for years from a thick tome that came to be known as the 'Sunderji Bible'. His principal claim was that nuclear weapons would bring stability to the subcontinent, and that there would be no Cold

War type nuclear racing. Certainly he had Pakistan on his mind—not China—when, in the 1980s, he pressed hard for weaponizing India's nuclear capacity. With infectious enthusiasm, Sunderji lectured that India needed only a handful of fission weapons to 'take out' major Pakistani cities. More was not better, he said. Like the other military men of his time, this rather simple and likeable man thought that these terrible weapons had now made war impossible.

My single encounter with Sunderji was at a Carnegie conference in Washington in 1993. He had just finished speaking on the absolute security that nuclear weapons would bestow upon the world. I had never before seen a man who loved the bomb more; his eyes would light up upon its mere mention. So, when I introduced myself to him as a Pakistani nuclear physicist, he was overjoyed and hugged me warmly saying: 'I was commanding officer at Pokharan in 1974 when the damn thing went off. Right away I told the bug that we should give it to them [the Pakistanis] because war will then become impossible.' I did not have the heart to tell him that Pakistan, inspired by India, was indeed well on its way to having more than a few of its own. Nor, for that matter, that his (Sunderji's) dangerous initiative, 'Operation Brasstacks', had nearly brought the two countries to blows in 1987. For all his heartiness and bonhomie, this man's irresponsible and dangerous antics could have led to the deaths of thousands.

Sunderji's infectious nuclear enthusiasm had already made its way across the border. In March 1990, long before the nuclear tests had been carried out, Pakistan's General K.M. Arif wrote in *The Globe*: Let India and Pakistan both become nuclear weapon states openly and without reservations. They are both mature nations which need no counselling on their international responsibilities and conduct.

Top Pakistani generals, whose mannerisms scarcely differ from that of Indians, are fairly nonchalant about nuclear weapons. They seem to view these bombs as just another kind of bomb, albeit an oversized one. They had no appreciation of what would happen to the country after a nuclear war, apart from a rather dim understanding that many people would die.

I have many tales to tell.

In late 1989, a group of seven senior military officers, then studying operational matters at the National Defense College, came to meet me at the physics department of Quaid-e-Azam University. Their term project was to write a paper on nuclear strategy and posture in the Pak–India context. Although Pakistan did not officially acknowledge possessing such weapons then, the process of inducting them into the forces had already begun. It was also a time when there was almost zero understanding of nuclear matters in the military and, quite sensibly, they were keen to learn technical details from every available source.

Since this group was larger than could fit into my little office, I led them to the physics department conference room (still called the 'tea room' by everybody because that's where we have our 10:30 am tea everyday). We spent the next two hours there, discussing everything: from blast radii and firestorms to electronic locks and PALS (Permissive Action Links). The officers took copious notes and appeared satisfied. As they prepared to leave I asked what circumstances, in their opinion, would warrant the use of nuclear weapons by Pakistan. After some reflection one officer spoke up: 'professor', he assured me, 'they shall be used only defensively if at all, and only if the Pakistan Army faces defeat. *We cannot allow ourselves to be dis-honoured.*' Around the table, heads nodded in agreement. Significantly, the calculus of destruction—that cities and populations would be obliterated on both sides—was not what mattered. Instead it was *ghairat*—the protection of honour—that was primary. Preserving a tribal value, probably acquired around Neolithic times, was considered more important than preserving life.

The same question put to Indian military officers would probably elicit the same answer. Historically, honour has driven armies to fight battles. Even as the officer spoke, my thoughts wandered to the charge of the Light Brigade. During the Crimean War of 1854, wave after wave of honour-charged British soldiers rode their horses into the mouths of Russian guns which, of course, promptly mowed them down. Tennyson later immortalized the slain men in his famous poem: *All the world wonder'd. Honour the charge they made! Honour the Light Brigade.*

In the same year that I encountered General Sunderji, I also met with General Shamim Alam Khan. He was then Chairman, Joint Chiefs of Staff. Frankly, it's a little scary to receive a call from the GHQ in Rawalpindi. Our generals usually don't deign to talk to professors, especially dissident ones. But here was a staff car, with a smart uniformed officer, that had been dispatched to fetch me from the university. I had to wait for an hour outside Gen. Alam's office. Dr A.Q. Khan, who walked past me (he did not know me at the time) had suddenly dropped in to meet him.

Once Dr Khan left, the general had many questions for me. He told me that the army was just learning to operationally integrate its newly acquired weapons into the command structure, and so wanted to know all about Permissive Action Links; command and control issues; possibilities of accidental nuclear war, etc. Although he was certainly aware of my opposition to the bomb, he was still sufficiently curious.

General Alam was a tough, short man who passionately hated India. He regaled me with various episodes. Once he had excused himself in 1985 from an order received from President General Zia-ul-Haq. Zia was about to embark for Delhi on his famous cricket diplomacy stint and had ordered Alam to accompany him there. Alam asked to be excused saying: 'Sir, if I ever enter Delhi it shall be only if I am sitting behind the turret of my tank.' He then told me how, borrowing a small propeller-driven army reconnaissance plane from his Army Aviation Unit, he had piloted it into Indian territory and flew around for a full half an hour before returning to base. The Indians duly protested; Pakistan duly denied. His purpose for this stint was to spite Zia for his peace initiative.

After Gen. Alam had quizzed me on technical matters for over two hours, towards the end I said something to the effect that nuclear war should never even be contemplated because it would wipe out Pakistan. Alam was visibly irritated: 'professor, what you are claiming is nonsense.' He then asked me to calculate roughly how many would die if one hundred Indian bombs were dropped on Pakistan. My rough estimation satisfied him: Pakistan would lose 13 per cent of its population of 130 million (as it was then; it's 200 million now). Gen. Alam was triumphant—this was a tolerable injury, and hence not sufficient reason to hold back from a nuclear war. In time Pakistan would recover!

General Alam's thinking was not very different from that of the late K.S. Subrahmanyam, India's most influential Indian defense analyst in the 1980s and 1990s. In one of his articles, Subrahmanyam wrote:

> Even the failure of deterrence will cause vast, but still finite damage, considering the kind of arsenal the two sides are likely to have for a long time to come, with the advantage being in favour of India if India were to exercise its option (to arm with nuclear weapons). It will not mean nuclear winter, rapid escalation involving the use of hundreds of warheads and loss of control over the war. It will be analogous to the situation between the superpowers in the early fifties. That situation will still be preferable to one of India remaining non-nuclear, facing the threat of humiliation, defeat and disintegration.[9]

In the early days of Indian and Pakistani nuclear development, minimal deterrence or 'just enough' had been the mantra of the times. South Asian nuclear proponents were wont to take personal insult upon mention of an arms race, which they debunked as fear mongering. Hawkish Indian defense strategists, following Subrahmanyam, vehemently asserted that arms racing is a Cold War concept invented by the western powers and totally alien to subcontinental thinking. Their Pakistani counterparts agreed. In the late 1980s and early 1990s, the nuclear philosophy of Mutually Assured Destruction (MAD) and of steady escalation were believed to be products of twisted western minds. South Asians were supposedly wiser and would limit destructive powers only to 'what was needed'.

Subrahmanyam and I had first clashed on the subject of India's nuclear intentions at a meeting held at the University of Chicago in

1992, held to commemorate the 50th anniversary of Enrico Fermi's nuclear reactor. We then crossed swords off and on at various meetings over the years. The last time, just before he died of cancer, I was in Delhi at a meeting held in 2010 at IDSA (Institute of Defense and Strategic Analysis) of which he had been director. I reminded him of his earlier belief that Pakistan could not develop nuclear weapons, and then argued that India's decision to test had shorn it of its earlier massive military advantage over Pakistan. Perhaps because of his illness, his response was weak and unconvincing. But the real reason is that events had proved the great guru of Indian nuclearization to be plain wrong.

Even if many Indians still refuse to see it that way, the fact is that India has been essentially paralyzed after choosing to go nuclear; its ability to respond to Pakistan was enormously reduced. Take for example the events of early 2002, when the build-up of troops had escalated on both sides of the border. The Indian Parliament had been attacked weeks earlier, on 13 December 2001, and a Pakistan-based group, Jaish-e-Muhammad, had taken responsibility before suddenly denying it. India growled threateningly again and again. But faced by the awful prospect of nuclear destruction, it failed to make any moves.

Still, those were tense times. Nuclear threats had started flying in all directions. As Pakistan Air Force fighter aircraft loudly circled Islamabad, in a public debate with me at SDPI (Sustainable Development Policy Institute), General Mirza Aslam Beg, former chief of the Pakistan Army, declared: 'We can make a first strike, and a second strike, or even a third.' The lethality of nuclear war left him unmoved. 'You can die crossing the street,' he observed, 'or you could die in a nuclear war. You've got to die someday anyway.' Of course, there was no war and, thanks to the hectic efforts of U.S. and British officials and diplomats, the crisis was eventually defused.

Times of tension have brought out the steel claws again and again. Mumbai had just been attacked (26 November 2008), and I was on the same television talk show as General Hamid Nawaz (retd.), who had also served as Federal Interior Minister and Defense Secretary of Pakistan. The general angrily attacked me for suggesting that one of the many Pakistan-based jihad groups could have been involved because, indeed, I said that attacking India is exactly what they had long promised and said they would do. But Gen. Nawaz recommended readying Pakistan's nuclear arsenal, and said that a nuclear first-strike should be among Pakistan's preferred options.

Clearly it didn't take much for this particular general to want to push the button. Hopefully others are very different from him, but then that is just a hope.

DON'T TRUST THE DIPLOMATS EITHER

Pakistan and India are, of course, different countries. When visitors say that they are similar, they risk offending their local hosts. But there is undeniably a critical symmetry between their peoples, politicians, and generals that overpowers their differences. Operations 'Brasstacks' and 'Cold Start' may have had different goals from that of Gibraltar and Kargil, but they competed in recklessness and readiness to needlessly provoke and kill. The symmetry in military minds is also present in the thinking of highly paid Pakistani and Indian diplomats and negotiators. The protagonists can often only be distinguished by their names—and that too not always because some Indian diplomats are Muslim!

Suave and westernized, their job is to don the mask of nuclear respectability. Having watched them at close quarters in arms control workshops and seminars for nearly two decades, I can vouch that they meet with amazing civility (and even a forced cordiality), and seem like men of the world. Fluent in the jargon of confidence-building measures and nuclear risk reduction measures, they have honed their skills to conceal their multi-layered mistrust and inner hostility towards the other side. Tasked to show that their country's nuclear weapons are in responsible hands, they will repeat their myth even if their leaders have screamed nuclear threats just days earlier. They must also perforce claim that their countries do not proliferate weapons; that their government is fully in control of its nuclear arsenal; and that they can handle nuclear weapons just as well as any western nation. Each side says it is a hapless victim of terrorism. But when the going gets rough; off come the velvet gloves and out comes the iron fist. Most diplomats probably believe their own national fiction. Only the rare exception among them is honest to his inner self, introspects, and takes an independent position— and that too mostly after retirement!

SO WHO TO TRUST?

The message: Pakistanis and Indians should not trust their respective establishments when it comes to nuclear matters. Nor should they look to the United States (or, now, China!). Instead, objective reality, self-protection, and self-observation need to be our guide. It is for my Indian friends to look at the reality on their side of the border; they will see something similar though not identical. As a Pakistani, I am obligated to look upon my side.

Here is what the facts around me say: Pakistan has just about every kind of problem that there is. At the core lies an exploding population without employable skills, and thus a perpetually staggering economy. Day after day, and for year after year, newspaper headlines and the audio-visual media have been consistently broadcasting some new disaster: suicide bombings, brutal assassinations, public lynchings, pogroms, and riots.

Less dramatic but more tragic is that the population is seriously deprived of essential needs. A 2011 Oxfam report says that nearly two-thirds of the Pakistani population spends between 50 to 70 per cent of its income on food.[10] A staggering 36 per cent are undernourished. This places Pakistan among the 21 undernourished nations of the world. In 2011, the London-based Legatum Institute 'Prosperity Index' ranked Pakistan at 107 out of the 110 surveyed: above Ethiopia, Zimbabwe, and the Central African Republic.[11] India, in spite of its booming economy and relative internal peace, does only marginally better.

Farrukh Saleem, an astute observer of Pakistan's economic scene, puts it this way:

For the first time in recent memory, net borrowing of the private sector has been negative—Rs81 billion—indicative of a shrinking private sector. For the first time ever every Pakistani man, woman and child is indebted to the tune of Rs61,000 . . . the day Syed Yousuf Raza Gilani was taking oath of office, there were an estimated 47.1 million Pakistanis living in extreme poverty. Over the past three years an average of 25,000 Pakistanis per day—every single day of the past three years—have been driven into extreme poverty. The total now stands at an estimated 72.9 million below the poverty line. . . . For the first time in recent memory Foreign Direct Investment (FDI) has suffered such a drastic fall over such a short period of time—from $5.4 billion in 2008 to around a billion. Public Sector Enterprises are now losing Rs100 crore a day, every day of the year, and no one is worried. Pepco, just by itself, is losing Rs50 crore a day, every day of the year, and no one is worried. The Pakistan Railways is about to add a colossal $600 million to our national debt . . .[12]

For Pakistan's political and military establishment, all this bad news is like water off a duck's back. It still glows with enthusiasm about its nuclear weapons and keeps making more. For them, these are Pakistan's greatest assets. General Musharraf called them 'our crown jewels', and commentators refer to the May 1998 tests as 'our finest hour'. But the truth lies elsewhere.

DREAMS OF A NUCLEAR BAYONET

Napoleon, in an enthusiastic moment, is said to have once remarked: 'Bayonets are wonderful! One can do anything with them except sit on them!' Indeed, following the 1998 nuclear tests, Pakistan's military and political leaders saw the bomb as a panacea for solving Pakistan's multiple problems. It became axiomatic that, in addition to providing total security, this would give Pakistan international visibility, help liberate Kashmir, create national pride and elevate the country's technological status.

The mass euphoria following the tests led to the emergence of new nuclear goals. Earlier, Pakistan had only one large reason for wanting the bomb—Indian nuclear weapons had to be countered by Pakistani ones. But a second purpose now emerged: a super-

confident military saw the bomb as a magic talisman. Having nukes-
for-nukes became secondary; the bomb could strip India of its
military advantage and neutralize its larger conventional land, air
and sea forces.

Thereafter, just months later, Pakistani troops and militants,
protected by a newly activated nuclear shield, were to cross the Line
of Control (LoC) in Kashmir into Kargil.[13] Earlier, across the length
and breadth of Pakistan, militant Islamic groups had organized
freely and built up a fearsome strength. They did so, protected by
an impregnable nuclear Pakistan that made impossible an Indian
strike on militant camps safely ensconced within Pakistan's borders.
When the Mumbai attacks eventually followed in 2008, India could
do little more than froth and fume. Then, years after the tests, a
third purpose was to emerge. No book or scholarly article talks
about it much because it operates only at the subjective level. But
this reason competes with earlier ones for having bombs. Bluntly
put: Pakistan's rulers began to see nuclear weapons as money
spinners—they could help generate income for a stumbling
economy and act as insurance against things going too far wrong.
But how so? Like North Korea, Pakistan feels the world shall not
allow a nuclear country to fail—no matter what. Indeed, hard times
have befallen the country: electricity and fuel shortages routinely
shut down industries and transport for long stretches; imports far
exceed exports; inflation lies at the double-digit level; foreign direct
investment is negligible because of concerns over physical security;
tax reform has failed; corruption remains unchecked; and the
country essentially survives on remittances earned by Pakistanis
abroad. And yet the feeling is that international financial donors
cannot afford to stop pumping funds into Pakistan's dysfunctional
economy. In the world's eyes, Pakistan is not some African country
like Somalia or Congo. Their collapse would be a local matter;
Pakistan's could be a global catastrophe.

Surely it would be the world's darkest nightmare if a collapsing
Pakistan was unable to prevent its 100 plus Hiroshima-sized bombs
from disappearing into the night. The bailout packages currently

given to Pakistan would be a pittance compared to the cost of dealing with loose weapons. The moral: keep the cash flowing!

Therefore, over time, Pakistan's nuclear bayonet gained more than just deterrence value; it became a dream instrument for its ruling oligarchy. The silent menace of the weapons is enough to make the faint-hearted quail. Napoleon's bayonet was painful to sit upon, but nuclear weapons offer no such discomfort. The world has no option but to support Pakistan and prevent it from a fate like that of Somalia. General Musharraf was an authentic spokesman for the Pakistani establishment when he declared that our 'crown jewels' were to be protected at all costs—even if this meant accepting American demands to dump the Taliban after the 9/11 episode.

POST OSAMA BIN LADEN THERE'S YET ANOTHER REASON

Pakistan's frequently argued position is that it needs to produce still more bombs—and hence more bomb materials—because of India. Its representatives in Geneva have, along with older issues related to verification problems and existing stocks, frequently cite the Deal[14]—a wide-ranging accord signed in 2008.

Indeed, the Deal is a strong argument: the U.S. has committed itself to nuclear cooperation with a state that is not a signatory to the Nuclear Non-Proliferation Treaty (NPT)—and one that made nuclear weapons surreptitiously. Moreover, it is currently using its new-found economic gains to expand its military capability, both nuclear and conventional. Reports exist that India, with support extended by the U.S., is inching towards membership of the Nuclear Suppliers Group. This would increase Pakistan's sense of embattlement by yet another notch.[15] Now that the sanctions imposed after the 1998 tests are long gone, India can import advanced nuclear reactor technology as well as natural uranium ore from diverse sources, Australia included. Although imported ore cannot be used for bomb-making, India can divert more of its scarce domestic ore towards military reactors.

But the Deal may actually be a fig leaf. Pakistan's rush for more bombs also comes from its changed relationship with the United States. The killing of Osama bin Laden on 2 May 2011 sharply increased the sense of vulnerability in Islamabad. American invaders had come and gone without even being challenged. The world's most prized fugitive had been discovered ensconced in an army town within walking distance of the famed Pakistan Military Academy in Kakul, and his dead body whisked away.

In spite of what columnist Ayaz Amir called the 'mother of all embarrassments', introspection and remorse were noticeably absent in the corps commanders conference held three days later. Threat and bluster dominated. America would get a befitting response should it once again violate Pakistan's territorial integrity through its 'unilateral military action'. Military chief, General Ashraf Parvez Kayani, said he would demand a 25–40 per cent cut in the number of U.S. Special Operations personnel based in Pakistan; soon thereafter U.S. military trainers were withdrawn from Pakistan.[16] Only a handful trickled back a year later.

The downward spiral became dizzyingly fast after the 2011 NATO attack on two Pakistani military check-posts along the Afghanistan–Pakistan border on Saturday, 26 November 2011. According to reports, two NATO Apache helicopters, an AC-130 gunship and two F-15E Eagle fighter jets entered the Pakistani border area of Salala, killing 24 Pakistani soldiers. The Americans later expressed regret, but refused to apologize. Pakistan cut off NATO land routes to Afghanistan, and refused permission for drones to be launched from Pakistani soil. It took eight months for supplies to resume, and then too only partially, after Secretary Hilary Clinton's rather ragged apology in early July 2012.

In the Pakistani military's mind, the Americans pose a rising threat, one that may become as serious as India's. They are certainly considered more of an adversary than the Pakistani Tehreek-e-Taliban (TTP) jihadists who, although, they have killed thousands of Pakistani troops and civilians, are not reviled with any comparable intensity. Even as the TTP released its gory video-taped executions of Pakistani soldiers, the Salala incident was freely allowed by the military to inflame public opinion.

Pakistani public views about the United States are easier to poll and document than those of the men in khaki: three quarters of respondents polled over the internet said 'the U.S. government does not respect Islam and considers itself at war with the Muslim world.' Only 16 per cent believe that Al Qaeda had anything to do with the 9/11 attacks, and 75 per cent disapproved of the killing of Osama bin Laden.[17]

Pakistani animosity rises as it sees America tightly embracing India, and standing in the way of a Pakistan-friendly government in Kabul. Once again 'strategic defiance' is gaining ground, albeit not through the regional compact suggested by General Mirza Aslam Beg in the early 1990s. This attitudinal shift has created a strong non-India reason that favours ramping up bomb production—the perceived threat emanating from the U.S. to Pakistan's nuclear weapons. This perception has been reinforced by the large amount of attention given to the issue in the U.S. mainstream press, and by war-gaming exercises in U.S. military institutes. Thus, redundancy is considered desirable—an American attempt to seize or destroy all warheads would have smaller chances of success if Pakistan had more. And America would have more to fear if there were more nukes left over.

But can Pakistan's nukes lose their magic? Get stolen, rendered impotent or lose their menacing image? More fundamentally, one must ask how and when they could fail to be the perfect protection they are imagined to be.

THE TIPPING POINT

One can easily imagine that a Pakistan-based cross border attack on India could cause a series of self-elevating crises. The military establishment's reluctance to clamp down on anti-India jihadi groups, or to punish those who carried out the 26/11 attacks in Mumbai, suggests that this lies well within the realm of possibilities. Although not officially assisted or sanctioned, a second Mumbai would raise fury in India and call for revenge. What then? How would India respond?

There cannot, of course, be a definite answer. But it is instructive to analyze 'Operation Parakram',[18] and India's response to the attack on the Indian parliament on 13 December 2001. This ten-month-long mobilisation of nearly half-a-million soldiers and deployment of troops along the LoC was launched to punish Pakistan for harbouring the Jaish-e-Mohammad, which, at least initially, had claimed responsibility for the attack.

A seminar held in August 2003 in Delhi brought together senior Indian military leaders and top analysts to reflect on Parakram. To quote the main speaker, Major General Ashok Mehta, the two countries hovered on the brink of war and India's 'coercive diplomacy failed due to the mismatch of India–U.S. diplomacy and India's failure to think through the end game.'[19] The general gave several reasons for not going to war against Pakistan. These included a negative cost-benefit analysis; lack of enthusiasm in the Indian political establishment; complications arising from the Gujarat riots of 2002; and 'a lack of courage'. That Parakram would have America's unflinching support also turned out to be a false assumption. The bottom line: when Parakram fizzled out, Pakistan claimed victory and India was left licking its wounds.

A second important opinion, articulated by the influential former Indian intelligence chief, Lt. Gen. Vikram Sood, was still harsher on India. He expressed regret at not going to war against Pakistan and said that India had 'failed to achieve strategic space as well as strategic autonomy.'[20] He went on to say that Musharraf never took India seriously after it lost this golden opportunity to attack a distracted Pakistan that was waging war against the Taliban on the Durand Line. Using the word 'imbroglio' for India's punitive attempt, he pointed out that no political directive had been provided to the service chiefs for execution even as late as August 2002. On the contrary, that month the Chief of Army Staff was asked to draw up a directive to extricate the army.

Now that the finger-pointing, recriminations, and stock-taking are over, one can be fairly sure that India will not permit a second Parakram. Indeed, a new paradigm for dealing with Pakistan was invented and embodied into the Cold Start doctrine.[21] This calls for quick, salami-slicing thrusts into Pakistan while learning to fight a conventional war under a 'nuclear over-hang' (by itself an interesting new phrase, used by General Deepak Kapoor in January 2010).

Revelations by WikiLeaks about Cold Start are worthy of consideration. In a classified cable to Washington in February 2010, Tim Roemer, the U.S. ambassador to India, described Cold Start as 'not a plan for a comprehensive invasion and occupation of Pakistan' but 'for a rapid, time- and distance-limited penetration into Pakistani territory.'[22] He wrote that, 'it is the collective judgment of the U.S. Mission that India would encounter mixed results.' Warning India against Cold Start, he concluded: 'Indian leaders no doubt realize that, although, Cold Start is designed to punish Pakistan in a limited manner without triggering a nuclear response, they cannot be sure whether Pakistani leaders will in fact refrain from such a response.'

Roemer is spot on. Implementing Cold Start, which might be triggered by Mumbai-II, may well initiate a nuclear disaster. Indeed, there is no way to predict how such conflicts will end once they start. Recognizing this, Gen. V.K. Singh came closer than any other Indian government official towards denying such an aggressive strategy: 'There is nothing like Cold Start. But we have a "proactive strategy" which takes steps in a proactive manner so that we can achieve what our doctrines and strategies (demand).'[23] A rational Indian leadership—if one exists at the crisis moment—is unlikely to opt for a Cold Start type of operation. But even if the Indians do not attack, another major Pakistan-based attack upon India would bring disaster to Pakistan. Yes, Pakistani nuclear weapons would be unhurt and unused, but their magic would have evaporated. The reason is clear: an aggrieved India would campaign—with a high chance of success—for ending all international aid for Pakistan, a trade boycott and stiff sanctions. The world's fear of loose Pakistani nukes hijacked by Islamist forces would likely lose out against the revulsion of yet another stomach-churning massacre.

An international trade boycott alone would cause Pakistan's economy, which has little fat to spare, to collapse like a pack of cards. The initial bravado, intense at first, would fast evaporate. Foodstuffs, electricity, gas and petrol would disappear. China and Saudi Arabia would send messages of sympathy and some aid, but they would not make up for the difference. With scarcity all around, angry mobs would burn grid stations and petrol pumps, loot shops, and plunder the houses of the rich. Today's barely governable Pakistan would become ungovernable. The government then in power, whether civilian or military, would exist only in name. Religious and regional forces would pounce upon their chances; hellish anarchy would be unleashed. It would be the end of Pakistan as a nation-state.

Napoleon's bayonet ultimately could not save him, and Pakistan's nuclear bayonet has also had its day. It cannot protect Pakistan. Instead, the country needs peace, economic justice, rule of law, tax reform, a social contract, education and a new federation agreement.

OUTLINE OF BOOK

Many of this book's chapters are new and intended to reflect realities as of the present time (2012). Others have been published elsewhere but were included because they have staying power and will be pertinent for years to come. They have been updated and modified to include new facts and developments. Original sources have been duly acknowledged.

India's development of a 'nuclear priesthood', and the tireless efforts of Dr Homi Bhabha to create an appetite for the bomb, is the subject of the first chapter. M.V. Ramana relates in detail how Bhabha consciously worked to overturn the notion of a Gandhian India by enthusing—and forcing—Indian nuclear scientists to work towards building the bomb. Rather than any external threat, the notion that great nations need big bombs was the driver. Decades later, the rise of Hindu nationalism, or *Hindutva*, led to India's quest for 'international status' through the May 1998 tests.

While there were only a few Indian scientists who opposed the bomb, some of these dissidents had exceptionally strong scientific reputations. Among them were Meghnad Saha, C.V. Raman, and D. Kosambi. In their view, Bhabha's efforts were misdirected and would lead India in the wrong direction. Ramana notes that, 'despite this relatively long history of opposition, anti-nuclear scientists in India have, for the most part, not made much use of their technical expertise. This has both good and bad consequences.' He says that dissident scientists tend to be of disparate backgrounds and are concerned with a huge range of social problems, which necessarily dilutes their impact. Well, maybe! One wonders if they had, or have, an alternative.

Zia Mian, in the second chapter, details how the atomic age came to Pakistan by way of the United States' Atoms for Peace program. His erudite essay recalls those heady days when atomic energy seemed to hold boundless promise. Pakistan's elite jumped upon the idea, receiving the country's first reactor in 1965. Although the U.S. now views Pakistani nuclear weapons with great alarm, this was not so earlier. According to Stephen P. Cohen, who has been an insider with the U.S. establishment for decades, Pakistani military officers were visited by an American nuclear-warfare team in 1957. He says that, 'Present-day Pakistani nuclear planning and doctrine is descended directly from this early exposure to Western nuclear strategizing; it very much resembles American thinking of the mid-1950s with its acceptance of first-use and the tactical use of nuclear weapons against onrushing conventional forces.'[24]

Mian also gives important details of just how nuclear enthusiasm was created in Pakistan, at a time when the country possessed less than a handful of persons who had at least some understanding of nuclear technology. Although he does not specifically mention Prof. Abdus Salam—who went on to win a Nobel Prize in 1979 for his work in high energy physics—the fact is that Salam had an essential role in convincing policy makers about nuclear energy, and later nuclear weapons as well. The idea that progress required nuclear development caught on: eventually it created a Pakistan that has nuclear weapons, nuclear power plants, and a nuclear complex that dwarfs all other areas of science and technology.

Pakistan's nuclear trajectory is the subject of the two subsequent chapters They trace the early development of Pakistan's nuclear weapons; discuss how nuclear philosophy has evolved over time; and go on to discuss the recurrent crises subsequent to their operation- alization after the 1998 tests. As a crisis escalates, both countries would walk up a nuclear escalation ladder. What might the rungs of that ladder look like? It is argued that false assumptions, mission creep, and high levels of risk-taking have made deterrence less effective over time. Using publicly available information, the current state of the nuclear arsenal, missiles, and aircraft is presented, together with a discussion of what constrains Pakistan's further nuclear expansion. An intriguing question is addressed: Pakistan has been surprisingly successful in creating a fairly large and diverse intermediate range missile force in a very short time. What made this possible, given its weak industrial and scientific infrastructure?

The third chapter discusses the topic of Kashmir and the bomb. Kashmir has almost always been quoted as a key reason, if not *the* reason, for Pakistan to want the bomb. What has been Pakistan's strategy in this dispute, and what kind of change did Pakistan expect could happen once the bomb came along? This essay argues that while Pakistan botched its chances of securing Kashmir— particularly after Kargil—India has not won either. Today's relative calm along the Line of Control could turn into a blaze of artillery any time. So what could be the long-term solution for Kashmir? An opinion will be found towards the chapter's end.

The essay 'Nationalism and the Bomb' explores whether public enthusiasm for the bomb can be strong enough to create a national identity around it. As a symbol of power, it can be used along with national holidays, anthems, flag carrying airlines, and displays of military might to build a national spirit. But will all this serve as acting positively or negatively towards alleviating Pakistan's multiple difficulties? Will it heal splits that exist within the country? Pakistanis have been told that if the country had a bomb in 1971, East Pakistan would have never been lost. But this is pure fantasy; the crisis of East Pakistan was fundamentally a political one and had no military solution. The bomb could not have saved Pakistan from breaking up. Certainly, Bangladeshis—who were Pakistanis in 1971 and formed the country's majority—are delighted that Pakistan did not have a bomb at the time! They show little regret at no longer being East Pakistanis. The chapter concludes with steps that would be needed for Pakistan to become a viable nation at peace with itself and the rest of the world.

Religion and the bomb are the focus of the next chapter. When Zulfikar Ali Bhutto introduced the term 'Islamic Bomb' into the nuclear lexicon, he seriously misled everyone. Pakistan had made its bomb to counter India's, not for the glory of Islam. But later, things took an interesting new twist. Pakistan's religio-political parties soon claimed the bomb for Islam, and a means of defending the *ummah* (Islamic Brotherhood).

More significantly, as religion played a greater role in the matters of Muslim states everywhere, the bomb began to acquire a sectarian touch. This may soon acquire even more prominence. Iran is at the threshold of making its own. What then? Certainly, this would be a powerful stimulus pushing the Kingdom of Saudi Arabia to follow and seek the first Sunni bomb.

Although Pakistan is the only Muslim country in the world specifically created in the name of religion, it built its bomb not for Islamic reasons but to counter India's nuclear arsenal. On the other hand, Sunni Saudi Arabia perceives Shi'a Iran as its primary enemy, not Israel. The two theocracies are bitter rivals after the Iranian revolution, and have been vying for influence in the Muslim world. Willy-nilly, Pakistan would then enter into yet another nuclear race, having to decide between two Middle Eastern Muslim countries. It is easy to see which side Sunni Pakistan would choose. Less easy is to guess the kind of assistance it would provide.

The safety and security of Pakistan's nuclear arsenal comes up for scrutiny next. Since 2004, Pakistan military officers, installations, equipment and weapons have been targeted by those it had trained to fight against the Soviet Union and, later, India. Hidden inside the ranks of the Army and ISI (Inter-Services Intelligence) are shadowy groups of various persuasions. It is therefore unsurprising that the hijacking of Pakistan's nuclear weapons, or fissile materials, is considered a serious possibility by much of the world.

The Pakistan Army, that has physical custody of nuclear weapons, and the various secret organizations that participate in their production process, all swear that this is impossible. While one fervently hopes that they are correct, nagging worries remain. The army was indeed a tightly disciplined force in earlier times and such worries could have then been dismissed outright. But its secular culture has dissipated over time, a direct cost of waging covert war against India with the help of religious proxies. This had opened the doors to the barracks of many Islamic organizations, each with its own political agenda. Some—such as the Tablighi Jamaat and Jamaat-i-Islami—operate freely within military ranks. Others, such as the banned Hizb-ut-Tahrir, are underground. They dream of establishing their own version of an Islamic state in Pakistan and have helped kill their own colleagues. Spectacular attacks from extremists, in collusion with inside partners, have forced attention on this issue. One striking example which caused alarm within Pakistan as well as globally, was that of the revenge attack on the Mehran Navy base subsequent to bin Laden's killing. The attack on the Pakistan Air Force base at Kamra in August 2012 reportedly also had support from insiders.

The issue of how nuclear weapons are commanded and controlled is taken up by Zia Mian in the subsequent chapter. At one level, this is a technical matter and involves setting up a military command structure with small response times and the smallest possible signalling error. Mian discusses the extensive, although, not completely foolproof procedures developed by the Americans and Russians over half a century. These embody much thinking and technology and therefore Pakistan and India have both sought technology, such as Permissive Action Links (PALs), from the other nuclear weapon states. This would reduce the possibility of unauthorised use. But, as the chapter points out, in the fog and friction of war the decision to unleash nuclear destruction ultimately may not be for South Asia's generals or prime ministers to make.

Four subsequent chapters by Zia Mian and his collaborators look at various technical aspects: whether early warning of a nuclear attack is technically possible in the Pakistan–India situation; the implications of introducing tactical (or theatre) nuclear weapons (TNWs) as part of Pakistan's war fighting strategy; the effect of nuclear war in South Asia; and Pakistan's nuclear diplomacy in relation to the fissile material cut-off treaty.

The 'Early Warning' chapter draws from the experience gained during the Cold War. It was extremely challenging, even with satellites stationed overhead, to decide whether a missile attack was imminent. But, on the subcontinent, with missile flight times of 5–10 minutes needed for traversing any two points, the technical challenges are much harder. The authors conclude: 'it appears that early warning satellites in South Asia will serve little useful purpose.' Even if the warning was communicated to decision-makers, there would be almost no time to consult or deliberate after receiving this warning. They note that an early warning system could actually be counter-productive because false alarms, combined with the short decision time involved, could increase the chances of an accidental nuclear war.

Short flight times become still shorter once nuclear weapons are deployed on the battlefield. This has become of high contemporary relevance now that Pakistan plans to deploy *Nasr*, a short-range battlefield missile, in the coming years. Therefore the next chapter considers the scenario where Pakistan deploys tactical nuclear weapons. Indeed, it has already sent signals that, in response to a quick thrust of Indian tanks into Pakistani territory, it may consider using nuclear weapons in response. But, quite apart from asking whether this use would escalate into a full-blown nuclear war, one can inquire about its efficacy. This is an interesting physics question: tanks are radiation hardened and, therefore, difficult to destroy in large numbers even with a nuclear weapon unless packed together. Using different inter-tank distances, the authors conclude that unless Indian tanks disperse widely—which then reduces their concentration of firepower—Pakistan may be able to destroy a significant proportion of any invading Indian armoured force. However, most of its arsenal would then be exhausted. This, of course, calls for building still more bombs!

The next chapter is on the effects of a nuclear exchange between Pakistan and India. Abstractions can hinder comprehension of reality. Therefore, it is important to have some understanding of what might actually happen. Being explicit is necessary because even generally well-informed people, including political strategists, know surprisingly little about the effects of nuclear weapons. On one end are extreme, apocalyptic views—that such a war would end all life on the subcontinent. The other end sees nuclear weapons as powerful but not catastrophic, and that nuclear war would leave manageable destruction behind.

These extreme views are deeply flawed. Instead, a scientific analysis is needed. Using physics formulas developed in the 1940s, a scientific assessment of casualty estimates is provided by McKinzie et. al. Their figures, clinically presented, do not convey the horrors of a nuclear war—it has to be imagined. They conclude that, 'The ultimate impact on both societies would extend well beyond the bombed areas in highly unpredictable ways. . . . Nothing would ever be the same again.'

In a more recent study, scientists assess the potential damage and smoke production associated with the detonation of small nuclear weapons in a modern megacity. They find that low yield weapons, roughly Hiroshima-sized, if targeted at city centres, can produce hundred times as many fatalities and hundred times as much smoke from fires per kiloton yield as previously estimated in analyses for full scale nuclear wars using high-yield weapons.[25] They also analyze the likely outcome of a regional nuclear exchange involving 100

15-kt explosions, which is roughly what one might expect in an Indo–Pakistan war. They find that such an exchange could produce direct fatalities 'comparable to all of those worldwide in World War II, or to those once estimated for a "counterforce" nuclear war between the superpowers. Megacities exposed to atmospheric fallout of long-lived radionuclides would likely be abandoned indefinitely.' Nuclear explosions have global effects because the explosions throw up major concentrations of soot into the stratosphere. These could remain up there long enough to cause unprecedented worldwide climate cooling, with major disruptive effects on global agriculture. While blast effects are relatively easily estimated, it is harder to calculate the impact of fires following an Indo–Pak nuclear war. That collateral damage may be capable of killing substantial parts of the Earth's population by injecting large quantities of soot into the upper atmosphere. Indeed, global dust storms on Mars and Titan are being studied with this in mind.

More bombs require more fissile materials—highly enriched uranium and weapons-grade plutonium. It appears that Pakistan has dug its heels in and will do all it can to prevent a global agreement for cutting off fissile material production from coming into effect. Its sustained diplomatic efforts to this end are taken up by Mian and Nayyar in their detailed article. They state what is obvious: Pakistan is blocking talks on an FMCT so that it may build up its fissile material stockpile. It wishes to highlight to the international community its concerns about a fissile material gap with India and the consequences of India's current military build-up, especially India's search for missile defenses, and the consequences of the U.S.–Indian nuclear deal. Faced with Pakistan's road-block, other states are exploring possible ways outside the framework of the Conference on Disarmament.

An uncertain situation leads to a cloudy crystal ball. Still, as in the next chapter, an attempt is made to anticipate probable futures of nuclear South Asia. This is increasingly wrapped up in great power politics. As U.S. and India move closer in their strategic partnership, a natural response will be for Pakistan to move towards

China and further away from the U.S. Beijing is considered an 'all-weather' friend in Islamabad, while Washington is considered a fickle ally—if at all an ally now. But China has also shown no sign that it is willing to shoulder the financial burden of propping up Pakistan that America has so far been willing to bear. Nor does it want too close a relationship—Pakistan's usefulness is limited to South Asia, whereas China has global aspirations. One can expect enhanced military and nuclear assistance, but Chinese caution will kick in if it sees the Pakistani state weakening and jihadism gaining strength.

The last chapter on nuclear weapons on the subcontinent takes up the issue of global zero. This is an initiative by a Washington-based group for the total elimination of nuclear weapons and, doubtlessly, an utterly laudable goal. Yet, it encounters deep suspicions. Given massive U.S. supremacy in conventional weapons, is global zero a means by which countries would be deprived of an equalizer? And, given that its proponents include former stalwarts of the American imperium, such as Henry Kissinger, does this announce a renewed desire for empire rather than a more equal world? In the South Asian context, Pakistan would be loath to give up its equalizer against India. Surely it is important to deal with these difficult issues upfront rather than just sweep them under the rug.

The book concludes with two chapters on nuclear electricity generation: one each for Pakistan and India. Although its focus is the bomb, to include the topic of power generation in the book is entirely appropriate. First, both countries built their weapon-making capacity around the civilian nuclear infrastructure. Second, the impetus for increasing the size of the two nuclear arsenals comes, to a large extent, from the two huge national nuclear establishments. Their large budgets were secured by the promise of delivering energy. But how real are these promises? Is nuclear energy cheap, reliable, and safe? While these questions can be asked anywhere in the world, in the subcontinent's context there are new elements involved that merit a closer look.

CONCLUSION

It is unlikely that this will be a popular book. Books published from Pakistan on the subject generally extol the virtues of the bomb while others, at best, feign to be analytical and neutral. Some are officially sponsored, whether secretly or openly, and others reflect the personal enthusiasm of their authors. They dwell upon the supposedly heroic efforts needed to create the bomb, its role as a stabilizer and strategic equalizer, and the absolute safety it supposedly brings. They also assume that the sleeping nuclear monster shall never wake up, which is a matter of faith and not fact. The inevitable conclusion is that the other side should disarm first. But since nobody believes this will happen, both sides continue to indefinitely possess, and expand their nuclear capabilities.

The perspective here is frankly different. The authors believe in a moral universe, where human life is to be valued and its destruction en masse to be abhorred. They do not, therefore, use the language of strategic double-speak which rarely adds nuance or encourages deeper discussions. Rather, pseudo-academic discourses often serve as a pretext for justifying nuclear weapons, and for increasing their numbers and potency. Depressingly often one sees scholars acting like policemen and soldiers in the service of their respective states instead of providing objective and analytical accounts. Nevertheless, while taking a position against nuclear weapons, it is not our intent to needlessly moralize. Facts are stated exactly as they happen to be. This is a responsibility that we owe both to our profession as scientists, and to our own selves as well.

To conclude, the intent of the book is to provide readers in Pakistan and India with a counter narrative that, hopefully, is well considered and well argued. If it has succeeded in raising questions in the reader's mind and increases self-scrutiny, then it shall have served its purpose.

REFERENCES

1. Notes of the Interim Committee, 31 May 1945, in Martin Sherwin, *A World Destroyed: Hiroshima and the origins of the Arms Race*, (Vintage Books, 1987), Appendix L, p. 303.
2. *A World Destroyed: Hiroshima and the origins of the Arms Race*, Martin Sherwin, (Vintage Books, 1987), p. xvii.
3. I heard Bethe say these words at a meeting organized by the Union of Concerned Scientists at Cornell University, U.S.A., in June 1997. They provoked outrage among some in the audience, myself included. But he responded to me directly saying that more Japanese lives would have been lost if the fire-bombing of cities had continued.
4. *Israel and the Bomb*, Avner Cohen, Columbia University Press, 1998, p. 11.
5. Cited in e.g., Zia Mian, 'Homi Bhabha Killed a Crow', in Zia Mian and Ashis Nandy, *The Nuclear Debate—Ironies and Immoralities*, (RCSS, 1998), pp. 12–13.
6. Nuclear test our biggest achievement: Advani, *India Today*, http://indiatoday.intoday.in/story/Nuclear+test+our+biggest+achievement:+Advani/1/40388.html
7. 'Arms Race of India, Pakistan Nothing New', *Los Angeles Times*, 14 May 1998.
8. 'A Science Odyssey: Pakistan's Nuclear Emergence', speech delivered by Dr Samar Mubarakmand at the Khwarizmic Science Society, Lahore, 30 November 1998.
9. *Critical Mass*, by William E.Burrows and Robert Windrem, 1994.
10. 'Undernourishment on the rise in Pakistan again: Oxfam', *The Express Tribune*, 4 August 2011.
11. http://www.prosperity.com/rankings.aspx
12. 'Economic meltdown 2012–2013', Farrukh Saleem, *The News* (Islamabad). 20 November 2011.
13. A nuanced history of the Kargil conflict, including discussions of the nuclear dimension, may be found in *Asymmetric Warfare in South Asia—The Causes and Consequences of the Kargil Conflict*, edited by Peter R. Lavoy, Cambridge University Press, 2009.
14. 'The U.S.–Indian Deal and Its Impact', *Arms Control Today*, July/August 2010.
15. 'U.S. works for India's membership in Nuclear Suppliers Group', *Times of India*, 22 June 2011.
16. Pakistan expels 90 U.S. military trainers, *Army Times*, 8 June 2011.
17. YouGov Siraj Survey Results, Pakistan Poll, May 2011, http://cdn.yougov.com/today_uk_import/yg-archives-pakistan-poll_0.pdf
18. Gen. Padmanabhan mulls over lessons of Operation Parakram', Praveen Swami, *The Hindu*, 6 February 2004.
19. 'Coercive Diplomacy: Operation Parakram—an Evaluation', Institute of Peace and Conflict, New Delhi, 30 August 2003.

20. Ibid.
21. India's Controversial New War Doctrine, Harsh V Pant, ISN Security Watch, 25 Jan. 2010.
22. 'India "unlikely" to deploy Cold Start against Pakistan', *Dawn*, 3 December 2010.
23. 'Revisiting Cold Start—Weighing Strategic Shifts in South Asia', CSIS, 12 February 2012.
24. *The Idea of Pakistan*, Stephen P. Cohen, Brookings Institute Press, 2004, p. 103.
25. 'Atmospheric effects and societal consequences of regional scale nuclear conflicts and acts of individual nuclear terrorism', O.B. Toon, R.P. Turco, A. Robock, C. Bardeen, L. Oman, and G. L. Stenchikov, *Atmospheric Chemistry and Physics*, 7, 1973–2002, 2007.

CHAPTER 1

SCIENTISTS AND INDIA'S NUCLEAR BOMB

M.V. Ramana

The bomb cult . . . [is] the rebellion of the rebelled against an insurgency of an elite.

Amitav Ghosh[1]

Speaking at the 1971 annual meeting of the American Association for the Advancement of Science, Alvin Weinberg, then the director of the Oak Ridge National Laboratory, United States, called for setting up an elite 'priesthood' that would manage the nuclear energy enterprise.[2] In India, a similar priesthood was set up in the late forties by Homi Bhabha, a theoretical physicist and architect of India's nuclear program. Starting at a small scientific laboratory, the Indian nuclear establishment progressively moved onto becoming the creators of India's 'nuclear option' and, more recently, a nuclear arsenal featuring weapons with varying destructive capabilities. Together with the Defense Research and Development Organization (DRDO), the designers of the missiles that would carry these explosives to their targets, the nuclear establishment constitutes what Itty Abraham has aptly termed a 'Strategic Enclave'.[3] The pressure exerted by this strategic enclave has been an extremely important factor in India's quest for nuclear weapons and shaping nuclear and security policy.[4] In this paper we will trace the history of the strategic enclave's involvement with the bomb in India and some prognosis of the future. Then we briefly chronicle opposition to nuclear weapons and militarisation on the part of Indian scientists. We first start with a quick overview of the involvement of scientists around the world in making nuclear weapons and defense policy, a short discussion of the political economy of science, and a brief overview of the sociological factors specific to the scientific community in India.

SCIENTISTS AND NUCLEAR WEAPONS

From the beginning of the Manhattan Project, scientists in general, and physicists in particular, have been seen as the makers of the bomb.[5] Given the prominence accorded to scientists, it should not be surprising that they have had an enormous influence, in different capacities, on nuclear policy around the world. This influence has been best studied in the case of the United States.[6] For the most part, what is available in the case of other countries that have developed nuclear weapons are general histories from which the role of scientists can be inferred.[7]

Among scientists the bombing of Hiroshima and Nagasaki led to two opposite reactions.[8] On the one hand, there was greater concern among scientists about the results of their activities and what uses it was put to by the state.[9] On the other hand, scientists were also seduced by the enormous increase in access to power that came about if they played along with, or better still, drove the state's obsession with using the latest technological devices for militaristic purposes.[10] As Solly Zuckerman argued: 'In the changed relationship between science and military affairs that has prevailed since the Second World War, the military man has never ceased to urge the scientist to intensify the technological exploitation of his knowledge in order to improve the armoury of available weapons; and within the economic restraints set them, the scientist and engineer have been only too ready to oblige, to the full extent of their abilities.'[11]

An example of how scientists not only obliged, but in fact actively promoted the application of science to military uses comes from the United States during the First World War. In 1916, upon instigation by George Ellery Hale, a distinguished astronomer and foreign secretary of the prestigious National Academy of Sciences (NAS), a delegation of scientists met with President Wilson. The meeting resulted in the setting up of the National Research Council (NRC) in secret, with the objective of encouraging pure and applied research for 'national security and welfare.' Hale's own reasons for this initiative resulted from his earlier experience as a student in Europe where he had learnt the lesson: 'to accomplish great results,' scientists had to 'enjoy the active cooperation of the leaders of the state.'[12]

Regardless of the actual percentages of scientists supporting or opposing such developments, there is little doubt that by and large it is such scientists who supported the application of science and technology to militaristic purposes that have wielded greater influence on government policy. To understand why scientists espouse such goals requires an examination of the political economy of science as well as the role that the state would like scientists to play.

Science is often seen as 'neutral' and detached from the forces that rule our everyday lives. But science, like all productive activities, is a social activity strongly influenced by social and political structures around it.[13] Because it is a human productive activity that takes time and money, science is guided by and directed by those forces in the country, or the world, that have control over money and resources. People earn their living by science—so the dominant social and political forces that fund this activity determine to a large extent what science studies and what the results of such studies are used for.

The most obvious reason why science is funded is because of its connection with technology and the production of new artefacts that benefit society in general, and the funding agencies in particular. Among such artefacts that the state, which is a major source of science funding everywhere—and, in many countries including India, practically the only source of funding—the state's desires are weapons. One characteristic of modern states is that they 'possess the material and organizational means of waging industrialized war.'[14] To obtain these means, they have invested heavily in science and technology.

In addition to this task, the state and dominant forces would also like scientists, and more generally intellectuals, to say and do things that legitimize and strengthen the existing social order. Though authors like Julien Benda have railed against this 'treason of the intellectuals',[15] intellectuals have by and large performed this task willingly. In the case of India, where the bulk of financial support for science came directly or indirectly from the state, it has been argued that science through its association with 'freedom and enlightenment, power and progress', contributed in a major way to the Indian state's efforts at legitimizing itself.[16]

The above-mentioned factors represent the 'structure' under which scientists operate. However, in its day-to-day functioning, as well as in how the truth-value and validity of scientific theories, models and experiments are determined, the scientific community has considerable autonomy.[17] Furthermore, political elites depend on scientists to inform them of the implications of the advances in science. Therefore, scientists—and here the conflicts between different fields and different approaches within each individual field come to the fore—can choose to term one area of research as promising and call for greater support. In short, scientists also have 'agency' in shaping the course science takes. But as the earlier discussion pointed out, there are strong constraints placed on this autonomy.

It is important to distinguish this formulation from more extreme criticisms of science that question the ontological and epistemological basis of the discipline. While social, economic and political factors do determine what kinds of science get privileged, they do not affect the subject matter of science, the 'objective world'. For example, American research in the 1940s and 1950s on quantum electronics was motivated in large part by potential military applications.[18] However, as Alan Sokal points out, these motivations or other extraneous factors have no effect on the underlying scientific question of whether atoms really do behave according to the laws of quantum mechanics.[19] There is a substantial body of convincing evidence that support the belief that the behaviour of atoms can indeed be described by quantum mechanics.

FACTORS SPECIFIC TO INDIA

In the context of Indian nuclear policy, historically there have been both elements of continuity and rupture. At the level of setting up the necessary infrastructure and the activities of the scientific and technological establishment one can discern continuity and a steady progression over the decades. This continuity is possible because nuclear scientists have been able to pursue programs that diverge in subtle ways from proclaimed policy; this ability, in turn, is related to the structure of nuclear policy making and implementation in India. Unlike most policy matters where the cabinet has the ultimate authority, the agency in charge of nuclear affairs is the Atomic Energy Commission, which was constituted under a special act of parliament, and is composed primarily of scientists and dominated by the top leaders of the Department of Atomic Energy (DAE). The DAE was set up in 1954 under the direct charge of the Prime Minister. In addition to the head of the DAE, it has 'been a tradition for several years to have the Principal Secretary to the Prime Minister, the Cabinet Secretary, Chairman, [and managing director of the] Nuclear Power Corporation, and Director, Bhabha Atomic Research Centre (BARC) as members of the AEC.'[20] Further, the structure of the DAE is hierarchical and not conducive to open dissent. Thus, even if junior scientists had qualms about working on some project, they would have few alternatives. In addition there are no institutions outside of the DAE that work on nuclear technology. With one exception, no university does research or offers a degree in nuclear engineering. Nuclear scientists, therefore, have no alternative to working in the DAE. This resulted in a situation where the 'majority of workers and administrators in the scientific establishments play only a marginal role.'[21]

Added to this is the fact that the DAE, like the larger scientific community in India, has had relatively few notable accomplishments. There have been, for example, no Nobel Prizes awarded to any scientist for work conducted in post-independence India. An important study of the scientific community in India found that most scientists were troubled by the marginal position of scientific activity in India in general, and of their own scientific research in particular.[22] The lack of relevance, perceived or real, of scientific research to the actual problems of India further accentuates the peripherality of scientists and results in widespread demoralisation. The shrill rhetoric, especially on the part of the nuclear and missile establishments, about self-sufficiency and indigenous development is indicative of the desire for wider recognition. Building nuclear weapons and thereby being seen as serving a national priority by the elite has, therefore, been an answer to the larger failure on the part of the DAE to either produce world class science or provide cheap and reliable electricity.

While, as mentioned earlier, there has been continuity in some aspects of Indian nuclear policy, at the level of doctrine there have been sharp differences between different governments across the years.[23] These differences influenced and were influenced by middle class and elite perceptions, both of nuclear weapons and, more generally, of India's position and role in the world. One of the clear discontinuities or ruptures is the difference between the 'official nationalism' of the Nehruvian period and that of the contemporary *Hindutva* moment.

During the Nehruvian phase, the attempts to consolidate society and to fashion a national identity produced an 'official nationalism' (generally upheld by the state and its directing personnel).[24] Given the elite notion that Indian independence was to lead to India finding its rightful place in the world, it was not surprising that it adopted a particular 'big vision'. Accordingly, postcolonial state-formation privileged 'Big Science, Big Development, Big Projects, and Big Goals'. This vision continues to be prevalent. Absent during the Nehruvian era, however, was a role for 'Big Weapons'. In other words, it was not a route to greatness through the acquisition of massive destructive capability.

The rise of Hindu nationalism or *Hindutva* in recent years is due to a new 'elite insecurity' arising from the increasing social and political assertion of marginalized groups and the uncertainties associated with economic liberalization.[25] *Hindutva's* answer to this is a quest for 'international status', through the deployment of symbolic gestures of 'great power status' such as the ability to acquire and test nuclear weapons. The May 1998 tests, or for that matter the destruction of a sixteenth century mosque, the Babri Masjid in Ayodhya in 1992, are acts that demonstrate how it envisions making India 'strong'.

The leaders of the various institutions comprising the strategic enclave are certainly part of the elite, and their views are shaped by these shifts in official ideology. In fact, these leaders were more than sensitive to such shifts so as to advance their respective institutional interests. While individual leaders did have their own personality traits and priorities, their actions are strongly constrained by the structural details explained above and their positions as heads of institutions. It is in this light that one must read the history of the involvement of scientists with the bomb in India.

HISTORY

Perhaps the first important event in the setting up of the Indian nuclear program was a letter written by Homi Bhabha in March 1944 to the Sir Dorab Tata Trust, requesting funds to set up a research institute. In his letter, Bhabha promised: 'When Nuclear Energy has been successfully applied for power production in say a couple of decades from now, India will not have to look abroad for its experts but will find them ready at hand.'[26] These experts were to form the priesthood that managed nuclear affairs.

The institution of the Indian Atomic Energy Commission (AEC) in early 1948, barely a few months after independence, speaks to Bhabha's influence and the prominence accorded by Jawaharlal Nehru, India's first Prime Minister, to the atomic energy enterprise. The bill enabling this was introduced at the Constituent Assembly by Nehru and made atomic energy the exclusive responsibility of the state.[27] Modelled on Britain's Atomic Energy Act, the act imposed even greater secrecy over research and development than did either the British or American atomic energy legislation.[28] Nehru gave two reasons for the imposition of secrecy. 'The advantage of our research would go to others before we even reaped it, and secondly, it would become impossible for us to cooperate with any country which is prepared to cooperate with us in this matter, because it will not be prepared for the results of researches to become public.'[29]

To say that U.S., Canada, England and so on, from whom India got much of its early nuclear know-how, would steal ideas from Indian research is disingenuous at the very least. Further, it is not clear why 'others' should not benefit from 'our research'. India, after all, was planning to benefit from the results of research carried out by western countries. But, in the post-independence milieu, such questions never arose in the Constituent Assembly. Neither were questions raised about the appropriateness of choosing nuclear energy as the path to India's development. As Zia Mian's nuanced analysis makes clear, the tone set by Nehru's arguments for investing in the program precluded any such doubts.

Nehru argued that by not having developed steam power and having thus missed out on the industrial revolution, India became a backward country. And what was the expression of that backwardness? In a clear reference to colonialism, he said, 'it became a slave country because of that.' The connection to atomic power became obvious. Nehru argued: 'the point I should like the House to consider is this, that if we are to remain abreast in the world as a nation which keeps ahead of things, we must develop this atomic energy.'[30]

But Nehru could not prevent censure on another count. At least one member of the assembly, Krishnamurthy Rao from Mysore, strongly criticized the secrecy provisions in the bill.[31] Though he claimed to support the act, Rao asserted that the bill did not allow for the oversight and the checking and balancing mechanisms contained in the U.S. Atomic Energy Act. He also pointed out that in the bill passed by the British, secrecy is restricted only to defense purposes and demanded to know if in the Indian bill secrecy was insisted upon even for research for peaceful purposes.

Nehru's response to this is surprising for someone who has spoken so eloquently about the peaceful uses of nuclear energy. He said: 'I do not know how to distinguish the two [peaceful and defense purposes].' Nehru's dilemma is clear from his statements while introducing the bill. On the one hand he said, 'I think we must develop it for peaceful purposes.' But he went on, 'Of course, if we are compelled as a nation to use it for other purposes, possibly no pious sentiments will stop the nation from using it that way.' Barely two years after the wholesale destruction of Hiroshima and Nagasaki, the 'other purposes' were obvious.[32]

Within the AEC itself, it was clear that the commission was created not only to generate nuclear electricity; its aims were explicitly to develop 'atomic energy for *all purposes*.'[33] [emphasis added.] M.R. Srinivasan, who headed the DAE in the 1980s, explicitly states the view within the commission: '[N]uclear technology was developed by a country to be solely available for its own benefit, whether for peaceful purposes or for military applications.'[34] Since the AEC fell directly under the direct personal oversight of the Prime Minister, which in practical terms meant that the head of the DAE called the shots, the DAE operated with no controls whatsoever.

The DAE's plans for the nuclear program were ambitious and envisaged covering the entire nuclear fuel cycle. Despite the rhetoric of indigenous development that pervaded, Bhabha and other leaders approached and accepted technical and financial aid from several countries such as the U.S., Britain and Canada.[35] *Apsara,* the first Indian reactor, for example, was based on a British design and used fuel rods manufactured in Britain. Likewise, it was an American firm, Vitro International, which was awarded the contract to prepare blueprints for the first reprocessing plant at Trombay. Between 1955 and 1974, 1104 Indian scientists were sent to various U.S. facilities; 263 were trained at Canadian facilities prior to 1971.[36]

Central to the effort to create the wherewithal to produce nuclear weapons was the second research reactor, CIRUS, a 40 MW heavy water moderated, light water cooled, natural uranium fuelled reactor using the same design as the NRX reactor at Chalk River in Canada.[37] Canada supplied the reactor as part of its Colombo plan—a plan that was, in the words of Robert Bothwell, 'premised on the relation between misery and poverty and communism.'[38] Initiated by Nik Cavell, administrator of the Colombo plan, the idea of donating a reactor to India was supported by W.B. Lewis, head of AECL, Canada, and a fellow student of Bhabha's at Cambridge. The occasion for the announcement of the gift was the 1955 Geneva Conference on the peaceful uses of atomic energy. Following shortly after the 1953 Atoms for Peace initiative by Eisenhower, the conference was the scene of much cold war era manoeuvring as well as an opportunity for countries to exhibit their nuclear wares and woo potential customers. [39]

A few Canadian diplomats realized that this could lead to potential acquisition of weapons useable plutonium by India. After all the NRX was an efficient producer of plutonium because of its high neutron economy. Nevertheless the initiative went through because it was assumed that India would be able to acquire a reactor from some other source. Despite consistent efforts on the part of the Canadians, India, led by Bhabha, adamantly refused to accept any kind of voluntary controls or safeguards on the spent fuel produced.[40]

The ostensible reason for this refusal was the three-phase nuclear power program for India that Bhabha had put forward. This program involved separating plutonium from the spent fuel produced in natural uranium reactors and setting up breeder reactors, which in turn could be used to utilize India's vast resources of thorium for energy production.[41] Separated plutonium, therefore, was an essential requirement. The leap of logic that was put forward was that the imposition of safeguards would disallow plutonium acquisition. Hence, safeguards were considered unacceptable.

It is worth clarifying that there is no *a priori* reason why the imposition of safeguards would prevent the development of a breeder program. For example, the Japanese breeder program runs fully under international safeguards. The more obvious and honest reason for opposing safeguards by Bhabha and subsequent leaders is the insistence on keeping the bomb option open, right from the inception of the nuclear program. But with practically no one in the country outside of the Atomic Energy establishment familiar with nuclear technology, questions about the proffered excuse were never raised.

When it suited his purposes, however, Bhabha also accepted safe-guards. Examples of this are the reactors at Tarapur (TAPS I and II) and Rawatbhata (RAPS I and II). Bhabha's speech in 1956 at a con-ference on the International Atomic Energy Agency's statute makes clear the strategy he adopted. '[T]here are,' Bhabha said, 'many states, technically advanced, which may undertake with Agency aid, fulfilling all the present safeguards, but in addition run their own parallel programs independently of the Agency in which they could use the experience and know-how obtained in Agency-aided projects, without being subject in any way to the system of safeguards.'[42] Thus, India would use international assistance to further its weapon and civilian applications of nuclear power.

At the same time as these developments were occurring, the fifties also marked Nehru's determined pursuit of global nuclear dis-armament. Prominent among his initiatives was the Comprehensive Test Ban Treaty (CTBT).[43] Nehru also supported the activities of the international peace movement, in particular British philosopher-mathematician Bertrand Russell's initiative to foster contact between American and Soviet scientists. For a time, it seemed that the Indian government would sponsor what eventually became the Pugwash conferences.[44] New Delhi was in fact chosen as the first conference site and in June 1956 Russell dispatched invitations for a conference there in January 1957.[45] That was not to be. As Russell lamented: '[Nehru] had been exceedingly friendly. But when I met Dr Bhabha, India's leading official scientist. . . . I received a cold douche. He had profound doubts about any such manifesto, let alone any such conference as I had in mind for the future (Pugwash). It became evident that I should receive no encouragement from Indian official scientific quarters.'[46] Not a single Indian nuclear scientist signed the famous Russell-Einstein manifesto.[47] Nehru, however, set up an official group to study the effects of nuclear explosions at Russell's suggestion.[48]

Balancing this concern of Nehru's in nuclear disarmament was Bhabha's interest in and awareness of weapons technology. As early as 1959, he told the Parliamentary Consultative Committee on Atomic Energy that India's atomic energy program had progressed to the point where it could make atomic weapons without external aid if called upon to do so.

More revealing is George Perkovich's account of a private meeting in 1960 between Nehru, Bhabha and an American military engineer, K.D. Nichols. After his forty-five minute presentation about the advantages of American reactors, Nehru, according to Nichols, turned to Bhabha and asked him if he could develop an atomic bomb and how long it would take him to build it. Bhabha replied that he could do it in about a year. Upon which Nehru turned to Nichols and asked him if he agreed with Bhabha. An astonished Nichols replied in the affirmative. Whereupon Nehru turned to Bhabha and said: 'Well, don't do it till I tell you to.' With the benefit of hindsight, and perhaps the scepticism that comes easily to anyone who examines the Department of Atomic Energy's record, Perkovich also notes that Bhabha's claim had 'no basis in fact'.[49] Even under the most optimistic assumptions a bomb could not have been made before 1963.[50]

The 1962 Indo–China war marked an early successful public attempt at integrating the nuclear enterprise with national security when Bhabha offered the services of the Atomic Energy Establishment at Trombay (now the Bhabha Atomic Research Centre) to help with defense systems. He also canvassed with the government and set up an Electronics Committee with himself as the chairman.[51] Political authorities were certainly favourable to this kind of nexus between science and military affairs. As early as 1946, Jawaharlal Nehru stated, 'Modern defense as well as modern industry require scientific research both on a *broad* scale and in *highly specialised ways*. If India has not got highly qualified scientists and up-to-date scientific institutions in large numbers, it must remain a weak country incapable of playing a primary part *in a war*.' [emphases added.]

Scientists and their institutions were thus portrayed as crucial components of the state in peace and especially in war.[52]

The year 1962 also marked the adoption of a revised Atomic Energy Act by the parliament. The act significantly tightened secrecy and the AEC's control over all activities related to atomic energy. What was also significant, as Itty Abraham notes, was that neither the act nor the debate that took place in parliament when introducing the act did not, for the most part, mention the by then traditional focus on 'peaceful uses'.[53] Tacitly, the connection between nuclear power and national security was being elevated.

Three events mark the shift in India's nuclear program during the next few years. The first was the death of Jawaharlal Nehru. While encouraging the development of a militarily capable nuclear infrastructure, Nehru had always opposed explicit weaponization. As late as 1957, when speaking at the Lok Sabha, Nehru declared that in no event would India use nuclear energy for destructive purposes.[54] During his tenure as the Prime Minister, there was only one instance when a parliamentarian ever called for the development of nuclear weapons. This was Ramachandra Bade, a member of the Jan Sangh, the precursor to the current Bharatiya Janata Party (BJP), who wanted the development of nuclear weapons to counter Russia and China.[55] The second event was the first Chinese nuclear test in 1964, barely two years after India lost the war with China. Third was the completion of a reprocessing plant at Trombay in 1964, which, along with the CIRUS reactor that became critical in July 1960, gave India the ability to extract plutonium and thus to make nuclear weapons.

By the time of the Chinese test, Bhabha had, for all practical purposes, began a public, though sometimes indirect, campaign for developing nuclear weapon capability. The campaign consisted of three elements. First, in response to one of the main objections against building nuclear weapons, Bhabha made exaggerated claims about how cheap nuclear weapons were. On 24 October 1964, for example, in a broadcast on the state-run All-India Radio (AIR), Bhabha quoted a paper published by the Lawrence Radiation

Laboratory, Livermore, U.S.A., to assert that a 10 kiloton (kT) bomb would cost only U.S.$350,000 or Rs17.5 lakhs. And on the basis of these figures he claimed that 'a stockpile of fifty atomic bombs would cost under Rs10 crores and a stockpile of fifty two-megaton hydrogen bombs something of the order of Rs15 crores and argued that this was 'small compared with the military budgets of many countries.'[56] The 'bomb lobby' repeatedly used this speech to claim that nuclear weapons could be produced quite easily and at a relatively low cost even by a poor country like India.[57]

Second was the technical claim about DAE's ability to build nuclear weapons. Speaking in London on 4 October 1964, nearly two weeks *before* the first Chinese test, Bhabha declared that India could explode an atom bomb within eighteen months of a decision to do so.[58] And, in an attempt to provoke Prime Minister Lal Bahadur Shastri, he went on to add, 'But I do not think such a decision will be taken.' Seemingly in response to this, Shastri, who was attending a conference of non-aligned nations in Cairo at that time, declared that India's nuclear establishment was 'under firm orders not to make a single experiment, not to perfect a single device which is not needed for peaceful uses of nuclear energy.'[59]

The last caveat was the basis of the third element of Bhabha's campaign—advocating work towards building Peaceful Nuclear Explosives (PNE). Indeed, in his crucial Lok Sabha speech on 27 November 1964 that sanctioned work towards a PNE, Shastri revealed that: 'Dr Bhabha has made it quite clear to me that as far as we can progress and improve upon nuclear devices, we should do so, as far as development is possible, we should resort to it so that we can reap its peaceful benefits and we can use it for the development of our nation.' What is also significant is that Shastri had met with Bhabha just before the Lok Sabha session.[60] Clearly, Bhabha played a crucial role in obtaining political support for the PNE program.

Earlier the same year, speaking at a Pugwash Conference in Udaipur, Bhabha gave a description of a deterrent relationship between two countries, even if one is much more powerful than the other. As though offering an example, Bhabha focussed on China: '[A] country with a huge population, such as China, must always present a threat to its smaller neighbours, a threat they can only meet either by collective security or by recourse to nuclear weapons to redress the imbalance in size.' Though he did not mention India by name, it is clear what he thought were the options available to India. Following from this, Bhabha suggested that the only possible collective security measure would be a guarantee from both the United States and the Soviet Union.[61] The astute Bhabha could not but have recognized that neither country was likely to offer such assurances. Relations between the U.S. and India were often tense and Russia had not extended a nuclear umbrella to any country outside of the Warsaw Pact. Given the only two options that he had laid out, it was easy to figure out what he was recommending for India's nuclear policy. In the audience were Vikram Sarabhai, who was soon to succeed Bhabha as the head of the atomic program, Prime Minister-to-be Indira Gandhi, and V.C. Trivedi, who was to go on to be the principal negotiator at the Nuclear Non-Proliferation Treaty (NPT) talks.

The momentum set off by Bhabha's pronouncements continued even after his sudden demise in a plane crash in 1966. Sarabhai, who took over after Bhabha, differed somewhat on the question of nuclear weapons. As George Perkovich put it: 'Sarabhai questioned the morality and utility of nuclear weapons for India and would soon take steps to reverse the peaceful nuclear explosives project.'[62] While the attempted reversals are a matter of record, Sarabhai's intentions may not have derived entirely from morality. Nor did he completely reject the idea of nuclear weapons for India. What he did not endorse was the particular PNE program envisioned by Bhabha and other senior DAE scientists. As Sarabhai himself was to declare: 'Let our emphasis be on reality and not on show. I am opposed to gimmicks.'[63] This view was at variance with the importance given to 'performative gestures' by Bhabha, Nehru, and especially the present ruling party, the BJP. For Sarabhai, then, developing the bomb carried no symbolic meaning; instead he evaluated it in concrete, military and economic terms.

In Itty Abraham's reading, 'Sarabhai was arguing, first, that India could not afford an atomic deterrent in order to be secure from external threats, as nothing short of a full-fledged atomic weapons arsenal with all its concomitant systems (delivery systems, second strike capability, command and control infrastructure) would provide that security. Second, and more subversively, he suggests that perhaps the more serious threat to national security came from within the country—and atomic weapons were certainly not going to be of help there.'[64]

Despite Sarabhai's attempts to shift the focus of India's nuclear policy, the PNE effort continued. As Raja Ramanna, one of the leaders of the 1974 test, acknowledged in a private interview, 'Sarabhai could not keep scientists from doing their work. He couldn't look over our shoulders.'[65] In other words, the normal autonomy accorded to scientists in their research helped the bomb makers.[66] Design work on the nuclear explosive tested at Pokharan began in 1968.[67] Under the leadership of R. Chidambaram and Ramanna, and in cooperation with B.D. Nag Chaudhuri, scientific adviser to the Minister of Defense and Director of the Defense Research and Development Organization (DRDO), about fifty to seventy-five scientists from DAE and DRDO were directly involved in the project.

On 18 May 1974, at the height of a nation-wide railway strike (led by George Fernandes, who was then a trade union leader and later became the Defense Minister), India conducted its first nuclear test at Pokharan in the desert in Rajasthan.[68] In domestic circles, enthusiastic reception followed the tests. The scientists were feted repeatedly. Popular magazines like the *Illustrated Weekly of India* and *Science Today* carried glowing reports on the scientists— Sethna, Ramanna, and Iyengar in particular—who made it happen.[69]

The role of the Atomic Energy establishment in pushing for the 1974 test was considerable. Apart from Bhabha, senior scientists like Homi Sethna, Raja Ramanna, P.K. Iyengar and R. Chidambaram—all of whom went on to head India's Atomic Energy Commission—played important roles in building up momentum to test. As summarized by Perkovich, 'Whatever Mrs [Indira] Gandhi's calculus [in conducting the test], the fact remained that conducting the PNE was not her idea. She disposed what others proposed: it was Ramanna, Sethna, Iyengar, Chidambaram, and, before them, Bhabha who made the PNE possible.'[70] To these leaders, observes Itty Abraham, the 1974 test was 'a symbol of the changing fortunes of the atomic energy establishment.'[71]

Soon after the 1974 test, scientists began lobbying for further nuclear tests involving more sophisticated designs. From statements after the 1998 tests, it seems likely that P.K. Iyengar and R. Chidambaram had developed a boosted fission design that they wanted to test in early 1983.[72] Scientists were also interested in making a hydrogen bomb. Conceptual work on this probably began in the late 1970s but may not have been pursued vigorously. In a private interview to W.P.S. Sidhu, Ramanna admitted that when he got back from Jodhpur after the 1974 test, he met Indira Gandhi and told her, 'madam now we'll have to work on the hydrogen bomb [H-bomb]. She said, 'I knew that pressure was coming but not that fast.' So, that settled it'.[73] What is more certain is that ever since the 1974 test, DAE and DRDO scientists were working quietly to produce more reliable neutron initiators, enhance the simultaneity of high explosive charges, miniaturizing a device and improve its yield-to-weight ratio. Work on the latter two areas demonstrates, even to those who believed that a meaningful distinction can be made between a 'Peaceful Nuclear Explosion' and a nuclear weapons test, that the purpose of the Department of Atomic Energy was not only the exploitation of 'atomic energy for . . . peaceful purposes.'[74]

Sometime in late 1982 or early 1983 Raja Ramanna and V.S. Arunachalam, director of the Defense Research and Development Organization, made their case for a nuclear test to Mrs Gandhi. Without portraying the test as the beginning of a nuclear weapons program, Ramanna and Arunachalam focused on the technical arguments for testing new designs. At the end of the meeting, Indira

Gandhi tentatively agreed for a nuclear test, only to change her mind within twenty-four hours.[75] One of the causes for the change is said to have been a conversation with M.K. Rasgotra, India's foreign secretary, who was reportedly confronted by an American official with satellite evidence displaying preparations going on at the test site. The conversation seems to have convinced Indira Gandhi that the U.S. reaction would be strong and it would impact on the economic troubles India was experiencing at the time.[76]

Instead it is reported that Mrs Gandhi wanted to test at 'the appropriate moment' and in the meanwhile she wanted to 'develop other things and keep them ready,' as well as to 'make further improvements in . . . [weapons] designs.'[77] The 'other things' that she had in mind were long range ballistic missiles to be developed under the aegis of the DRDO (Defense Research and Development Organization).

Set up in 1958 as a department of the Ministry of Defense, the Defense Research and Development Organization (DRDO) is the primary source of Indian military research and development.[78] As early as 1962, under 'Project Indigo,' an Indo–Swiss agreement was signed to design and manufacture a Surface-to-Air Missile (SAM). But with the purchase of SA-2 SAMs from the Soviet Union, the project was cancelled.[79] It was in February 1972 that the DRDO embarked on its first missile development undertaking, 'Project Devil', which aimed at reverse engineering the SA-2 missile. The project was managed by Air Commodore V.S. Narayanan, who went on to become the director of the Defense Research and Development Laboratory (DRDL).[80] The project reportedly had a budget of about US$700 million and employed between 700 and 800 technical personnel.[81] By 1974, two liquid propulsion rocket motors had reportedly been developed. However, after the failure of several prototypes, the project was cancelled in 1978. Though it failed to create a complete system, the Devil project led to the development of several critical technologies and components that formed the basis of the *Prithvi* and *Agni* missiles.

In 1983, shortly after the aborted nuclear test, the Integrated Guided Missile Development Program (IGMDP) was set up. From the beginning the program had high bureaucratic priority and many standard procurement and funding procedures were overridden.[82] The program started with the development of five missile systems— the short range *Prithvi* (earth); the intermediate range *Agni* (fire); the surface to air missiles *Akash* (sky); *Trishul* (trident); and the guided anti-tank *Nag* (snake). By 1988, the results of the new program were visible with the first test of *Prithvi* on 25 February.[83] This was followed the next year with a test of *Agni*. Other missile systems are also reportedly under development such as the *Pinaka*, the *Sagarika* and the *Astra*.

Unlike earlier efforts to develop missiles, the missile program borrowed expertise and personnel from the Department of Space, most prominently in the form of Abdul Kalam, who was chosen to head IGMDP (Integrated Guided Missile Development Program). Kalam had earlier led the Space Launch Vehicle Program and thus was intimate with the details of solid propellant technology that was used for the first stage of the *Agni* missile. Kalam's greater contribution, however, may have been the way he chose to run the project. In a break with earlier 'autistic' practices, the IGMDP involved not only the defense laboratories, but also technical institutions, universities, ordnance factories belonging to the Ministry of Defense, and public and private sector firms.[84] Following the nuclear tests of May 1998, this network has been feted. In January 1999, on the eve of Republic Day, a government press release proudly proclaimed that, 'DRDO laboratories with a partner network of R&D organizations, academic institutions and industries, have been and are progressing high technology systems, against all possible difficulties. Today the nation is proud of DRDO . . .'[85]

The missile efforts and the development of more advanced designs were continued by Rajiv Gandhi when he took over the leadership of the country. Rajiv Gandhi brought in two contrasting tendencies into policy making. The first was an unprecedented expansion of military spending and defense modernization.[86] The second was a youthful ardour in pursuing nuclear disarmament. The latter resulted in the proposals like the plan for a world free of nuclear weapons that Rajiv Gandhi presented to the Special Session on Disarmament of the United Nations General Assembly in June 1988.[87] But, at the same time, Rajiv Gandhi also formed a small group, including scientists like Raja Ramanna, R. Chidambaram and Abdul Kalam, to 'sketch India's nuclear weapon requirements and the anticipated costs required to meet them.'[88] The task force concluded that India could have a nuclear force that would 'include the *Agni* and *Prithvi* missiles, aircraft and an appropriate number of warheads in low three digit figures.'[89]

According to K. Subrahmanyam, shortly after putting forward his plan for nuclear disarmament at the United Nations in 1988 and being disappointed with the lack of positive response, Rajiv Gandhi gave the go-ahead to the DRDO under Arunachalam and the BARC under P.K. Iyengar to proceed with the Indian nuclear weapons program. Soon after that V.P. Singh, the new Indian Prime Minister, named Raja Ramanna Minister of State for Defense, signalling, perhaps, that the government was interested in pursuing the nuclear weapons program. This was strengthened with the appointment of P.K. Iyengar, who had been an important member of the team involved in the 1974 Pokharan test, as chairman of the Atomic Energy Commission in 1990. The first 'Indian nuclear deterrent'— the ability to quickly assemble nuclear weapons that could be delivered by air—is said to have come into existence around this time.[90] Nevertheless, even well into the 1990s, prominent scientists such as R. Chidambaram claimed that India had not 'stockpiled' or 'deployed' nuclear weapons.[91]

Retired scientists, however, were more forthright, perhaps in an attempt to further the nuclear weapons effort. Thus, for example, in his 1991 autobiography, Raja Ramanna, in contrast to official claims that the 1974 test was a peaceful nuclear explosion, described how he had 'been involved in the development of a *prototype weapon.*'[92] [emphasis added.] P.K. Iyengar, in his 1993 retirement speech, raised the profile of the program by claiming that 'to have been able to put together an atomic device in 1974 was the most exhilarating experience of my career.'[93] M.R. Srinivasan advised the Indian government to become more 'hawkish' on the nuclear issue.[94]

In 1994, official scientists like AEC chairman Chidambaram and DRDO chief Abdul Kalam started a media campaign to counter American non-proliferation initiatives. Breaking a long-standing rule of the establishment, Chidambaram, in an interview to *India Today*, boasted about 'how good our bomb was' when asked about the 1974 test.[95] Former AEC chairman M.R. Srinivasan declared in an interview in the *Indian Express* that, '[t]here are responsible persons who know we have the nuclear weapons capability,' and suggested that '[w]e should have followed the Chinese example of open defiance and cultivation of force.'[96]

Other media hawks, fed with material by scientists, added to the pressure for full-scale tests. By August 1995, the test site at Pokharan was being prepared for nuclear tests. According to former top-level scientists and policy advisors, 'the strategic enclave did not need explicit political authorization to maintain the site or make other test preparation.'[97] According to interviews conducted by Perkovich, the scientists justified their pressure for further tests on three grounds: 'they needed to perfect and demonstrate their technological innovations; they believed that only full-scale explosive tests could validate their work, and therefore the nuclear deterrent; they needed explosive tests to both recruit and retain talented scientists and engineers in the nuclear and defense programs when higher paying jobs awaited them in the commercial sector.' However, the planned test was called off.

Shortly thereafter the Bharatiya Janata Party (BJP) came to power in May 1996 on a hawkish platform. Scientists sought to seize the opportunity afforded by the BJP's nuclear hawkishness as soon as possible and increased preparations even before the BJP formed the government. Once again the tests were cancelled, this time because the BJP lost the vote of confidence in the parliament.

The debate over the Comprehensive Test Ban Treaty (CTBT) in 1996 was a crucial turning point in Indian nuclear policy. Even as late as March 1996, the Indian Foreign Secretary, Salman Haider said, 'We do not believe that the acquisition of nuclear weapons is essential for our national security and we have followed a conscious decision in this regard.' This was completely in line with the traditional Indian view on not relying on nuclear weapons for its security. But, on 20 June 1996, when Arundhati Ghose, then the Indian Ambassador to the Conference on Disarmament, rejected the CTBT in the present form, she said that the CTBT was not 'in India's national security interest' and 'our national security considerations (have) become a key factor in our decision-making.'

Scientists, who realized that signing the CTBT would enormously hamper their nuclear weapons efforts, lobbied behind the scenes and publicly adopted the position that the CTBT should be linked with 'a time-bound program for total elimination of all nuclear weapons.'[98] Opposing the CTBT represented a public relations opportunity for the nuclear establishment to counter publicly aired doubts about the functioning of the nuclear establishment and to provide its personnel with continued incentives for furthering nuclear weapons work.[99]

Having succeeded in getting India to vote against the CTBT, the nuclear establishment approached the Indian Prime Minister H.D. Deve Gowda for permission to conduct tests. In his own words, Deve Gowda declined, 'not because of the adverse reaction from the international community but because of my concern for improving the economic situation of the country.'[100]

With the BJP coming back to power in 1998, scientists busied themselves with preparing for the expected tests. Even before the election results came out, while talking to a journalist about nuclear tests, R. Chidambaram came as close to publicly advocating nuclear weapon tests as any serving AEC chairman had.[101] First Chidambaram claimed that, 'we are prepared . . ., but it is [for] the policy makers to decide whether to go nuclear or keep the options open.' Then, when asked about the possibility of using computer simulations to develop nuclear weapons, Chidambaram responded, '[T]hen what was the use of some countries going for 2000 explosions?' And further added, '[the] higher the database, [the] better the simulations.'[102]

With the tests of 11 and 13 May 1998, India's nuclear weapon scientists finally achieved 'their dreams'. Speaking at a joint DAE–DRDO press conference, Abdul Kalam proclaimed that, 'weaponization is now complete.' There have also been statements that the tests have 'significantly enhanced our capability in computer simulations of new designs and taken us to the stage of sub-critical experiments in the future, if considered necessary.' Regardless of the accuracy of these claims, the implicit reference to the example of the Stockpile Stewardship Program in the United States suggests that the leaders of the Indian nuclear program now think of it as being similar to those of Los Alamos and Lawrence Livermore.

Soon after the May 1998 tests, the Indian Prime Minister Atal Behari Vajpayee publicly celebrated the role of the scientists who designed the weapons and conducted the explosions, raising science to the level hitherto reserved for those who protect the nation and feed its citizens. Though left unsaid, as must be obvious from the context, it is the kind of science practiced by the strategic enclave that he sought to place on a pedestal. Shortly thereafter, this felicitation also translated to massive budget increases for these establishments as well as several national awards to these scientists.

The nuclear and missile establishments have used their current influence and increased funding to further weapons programs. Research on nuclear weapons with the aim of qualitative improvements and development of new designs continues. One weapon system that seems to be receiving a lot of attention is the neutron bomb; according to R. Chidambaram, India can make one.[103] Following this claim, P.K. Iyengar called for testing one.[104] Abdul Kalam, drawing on the infamous Star Wars program of the United States, proposed building a missile shield around New Delhi.[105] Another 'futuristic' weapon being pursued is a 'beam weapon' that uses bursts of microwaves.[106]

Hand-in-hand with these qualitative developments, the nuclear establishment has also pushed for the increase in quantity of nuclear weapons material. Accordingly, in December 1999, India's Minister of State for Atomic Energy announced plans to construct a new plutonium production reactor comparable to its 100 MW Dhruva plant.[107] All these suggest that the pressure from the nuclear and missile establishments will contribute greatly to an arms race in South Asia, with disastrous consequences to the inhabitants of the region.

OPPOSITION

Alongside this history of canvassing for, propelling and building the bomb and the associated means of delivery, what must also be mentioned is the role of the, unfortunately few, scientists in resisting these efforts.

Despite the Nehruvian commitment to big science, the contours and institutional focus of the nuclear establishment was by no means pre-determined. Much before Bhabha became a force to reckon with in Indian science policy, the scientist who dominated discussions and formulations of science policy was the prominent physicist and astrophysicist Meghnad Saha. As early as 1938, the then president of the Indian National Congress Subash Chandra Bose had invited Saha to join the National Planning Committee. Saha became the Chairman of the Power and Fuel Sub-Committee as well as a member of the River Transport and Irrigation Sub-Committees.[108] Prior to that Saha had started the influential science and science policy journal, *Science and Culture*, and used it to espouse his views on science planning. Saha's notions about the role of science in society were quite different from Bhabha's. Saha 'emphasized "judicious and equitable distribution" and advocated participatory democracy even in engineering projects that involve highly technical information and his nationalism was 'based on the rights and aspirations of the majority with little affiliation or identification with the Indian 'aristocratic classes'.'[109] Despite the deep political roots in the Indian nationalist movement that Saha and his group had, the more elitist group led by Bhabha prevailed over the more open and democratically disposed group led by Saha.[110]

Though ousted from power, Saha continued to argue for open and university-based research in nuclear physics. He opposed the AEC because it had 'enveloped itself in a cloud of secrecy.' In a memorandum to Nehru, Saha suggested that, 'the true facts of atomic energy and its implications should be placed before the country; discussion and expert knowledge and viewpoints of different groups will enable a policy to be shaped.' But all that was of no avail. Indian nuclear policy continued to be fashioned by a small coterie of decision-makers and scientists.

Saha was not alone among the ranks of well-known scientists who opposed Bhabha and the AEC. Throughout the same period, the well-known physicist C.V. Raman was very critical of nuclear weapons and of the militarization of science.[111] D.D. Kosambi, a prominent mathematician, also made an unsuccessful attempt at trying to maintain an open and participatory system and questioned high expenditures on atomic energy research and development. Unlike Saha and Raman, however, Kosambi did not head his own institution; in 1962 he was removed from his position as senior fellow at the Tata Institute of Fundamental Research.[112]

Though without much success, opposition to the activities of the DAE has continued. In the 1980s, Amulya Reddy, a physical chemist who turned his attention to energy and rural development issues, assessed the costs of nuclear power in India and discovered several problems with the way the AEC was calculating the costs. In contrast to the claims of the AEC, Reddy concluded that other options like coal and hydroelectric power were cheaper than nuclear power under realistic, rather than optimistic, assumptions.[113] Later, he became one of the important figures in opposing the 1998 nuclear tests.

A completely different kind of engagement was demonstrated by members of the people's science movement and scientist-activists like Surendra and Sanghamitra Gadekar.[114] Surendra, a trained physicist, and Sanghamitra, a physician by training, brought out

Anumukti, South Asia's only anti-nuclear magazine. Apart from attacking different aspects of Indian nuclear policy, they carried out detailed health surveys of people living near nuclear facilities.

With the Indian nuclear tests of May 1998, opposition to nuclear weapons, and to a lesser extent nuclear energy, became much more prevalent, both among society at large and among many scientists. At least two groups of scientists launched petitions signed by hundreds of individuals condemning the action by the government. As a result, an organization by the name of 'Indian Scientists Against Nuclear Weapons' came into being.[115] Prominent among these scientists was T. Jayaraman, a faculty member at the Institute of Mathematical Sciences (IMSc) who went on to becoming one of the vocal critics of the BJP government's nuclear weapons efforts. Through his articles in Indian magazines and journals like, *Frontline* and *Seminar*, he raised difficult questions about the capabilities of the Indian nuclear establishment, the draft nuclear doctrine, the efficacy of deterrence and so on.

The May 1998 nuclear tests drew flak from even within the nuclear establishment. Dr N. Srinivasan, a former member of the Atomic Energy Commission and the first director of the Reactor Research Centre (now the Indira Gandhi Centre for Atomic Research) rued the impact of the 1998 tests on the nuclear power program: 'I have a sad feeling that the first nail was driven in the coffin of the nuclear power program in May '74 and the last nails have now been hammered in, in May '98. I fervently hope I am wrong.'[116]

Despite this relatively long history of opposition, anti-nuclear scientists in India have, for the most part, not made much use of their technical expertise. This has both good and bad consequences. In the West the peace and anti-nuclear movement was, in the words of Eqbal Ahmad, '. . .nuko-centric, phobo-centric (creating fear rather than understanding), techno-centric (concerned with the technology rather than causes) . . .'[117] This happened in part because of the privileging of the expertise of scientists. In India, on the other hand, scientists involved in anti-nuclear activities have, for the most part, come with significantly different political biographies. They are, therefore, more likely to pay heed to a vaster range of social problems, of which nuclear weapons are only one symptom, and not focus completely on technical issues.[118]

At the same time, there are, after all, technical issues related to nuclear weapons that have to be addressed through technical means.[119] Thus, there is a relative lack of independent technical expertise that could challenge statements and claims made by official scientists about various aspects of the nuclear weapons, and energy programs—for example, the technical feasibility, the economic viability, the safety of reactors, or the environmental impacts of the nuclear program. This would be very valuable. As Joel Primack and Frank von Hippel argued in their 1974 book, *Advice and Dissent*, '[The] way in which technical experts make their services available to society can significantly affect the distribution of political power.'[120]

Historically, there have been many differences between how scientists have responded to and affected nuclear policy in the U.S. and India. Apart from their contributions to building the nuclear complex, scientists in India have largely played only two kinds of roles: advisors supportive of government policy, often being even more hawkish, and dissidents. There are practically no examples of scientists who, as advisors, have exerted a moderating and disarming influence on the government.[121] To a small extent Vikram Sarabhai and M.R. Srinivasan played this role but their dual role as purveyors of the nuclear energy program imposed limits on their effectiveness in moderating policy. Further, as mentioned earlier, Sarabhai was not opposed to nuclear weapons *per se*. He was only opposed to symbolic acts without enough substance. Similarly, M.R. Srinivasan's concerns were only that India would 'get on to a vast weaponization program which is harmful to the interests of the common man in this country and to the people in the region generally.'[122] Nevertheless, he felt that weaponization is 'inevitable.'

In the wake of calls by the leaders of the strategic enclave to 'build up a military industrial complex',[123] it is imperative that scientists and society in general resist the pressures to turn all of science into 'the handmaid of the war machine'. In the United States, the combined effects of a large scale military industrial complex and what David Dickson terms: 'The New Politics of Science', has led to a situation wherein 'planning for science is now exclusively based— whether in the short, the medium, or the long term—on the needs of the military and the marketplace. Social objectives (such as the protection of health or the natural environment) . . . are accepted only to the extent that they are compatible with increased military strength or commercial profits.'[124] However, opposition to nuclear weapons or energy must not be seen as just that. It must be viewed as part of developing alternative sources of technical expertise, grounded in local realities and reflecting the aspirations of the vast majority of people.

CONCLUSION

India's nuclear program started with the promise of producing cheap electricity that was assumed to be necessary and, to a large extent, sufficient for 'progress'. Failing in this task, the program, or more precisely the institutions that ran the program, invented a different rationale to ensure continued funding. This was by entering the 'national security' business, clearly a goal certain to gain support from political elites. The nuclear establishment along with the DRDO, i.e., the strategic enclave, performed this task with enthusiasm. Their contributions are not confined merely to designing and manufacturing the bomb but also included lobbying with political leaders and mobilizing elite constituencies, often indirectly, but also directly through public advocacy for nuclear weapons and missiles. By seeking power through their claims of knowledge and expertise, the strategic enclave, and to some extent the larger scientific community, cannot escape responsibility for the enormous impacts on the 'one-sixth of humanity' that Prime Minister Vajpayee invoked to justify his decision to conduct the May 1998 nuclear tests. It is up to this one-sixth of humanity, i.e., the people of India, to hold them responsible.

Because the responsibility flows from the connection between knowledge and power, the road out of the bomb's shadow passes through the fields of power and knowledge. The challenge to the power of the elites comes from the 'new' social movements and the much older labour movements, which have been attempting to bring democracy and justice as the basis of decision making.[125] Scientists, as well as other professionals, with their knowledge and expertise must join this caravan.

REFERENCES

1. Amitav Ghosh, 'Countdown,' *Himal*, November 1998, pp. 16–27.
2. Alvin M. Weinberg, 'Social Institutions and Nuclear Energy,' *Science*, 7 July 1972, pp. 27–34. The choice of the term 'priesthood' to describe nuclear engineers is appropriate in ways other than Weinberg intended. As Antonio Gramsci argued: 'In the absence of [a sentimental connection], the relations between the intellectual and the people-nation are, or are reduced to, relationships of a purely bureaucratic and formal order; the intellectuals become a caste, or a priesthood.' See Antonio Gramsci, *Selections from the Prison Notebooks* (New York: International Publishers, 1971), p. 418.
3. 'The guided missile and nuclear programs in India . . . constitute a "strategic enclave." This enclave is defined as a subset of the Indian military-security complex—specifically, the set of research establishments and production facilities that are responsible for the development of these new programs. It is 'strategic' because the end product of the efforts forms the most advanced technological means toward the goal of national security and represents the currency of international prestige and power today. It is an "enclave" because institutionally, spatially and legally, the high-technology sectors of space and nuclear energy are distinct and different from the existing structure of the Indian military-security complex.' Itty Abraham, 'India's "Strategic Enclave": Civilian Scientists and Military Technologies,' *Armed Forces and Society* 18, no. 2 (Winter 1992), pp. 231–52, p. 233.
4. See for example George Perkovich, *India's Nuclear Bomb: The Impact on Global Proliferation* (Berkeley: University of California Press, 1999), pp. 458–59.
5. There is, of course, a difference between science and technology, and the vast majority of work that goes on in designing and manufacturing nuclear weapons would fall under the rubric of technology than science. Nevertheless, we use the terms science and scientists in a generic fashion without distinguishing them from technology for three reasons. First, public pronouncements about the bomb often portray it as a triumph of science rather than as an expression of technological prowess. Following the 1998 nuclear tests, practically all political parties showered praise on 'our

scientists' rather than 'our engineers'; Prime Minister Vajpayee, in fact, added *Jai Vigyan* (Hail Science) to the old slogan: *Jai Jawan, Jai Kisan* (Hail the Soldier, Hail the Farmer). Thus, in public consciousness, the makers of nuclear weapons are identified as scientists rather than engineers. Second, more often than not, the leaders of nuclear weapons programs around the world have been physicists rather than, say, engineers. Third, a substantial portion of the actual technical work done to develop a bomb can legitimately be considered scientific, including, for example, modelling the neutronics as a function of time or calculating the intensity of radiation pressure.

6. See for example Robert Gilpin, *American Scientists and Nuclear Weapons Policy* (Princeton: Princeton University Press, 1962); Lawrence Badash, *Scientists and the Development of Nuclear Weapons: From Fission to the Limited Test Ban Treaty 1939–1963*, (Atlantic Highlands: Humanities Press, 1995); and Matthew Evangelista, *Unarmed Forces: The Transnational Movement to End the Cold War*, (Ithaca: Cornell University Press, 1999). There are few similar studies about scientists in other nuclear weapon states.

7. See for example: David Holloway, *Stalin and the Bomb* (New Haven: Yale University Press, 1994); Margaret Gowing, *Independence and Deterrence: Britain and Nuclear Energy, 1945–1952* (London: Macmillan, 1974); Laurence Scheinman, *Atomic Energy Policy in France Under the Fourth Republic* (Princeton: Princeton University Press, 1965); John Wilson Lewis and Xue Litai, *China Builds the Bomb* (Stanford: Stanford University Press, 1988); and Avner Cohen, *Israel and the Bomb*, (New York: Columbia University Press, 1998).

8. Robert Jay Lifton and Greg Mitchell, *Hiroshima in America: A Half-Century of Denial*, (New York: Avon Books, 1995), p. 251.

9. Alice Kimball Smith, *A Peril and a Hope: The Scientists' Movement in America 1945–47*, 2nd ed., (Cambridge, U.S.A.: M.I.T. Press, 1970).

10. See for example Bruno Vitale, 'Scientists as Military Hustlers,' *Issues in Radical Science* (London: Free Association Books, 1985), pp. 73–87.

11. Solly Zuckerman, *Scientists and War: The Impact of Science on Military and Civil Affairs*, (London: Hamish Hamilton, 1966), p. 29.

12. Daniel J. Kevles, *The Physicists: The History of a Scientific Community in Modern America*, (Cambridge: Harvard University, 1995), p. 111.

13. This formulation draws on Richard Lewontin, *Biology as Ideology*, (New York: Harper Collins, 1992).

14. Anthony Giddens, *The Nation-State and Violence*, (Berkeley and Los Angeles: University of California Press, 1987), p. 293.

15. Julien Benda, *The Treason of the Intellectuals (La Trahison des Clercs)* (New Jersey, U.S.A.: Transaction Publishers).

16. Gyan Prakash, *Another Reason: Science and the Imagination of Modern India*, (Princeton: Princeton University Press, 1999), p. 3.

17. It has been argued that this 'independence' or 'detachment' makes science seem objective and authoritative, giving it the legitimating power that makes science a resource for the state. Chandra Mukerji, *A Fragile Power: Scientists and the State*, (Princeton: Princeton University Press, 1989), p. 191.

18. Paul Forman, 'Behind Quantum Electronics: National Security as Basis for Physical Research in the United States, 1940–1960', *Historical Studies in the Physical and Biological Sciences* 18, (1987), pp. 149–229.

19. Alan Sokal, 'What the *Social Text* Affair Does and Does not Prove', in: *A House Built on Sand: Exposing Postmodernist Myths about Science*, Noretta Koertge (ed.), (Oxford: Oxford University Press, 1998).

20. 'Atomic Energy Commission', available on the internet at http://www.dae.gov.in/aec.htm.

21. Ashok Kapur, 'India: The Nuclear Scientists and the State, the Nehru and Post-Nehru Years', in: *Scientists and the State: Domestic Structures and the International Context*, Etel Solingen (ed.), (Ann Arbor: The University of Michigan Press, 1994), pp. 209–29.

22. V. Shiva and J. Bandyopadhyay, 'The Large and Fragile Community of Scientists in India', *Minerva*, 18 (1980), pp. 575–94.

23. Praful Bidwai and Achin Vanaik, *South Asia on a Short Fuse: Nuclear Politics and the Future of Global Disarmament*, (New Delhi: Oxford University, 1999), p. 235.

24. Achin Vanaik, 'Ideologies of the State: Social-Historical Underpinnings of the Nuclearization of South Asia', (paper presented at workshop on 'Nuclear Understandings: Science, Society and the Bomb in South Asia', Dhaka, Bangladesh, 17 February 2000). On 'official nationalism' see, Benedict Anderson, *Imagined Communities: Reflections on the Origin and Spread of Nationalism*, (London: Verso, 1983).

25. Achin Vanaik, 'Ideologies of the State: Social-Historical Underpinnings of the Nuclearization of South Asia'.

26. G. Venkatraman, *Bhabha and his Magnificent Obsessions*, (Hyderabad: Universities Press, 1994), p. 141.

27. Itty Abraham, 'Towards a Reflexive South Asian Security Studies,' in: *South Asia Approaches the Millenium: Reexamining National Security*, ed. Marvin G. Weinbaum and Chetan Kumar, (Boulder: Westview Press, 1995), pp. 17–40.

28. George Perkovich, *India's Nuclear Bomb: The Impact on Global Proliferation*, p. 18.

29. Shyam Bhatia, *India's Nuclear Bomb*, (New Delhi: Vikas Publishing House, 1979), p. 84.

30. Zia Mian, 'Homi Bhabha killed a Crow', in *The Nuclear Debate: Ironies and Immoralities*, Zia Mian and Ashis Nandy, (Colombo: Regional Centre for Strategic Studies, 1998), p. 12.

31. Itty Abraham, 'Towards a Reflexive South Asian Security Studies'.

32. Zia Mian, *Homi Bhabha Killed a Crow*, p. 12.

33. Raja Ramanna, *Years of Pilgrimage*, (Delhi: Viking, 1991), p. 60.

34. M.R. Srinivasan, 'India's Atomic Adventure', *Frontline*, 15 August 1997, pp. 142–43.

35. The word indigenous was often applied to even minor modifications of imported systems. One ironic example of this practice is Abdul Kalam's description of an effort at reverse-engineering a Russian rocket-assisted take-off system as 'indigenous development.' See, A.P.J. Abdul Kalam with Arun Tiwari, *Wings of Fire: An Autobiography* (Hyderabad: Universities Press, 1999), p. 51.

36. George Perkovich, *India's Nuclear Bomb: The Impact on Global Proliferation*, p. 30, 482.

37. W.B. Lewis and H.J. Bhabha, 'The Canada–India Reactor: An Exercise in International Co-operation', in: 'Proceedings of the Second United Nations International Conference on the Peaceful Uses of Atomic Energy', vol. 1, *Progress in Atomic Energy*, (Geneva: United Nations, 1958), pp. 355–58. CIRUS stands for Canadian Indian Reactor; the U.S. was added later on when the U.S.A. supplied heavy water for the reactor.

38. Robert Bothwell, *Nucleus: The History of Atomic Energy of Canada Limited*, (Toronto: University of Toronto Press, 1988), pp. 350–71.

39. See for example the description in Peter Pringle and James Spigelman, *The Nuclear Barons*, (New York: Holt, Rinehart and Winston, 1981), pp. 165–78.

40. Ruth Fawcett, *Nuclear Pursuits: The Scientific Biography of Wilfrid Bennett Lewis*, (Montreal & Kingston: McGill-Queen's University Press, 1994), pp. 110–14.

41. See for example H.J. Bhabha and N.B. Prasad, 'A Study of the Contribution of Atomic Energy to a Power Program in India', in: *Proceedings of the Second United Nations International Conference on the Peaceful Uses of Atomic Energy*, vol. 1, *Progress in Atomic Energy*, (Geneva: United Nations, 1958), pp. 89–101. A careful assessment shows that the breeder reactor program is not likely to contribute significantly to India's electricity needs; see Rahul Tongia and V.S. Arunachalam, 'India's Nuclear Breeders: Technology, Viability and Options', *Current Science* 75, no. 6, 25 September 1998, pp. 549–58.

42. Statement by H.J. Bhabha at the Conference on the IAEA Statute, 27 September 1956, reprinted in J.P. Jain, *Nuclear India*, vol. 2, (New Delhi: Radiant Publishers, 1974), pp. 39–49.

43. Statement in the *Lok Sabha*, 10 May 1954, reprinted in *India and Disarmament: An Anthology of Selected Writings and Speeches*, (New Delhi: Government of India/Ministry of External Affairs, 1988), pp. 33–7.

44. Lawrence Wittner, *The Struggle Against the Bomb*, vol. 2, *Resisting the Bomb* (Stanford: Stanford University Press, 1997), p. 100.

45. Lawrence Wittner, *The Struggle Against the Bomb*, vol. 2, *Resisting the Bomb*, p. 34.

46. Bertrand Russell, *The Autobiography of Bertrand Russell*, vol. 3, London: Allen & Unwin, 1969, (ed.), p. 80; Cited in Dhirendra Sharma, 'Politics of the Atomic Energy', *Philosophy and Social Action* 24, no. 3, (1998).

47. Dhirendra Sharma, 'Science and Control: How Indian Atomic Energy Policy Thwarted Indigenous Scientific Development', in: *The Revenge of Athena: Science, Exploitation and the Third World*, Ziauddin Sardar, (ed.), (London: Mansell Publishing, 1988), pp. 73–80.

48. Lawrence Wittner, *The Struggle Against the Bomb*, vol. 2, *Resisting the Bomb*, p. 100.

49. George Perkovich, *India's Nuclear Bomb: The Impact on Global Proliferation*, pp. 36–7.

50. Leonard Beaton and John Maddox, *The Spread of Nuclear Weapons* (London: Chatto & Windus, 1962), pp. 138–40; cited in W.P.S. Sidhu, 'The Development of an Indian Nuclear Doctrine since 1980', (PhD dissertation, Emmanuel College, Cambridge University, 1997).

51. G. Venkatraman, *Bhabha and his Magnificent Obsessions*, p. 172.

52. Jawaharlal Nehru, 'Defense Policy and National Development,' note of 3 February 1947, in: *Selected Works of Jawaharlal Nehru*, vol. 2, Second Series, (Delhi: Jawaharlal Nehru Memorial Fund), p. 364; cited in Itty Abraham, *The Making of the Indian Atomic Bomb: Science, Secrecy and the Postcolonial State*, (London and New York: Zed Books, 1998), p. 49.

53. Itty Abraham, *The Making of the Indian Atomic Bomb: Science, Secrecy and the Postcolonial State*, pp. 114–20.

54. Praful Bidwai and Achin Vanaik, *South Asia on a Short Fuse: Nuclear Politics and the Future of Global Disarmament*, p. 64.

55. Shyam Bhatia, *India's Nuclear Bomb*, p. 109.

56. Broadcast by H.J. Bhabha over All India Radio on United Nations Day, 24 October 1964, reprinted in J.P. Jain, *Nuclear India*, pp. 158–61.

57. Shyam Bhatia, *India's Nuclear Bomb*, pp. 113–14.

58. George Perkovich, *India's Nuclear Bomb: The Impact on Global Proliferation*, p. 65.

59. Ibid.

60. George Perkovich, *India's Nuclear Bomb: The Impact on Global Proliferation*, pp. 82–3.

61. Homi Bhabha, 'Safeguards and the Dissemination of Military Power', (paper Presented by H.J. Bhabha to the 12th Pugwash Conference on Science and World Affairs, 27 January—1 February 1964), reproduced in J.P. Jain, *Nuclear India*, pp. 139–45.

62. George Perkovich, *India's Nuclear Bomb: The Impact on Global Proliferation*, p. 114.

63. K.D. Kapur, *Nuclear Non-Proliferation Diplomacy: Nuclear Power Programs in the Third World*, (New Delhi: Lancers, 1993), p. 309.

64. Itty Abraham, *The Making of the Indian Atomic Bomb: Science, Secrecy and the Postcolonial State*, p. 144.
65. George Perkovich, *India's Nuclear Bomb: The Impact on Global Proliferation*, p. 123.
66. While this may seem at odds with the lack of control over their work in the case of junior personnel, it must be remembered that Ramanna was, by then, fairly high up in the DAE.
67. R. Chidambaram and C. Ganguly, 'Plutonium and Thorium in the Indian Nuclear Program', *Current Science* 70, no. 1, 10 January 1996, pp. 21–35.
68. R. Chidambaram and Raja Ramanna, 'Some Studies on India's Peaceful Nuclear Explosion Experiment', *Peaceful Nuclear Explosions IV: Proceedings of a Technical Committee on the Peaceful Uses of Nuclear Energy organised by the International Atomic Energy Agency*, January 20–4, 1975, pp. 421–36.
69. Khushwant Singh, 'Explosions in the Desert: Meet the Scientists,' *The Illustrated Weekly of India*, 14 July 1974, pp. 6–13; 'Where do we go from Pokharan?,' *Science Today*, June 1974, pp. 19–21.
70. George Perkovich, *India's Nuclear Bomb: The Impact on Global Proliferation*, p. 176.
71. Itty Abraham, *The Making of the Indian Atomic Bomb: Science, Secrecy and the Postcolonial State*, p. 149.
72. George Perkovich, *India's Nuclear Bomb: The Impact on Global Proliferation*, p. 242.
73. W.P.S. Sidhu, 'The Development of an Indian Nuclear Doctrine since 1980'.
74. The 1962 Atomic Energy Act claims to provide for the development, control and use of atomic energy for the welfare of the people of India and for other peaceful purposes and for matters connected therewith. See http://www.dae.gov.in/rules/aeact.htm
75. George Perkovich, *India's Nuclear Bomb: The Impact on Global Proliferation*, pp. 242–43.
76. Raj Chengappa, *Weapons of Peace: The Secret Story of India's Quest to be a Nuclear Power*, (New Delhi: Harper Collins, 2000), pp. 255–61.
77. Raj Chengappa, *Weapons of Peace: The Secret Story of India's Quest to be a Nuclear Power*, p. 260.
78. Timothy V. McCarthy, 'India: Emerging Missile Power', in *The International Missile Bazaar*, ed. William C. Potter and Harlan W. Jencks, (Boulder: Westview Press, 1994), pp. 201–33.
79. For details about the orders and deliveries see Steven I. Zaloga, *Soviet Air Defense Missiles*, (Alexandria, U.S.A.: Jane's Information Group, 1989).
80. A.P.J Abdul Kalam with Arun Tiwari, *Wings of Fire: An Autobiography*, p. 73.
81. S.M. Flank, 'Reconstructing Rockets: The Politics of Developing Military Technology in Brazil, India and Israel', unpublished PhD dissertation, Massachusetts Institute of Technology, 1993.
82. Anand Parthasarathy, 'A Firm Purpose', *Frontline*, 10–23 June 1989, pp. 9–14.

83. Timothy V. McCarthy, 'India: Emerging Missile Power'.

84. 'A Man and his Mission: Interview with A.P.J. Abdul Kalam', *Frontline*, 25 September 1998, pp. 88–90; Timothy V. McCarthy, 'India: Emerging Missile Power', p. 204; A recent example of this practice was the Memorandum of Understanding that DRDO signed with Bharathiar University to collaborate on, *inter alia*, 'plasma engineering and special coatings', which are clearly topics related to problems faced when missiles re-enter the atmosphere from space. 'DRDO Signs MOU with Bharathiar University', *Current Science* 74, no. 9, (10 May 1998), p. 723.

85. 'DRDO Institutes Ten New Award Schemes: Awards for 1998 Announced', *Current Science*, 76, no. 6 (25 March 1999), p. 719.

86. Between 1983 and 1987, the Indian defense budget increased by 50 per cent. See Neeraj Kaushal, *India's Defense Budget: Can it be Reduced?* ACDIS Occasional Paper, University of Illinois at Urbana Champaign, June 1995, p. 4.

87. Rajiv Gandhi, 'A World Free of Nuclear Weapons', Speech at the United Nations General Assembly, 9 June 1988; reproduced in *India and Disarmament: An Anthology*, (New Delhi: Ministry of External Affairs, Government of India, 1988), pp. 280–94.

88. George Perkovich, *India's Nuclear Bomb: The Impact on Global Proliferation*, pp. 273–74.

89. K. Subrahmanyam, 'India's Nuclear Policy—1964–98 (A Personal Recollection)', in: *Nuclear India*, ed. Jasjit Singh, (New Delhi: Knowledge World in association with Institute for Defense Studies and Analyses, 1998), pp. 26–53.

90. K. Subrahmanyam, 'India's Nuclear Policy—1964–98', p. 44.

91. See for example, Steve Coll, 'India Faces Nuclear Watershed', *The Washington Post*, 7 March 1992.

92. Raja Ramanna, *Years of Pilgrimage*, p. 100.

93. P.K. Iyengar, 'Forty Years with Atomic Energy', farewell address, 4 February 1993, in: *Collected Scientific Papers of Dr P.K. Iyengar*, vol. 5, (Bombay: Bhabha Atomic Research Centre, Library and Information Services Division, 1993), p. 85.

94. Rahul Bedi, 'India should own up to Atom Bomb', *The Daily Telegraph*, 20 September 1994.

95. 'Say No to Regional Capping,' Interview by Raj Chengappa, *India Today*, 30 April 1994, p. 46.

96. *Indian Express*, 19 September 1994, reproduced in *FBIS-NESA*, 23 September 1994.

97. George Perkovich, *India's Nuclear Bomb: The Impact on Global Proliferation*, p. 365.

98. 'Budget Doubled, Target Elusive: Interview with R. Chidambaram', *Frontline*, 26 January 1996.

99. Dinshaw Mistry, *India and the Comprehensive Test Ban Treaty* ACDIS Research Report, University of Illinois at Urbana-Champaign, September 1998, p. 30.
100. Parvathi Menon, 'A Former Prime Minister Speaks Out', *Frontline*, 20 June 1998.
101. George Perkovich, *India's Nuclear Bomb: The Impact on Global Proliferation*, p. 407.
102. AEC Chief Says India Ready "To Go Nuclear" *Deccan Herald*, 4 March 1998, reproduced in *FBIS-NES*, 98–063.
103. 'India can make neutron bomb: Chidambaram', *The Hindu*, 17 August 1999.
104. 'India must test N-bomb before signing CTBT', *The Hindu*, 2 May 2000.
105. 'India to Design ABM on U.S. lines: Kalam', *The Times of India*, 5 January 2000.
106. 'Beam Weapon in Final Stages', *The Hindu*, 19 August 1999.
107. 'Questions in Lok Sabha: Govt proposes to build another nuclear reactor', *Hindustan Times*, 16 December 1999.
108. Robert Anderson, *Building Scientific Institutions in India: Bhabha and Saha*, (Montreal: Center for Developing Area Studies, 1975), pp. 26–8.
109. Abha Sur, 'Egalitarianism in a World of Difference: Identity and Ideology in the Science of Meghnad Saha', (Forthcoming).
110. T.V. Satyamurthy, 'India's Post-Colonial Nuclear Estate,' in: *No Clear Reason: Nuclear Power Politics*, edited by the Radical Science Collective, (London: Free Association Books, 1984), pp. 110–11.
111. M.V.N. Murthy, Madan Rao, R. Shankar, J. Samuel and A. Sitaram, 'Voices against the Militarization of Science', *Current Science* 75, no. 11, (10 December 1998), pp. 1110–1111.
112. Dhirendra Sharma, 'India's Lopsided Science', *Bulletin of the Atomic Scientists* 47, no. 4 (May 1991), pp. 32–6; available on the internet at http://www.thebulletin.org/issues/1991/may91/may91sharma.html
113. Amulya Kumar N. Reddy, 'Nuclear Power: Is it Necessary or Economical?', *Seminar*, June 1990, pp. 18–26.
114. On people's science movements, see Vinod Raina, 'Promoting People's Science', *Seminar*, May 1999, pp. 39–43.
115. http://www.freespeech.org/isanw/
116. N. Srinivasan, 'Nuclear Tests and our Power Program', *Voices Against Nuclear Weapons* (Chennai: Indian Scientists Against Nuclear Weapons/Tamil Nadu Science Forum, August 1998), p. 10.
117. Quoted in Beena Sarwar, 'Peace Workshop Stresses Need for New Strategies', Inter Press Service Report; available on the internet at http://no_nukes_sa.tripod.com/beena_workshop.html
118. For an elaboration of this argument, see M.V. Ramana, 'For a Just Peace—The Anti-nuclear Movement in India', *Social Science Research Council Newsletter* 12 May 1999.

119. H.A. Feiveson, 'Thinking About Nuclear Weapons', *Dissent*, Spring 1982, pp. 183–94.

120. Joel Primack and Frank von Hippel, *Advice and Dissent: Scientists in the Political Arena*, (New York: Basic Books, 1974), p. ix.

121. On the role of scientist-advisors in the U.S. see Joel Primack and Frank von Hippel, *Advice and Dissent: Scientists in the Political Arena*.

122. Sukumar Muralidharan, 'Weaponisation is Harmful': Interview with M.R. Srinivasan,' *Frontline*, June 6, 1998.

123. T. Jayaraman, 'Indian Science After Pokhran II', *Seminar*, August 1998, pp. 60–4.

124. David Dickson, *The New Politics of Science*, (Chicago: The University of Chicago Press, 1988), p. 18.

125. On the 'new' social movements, see for example Arthur Bonner, *Averting the Apocalypse: Social Movements in India Today*, (Durham: Duke University Press, 1990); and Gail Omvedt, *Reinventing Revolution: New Social Movements and the Socialist Tradition in India*, (Armonk: M.E. Sharpe, 1993).

CHAPTER 2

THE COMING OF THE ATOMIC AGE TO PAKISTAN
Zia Mian

Too little attention has been paid to the part which an early exposure to American goods, skills, and American ways of doing things can play in forming the tastes and desires of newly emerging countries.
President John F. Kennedy, 1963*

On 19 October 1954, Pakistan's prime minister met the president of the United States at the White House in Washington. In Pakistan, this news was carried alongside the report that the Minister for Industries, Khan Abdul Qayyum Khan, had announced the establishment of an Atomic Energy Research Organization. These developments came a few months after Pakistan and the United States had signed an agreement on military cooperation and launched a new program to bring American economic advisors to Pakistan. Each of these initiatives expressed a particular relationship between Pakistan and the United States, a key moment in the coming into play of ways of thinking, the rise of institutions, and preparation of people, all of which have profoundly shaped contemporary Pakistan.

This essay examines the period before and immediately after this critical year in which Pakistan's leaders tied their national future to the United States. It focuses in particular on how elite aspirations and ideas of being modern, especially the role played by the prospect of an imminent 'atomic age', shaped Pakistan's search for U.S.

---

* Epigraph quote from H. Magdoff, *The Age of Imperialism*, (Monthly Review, 1969), p. 133.

military, economic and technical support to strengthen the new state.

The essay begins by looking briefly at how the possibility of an 'atomic age' as an approaching, desirable global future took shape in the early decades of the twentieth century. It then sketches the way that this vision was expressed in the American elite imagination after World War II, and how, with the coming of the Cold War, it became a central element of U.S. foreign and security policy. The essay goes on to examine how, against this background, those of the emergent elite of newly independent Pakistan sought to end their sense of national insecurity, poverty and backwardness, and secure their position and that of the state, both within their own society and internationally, by developing military allies and capabilities, planning economic development, and establishing a scientific community and a public sensibility that would be appropriate to the atomic age. Their aspirations and decisions exemplify a broader pattern that Eqbal Ahmad identified as characteristic of Third World societies, where people find themselves, 'living on the frontier of two worlds—in the middle of the ford haunted by the past, fevered with dreams of the future.'[1]

Pakistan's elite has succeeded, at great cost and with help from the United States, in making its dreams come true. They have created a Pakistan that has nuclear weapons, nuclear power plants, and a nuclear complex that dwarfs all other areas of science and technology. But in this fifty-year-long effort, Pakistan's elite has failed to meet many of the basic political, social, and economic needs of its citizens. The essay concludes by looking at the aftermath of the 1998 nuclear tests and the state's promotion of nuclear nationalism as the basis for a shared sense of identity and achievement. My argument is that the peace movement in Pakistan, if it is to prevail, needs to look beyond a simple opposition to nuclear weapons. It must also offer a vision of an alternative future.

ATOMIC FUTURES AND AMERICAN DREAMS

The idea of an 'atomic age' is as old as atomic science. In 1901 Fredrick Soddy and Ernest Rutherford discovered that radioactivity was part of the process by which atoms changed from one kind to another and involved the release of energy. Soon Soddy was writing in popular magazines that radioactivity was a potentially 'inexhaustible' source of energy, that atomic science meant 'the future would bear . . . little relation to the past,' and offering a vision of an atomic future where it would be possible to 'transform a desert continent, thaw the frozen poles, and make the whole earth one smiling Garden of Eden.'[2] Soddy, along with other scientists and commentators, also talked of how atomic energy could possibly be used in weapons to wage war, and this soon became the stuff of science fiction in the hands of writers such as H.G. Wells, whose novel, *The World Set Free*, was dedicated to Soddy and described 'atomic bombs', the idea of a 'chain reaction', and the effects of an atomic war.[3]

The future hurtled closer with the 1939 discovery of atomic fission, the process that underlay radioactivity, and as one historian of the nuclear age has observed, 'journalists and scientists everywhere were caught up in the excitement' and there were countless 'awestruck stories' of what might be possible. Part of this future became all too real when in 1945 United States built the first atomic bombs and used them to destroy the Japanese cities of Hiroshima and Nagasaki. The U.S. soon deployed its new weapons to confront the Soviet Union in a divided Europe, and in 1949 the Soviet Union tested its first atomic bomb. The Korean War broke out in June 1950, and on the first day of that war U.S. leaders privately discussed the use of nuclear weapons; in subsequent months the question was raised repeatedly in the press, with President Truman inciting international uproar by announcing in November that, 'there has always been active consideration of its use.'[4]

The development of nuclear weapons proceeded at a furious pace. Britain became the third nuclear armed state when it conducted its first nuclear test in 1952. That same year, the United States developed and tested the hydrogen bomb, with a yield many hundreds of times that of the bombs that had destroyed Hiroshima and Nagasaki, and the Soviets tested theirs a year later. By 1953 the United States had over one thousand nuclear weapons, roughly ten times as many as the Soviet Union, and by 1955 both had twice that number.[5] As ever larger bombs were tested year after year, it became hard to ignore the importance of nuclear weapons and the threat of nuclear war.

In these years the United States also led the way in shaping the ideas and hopes for an atomic-powered utopia. The day after the bombing of Hiroshima, *The New York Times* wrote: 'We face the prospect either of destruction on a scale that dwarfs anything thus far reported or of a golden era of social change which could satisfy the most romantic utopian.'[6] Three days after Nagasaki was destroyed, the *New York Times* editorialised that atomic technology 'can bring to this earth not death but life, not tyranny and cruelty, but a divine freedom,' and could bring 'dazzling gifts' to the 'millions of China and India, bound for so many ages in sweat and hunger to the wheel of material existence.'[7] Books soon began to appear about the wondrous prospects made possible by atomic technology; a 1947 book, *Atomic Energy in the Coming Era*, claimed that the future would be 'as different from the present as the present is from ancient Egypt,' and captured some of the practical qualities of the atomic dream:

> No baseball game will be called off on account of rain in the Era of Atomic Energy. No airplane will bypass an airport because of fog. No city will experience a winter traffic jam because of heavy snow. Summer resorts will be able to guarantee the weather, and artificial suns will make it as easy to grow corn and potatoes indoors as on the farm. . . . For the first time in the history of the world, man will have at his disposal energy in amounts sufficient to cope with the forces of Mother Nature.[8]

The possibilities seemed both limitless and immediate. *The New York Times* told its readers in 1947 that Africa 'could be transformed into another Europe,' and the *Woman's Home Companion* explained in 1948 that it would be possible to 'make the dream of the earth as the Promised Land come true in time for many of us already born to see and enjoy it.'[9] Contemporary surveys suggested these ideas were championed by nuclear scientists, parts of the media, some in government and some industrialists, with support largely limited to affluent and well-educated Americans, while the general public focused more on the threat of nuclear weapons.[10] It was these groups, however, with their shared vision of saving the world through atomic science that quickly came to dominate the debate in the United States.

The idea of the atomic future soon came to play an important role in U.S. foreign policy. America's determination to save the world— from the Soviet Union, from Communism and from poverty and suffering, through the application of its military strength and its technology—had been laid out by President Truman in his inaugural address in January 1949. He declared:

> The American people desire, and are determined to work for, a world in which all nations and all peoples are free to govern themselves as they see fit, and to achieve a decent and satisfying life. . . . In the pursuit of these aims, the United States and other like-minded nations find themselves directly opposed by a regime with contrary aims and a totally different concept of life. . . . We will provide military advice and equipment to free nations which will cooperate with us in the maintenance of peace and security . . . [And] we must embark on a bold new program for making the benefits of our scientific advances and industrial progress available for the improvement and growth of underdeveloped areas.[11]

It was left to Truman's successor, Dwight Eisenhower, to bring the peaceful atom into the Cold War and onto the global stage. In a speech to the U.N. General Assembly in December 1953, President Eisenhower detailed the destructive power America could now wield with its atomic weapons, and announced that America wished all to share in the bounty of the atomic future that had now arrived.[12] He declared:

Today, the United States' stockpile of atomic weapons, which, of course, increases daily, exceeds by many times the explosive equivalent of the total of all bombs and all shells that came from every plane and every gun in every theatre of war in all of the years of World War II. . . . But the dread secret, and the fearful engines of atomic might, are not ours alone. The United States knows that if the fearful trend of atomic military build-up can be reversed, this greatest of destructive forces can be developed into a great boon, for the benefit of all mankind. The United States knows that peaceful power from atomic energy is no dream of the future. That capability, already proved, is here—now—today.[13]

The speech was broadcast around the world and the U.S. government used it as part of an intense international effort in the years that followed to show that, unlike the Soviet Union, it believed in developing and sharing the peaceful uses of atomic energy. The atomic dream was an American dream, and America would ensure every nation could have a share in it.

It must be said, however, that there was little evidence to support Eisenhower's grand claim that the atomic future was 'here—now—today.' In late 1951 the Argonne National Laboratory had generated a token amount of electricity from a small experimental reactor, which had been widely publicized, and had led to suggestions that nuclear power was 'imminent'.[14] In June 1953, the U.S. Atomic Energy Commission, under pressure to speed up the development of nuclear power, had decided that the quickest way to build a full-scale nuclear power plant was to allow Admiral Hyman Rickover to modify the pressurized water reactor that had been under development for use in aircraft carrier propulsion.[15] It only began operation in 1957. The imagined peaceful and prosperous atomic future was still just a vision. Nuclear weapons, the 'fearful engines of atomic might,' were all too real.

SECURING THE STATE

While the atomic age was taking shape, Pakistan, too, was no more than an idea and a hope. The Muslim League, founded in 1906, and led by Mohammad Ali Jinnah, eventually succeeded in establishing the state of Pakistan.[16] The history and geography of India's Muslims, their encounter with British colonialism, and their relationship with India's struggle for independence, combined with the nature of the Muslim League movement, left important legacies that shaped the early years of Pakistan, and to some degree has continued to have an influence. These included what has been called a 'low level of political culture' in the feudal and tribal leaderships that dominated much of the Muslim majority areas that became Pakistan, the 'poor institutionalisation' of the Muslim League as a mass-based political movement in these areas; the conflict between diverse local and regional identities and the new national identity; and the simple fact that to create a large constituency the League had been 'deliberately vague about the nature of a future Pakistani state.'[17]

On this basis the new leadership set about to achieve what it considered as its primary task, to create a nation-state.[18] The leadership's ability to exercise power at the national level was limited, and a sense of direction was in short supply. As one historian has observed:

> The chaos that overwhelmed Pakistan independence was a consequence of little planning and virtually no conceptualization . . . neither Jinnah nor any of his immediate circle was moved to lay out on paper the blueprint for the state they intended to create. There is nothing in the archives to even hint that someone was responsible for defining the nature and structure of the state, its purposes and functions, its powers and limitations.[19]

A measure of the chaos may be seen in the effort to create a new constitution through a constituent assembly. Established in August 1947, the assembly never managed to gather all of its sixty-nine members—some chose to go to India and were never replaced and others simply did not show up at meetings. It met for only four days the rest of that year, a mere eleven days the subsequent year, and eventually was dissolved in 1954, having met for a total of a hundred and sixteen days.[20]

There were other problems. The thoughtless and hurried partition of British India into the new states of West and East Pakistan and India created millions of refugees who trekked in opposite directions across the new borders, seeking new identities and the promise of justice and security. Within months, a war erupted over Kashmir. It ended in a stalemate, with India and Pakistan each controlling parts of Kashmir. Crisis followed crisis. Mohammad Ali Jinnah, who had centralized political and bureaucratic power by appointing himself Governor General of Pakistan, died in 1949, leaving behind a leadership vacuum. Then, in 1951, it was revealed that Maj. Gen. Akbar Khan had been working with a group of left-wing officers and a handful of activists of the Pakistan Communist Party since 1949 in an effort to seize power.[21] The first Prime Minister, Liaquat Ali Khan, was killed in October 1951 as he was about to address a public meeting in Rawalpindi. There were to be three governor generals and six prime ministers before a coup in 1958 led to more than a decade of military government.

As the new national elite in Pakistan struggled to establish itself and to create institutions that it could call its own, it is easy to see why it sought access to resources and support from powerful international allies. In the immediate aftermath of partition, Pakistan sought to develop a strategic relationship with Britain. Morris James, the British Deputy High Commissioner noted that the Pakistanis, 'in those early years were willing to range themselves at the side of Britain, then still a major world power, if in return we would help them to redress the strategic balance between themselves and the Indians. They sought a powerful outside friend and patron.'[22] The search for a 'friend and patron' to help counter India can be understood in large measure as a 'continuation of the political struggle before partition' that Pakistan's eventual leaders had waged against the Congress Party, and for whom 'the habit of criticism could not be effaced by the drawing of a new boundary.'[23] It was this sensibility that led them to interpret and respond to disputes over Kashmir, the division of rivers, the distribution of financial and military resources, refugees etc., as proof of Indian hostility.[24] This sensibility has crystallized in the education system and is present in the national curriculum and school textbooks in Pakistan even today.[25]

Although Britain was not able to play a role as patron, the Cold War eventually offered both Pakistan and the United States an opportunity for such a relationship. Whereas British India had been vital to the British Empire, the United States saw Pakistan as, 'the hastily created by-product of Britain's retreat from empire, a nation plagued by such immense internal and security problems that it offered little promise for future international prominence.'[26] As the Cold War set in, however, the U.S. military planners began to see Pakistan as important because of its 'proximity to the Soviet Union; its proximity to the oil fields of the Middle East; its potential role in the defense of both the Indian Ocean area and the Indian subcontinent; its position as the largest Muslim nation in the world; and its army.'[27] Despite this, nothing substantial happened. The U.S. did not want to undermine the possibility of a good relationship with India and so left Pakistan on the margins of the Cold War.

Pakistan's representatives for their part tried to incite the U.S. to reach out. They 'carefully couched all appeals to the United States in a virulently anti-Soviet rhetoric that they hoped would strike a chord with the Truman administration's Cold War planners.'[28] Success came not because of their entreaties but with the outbreak of the Korean War in 1950. By late 1951 the U.S. had decided to sell military equipment to Pakistan, and in early 1952 Pakistan and the U.S. signed the first of a number of supplementary agreements on security, which Pakistan soon tested by asking for $200 million in military aid.

Unites States' concerns and interests in Pakistan were summed up in an August 1953 Memorandum to the National Security Council from the Acting Secretary of State. The Memorandum observed:

> There was a noticeable increase in the activities of the mullahs (orthodox religious leaders) in Pakistan. There was reason to believe that in face of growing doubts as to whether Pakistan had any real friends, more and

more Pakistanis were turning to the mullahs for guidance. Were this trend to continue the present government of enlightened and Western-oriented leaders might well be threatened, and members of a successive government would probably be far less cooperative with the west than the present incumbents.[29]

In February 1954, the U.S. announced that it would be giving military aid to Pakistan. This was followed, in May 1954, by Pakistan formally signing the Mutual Defense Assistance Agreement with the United States. A U.S. Military Assistance and Advisory Group was created, and these military advisors moved into the General Headquarters of Pakistan's armed forces.

The consequences for Pakistan of this new relationship with the U.S. were enormous. Since independence, Pakistan's political and military leaders had been spending an extraordinary share of available government resources on the military and it was unsustainable. In both 1948 and 1949, over 70 per cent of government expenditure went to the military. This fraction did not fall to 50 per cent in any year in the first decade of independence, and the military only consumed less than half of government spending for two years in the early 1960s before the 1965 war caused the military share to rise again.[30]

The new strategic relationship with the U.S. had a strong impact on Pakistan's military. United States' training and techniques flowed in along with military aid: 'The United States connection led to the complete revision of tables of organization [of the Pakistan Army], the addition of several entirely American-equipped divisions . . . and the adoption of American techniques (in gunnery for example).'[31] Along with this went training for the Pakistani military, with hundreds of Pakistani officers attending U.S. military schools between 1955 and 1958. Some of these officers who trained in the U.S. became very prominent. General Zia-ul-Haq, who became chief of the Army Staff in 1976, and in 1977 staged a coup and ruled until his death in 1988, was an early graduate of the Command and Staff College and trained at Fort Leavenworth (where he took the Associate Command and General Staff Officer Course). General K.M.

Arif, who trained at the U.S. Armour School, at Fort Knox, Kentucky, went on to become Chief of Staff to General Zia in 1977 and in 1984 became vice-chief of army staff.[32]

The American support for Pakistan apparently 'made a deep impression on thousands of Pakistani officers.'[33] Eqbal Ahmad suggested that this training left a legacy of officers who 'have come to respect American technology, crave for contemporary weapons systems, and favour alliances which promise hardware.'[34] Not surprisingly, the Pakistani military began to turn its attention to the role of nuclear weapons. By the time of the Korean War, the U.S. had started to incorporate nuclear weapons into its military strategy and tactics, from bombs, short- and intermediate-range missiles, to an early nuclear howitzer.[35]

In 1954, Maj. Gen. M.A. Latif Khan became the first Pakistani Commandant of the Military Command and Staff College, Quetta. In the official history of the College, he recalled that,

On taking over as Commandant I found that the study of the various operations of war under nuclear warfare conditions was carried out in an elementary form and a few enquiries made by me soon revealed the fact that this subject had not received the attention it deserved. The time had come for us to start making a serious study of fighting the next war which would, whether we liked it or not, be fought with nuclear weapons.[36]

Gen. Latif Khan appointed a senior officer to deal with 'future warfare' and thus began the practice whereby, 'during the study of each operation of war, the same problem was considered under nuclear conditions.'[37] These exercises included tactical war games without the use of troops, in which hypothetical scenarios were tested out on actual terrain and the existing military doctrines rehearsed.

The United States played a direct role in this training. In the years that followed, Pakistan's Staff College was visited from time to time by a special U.S. Nuclear Warfare Team. The history of the college notes approvingly that, 'this visit proved most useful and resulted in modification and revision of the old syllabus to bring it into line with the fresh data given by the team.'[38] This was to be part of a more enduring program, the history notes there were 'periodic visits by American nuclear experts.'[39] General Khan noted that, 'it was generally agreed that this subject required serious study, even if we ourselves were not going to be likely to possess nuclear weapons for many years.'[40]

These military exercises were among the first nuclear practices in Pakistan. It is difficult to fathom these rehearsals for nuclear war, in which Pakistanis planned and imagined the use of a weapon that no Pakistani had actually seen or experienced. The psychological and institutional implications of several generations of young Pakistani military officers playing these fantasy nuclear war games merit further study.

How the Pakistani military thought they would eventually acquire nuclear weapons is not clear. Perhaps they believed that these weapons would come to Pakistan as part of the alliance with the United States. In 1956, the U.S. Joint Chiefs of Staff compiled a list of states which they wanted to serve as bases for intermediate-range ballistic missiles, armed with nuclear weapons. The 'most desirable' states for such deployments were Turkey, Norway, Britain, Japan, Okinawa, and France. States considered merely 'desirable' states were Pakistan, Greece, Iran, Taiwan, Denmark, West Germany, the Philippines, Spain, Italy and Libya.[41] The U.S. went on to base its nuclear weapons in Turkey, Britain, Okinawa, Greece, Taiwan, Denmark (actually in Greenland, which was part of Denmark until 1979), West Germany, the Philippines, and Italy. Other nuclear weapons were stored in Spain.[41]

Apparently, for reasons that are not clear, Pakistan, Iran, and Libya were the only states from the original list where no U.S. nuclear weapons were placed. There may have been concern about these countries' stability. As suggested in the 1953 National Security Council memorandum cited earlier suggested, U.S. policy makers feared that the pro-Western government in Pakistan might not last.

What is clear is that after the 1958 coup by General Ayub Khan, which put in place a military government that lasted until 1971, the armed forces apparently did not pursue a focused nuclear weapons program. They seemed to have been content with their strong relationship with the U.S. and access to American military aid and high-tech conventional weapons. The political decision to pursue nuclear weapons had to wait until the end of military rule, and ultimately was taken in early 1972 by Zulfikar Ali Bhutto, a civilian leader. Also curious is that even though Pakistan had completed its development of nuclear weapons by the early 1980s, the military government of General Zia-ul-Haq resisted calls for testing these weapons. Instead, he preferred keeping them under wraps and maintaining ties with the United States, receiving military aid and modern American weapons such as F-16 fighters. Only in 1998 did Prime Minister Nawaz Sharif decide to test nuclear weapons. Pakistan's last military ruler, Gen. Pervez Musharraf, also emphasized the need to maintain a relationship with the U.S. and obtain American military aid and weapons.

PLANNING THE FUTURE

The challenge and pattern of economic development has been of central concern for Pakistan's decision-makers since independence. They recognized the weak economic foundations of the new state carved out of the western and eastern peripheries of British India. Indeed, Pakistan's economic prospects were uncertain even before its independence in 1947.[43] In March 1946, at a meeting in Calcutta, Jinnah was asked about the relative backwardness of the country he envisioned: 'What of the economic situation in Pakistan? There is no iron, no coal, no hydro-electric power, no industries.' Jinnah replied, 'I am fully aware of these things. Our people have had no opportunity to develop these things. I have every faith . . . that, given the opportunity, they will achieve all this.'[44] At other times, Jinnah was less optimistic: 'If the worse comes to the worst, like a sensible man we will cut our coat according to our cloth.'[45]

Pakistan's first efforts at planning its economic development were launched in 1948, when the government set up two official bodies, a Development Board and a Planning Advisory Board.[46] The former began its task by asking government ministries to 're-examine and update' projects planned for the area that was now Pakistan by the Department of Planning and Development of the Government of British India. The Board dealt with one project at a time and 'made no attempt to prepare a plan or even to relate projects to one another.'[47] In 1950, however, as part of the agreement to create coordinated six-year development plans for the members of the Colombo Plan for Cooperative Economic Development in South and Southeast Asia, the Board did put together a larger plan. Still, the plan was little more than a set of 'projects which had been selected on an ad hoc basis without reference to available resources and the requirements of the economy.'[48]

In 1951 the Development Board and the Planning Advisory Board were combined to form a new Planning Commission, but this, too, quickly failed to find its feet. This led, in 1952, to the creation of an Economic Appraisal Committee that believed no harm had been done so far by the failure to plan properly but advised that, 'an adequate and efficient planning [o]rganization is essential.'[49] The government responded in July 1953 by establishing a Planning Board that was to come up with a five-year development plan to begin in April 1954.

The evidence that Pakistan's economic planners and managers were failing was abundant. Economic growth had been poor: from 1949 to 1954 GNP per capita had risen barely 1 per cent, and per capita rural incomes (reflecting the livelihoods of a great majority of the population) had fallen by 3 per cent.[50] The arbitrary character of the plans suggested a lack of coherent goals in the planning process. Economists were also in short supply, in fact, a history of the discipline notes that, 'at independence, there were hardly any economists in Pakistan.'[51] The first chief economist of the Planning Commission had actually been a chemistry teacher at the Delhi

University before 1947, and, out of his own interest, had obtained an MA in economics.[52]

The chairman of the Planning Board looked for help outside the country and found it in the United States. In February 1954 the Ford Foundation agreed to fund a program whereby Harvard University's Graduate School of Public Administration would 'recruit and guide a group of experts who would assist Pakistan's Planning Commission.'[53] It should be noted here that Pakistan was not alone in turning to American economists for help with planning; India did the same.[54] The first economic advisors for Pakistan arrived in April 1954 (around the same time as the military advisors); their work was expected to be mostly completed in about eighteen months. The program grew with time, however, and lasted much longer than anticipated. The last adviser left Pakistan in mid-1970.[55]

The planners saw their task as guiding the transformative movement of the economy, society and culture of Pakistan along a technological axis. The opening page of the first five-year plan declared:

> Planning in the present stage of our society means the formulation of programs and policies designed to lead it by a consciously directed and accelerated movement from a largely technologically backward and feudalistic stage into the modern era of advanced technology now on the threshold of atomic age.[56]

The idea of a planned 'accelerated movement' from a 'stage' that is 'backward' to one that is 'modern' is premised on a notion that the difference between societies and economies is not one of history, geography, and culture but rather of different points along a single trajectory. Development meant catching up with the United States.

For the planners, speed was of the essence in this endeavour. Their passion to achieve their goal quickly seemed to overwhelm any reasonable sense of how to accomplish the complex and unprecedented task of economic, social and cultural transformation. The planners insisted that,

A country which has a leeway of centuries to make up cannot think of rest periods. . . . Consolidation and development must proceed simultaneously; the very idea of a breathing time to look back, take stock, settle down comfortably, and then think of the next stage is inconsistent with the speed and tempo of the atomic age.[57]

In addition to its role in planning the economy and advising the government, the Harvard Advisory Group (HAG) was also charged with training Pakistani economic planners. To this end, HAG members worked closely with their Pakistani counterparts to set up a graduate training program for Pakistani economists at leading U.S. universities, including Harvard, Yale and Princeton. The result was a group of Pakistani economists who shared the values of the HAG as well as an understanding of planning priorities. These economists became dominant figures in Pakistan's economic decisions making for the next several decades. One of the most prominent among them, Mahbub-ul Haq, served as Chief Economist of the Planning Commission during 1957–1970 and went on to be Minister of Finance, Planning and Commerce from 1982–1988.

The new economists shared with their mentors a clear perception of the state's role in the economy; the need for a 'modernizing elite' to manage it; and the role nuclear energy could play. Indeed, the latter seems to have overwhelmed their economic rationality. The first study on the economic viability of nuclear power in Pakistan was undertaken in 1955 by Maurice Kilbridge, a HAG member, with input from other members. Kilbridge concluded not only that, 'there does not seem to be much of an economic case for the use of large-plant nuclear power in either East or West Pakistan,' but that the pursuit of such a goal was unrealistic for the foreseeable future, noting that, 'probably not more than 10 persons in all Pakistan . . . have any extensive training in nuclear technology, and . . . not many more [have] the basic education necessary to absorb such training.'[58]

The Kilbridge study should have dampened the enthusiasm to develop nuclear power in Pakistan, but it did not. The determination to hasten Pakistan over the threshold into the atomic age remained strong. Even a decade later, in 1966, at meetings of the Planning

Commission, 'those in charge argued vehemently that nuclear energy was the wave of the future, that we could develop many peaceful uses of nuclear energy, and that we would be left behind in the race of modern science and technology unless nuclear research was given adequate funds.'[59] Forty years later this vision continues to drive the allocation of large funds into nuclear energy projects that provide electricity at much higher costs than other available energy sources, and are located at unsafe sites that add to the risk of catastrophic accidents.[60] It is ironic that Pakistan's decision-makers remain intent on the nuclear dream when in the United States, the home of that dream, no new nuclear reactor has been built in three decades.

SCIENCE AND THE NATION-STATE

Kilbridge had pointed out in his study that perhaps fewer than a dozen scientists in Pakistan were trained in the nuclear sciences, and few more had the ability to take advantage of this training. This reflected the general state of science in the areas that became Pakistan. Before partition, India had a Directorate of Scientific and Industrial Research modelled on the British structure for integrating research with the needs of industry. All its laboratories, however, were in cities that remained part of India.

After independence, Pakistan had set up its own Directorate of Scientific and Industrial Research, and in April 1953, this body, headed by Salimuzzaman Siddiqui, set up a Council of Scientific and Industrial Research (CSIR). This council then set up a Planning Committee, headed by Nazir Ahmad (who had trained as a physicist in Britain in the 1920s), to determine where and what kinds of government research laboratories should be built to aid in national development. Ahmad's task was soon made easier, at least in part. United State's President Dwight Eisenhower in his December 1953 'Atoms for Peace' speech, declared that, 'experts would be mobilized to apply atomic energy to the needs of agriculture, medicine, and other peaceful activities. A special purpose would be to provide abundant electrical energy in the power-starved areas of the world.'[61]

Pakistan's media welcomed the speech and the promise of the wondrous prospects of atomic energy. In the days that followed the speech, *Dawn*, Pakistan's leading English-language daily newspaper (which was read by the national elite) carried many reports on current and future possibilities. These were illustrated with photographs and elaborate graphics obviously produced by U.S. and British atomic establishments. The stories included U.S. proposals for the use of radioactive waste;[62] British ideas on using nuclear materials in industry;[63] the economics of nuclear power;[64] surveys of how the U.S. Atomic Energy Commission was assisting countries worldwide;[65] Britain's plans to produce nuclear electricity within a few years;[66] an introduction to Britain's atomic establishment;[67] the announcement by the American company RCA that it had invented an 'atomic battery' that converted atomic energy into electricity;[68] and an introduction to the physical principles underlying atomic energy.[69]

Pakistan, however, could hardly take advantage of these technological prospects. As Vice Chancellor of Peshawar University Raziuddin Siddiqui explained in his Presidential address to the Sixth Pakistan Science Conference in Karachi in January 1954, even though Pakistan's scientific community was in poor shape, it wanted to play its role in building the nation.[70] Siddiqui claimed that science was being neglected, with scholars 'at the mercy of petty officials and clerks'—this despite the fact that science and education were a 'defense against ignorance and the consequent poverty and disease.' But, Siddiqui argued, science and education were more than that: 'scientific research education and research is the real and only defense of a country in these days, as modern defense is mainly a technical affair requiring skill scientific skill and knowledge of a fairly advanced type.' With the Manhattan Project barely a decade old, and the Cold War arms race raging, not to mention the struggle for independence from colonialism still fresh in people's minds, it is clear Siddiqui was making the case for the role of science in Pakistan's national security. He went on:

It cannot be denied that in this age of power politics not only the security but even the free existence of the eastern countries is at stake, because of their backwardness in scientific and technical knowledge. . . . Hence we must have a vast army of those trained in all the fundamental and important scientific and technical subjects.

The first evidence that Pakistan's government was thinking of taking a scientific interest in the 'Atoms for Peace' program came in late September 1954. The U.S. National Planning Association announced it was to conduct a series of country studies to look at the 'economic problems and policy issues raised by the rapid increase in technological knowledge of atomic energy and its potential contribution to industrial and agricultural development and improved standards of living.'[71] Pakistan was chosen to be one of the countries for study, along with Japan, Korea, Brazil and Israel, because the Planning Association claimed that, 'all these countries [have] 'special institutions' which might make nuclear development interesting.'[72] Oddly, however, Pakistan had no 'special institution' at that time working on nuclear research. The report becomes understandable if a decision had been made in principle to start work on atomic energy in Pakistan at this time but had not yet been made public.

The announcement that Pakistan was looking toward atomic energy came some weeks later, at the second meeting of the Pakistan Council for Scientific and Industrial Research in Karachi on 19 October 1954. Khan Abdul Qayyum Khan, Pakistan's Minister of Industries announced:

The government is conscious that with the enormous progress the world is making towards the utilization of atomic energy for civil uses, adequate steps have to be taken without delay in Pakistan to work out a phased program of survey, research and ultimate developments in this field.[73]

Apparently, at least at this stage, atomic science was to fall within the purview of scientific and industrial research, suggesting that starting an atomic science program may have been driven partly by the desire of the Pakistani scientific community to gain access to what looked like major new sources of funding, overseas training, and so on, in order to gain more advanced ideas about science, technology, and development. In this they were using the same strategy as their peers within the economic planners and the military, completing the triumvirate of the state-modernizing elite.

It was left to Saleemuzzaman Siddiqui, the head of CSIR, to establish a committee that would draw up a 'detailed, phased Atomic Energy Program.' According to Siddiqui, the first task 'was to survey and assess the country's resources in radioactive minerals.' However, any effective program, he pointed out, would require a large nuclear science community and that meant having to send 'young scientists abroad for specialized training.'[74]

The extreme need for scientists of all kinds was clear, but Pakistan's educational system was not equipped to produce them domestically.[75] In 1953 Pakistan had only six universities—two in East Pakistan and four in West Pakistan—and not until 1961 would four new universities be created. In these six universities and associated colleges, 57,654 students were enrolled in arts and sciences courses and 2138 in engineering.[76] A total of 680 students graduated in 1953–1954 with a Bachelor of Science degree, and 107 students graduated with a Master of Science degree. In contrast, 2122 Bachelor of Arts degrees were awarded that year, and 241 Master of Arts degrees. Not one PhD was awarded—two had been awarded in science in 1949 and in 1950 by the University of Dacca [Dhaka], and another was awarded in 1954–1955, but no others until 1965.

The first opportunity to take advantage of the Atoms for Peace program came a month or so later. The Raw Materials Sub-Committee of the U.S. Congress Joint Committee on Atomic Energy visited Pakistan as part of a whistle-stop tour that included New Zealand, the Philippines, Formosa, Thailand, India, Iran, Turkey, Greece, Spain, and Australia. The U.S. delegation described their visit to Pakistan in effusive terms:

In Karachi we had the very real pleasure of meeting first with Prime
Minister Mohammed Ali, and later with the Council of Scientific and
Industrial Research for Pakistan. Long and hard though the road ahead
is for the people of Pakistan, they see and are attempting to grasp the
opportunities to make their passage along that road faster and better
through the use of atomic energy.'[77]

Their Pakistani hosts did not lose an obvious opportunity to make
a case for the importance of U.S. help in their endeavour to set up
atomic energy facilities. The Committee wrote, 'scientists and
government administrators alike made it clear to us while we were
there conferring with them that they must have assistance and
would welcome it particularly from the United States.'[78] They praised
the efforts of Pakistan's would-be nuclear scientists, 'men of
scientific and technical stature who are trying . . . with their limited
means to bring their country the benefits of this most revolutionary
science.'

The major public announcement of Pakistan's nuclear plans came
on 1 January 1955, in Prime Minister Mohammad Ali's 'first of the
month' broadcast to the nation. After laying out a number of
decisions taken by the government on constitutional and economic
issues, he declared:

While concentrating our attention on matters of vital interests to your
daily life we have not been unmindful of the need for the country's
progress and development in other spheres. A step forward in the
scientific field was the formulation of a scheme to set up a Nuclear
Research Centre for exploring the possibility of obtaining uranium from
the mountainous regions of our country with a view to production of
atomic energy for the country's economic development.[79]

The visit of the Congressional Joint Committee was viewed as a
certificate of approval for Pakistan's plans. The Prime Minister
announced that, 'four members of the United States Joint Committee
on Atomic Energy visited us. . . . I am happy to state that the U.S.
delegation has not only given us encouragement but has expressed
their appreciation of our efforts in this direction.[80]

The public also was soon provided opportunities to glimpse the dawn of the nuclear age. In January 1955 the U.S. ambassador opened a travelling public exhibition on the Atoms for Peace program, created by the U.S. Information Agency.[81] The exhibition, occupying 3000 square feet, used pictures, films and models to show the development and possibilities of nuclear science and technology. The show opened in Bahawalpur and was reported to be a 'smash hit,' with more than 2500 people viewing it within the first two hours of its opening, and as many as 6000 visitors two days later.[82] Eventually 50,000 people were reported as have seen it.[83]

After Bahawalpur the exhibition, now jointly sponsored by the Pakistan Atomic Energy Committee and the U.S. Embassy, moved to Karachi, the capital, where it was opened by Finance Minister Chaudhri Mohammad Ali.[84] It drew an audience of 300,000 people during the two weeks of the exhibition.[85] It then went on to Lahore and Peshawar, and toured most of the other major cities, drawing large enthusiastic crowds. The atom was now firmly part of the public consciousness of a significant number of urban, middle-class Pakistanis.

On 11 August 1955 Pakistan and the U.S. signed a five-year Agreement for Cooperation on the Civil Uses of Atomic Energy. The U.S. provided funding for a small research reactor, fissile material to fuel it, an archive of technical reports and papers on many aspects of nuclear science and engineering, and a training program for scientists and engineers. By 1961 the newly created Pakistan Atomic Energy Commission (PAEC) had 144 scientists and engineers, who either had already received training abroad or were currently bring trained abroad. Among those trained in the U.S. was Munir Ahmed Khan, who would return to Pakistan and in 1972 become Chairman of PAEC, and was given the responsibility of launching Pakistan's nuclear weapons program. The program took on more urgency after India's May 1974 nuclear weapons test, and continued despite U.S. sanctions and pressure in the late 1970s. This pressure was eased after Pakistan joined the U.S. in a proxy war against the Soviet Union when it invaded Afghanistan. The program succeeded in the early

1980s and, following additional nuclear tests by India, Pakistan tested its nuclear weapons in May 1998.

CONCLUSION

This essay argues that the ideas of an atomic future that were developing in the United States became a central element in its relationship with Pakistan as soon as the U.S. began to engage with that country. The relationships between Pakistan's military, economic planning, and scientific institutions and the United States were all informed at some level by the idea of this imminent atomic future. For Pakistan's new national elite, embracing this future offered a way to affirm a shared perspective on what it meant to be a modern state and society in the contemporary world and what the future would be like. The pursuit of this future also privileged those who could operate at the national level and with the United States.

The embrace of an atomic future essentially distinguished those who saw a way for the country to become modern at home and part of the modern world from those who were rooted in the past and locality, clung to tradition, and did not believe in rapid social change. In this respect, the idea and ideal of an atomic future may be read as representing both the future and the universal as opposed to the local and the present. Based on this radical vision of a future world, these new bureaucracies of economy, violence and technology, exposed at a formative stage to American goods, skills, and ways of doing things, imbued with certain American tastes and desires, and all privileging 'technical superiority', set about creating the necessary conditions for the exercise of their power.

For those Pakistani elites able to create and take advantage of them, ties to the United States offered preferential access to power, resources and privilege. Pakistan's army saw in the U.S. a source of money, weapons, training, strategic support, and the future of warfare. Its economic planners saw development as stemming from access to U.S. aid and knowledge and aimed at creating a society modelled after a United States that was entering the nuclear age. For the scientists, a path was opened by President Eisenhower's

Atoms for Peace plan with its vision of a short-cut to a nuclear future, with scientists as the indispensable guides.

These ideas of past, present and future, of change, progress and possibility, and the institutions that claimed to embody them were to have an impact comparable in some respects to the much earlier experience of some nominally independent countries importing European ideas and institutions during the colonial period.[86] Pakistan was to see the emergence of a military that dominates national politics and the allocation of national resources, one that has seized power three times and ruled directly for over half of Pakistan's history so far. It has had a process of economic planning and management that has failed to provide basic needs to a large proportion of citizens, and remains dependent on international aid to meet its most basic developmental needs. Pakistan has witnessed the creation of a nuclear estate of nuclear power plants, nuclear weapons, and nuclear science and technology research and development. But Pakistan's nuclear estate can offer only a nuclear nationalism, evident in the models of the nuclear weapons test site and ballistic missiles that were put up in major cities, as well as the annual celebration of the anniversary of the May 1998 nuclear tests.

The narratives and displays that initiated the 28 May celebrations in 1999 are revealing. The plans for what the government called a celebration of 'self reliance', and of an 'impregnable defense' included 'a competition of ten best Milli songs, seminars, fairs, festive public gatherings, candle processions, sports competitions, bicycle races, flag hoisting ceremonies etc. People will offer Namaz-e-Shukrana as well. Apart from this special programs for children would be arranged. Debates would be held among school children.'[87]

To make sure that no one missed out on this new common sense about the meaning of Pakistan's nuclear weapons and those who manufactured them, there were to be programs 'broadcast on national network as well as locally by all 24 stations of the radio. In addition to the national language Urdu, programs in regional languages, including Punjabi, Sindhi, Pushto, Balochi, Brahui, Saraiki, Potohari, Hindko, Balti and Shina will also be broadcast.

The external service and world service will air special programs in fifteen foreign languages for listeners in Europe, Middle East, Africa and South East Asia. The Azad Kashmir Radio will also broadcast special programs on the occasion in Kashmiri, Gojri, Pahari and English languages.'[88] This would ensure that everybody could hear and understand the new national story of nuclear Pakistan. The audience was also meant to be global; as Information and Culture Minister Mushahid Hussain proudly put it, the nuclear test site at Chagai 'has become a symbol of Pakistan's identity all over the world.'[89]

Absent from these celebrations was the recognition that the world has long struggled to eliminate these weapons of mass destruction after they had been first created. It was wrongfully asserted that Pakistan's nuclear achievements were a proof of national self-reliance. In fact, the nuclear project from its inception relied on outside support. Pakistan's nuclear scientists were trained abroad, at the expense of others. Its nuclear research and nuclear power reactors were imported, the key technology for producing the fissile material for its nuclear weapons was bought abroad covertly by A.Q. Khan, and even the design of its bomb may have come from China.

Rather than proving national strength and self-reliance, the coming of the bomb exposed Pakistan's fundamental weaknesses. Indeed, the events after the May tests provided clear evidence of just how weak Pakistan actually is. The sanctions imposed by the international community in response to the nuclear tests were quickly lifted not because the world was awed by Pakistan's new nuclear might, but because they saw its fragility. It appeared that the country was about to fall apart and no one wanted to see that happen.

Pakistan's claims to national technological and military prowess through mastery of the bomb, the reactor, and the missile provide a flimsy veil over its many basic failures as a state and society. It is this recognition that shapes the efforts of the small, emerging anti-nuclear movement in Pakistan to embed its prudential and moral critique of nuclear weapons and nuclear power in a broader challenge to prevailing ideas and practices of national security, development and the politics of knowledge.[90] To repeat the call made in, *Out of the Nuclear Shadow*:

> The tasks that confront the peace movements in India and Pakistan are unprecedented. Not only must they educate their fellow citizens in what it means to live with nuclear weapons in their midst, they must do so without creating such fear that people are immobilised. They must organise to abolish nuclear weapons but cannot concentrate simply on the technology, politics, economics and culture of nuclear weapons because nuclear weapons cannot be abolished from South Asia or globally while leaving everything else unchanged.[91]

This means imagining and building a future that goes beyond emulating the states, economies, societies and knowledge systems of the 'developed' societies. It requires new dreams.

REFERENCES

1. Eqbal Ahmad, 'From Potato Sack to Potato Mash', in: *Between Past and Future (Selected Essays on South Asia by Eqbal Ahmad)*, Dohra Ahmad, Iftikhar Ahmad, Zulfiqar Ahmad, and Zia Mian, (eds.), (Karachi: Oxford University Press, 2004), p. 11.
2. Spencer R. Weart, *Nuclear Fear: A History of Images*, (Cambridge, Mass.: Harvard University Press, 1988), p. 6.
3. Ibid., pp. 25–6.
4. Richard K. Betts, *Nuclear Blackmail and Nuclear Balance*, (Washington, D.C.: Brookings Institution, 1987), pp. 32–3.
5. 'Global Nuclear Stockpiles 1945–2000', *Bulletin of Atomic Scientists* March/April 2000, p. 79.
6. 'Science and the Bomb', *The New York Times*, 7 August 1945, cited in Paul Boyer, *By the Bomb's Early Light: American Thought and Culture at the Dawn of the Atomic Age*, (Chapel Hill, N.C.: University of North Carolina Press, 1994), p. 125.
7. 'One Victory Not Yet Won', *New York Times*, 12 August 1945, cited in Boyer, *By the Bomb's Early Light*, p. 122.
8. Cited in Boyer, *By the Bomb's Early Light*, p. 112.
9. Weart, *Nuclear Fear*, p. 159.
10. Ibid., p. 162.
11. Available at http://www.trumanlibrary.org/whistlestop/50yr_archive/inagural20jan1949.htm

12. For a history of this speech, see Richard G. Hewlett and Jack M. Holl, *Atoms for Peace and War 1953–1961: Eisenhower and the Atomic Energy Commission*, (Berkeley, CA.: University of California Press, 1989).

13. 'President Dwight D. Eisenhower's 'Atoms for Peace' Address to the United Nations General Assembly, 8 December 1953', in: *The American Atom: A Documentary History of Nuclear Policies From the Discovery of Fission to the Present 1939–1984*, Robert C. Williams and Philip L. Cantelon, (eds.), (Philadelphia, PA: University of Pennsylvania Press, 1984), pp. 104–11.

14. R.G. Hewlett and J.M. Holl, *Atoms for Peace and War 1953–1961*, p. 190.

15. Ibid., p. 192.

16. Ayesha Jalal, *The Sole Spokesman: Jinnah, The Muslim League and The Demand for Pakistan*, (Cambridge: Cambridge University Press, 1985).

17. Ian Talbot, *Pakistan: A Modern History*, (Karachi: Oxford University Press, 1998), pp. 94–5.

18. For a history of the early efforts at creating a national, central authority see e.g. Ayesha Jalal, *The State of Martial Rule: The Origins of Pakistan's Political Economy of Defense*, (Lahore: Vanguard Books, 1991).

19. Lawrence Ziring, *Pakistan in the Twentieth Century: A Political History*, (Karachi: Oxford University Press, 1997), p. 98.

20. Keith Callard, *Pakistan: A Political Study* (London: Allen and Unwin, 1957), p. 80.

21. Hasan Zaheer, *The Times and Trial of the Rawalpindi Conspiracy 1951, The First Coup Attempt in Pakistan*, (Karachi: Oxford University Press, 1998).

22. Morris James, *Pakistan Chronicle*, (New York: St. Martin's Press, 1993), p. 5.

23. Callard, *Pakistan*, p. 15.

24. Pervaiz Iqbal Cheema, *Pakistan's Defense Policy, 1947–1958*, (London: Macmillan, 1990); and more broadly, Hasan Askari Rizvi, *Military, State and Society in Pakistan*, (London: Macmillan, 2000).

25. A.H. Nayyar and Ahmed Salim, (eds.), *The Subtle Subversion: The State of Curricula and Textbooks in Pakistan*, (Islamabad, SDPI, 2004).

26. R.J. McMahon; *The Cold War on the Periphery: The United States, India and Pakistan*, (New York: Columbia University Press, 1994), p. 36.

27. Ibid., p. 69.

28. Ibid.

29. 'Memorandum by the Acting Secretary of State to the Executive Secretary of the National Security Council', 19 August 1952, *FRUS, 1952–1954, Vol. XI, Pt. 2* (USGPO, Washington, D.C., 1983), p. 1059.

30. *50 Years of Pakistan in Statistics*, Federal Bureau of Statistics, Government of Pakistan, 1997.

31. S.P. Cohen, *The Pakistan Army*, (Berkeley, CA: University of California Press, 1984), p. 64.

32. K.M. Arif, *Khaki Shadows: Pakistan 1947–1997*, (Karachi: Oxford University Press, 2001), pp. 140–45.

33. Cohen, *The Pakistan Army*, p. 66.
34. Eqbal Ahmad, 'Signposts to a Police State', in: Dohra Ahmad, Iftikhar Ahmad and Zia Mian (eds.), *Between Past and Future*, p. 54.
35. Thomas B. Cochran, William M. Arkin, Milton M. Hoenig, *U.S. Nuclear Forces and Capabilities*, (Cambridge, Mass.: Ballinger, 1984).
36. Maj. Gen. M.A. Latif Khan, 'The Staff College as I Saw It', in: *Command And Staff College Quetta 1905–1980*, edited and compiled by Command and Staff College, Quetta, (Command and Staff College, Quetta: 1982), pp. 139–40.
37. Ibid., p. 139–40.
38. Ibid., p. 88.
39. Cohen, *The Pakistan Army*, p. 65.
40. Khan, 'The Staff College as I Saw It', pp. 139–40.
41. K.W. Condit; *History of the Joint Chiefs of Staff*, vol. VI: *The Joint Chiefs of Staff and National Policy 1955–1955*, (Historical Division, Joint Chiefs of Staff, Washington D.C.: 1992), p. 146.
42. Robert S. Norris, William M. Arkin, William Burr, 'Where They Were', *Bulletin of the Atomic Scientists*, November/December 1999, pp. 26–35.
43. For the debates prior to independence on the economic viability of Pakistan, see Naureen Talha, *Economic Factors in the Making of Pakistan 1921–1947*, (Karachi: Oxford University Press, 2000), see especially, pp. 145–57.
44. Hector Bolitho, *Jinnah: Creator of Pakistan*, (Karachi: Oxford University Press, 1954), pp. 158–59.
45. Cited in Talha, *Economic Factors in the Making of Pakistan*, p. 152.
46. Albert Waterston, *Planning in Pakistan: Organization and Implementation*, (Baltimore: Johns Hopkins Press, Baltimore, 1963), p. 13.
47. Ibid., p. 15.
48. Ibid.
49. Ibid., p. 21.
50. Omar Noman, *The Political Economy of Pakistan 1947–1985*, (London: Kegan and Paul), 1980, p. 10.
51. Nadeem ul Haque and Mahmood Hasan Khan, 'The Economics Profession in Pakistan: A Historical Analysis', in: *50 Years of Pakistan's Economy— Traditional Topics and Contemporary Concerns*, Shahrukh Rafi Khan, ed., (Karachi: Oxford University Press, 1999), p. 471.
52. Ibid., p. 471.
53. *Design for Pakistan: A Report on the Assistance to the Pakistan Planning Commission by the Ford Foundation and Harvard University*, Ford Foundation, New York, 1965, p. 2.
54. For a comparative history see George Rosen, *Western Economists and Eastern Societies: Agents of change in South Asia, 1950–1970*, (Baltimore: Johns Hopkins University Press, 1985.
55. Dickson Keith Smith, 'Foreign Aid and Economic Development in Pakistan— The Ayub Years (1958–1969)', PhD thesis, University of Utah, 1974, p. 106.

56. *The First Five Year Plan 1955–1960*, National Planning Board, Government of Pakistan, Karachi, 1957, pp. 1–2.
57. Ibid., p. 395.
58. Maurice D. Kilbridge, *The Prospect for Nuclear Power in Pakistan*, National Planning Association, Washington, D.C., 1958, p. 55.
59. Mahbub ul Haq, 'Wasted Investment in Scientific Research', in: *Science and the Human Condition in India and Pakistan*, Ward Morehouse (ed.), (New York: Rockefeller University Press, 1968), p. 128.
60. Zia Mian and A.H. Nayyar, 'Another Nuclear White Elephant', *Dawn*, 25 July 2004.
61. 'President Dwight D. Eisenhower's "Atoms for Peace" Address to the United Nations General Assembly, 8 December 1953.'
62. R.C. Cowen, 'Radioactive wastes now marketable,' *Dawn*, 13 December 1953.
63. H. Seligman, 'Atoms for Peace', *Dawn*, 17 December 1953.
64. G. Hutton, 'Economics of the Atom', *Dawn*, 15 January 1954.
65. 'Atom for Prosperity', *Dawn*, 17 January 1954.
66. 'A-energy to Generate Electricity: British Plan', *Dawn*, 19 January 1954.
67. K.E.B. Jay, 'We are on the Brink of a Profound Change,' *Dawn*, 24 January 1954.
68. 'Atoms for Peace', *Dawn*, 2 February 1954.
69. L. Amour, 'Backdrop to the Atom', *Dawn*, 2 February 1954.
70. 'Dr Raziuddin's Address,' *Dawn*, 19 January 1954.
71. 'A-Energy for Peaceful Uses: 2-Year Probe Opens in U.S.A.: Pakistan Likely to be Among "Selected Areas"'. *Dawn*, 28 September 1954.
72. Ibid.
73. *Dawn*, 20 October 1954.
74. Ibid.
75. *50 Years of Pakistan in Statistics, Volume II, 1947–1972*, Federal Bureau of Statistics, Government of Pakistan, 1997.
76. Ibid., Table 13.17, p. 240.
77. *Report of the Raw Materials Subcommittee on its Visit to Australia*, Joint Committee on Atomic Energy, 9 February 1955.
78. Ibid.
79. 'Immediate Steps for Popular Rule in E. Wing, Atomic Schemes to be Pursued', *Dawn*, 2 January 1955.
80. Ibid.
81. 'Atoms for Peace Exhibit Opens', *Dawn*, 22 January 1955.
82. 'Atoms for Peace Exhibition—Great Success at Bahawalpur', *Dawn*, 25 January 1955.
83. 'Atoms for Peace Exhibit popular at Bahawalpur', *Dawn*, 1 February 1955.
84. 'Finance Minister Opens Atom Exhibition', *Dawn*, 6 February 1955.
85. 'Over 2 Lakhs People Visited Atomic Show in Karachi', *Dawn*, 21 February 1955.

86. David B. Ralston, *Importing the European Army: The Introduction of European Military Techniques and Institutions into the Extra-European World, 1600–1914*, (Chicago: University of Chicago Press, 1990).
87. 'PM says May 28 Reminds of Objectives of National Agenda', APP, 8 May 1999.
88. 'PBC to Broadcast Special Programs on 28th', *The News*, 22 April 1999.
89. 'May 28 to Go Down in History as Symbol of National Pride', *The News*, 22 April 1999.
90. See, for instance, in: *Out of the Nuclear Shadow*, Smitu Kothari and Zia Mian, (eds.), (Karachi: Oxford University Press, 2003).
91. Ibid. pp. 9–10.

CHAPTER 3

PAKISTAN: CLIMBING THE NUCLEAR LADDER
Pervez Hoodbhoy

This chapter traces the early development of Pakistan's nuclear weapons; follows the subsequent evolution of its nuclear objectives and postures; identifies the stages by which a Pakistan–India nuclear crisis could escalate; and examines whether mutual deterrence can be considered robust.

South Asia's nuclear history begins in 1948, a year after Partition. Prime Minister Jawaharlal Nehru, on the advice of the brilliant Cambridge-educated nuclear physicist, Dr Homi Jehangir Bhabha, who was both his confidante and scientific advisor, ordered the establishment of the Atomic Energy Agency Commission of India. While the AEC's public position was to work towards generating nuclear energy for electricity generation, earth excavation, medical technology, and other peaceful purposes, Bhabha struggled to keep its mandate deliberately ambiguous so that the AEC could also conduct secret weapons-related research.[1,2] Nehru agreed, though he was less enthusiastic about nuclear weapons. Bhabha's carefully argued freedom would eventually lead to the development of India's nuclear weapons. A new nuclear vigour came with the Sino–Indian border war in 1962, and soon India quietly embarked on its quest for the bomb. Violating the terms on which Canada had provided the Cirus CANDU-type nuclear reactor, plutonium was stealthily reprocessed from its spent fuel. In 1974, just as Prime Minister Indira Gandhi was in deep political trouble, the 'Buddha smiled' over the Pokharan nuclear test site.

In Pakistan under General Ayub Khan (1958–1968), there was no movement or enthusiasm for the bomb. Ayub reportedly said that,

'We will buy the bomb off the shelf if India goes nuclear,'[3] but his foreign minister, Zulfikar Ali Bhutto knew that doing such a thing was impossible. Bhutto, a brilliant politician who appealed to anti-Indian sentiment, had for long aspired for the bomb. In 1966 he wrote that, 'It would be dangerous to plan for less and our plans should, therefore, include the nuclear deterrent.'[4] Five years later Pakistan was decisively defeated by India whose military intervention tipped the balance in the bloody civil war between East and West Pakistan. Bangladesh emerged, leaving the 'Two-Nation Theory'— the basis on which Pakistan had come into existence—in tatters.

Serious, but still preliminary, thinking about the bomb began in 1972, a year after the crushing blow of defeat in the Indo–Pak War of 1971 which led to the break-up of Pakistan and the creation of Bangladesh. In the city of Multan, an emotionally charged Bhutto, now prime minister, called a meeting on 20 January 1972 to which senior scientists and engineers were invited. Bhutto exhorted them to build the bomb, fired the existing chairman of the Pakistan Atomic Energy Commission, Dr Ishrat Hussain Usmani and hired an ambitious new one, Munir Ahmad Khan.

But 1972 was still not the actual starting point for Pakistan's quest for the bomb although Indian analysts often justify acquisition of their bomb by pointing fingers at Pakistan. According to some of my senior physics colleagues present at that meeting—including Dr Riazuddin, who later received a high Pakistani award for being the bomb's chief theoretician—there were no clear ideas of what it took to make a bomb and what had to be done. But just two years later the shock waves from India's nuclear test hit Pakistan, which had now been reduced to half its former size.

An all-out 'Manhattan-style' effort in Pakistan began just days later.[5,6,7] Bhutto raised money from Arab states such as Libya and Saudi Arabia. It is rumoured that bales full of dollars were brought in on Pakistan International Airline flights from the Middle East. Funds donated for helping the victims of the 1974 earthquake that hit the Karakoram Mountains are alleged to have been diverted into the nuclear program. Those who knew the precise details, like

Ghulam Ishaq Khan and H.U. Beg, took these secrets to their graves. The truth shall never be known.

Bhutto also elicited crucial nuclear help from China. Alarmed at India's nuclear success, China was willing to share the designs of its first weapon with Pakistan. This bomb had first been tested in Lop Nur in 1964.[8] China had also allegedly supplied UF_6 (uranium hexafluoride) gas for testing the centrifuges before a UF_6 plant was secretly imported from Germany.[9] This gas is the raw material from which the bomb material is ultimately extracted. It is quite likely that the development of nuclear weapons by Pakistan would have eventually succeeded, but without Chinese assistance this would have taken longer.

Some details about Chinese involvement have been confirmed by Dr A.Q. Khan, the metallurgist who headed the uranium enrichment plant at Kahuta and is famed for having brought back centrifuge designs from his earlier employment at URENCO in Belgium. Publically disgraced in January 2004 after his global business enterprise of selling nuclear technology surfaced, he was put under house arrest but still succeeded in giving interviews. In a dejected moment he revealed that China had supplied 50 kilograms of highly enriched uranium together with a blueprint for a simple weapon that China had already tested, thus supplying a virtual do-it-yourself kit.[10] But Khan, who has launched his own political party and is now aspiring to becoming the president of Pakistan, says that Pakistan was not a passive recipient. He says that the traffic was both ways and Pakistani experts were dispatched to Hanzhong in central China, where they helped 'put up a centrifuge plant' and that, 'We sent 135 C-130 plane-loads of machines, inverters, valves, flow meters, pressure gauges. . . . Our teams stayed there for weeks to help and their teams stayed here for weeks at a time.'[11]

That China tested for Pakistan its first bomb in 1990 has been claimed in a recent book co-authored by former U.S. Air Force Secretary Thomas Reed. Reed had earlier worked at Livermore National Laboratory as a weapons designer.[12] According to Reed, the Chinese did a massive training of Pakistani scientists, brought them to China for lectures, and even gave them the design of the CHIC-4 device, which was a weapon that was easy to build a model for export. Together with the other author, Danny Stillman, who was director of the technical intelligence division at Los Alamos National Laboratory, Reed argues that the reason Pakistan could respond so quickly and confidently after the Indian tests was because it was already tested in 1990, eight years before the tit-for-tat tests. Pakistani weaponeers vigorously deny this.

By 1986, or possibly a year earlier, Pakistan had some form of weapon. Delivery capability came some years later but, of course, preparations for testing could be made independently. A team headed by Dr Samar Mubarakmand was put in charge of preparing nuclear test sites at Chaghai and Koh Ras. And so, just seventeen days after the Indian tests, on 28 May 1998, the Chaghai mountains in Balochistan turned white from five nearly simultaneous atomic blasts. Prime Minister Nawaz Sharif had initially been hesitant because he feared crippling sanctions but finally decided to cross the bridge.[13] To jubilant crowds he announced: 'Today we have settled scores with India by detonating five nuclear devices of our own. We have paid them back.'[14]

While Nawaz Sharif claimed credit, so did his arch-rival and opposition leader, Benazir Bhutto. Before Pakistan tested she demanded that the U.S. should bomb India. In an article published in the *Los Angeles Times*, she wrote: 'Rogue nations that defy world opinion ought to be taught a lesson,' and hence, 'If a pre-emptive military strike is possible to neutralize India's nuclear capability, that is the response that is necessary.'[15] Addressing a public rally she made a grand theatrical gesture, tossing her glass bangles on the ground and taunting Nawaz Sharif that he was a *na-mard*, i.e., not man enough to respond to India's nuclear provocation. Thereafter, whatever restraining doubts Sharif might have had quickly vanished.

Pakistan's initially reluctant political leaders now feasted on their new-found glory. Massive celebrations, organized as well as spontaneous, erupted across Pakistan. Celebrations on the West Bank, and in some Muslim countries, broke out. The bomb makers became celebrities; school children were handed free badges with mushroom clouds; and poetry competitions extolled the great national achievement. Missile and fibreglass replicas of the nuclear test site mushroomed across the country. Most were removed several years later but some still stand in Pakistan's public squares and at crossroads. They are testimony to the delirium that had overpowered the country at a time when, for the man on the street, they stood as symbols of national glory and achievement rather than instruments of wholesale death and destruction.

The exhilaration overpowered the rational sensibilities of national leaders, both military and civil. Soon Pakistan was to see nuclear weapons as a talisman, able to ward off all dangers. Countering India's nuclear weapons with Pakistani nuclear weapons became secondary. Instead, the latter became the means for neutralizing India's far larger conventional land, air, and sea forces. Size no longer mattered. Zulfikar Ali Bhutto's dream of avenging East Pakistan, and of liberating Kashmir, now seemed to lie within the realm of possibilities.

EVOLUTION OF PAKISTAN'S NUCLEAR POSTURE

Although India's nuclear weapons had been conceived primarily as a means to counter China and fulfil notions of national grandeur, they inevitably created new dynamics of hostility in Pakistan–India relations. A fearful Pakistan originally acquired its own weapons largely for a single purpose: that of balancing every Indian nuke with a Pakistani nuke, or as close to that as possible. At one level this is understandable; living with a nuclear neighbour—especially an unfriendly one—cannot ever be comfortable for any country.

But the goal post was soon to shift. As early as 1966, just after 'Operation Gibraltar' had failed to reach its objectives, Bhutto had wanted the bomb as a deterrent that would work even if Pakistan was to be proactive again in Kashmir. Now, after their successful 1998 nuclear tests, Pakistani generals instantly saw that the calculus of power had changed in their favour. The NATO–Warsaw Pact experience had already established that parity could be obtained even with a much larger conventional force on the other side. So the fact that India had 1.3 million personnel in military uniforms, and Pakistan had only 0.6 million mattered much less. Now nuclear weapons could be used for more than just a boring stand-off with India. Convinced of an impregnable defense, Pakistani military planners embarked on what they thought was a brilliant covert operation in Kashmir.

Just months after Pakistan had established its nuclear credentials, the Chief of Army Staff, General Pervez Musharraf, sent troops out of uniform along with Islamist militant fighters across the Line of Control (LoC) in Kashmir. They seized strategic positions in the high mountains of the Kargil area on the Indian-controlled side in early 1999, setting off a war that left approximately two to four thousand personnel dead on both sides. Arguably, it was the first war in history to have been caused by nuclear weapons; the belief that Pakistan now possessed an impregnable defense meant that it could take much bigger risks against a superior military adversary.

To Pakistan's surprise (what truly surprises is that its leaders were surprised!) India poured troops and artillery into Kargil and vigorously counter-attacked once it realized the seriousness of the secret invasion. A military disaster for Pakistan loomed ahead and, worse, it stood diplomatically isolated.[16,17] With a tense situation threatening to spiral into all-out war, western diplomacy went into overdrive. Gloomy and worried, Prime Minister Nawaz Sharif contacted the Americans. But even before he flew to Washington on 4 July 1999, he had been bluntly told to withdraw Pakistani forces or be prepared for full-scale war with India. Bruce Reidel, Special Assistant to President Clinton, writes that he was present in person when Clinton informed Nawaz Sharif that the Pakistan Army had mobilized its nuclear-tipped missile fleet.[18] (If this is true, then the preparations for nuclear deployment and possible use could only have been ordered by General Pervez Musharraf at either his own initiative or in consultation with the army leadership.)

Riedel writes:

> Was that what Sharif wanted, Clinton asked? Did Sharif order the
> Pakistani nuclear missile force to prepare for action? Did he realize how
> crazy that was? You've put me in the middle today, set the U.S. up to
> fail and I won't let it happen. Pakistan is messing with nuclear war.
> Sharif was getting exhausted. He denied that he had ordered the
> preparation of their missile force, said he was against that but he was
> worried for his life now back in Pakistan.[19]

Unnerved by Clinton's revelation and the closeness to disaster,
Nawaz Sharif agreed to immediate withdrawal, abandoning earlier
assertions that Pakistan's army had no control over the invaders.
The order to retreat was to poison relations between him and
Musharraf, leading to Sharif's ouster just months later, on 12
October 1999. However, contrary to claims that he made a decade
later, Sharif had not opposed the venture. While he may not have
been fully on board, television footage shows him visiting forward
army posts near the Kargil area where he had given rousing speeches
to soldiers.[20]

One does not know if there was any actual move towards readying
nuclear forces on either side; this will be forever debated and
disputed. But even if there had been none, Kargil had impacted
strategic behaviour in the subcontinent in a significant manner.
Timothy Hoyt, writing on the nuclear dimensions of Kargil, puts it
as follows:

> Prior to Kargil, Indian and Pakistani elites viewed their nuclear
> capabilities as largely political, rather than military tools, and assumed
> that they would stabilize their longstanding competition. Leaders of
> each country made assumptions about the impact nuclear arsenals
> would have on the other side's behaviour, but these assumptions were
> mutually contradictory, and ultimately failed to account for the attitudes
> and responses of the other side. As a result, nuclear weapons did not
> deter war.[21]

Despite the Kargil defeat, Pakistan political and military leaders insisted that Pakistan had prevailed in the conflict and that its nuclear weapons had deterred India from crossing the Line of Control or the international border. The information minister, Mushahid Hussain, claimed that the Indian forces had been given a sound drubbing.[22] This belief still exists in the military, which is reluctant to admit that the philosophy behind the Kargil invasion was flawed. Internationally, Pakistan was branded the aggressor. The conflict eventually wound down after Pakistan ordered the withdrawal of its forces.

After Kargil, it did not take long to get back to the brink. On 13 December 2001, Islamic militants based in Pakistan struck at the Indian parliament in Delhi, sparking off a crisis that lasted for about seven months. While it is probably true that Musharraf's government did not order, and was unaware of the planned attack, there is little doubt that a free hand had been given to jihadists in Pakistan-controlled Kashmir. Indian tempers soared again. Prime Minister Atal Bihari Vajpayee exhorted his troops in Kashmir to prepare for sacrifices and 'decisive victory'. This set off widespread alarm. It seemed plausible that India was preparing for a 'limited war' to flush out Islamic militant camps in Pakistan-administered Kashmir. That nuclear weapons were put on enhanced alert by both sides is a strong possibility, although, direct proof appears unavailable.

Tensions kept mounting during the stand-off. Sensing a global climate deeply hostile to Islamic militancy after the 11 September 2001 attack on New York's World Trade Centre, India's ruling BJP echoed the 'War on Terror' slogan as a way to garner international support for their military campaign in Kashmir. In response, Pakistan's ambassador to the U.N. in Geneva, Munir Akram, sent a threatening message by reiterating Pakistan's refusal of a no-first-use policy. He said that given India's armed forces are larger than Pakistan's; anyone asking Pakistan to rule out first-strike of nuclear weapons would be 'asking us in fact to accept the use of conventional force by India.'[23]

Indian aggressiveness was also on full display. Defense Minister George Fernandes told the *International Herald Tribune*: 'India can survive a nuclear attack, but Pakistan cannot.'[24] Indian Defense Secretary Yogendra Narain took matters a step further in an interview with *Outlook Magazine*: 'A surgical strike is the answer,' adding that if this failed to resolve issues, 'We must be prepared for total mutual destruction.[25] Indian security analyst, Brahma Chellaney, claimed: 'India can hit any nook and corner of Pakistan and is fully prepared to call Pakistan's nuclear bluff.'[26] Fortunately, good sense prevailed and once again international mediation helped wind tensions down after a tense, months-long standoff.

Then came the Mumbai massacre. Carried out by over 30 Pakistan-based attackers, it began on 26 November 2008 and lasted three days, killing 164 and wounding at least 308. This incident is considered as their 9/11 by Indians. In the first few days, it seemed that the Pakistani state, embattled as it was by other jihadist groups it was fighting, could not have ordered the attacks. With the revelations of David Headley, a Chicago-based Pakistani-American who was working with an ISI operative, the situation has become murkier. It appears that parts of the Pakistani establishment might have been involved without knowledge of those at the top. Between 2006 and 2008, Headley admitted to performing five spying missions in Mumbai scouting targets for the 2008 attacks, on behalf of Lashkar-e-Taiba and Pakistani ex-military officers. Indian temperatures soared when Pakistan vociferously denied that its nationals were involved—a manifest untruth after the capture of Ajmal Kasab belonging to Faridkot, Pakistan. The media in both countries poured fuel over the fire, with Indian television anchor persons repeatedly calling for military action against Pakistan. Tensions simmered for long, dying away only gradually.

As of 2012, the Pakistani government has not acted against the Mumbai perpetrators. Hafiz Saeed roams the land, exonerated by Pakistani courts, delivering fiery speeches against India and the U.S. Indian allegations of Pakistan's official involvement became more pointed after the capture of Abu Jindal in June 2012; the Indians described the event as hitting a gold mine which proves official involvement through the ISI. Pakistan routinely denied the charges.

A POSSIBLE CRISIS ESCALATION LADDER

Now let's suppose that Mumbai-II were to happen and tensions were once again to rise to some dizzying level. What are possible Pakistani responses to an Operation Parakram, Cold Start, or some similar operation designed to punish Pakistan? One can imagine the following rungs of escalation each leading to the one above, or perhaps, even skipping to the next one:

1. Strong statements by the Pakistan Army and political leaders, similar to those made during previous crises, with open threats that a nuclear showdown is imminent.
2. Mobilization of a few missiles and nuclear-capable aircraft. This would be detectable by India's RISAT's (Radar Imaging Satellite) which, while in a 540-mile high orbit, uses a synthetic aperture that gives it day-night all-weather reconnaissance capability.[27] Thereafter one expects India to respond with a similar mobilization. But Pakistan would have to rely on China for intelligence information as it does not have such satellite capability.
3. An underground nuclear test by Pakistan. This would be a powerful signal that nuclear temperatures have sharply increased. Such a test is certainly technically possible, and one presumes that Pakistan has already prepared an appropriate site (probably again in Balochistan). Since Pakistan has not signed the CTBT (Comprehensive Nuclear Test Ban Treaty), this would not violate any international law. The Indian response could be tit-for-tat: those Indian scientists long spoiling for a chance to fine-tune their thermonuclear weapons will have their wish fulfilled.[28]
4. Air-dropping a bomb on some uninhabited desert area within Pakistan. The psychological impact would be enormously larger than that of an underground test; the flash would be detected by

aircraft and satellites, and the mushroom cloud would carry radioactivity long distances in directions determined by winds prevailing at that time. The fact that even desert areas are not completely uninhabited would be a consideration, but would not rule out this option. It is unlikely that India would follow suit (although underground testing will remain an option). Pakistan's action would arguably not be a violation of any NFU (No First Use) principle.[29] However, massive alarm would be created by this action and Pakistan might be seen to have nuclearized the conflict. Thereupon India would seek to have a total international boycott imposed upon Pakistan.

5. Use of tactical nuclear weapons against invading Indian troops. The development of short-range battlefield nuclear weapons such as *Nasr* and *Abdali* suggests that Pakistani planners have accepted this as a plausible scenario and thus worth preparing for. A Pakistani Inter-Services Public Relations (ISPR) press release in May 2012 stated: '*Nasr*, with a range of 60 km, carries nuclear warheads of appropriate yield with high accuracy, shoot and scoot attributes. This quick response system addresses the need to deter evolving threats.'[30] The Indian response to a TNW attack could be: a) An all-out attack using conventional weapons and a sea-embargo of Pakistani ports; b) A demonstrative nuclear attack on some military target within Pakistan. If the latter, then there would be a real question of whether further escalation can be limited.

Although much is made of TNW's, they may not be very effective militarily—invading front-line combat units can be expected to be sufficiently well dispersed and mobile so as to not make good nuclear targets.[31] Moreover, the sub-kiloton warheads are expensive: in spite of a yield 10–15 times lower than a 'city-buster', they consume 3–4 times more fissile material. This fact could be important for a country that has limited fissile stocks. But the very fact that nuclear weapons were used—even if on Pakistani soil rather than Indian—would have broken a taboo and brought the danger level to the very highest level; cities on both sides would now stand in mortal danger.

After the first weapon has been used, can anything be done to prevent catastrophe and prevent all available ones from being used? Given the extreme passions that would then rage, it is difficult to be optimistic. But, anticipating that such a situation could arise, in these calmer times, India and Pakistan would do well to give some thought to the management of a nuclear conflict should it start, for whatever reason.

At the very least both countries need to declare a policy of proportionate response. Rather than deliberately cultivating a 'madman image', it is better to go for 'an eye for an eye, a tooth for a tooth' policy. For this reason, nuclear crisis diplomacy must be kept alive. If India–Pak communication breaks down at some point in a crisis, third-party interlocution is going to be vital for averting a disaster. This is a complex issue. Until Musharraf's departure, Pakistan's nuclear program has been relatively transparent to the U.S., although, India's had been relatively opaque. Pakistan had an abiding faith in the U.S. to keep the Pak–India conflict from getting out of control in spite of the fact that the U.S. did not come to its aid in the 1965 and 1971 wars. India, on the other hand, had long presumed that the U.S. would give primacy to Pakistan and so distrusted it. But events over the last two decades have moved India towards, and Pakistan away from the U.S. While this reduces the importance of U.S. diplomacy in mediating conflicts, it still remains the best option.

Who would make nuclear decisions on the Pakistani side and according to what procedure? Opacity is part of the strategy of every nuclear state, and so no definitive answer can be given. But some facts seem well established. While General Musharraf was simultaneously President and Chief of Army Staff, he was the central person. The Strategic Plans Division (SPD) was created on his orders in February 2000, and became the sole organization authorised to have custody of nuclear weapons. It was overseen by the Nuclear Command Authority (NCA) whose members were the President,

Prime Minister of Pakistan (Vice Chairman), Minister for Foreign Affairs; Minster for Defense; Minister for Finance; Minister for Interior; Chairman, Joint Chiefs of Staff Committee; Chief of Army Staff; Chief of Naval Staff; and the Chief of Air Staff. The Director General (DG) of SPD, Gen. Khalid Kidwai, was the NCA's Secretary. Kidwai was set to retire in 2006, but Musharraf gave him a one-year extension, reportedly because of his technical assignment; he remains DG as of the end of 2012.

Post-Musharraf, it became clear that the army had little patience for the civilian leadership, especially in nuclear affairs. In November 2009, President Asif Ali Zardari quit his position as the NCA chairman, transferring his powers to Prime Minister Yousuf Raza Gilani. One expects that these powers were transferred on to Raja Pervez Ashraf, his replacement. Of course, no one really believes that Pakistan's civilian governments have any substantial control over nuclear matters.

IS NUCLEAR DETERRENCE ROBUST?

The rhetoric during each new Pakistan–India crisis has been fierce, suggesting a lessening of political restraints and ever greater nuclear brinksmanship. During earlier crises, high-ranking Indian officials conveyed publicly what they believed to be a powerfully convincing deterrent message—one that Rawalpindi took all too seriously. For example, during the 2001–2002 'Twin Peaks' crisis, Defense Minister George Fernandes famously responded to belligerent Pakistani statements in this manner: 'We could take a strike, survive, and then hit back. Pakistan would be finished.' During this crisis, the President of the ruling Bharatiya Janata Party, Jana Krishnamurthy, issued the same warning: If Pakistan escalated to nuclear weapons' use, 'its existence itself would be wiped out of the world map.' The Indian Chief of Army Staff, S. Padmanabhan, sang the same tune— that if Pakistan resorted to first use, 'the perpetrator of that particular outrange shall be punished so severely that their continuation thereafter in any form will be doubtful.'

Various Indian strategic analysts have also echoed this deterrent threat. For example, Bharat Karnad says that the problem 'is not one of preventing nuclear war, but with believing that Pakistan can annihilate India, which is not possible, even as the reverse is eminently true.'[32] Gurmeet Kanwal asserted that, 'if Pakistan were to . . . resort to the unthinkable, then India might as well insure that Pakistan finally ceases to exist as a nation state. . . . In an imperfect world . . . it does not pay to be squeamish.'[33]

Nonetheless, in spite of such pronouncements, there been no actual use of nuclear weapons since Hiroshima and Nagasaki. Although Pakistan and India have viciously clawed at each other, each time they have stepped back from the brink. Doesn't this constitute proof that deterrence 'works'? On the face of it, the answer is 'yes'. But what has worked a few times might, or might not work the next time. Repeated cycles increase fear-fatigue, reducing the value of deterrence. Indeed, the efficacy of nuclear deterrence rests upon the ability of these weapons to induce terror. It also presupposes a rational calculus, as well as actors who, at the height of tension, will give primacy to logic over emotion. Events in South Asia have put these assumptions into question. Countries loitering close to the brink may begin to feel that they cannot fall into it.

The conflict in early 2002, which came in the background of crises in 1977 and 1990, showed a remarkable public indifference to the tense situation on the ground. A million troops had mobilized and leaders in both India and Pakistan threatened nuclear war. World opinion responded fearfully seeing a fierce, possibly suicidal, struggle up ahead. Foreign nationals streamed out of both countries. But even at the peak of the crisis, few Indians or Pakistanis lost much sleep. Stock markets flickered, but there was no run on the banks or panic buying. Schools and colleges, which generally close at the first hint of disturbances, functioned normally. The indifference to nuclear annihilation shocked the rest of the world.

The nonchalance has a strong reason. India and Pakistan are still largely traditional, rural societies, albeit undergoing rapid economic and social transformation. The fundamental belief structures of such societies (which may well be the last things to change), reflect the realities of agricultural economies dependent on rains and good weather—precisely the factors that brought the Rain God and other deities into being. These pre-scientific beliefs encourage surrender to larger, supernatural forces. Conversations and discussions often end with remarks to the effect that fate shall triumph, or that it shall be as Allah wills, after which people shrug their shoulders and move on. Risk-taking is natural once unseen forces can be brought to your defense.

Nuclear ignorance partially explains this cavalier attitude. In either country, most people lack any real understanding of the catastrophe that would follow the use of even a single, small 15KT nuclear weapon in a populated area. In India, a November 1999 post-election national opinion poll survey found just over half of the population had not even heard of the May 1998 nuclear tests.[34] In the middle of the spring 2002 crisis, the BBC reported the level of awareness of the nuclear risk among the Pakistani public was 'abysmally low'.[35] In India, it found 'for many, the terror of a nuclear conflict is hard to imagine.'[36]

First-hand evidence bears out these judgments. Even educated people seem unable to grasp basic nuclear realities. Some physics students (and faculty!) in my university's physics department think that a nuclear war would be the end of the world. Others see nuclear weapons as just bigger bombs. Many said it was not their concern, but the army's. Almost none know about the possibility of a nuclear firestorm, about residual radioactivity, or damage to the gene pool. The media has not attempted to change the public's ignorance of nuclear dangers. Critical discussions of nuclear weapons and nuclear war are strictly off limits in both countries.

Terror of nuclear weapons was fundamental in moving the Cold War adversaries towards nuclear treaties such as SALT (Strategic Arms Limitation Talks), and the winding down of their aggressive military posturing. But this feeling of fear is not to be found in the Pakistan–India nuclear situation. Instead, oftentimes one finds a casual denial of reality and an almost blasé indifference to what nuclear weapons do. This means that military and civil leaders are not constrained from hurling belligerent threats or taking rash actions.

Pakistani political leaders and analysts are also remarkably ignorant of nuclear matters. It is well known that Benazir Bhutto was kept out of the nuclear loop. Knowing how difficult it would be to persuade the generals, she displayed no desire to be informed of nuclear secrets, much less challenge the generals over whom she supposedly had authority.[37] President Asif Ali Zardari, after a faux pas in which he said Pakistan believed in NFU (No First Use) of nuclear weapons, quickly resigned from presiding over the nuclear command authority and delegated his authority to the prime minister.[38]

On the Indian side, serious misconceptions about Pakistan's capabilities prevailed even after the 1998 nuclear tests. Even later, several senior Indian military and political leaders continued to express doubts on the operational capability and usability of the Pakistani arsenal. As detailed earlier, after Pakistan's incursion into Kargil, India began to seriously consider making cross-border strikes on militant camps on the Pakistani side of the Line of Control. This gained support in Indian ruling circles, increasing risks of a mis-judgment that could have led to serious miscalculations.

Many Indians have also held the false belief that Pakistan, as a client state of the U.S., had been forced to put its nuclear weapons under the control of the U.S. Thus the U.S. would either restrain their use by Pakistan or, if need be, destroy them. At a meeting in Dubai which I attended in January 2002, senior Indian analysts said they were 'bored' with Pakistan's nuclear threats and no longer believed them. K. Subrahmanyam, an influential Indian hawk who has long advocated Indian nuclearization said that India can 'sleep in peace'. Although the current tension between the U.S. and Pakistan puzzles various Indian commentators, such beliefs continue to be held by many Indians—including those in high positions.

The presumption is misplaced. Even if the United States had the political will it would not have the capability to locate and destroy

Pakistani nuclear weapons. To faithfully track even a handful of mobile nuclear-armed missiles is extremely difficult. During the Cuban missile crisis, the U.S. Air Force had aerial photos of the Soviet missile locations and its planes were only minutes away, yet it would not assure that a surprise attack would be more than 90 per cent effective. In the first Gulf War, U.S. efforts to destroy Iraqi Scuds' had limited success. For all the talk and threats issued from time to time, the U.S. is extremely reluctant to move on Iran's nuclear weapons—or allow Israel to go for them. No country has ever tried to take out another's nuclear bombs. The consequences of a botched operation can be severe.

HOW MANY ARE ENOUGH?

The number of nuclear weapons that Pakistan 'must have' is generally left open by defense analysts; it is rare to find explicit numbers. It is therefore of some interest to consider the figures used by a retired Pakistani air force officer, Air Commodore Jamal Hasan.[39] His logic is reproduced below.

> We assume that destruction of two enemy cities will meet our minimum deterrence needs and each city would need to be hit with five nuclear bombs, that our delivery means have a 50% probability of successfully penetrating the enemy defenses, and finally the enemy has the capability of destroying 50% of our nuclear assets in a pre-emptive first strike. Now with these sets of assumed determinants, the number of weapons needed to ensure minimum deterrence would be:
>
> * Number of bombs required to take out two cities @ 5 per city: 10 bombs
> * After factoring in enemy's 50% intercept capability: 20 bombs
> * Enemy can take out 50% of our force in a pre-emptive strike. So we would need 40 bombs to maintain our minimum deterrence under the given set of assumptions.

This relatively modest figure of 40 bombs then jumps to a staggering 1000 under a different set of assumptions made by the same writer:

Let us now assume that the enemy has enhanced his offensive and defensive capability. Now, he can intercept 90% of our nuclear weapons because of better NMD system. He also has increased his offensive potential through greater number of nuclear weapons with enhanced accuracy and now can take out 90% of our nuclear arsenal in a pre-emptive strike. Now the fresh calculation would be:

* Number of bombs required to take out 2 cities @ 5 per city: 10 bombs

* After factoring in enemy's 90% intercept capabilities: 100 bombs

* After factoring in 90% of enemy's riposte capability: 1000 bombs[40]

A degenerative logic is apparent above. Tweaking input parameters arbitrarily generates arbitrary outputs—you can get the result you want, and yet it can be made to appear as the end product of a logical process.

Similar leaps of logic can be found on the Indian side. Like Pakistan, India refuses to set an upper limit on its arsenal. Instead, it enhances Pakistani fears by claiming advances on its side. DRDO's announcement[41] in 2012 that 'Delhi and Mumbai, the two most vital metros of India, have been chosen for ballistic missile defense shield' feeds into Pakistani fears, although, this gives incentive to Pakistan to step up its warhead production, the missile shield gives little real protection.

In the context of South Asia, missile defense is a technical impossibility because of extremely short 4 to 6 minute warning times, easily manufactured decoys, and various electronic counter measures. To attack with missiles is relatively easy but to defend specific targets against missiles in the mid-course and terminal phase is very hard. A report of the American Physical Society says that destroying missiles in even the (much easier) boost phase is dauntingly difficult.[42]

Nevertheless, the Indian establishment's security paradigm has not shifted fundamentally and more Indian missiles are on their way. Marking a quantum escalation, in July 2009, India began sea trials of its 7000-ton nuclear-powered submarine, the *Arihant*, with underwater ballistic missile launch capability. The submarine is the first in a planned fleet of five, and is to be supplemented by a hunter-killer nuclear submarine soon. While the *Arihant* is not yet operational, DRDO has claimed a recent success: after the maiden test of the 5000 km *Agni* V, DRDO's head, V.K. Saraswat, noted that several *Agni* variants could eventually be mated with multiple independently targetable re-entry vehicles (MIRVs), or multiple nuclear warheads. On 10 May 2012 he explained: 'Where I was using four missiles, I may use only one missile. So it becomes a force multiplier given the damage potential.'[43]

A booming Indian economy has fed India's rapid militarization. With only a sixth of India's budget, Pakistan obviously cannot match India weapon-for-weapon. Nevertheless, historically every Indian move somehow finds a counter move. Predictably, news of India's new weapon systems is badly received in Pakistan. What should it do? Tariq Osman Hyder, a former diplomat who headed Pakistan's delegation in 2004–2007 talks with India on nuclear and conventional CBMs, gave his answer:

> What should Pakistan do? First of all develop its own second strike nuclear submarine based capability on which it must have given some thought having been long aware of the Indian program. Secondly, equip its conventional submarines with nuclear-tipped cruise missiles. Thirdly, as the Russian assistance to India for this project, and the lack of any objection from the U.S. or any other party has shown that both leasing of nuclear submarines and technology for their production are completely compatible with the global non-proliferation regime, Pakistan should explore such possibilities.[44]

The long and short is that the Pakistan–India nuclear race is open-ended; the sky is the limit. Of course, this is not particular to the subcontinent. Escalation lies in the nature of the nuclear beast: the Cold War saw the U.S. warhead-count reach a peak of 31,255 in 1967.[45] Just one of these bombs—even one on the smaller side—dropped on a city can easily kill a hundred thousand and the fallout would render the city uninhabitable for years.

Praful Bidwai, an astute observer of the Indian nuclear scene, sums up South Asia's current situation as follows: 'Today, both countries refuse to restrict themselves to any specific number of weapons. Similarly, for delivery vehicles and 'flexible response' is kept undefined. Tactical nuclear war-fighting, once considered escalatory and way beyond minimal deterrence, is said to have been incorporated into current Indian military doctrine. . . . Taken together, Indian military options and Pakistani planning would seem to ensure that that any major India–Pakistan conflict would inexorably lead to the use of nuclear weapons.'[46]

Perhaps it might be slightly more scientific to insert 'likely' instead of 'inexorably' in Bidwai's sobering assessment. But then, that's only a quibble.

REFERENCES

1. Perkovich, George, *India's Nuclear Bomb*, University of California Press, (2002).
2. M.V. Ramana, in this volume.
3. 'Pakistan's Nuclear Development', Ashok Kapur, Croom Helm, London, 1987, p. 54.
4. 'Myth of Independence', *Z.A. Bhutto*, Oxford University Press, Karachi, 1969, p. 54.
5. Shahid-ur Rahman, *The Long Road to Chaghi*. This is an insider account of Pakistan's bomb history, probably written with the encouragement of the Pakistan Atomic Energy Commission as part of its effort to counter Dr A.Q. Khan's claims to being the father of the bomb.
6. Matin Zuberi, in: *Pakistan: At the Crossroads*, edited by K.K. Nayyar, Rupa & Co, 2003.
7. Zia Mian, in this volume.
8. Munir Ahmad Khan, former chairman of the Pakistan Atomic Energy Commission, private communication to the author *c.*1993. Although it was highly confidential information then, it is no longer considered controversial or confidential today.
9. German Firm Cited in Case Involving Sale of Fluoride Conversion Plant to Pakistan, Nuclear Fuel, 20 July 1981, Section: vol. 6, No. 15; p. 3.
10. Pakistani nuclear scientist's accounts tell of Chinese proliferation, R. Jeffrey Smith and Joby Warrick, *The Washington Post*, Friday, 13 November 2009.
11. Ibid.
12. *The Nuclear Express: A Political History of the Bomb and its Proliferation*, Thomas C. Reed and Danny S. Stillman, Zenith Press, 2009.

13. Riaz Khokhar, who was Pakistan's ambassador to the U.S. at the time of nuclear tests, had been summoned for consultations back in Islamabad. He told me in early June 1998 that there were sharp differences within the cabinet over whether Pakistan should test or not. Sartaj Aziz, then foreign minister, confirmed this to me as well many years later.

14. *Nawa-i-Waqt*, 30 May 1998.

15. Pakistan in 'No Haste' to Test Bomb, U.S. Told *Los Angeles Times*, 16 May 1998.

16. Editorial, *The Washington Post*, 28 June 1999; Editorial, *Economist*, 1 July 1999; Editorial, *The New York Times*, 5 July 1999.

17. *Asymmetric Warfare in South Asia—The Causes and Consequences of the Kargil Conflict*, edited by Peter R. Lavoy, Cambridge University Press, 2009.

18. Bruce Riedel, (2002), *American Diplomacy and the 1999 Kargil Summit at Blair House,* Centre for the Advance Study of India Policy Paper, University of Pennsylvania, 2002. Reproduced in Lavoy op. cit. and available on the internet at http://www.sas.upenn.edu/casi/reports/RiedelPaper051302.htm

19. Ibid.

20. Video footage of Nawaz Sharif in: 'Crossing The Lines—Kashmir, Pakistan, India', http://www.youtube.com/watch?v=3LLnuglrW34, Pervez Hoodbhoy and Zia Mian.

21. Timothy D. Hoyt, Kargil: The Nuclear Dimension, published in Lavoy, op. cit.

22. 'Pakistan and India under the Nuclear Shadow', http://www.youtube.com/watch?v=EeBRVFxe5oQ

23. 'Islamabad refuses to accept "no first strike" doctrine', *Dawn*, 31 May 2002.

24. Michael Richardson 'India and Pakistan are not "imprudent" on nuclear option; Q&A/George Fernandes', *The International Herald Tribune*, 3 June 2002.

25. Yogendra Narain, 'A Surgical Strike is the Answer: Interview with Defense Secretary Yogendra Narain', *Outlook*, 10 June 2002.

26. 'India Tests Nuclear-Capable Missile, Angers Pakistan', *Agence France Presse*, 25 January 2002

27. 'RISAT-1's radar can see through clouds and work in darkness', *The Hindu*, 25 April 2012.

28. 'No CTBT, India needs more nuclear tests: Santhanam', *Hindustan Times*, 27 August 2009.

29. China is apparently also taking the position that nuclear weapons exploded on its own territory does not constitute a first use.

30. *Hatf IX* Nasr Missile Tested by Pakistan, 29 May 2012, ISPR, Source: http://www.defense.pk/forums/pakistan-strategic-forces/183325-hatf-ix-nasr-missile-tested-pakistan-9.html#ixzz1y5f4umlA

31. Zia Mian and A.H. Nayyar, this volume.

32. Bharat Karnad, in: *Nuclear Weapons and Indian Security*, (2002).

33. Gurmeet Kanwal, *Nuclear Defense: Shaping the Arsenal*, (2001).

34. Yogendra Yadav, Oliver Heath, and Anindya Saha, (1999), 'Issues and the Verdict', *Frontline*, November 13–26.

35. Singh, Jyotsna, (2002), 'South Asia's Beleagured Doves', *BBC*, June 4.
36. Sen, Ayanjit, (2002) 'Indians Vague on Nuclear Terrors', *BBC*, June 3.
37. Pakistan: Political Transitions and Nuclear Management', a paper by Feroz Khan presented at NPEC's meeting, 'Securing Nuclear Arsenals for the Next Half Century: What Does History Recommend?', Feroz Khan 27 February 2012.
38. 'Asif Ali Zardari delights India with "no first strike" policy', *The Australian*, 25 November 2008.
39. 'Deterrence in a Nuclear Environment', Air Commodore (Retd.) Jamal Hussain, http://www.defensejournal.com/2003/mar/deterrence.htm
40. Ibid.
41. 'Delhi, Mumbai selected for ballistic defense missile shield', *Times of India*, 24 June 2012.
42. 'Report of the American Physical Society Study Group on Boost-Phase Intercept Systems for National Missile Defense: Scientific and Technical Issues', Rev. Mod. Phys. 76, S1–S424, (2004).
43. 'Agni-V may be equipped with multiple warheads: DRDO chief', *The Economic Times*, 10 May 2012.
44. Tariq Osman Hyder, 'Strategic stability in South Asia', *The News*, 1 August 2009.
45. 'Nuclear weapons and the U.S.', *Wikipedia*.
46. 'India: A dangerous high', Praful Bidwai, *Frontline*, Volume 29, Issue 18 May 2012.

CHAPTER 4

PAKISTAN: UNDERSTANDING THE 'WORLD'S FASTEST GROWING ARSENAL'
Pervez Hoodbhoy

The goal of this chapter is to summarize the current Pakistani warhead, missile, and aircraft situation—to the extent that it is known from published sources—and then to enumerate various constraints that might limit a still larger increase. The forces pushing expansion are discussed.

Claims that Pakistan's nuclear arsenal has become the world's fastest growing one have reverberated around the world. In 2011, *The Washington Post*[1] put Pakistan's stockpile at more than 100 deployed weapons, a doubling over the past several years. Those figures made Pakistan the world's fifth-largest nuclear power. A second estimate, published in the *Bulletin of Atomic Scientists* report entitled: 'Pakistan's Nuclear Forces—2011'[2] by the Federation of American Scientists, states that although the numbers of Pakistani warheads and delivery vehicles is a closely held secret, yet 'we estimate that Pakistan has a nuclear weapons stockpile of 90–110 nuclear warheads, an increase from the estimated 70–90 warheads in 2009.' The authors reckon that if the expansion continues, Pakistan's stockpile could reach 150–200 in a decade.[3] By this count, Pakistan's arsenal may have already exceeded India's, and will soon rival Britain's.

Similar statements have been made earlier as well. A former top official of the CIA is quoted in the September 2009 *Bulletin of the Atomic Scientists* as saying, 'It took them roughly 10 years to double the number of nuclear weapons, from roughly 50 to 100.'[4]

The first question is: how do these Western analysts and officials arrive at these estimates? Why should we believe their numbers?

Obviously all nuclear activities is inside buildings to which access is strictly forbidden, and every precaution is made to shield them from prying eyes in the sky (and sometimes on the ground). The security around nuclear installations can be quite fearsome. So, for example, on 26 June 1979 France's ambassador to Pakistan had his teeth knocked out while trying to drive by the forbidden area near the Kahuta Research Laboratory (KRL). In addition to many other security requirements, KRL workers are required to report not just on those colleagues who spend too much time with friends, but also on those who stare outside the narrow windows for too long.

Still, some things are impossible to hide from prying eyes: there are tell-tale signatures of nuclear activities and the trained analyst knows just what to look for. High resolution satellite pictures can give overall physical details of buildings, plants, and machinery; electricity consumption results in a thermal signature detectable by infrared satellite cameras; sensors secretly placed around a plant can detect various kinds of gases; trucks and cars going in and out can be seen; communications can be electronically monitored; and movements of materials can be monitored. And, of course, there are spies—euphemistically called HI or 'human intelligence'. Professionals can then piece together the various evidences available.

Estimations can be inaccurate at times for a variety of reasons. A country can use subterfuges to conceal fissile material—the stuff out of which bombs are made. Their quantity and purity, as well as warhead and missile details are hard to know from afar. High resolution satellites can also be fooled, and human intelligence can be used in a way to manipulate figures. Thus, at the end of the day, one has only estimates and preconceptions by which to go on. But, strangely enough, these estimates have turned out to be rather good in some cases—as when they were made for the U.S. and France. The in-depth penetration of Iran's program, proved by the U.S.'s engineered destruction of Iranian centrifuges using the Stuxnet virus, is another example of intelligence success. This rather tenuous argument does not guarantee, of course, that estimates made by U.S. analysts will resemble reality for India, Pakistan,

China, or Israel. But since governments generally do not divulge atomic secrets, perhaps it is better to have ballpark figures rather than no figures.

Pakistan has not denied *The Bulletin's* report. Its stockpile of bomb-grade HEU (Highly Enriched Uranium) is increased daily by the unknown thousands of centrifuges whirring away at the enrichment facility at Kahuta (KRL) some forty miles from Islamabad, as well as those rumoured to be elsewhere. A different kind of bomb material, plutonium, is produced by reactors located at Khushab in the province of Punjab. Two reactors are already at work and a third is undergoing trials. A fourth one is under construction, as anyone who can use Google Earth will confirm. The plutonium has no commercial purpose. Instead, the goal is to produce lighter and more compact bombs to be fitted on to missile tips.

In Graph I the current estimate of Pakistan's nuclear arsenal is given. It is, of course, subject to the caveats mentioned above. The numbers for earlier years appear to be underestimated; the first nuclear weapon dates to 1985–1986, and six had been tested in 1998.[2] Clearly there could not have been just two bombs left in the

Graph 1: Growth of Pakistan's Nuclear Arsenal

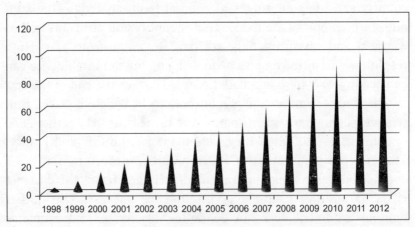

Data from *Bulletin of the Atomic Scientists* 2011 67: 91 by Hans M. Kristensen and Robert S. Norris in: 'Pakistan's Nuclear Forces, 2011'.

arsenal after the test. So a pinch of salt is called for! The subsequent rate of growth appears plausible, however.

Given that most nuclear states choose not to announce limits upon the size of its nuclear arsenal, one can safely assume that Pakistan's targets are similarly open-ended. Subject to material and technical constraints, Pakistan will seek to make as many warheads as possible, as well as make them more powerful and efficient. Hence more bomb material is being sought.

India's push for nuclear improvements and changing military doctrines almost immediately draw Pakistani reaction. A Wikileaks cable sent to Washington from the U.S. embassy in Islamabad said that Indian missile defense is a cause for worry in Pakistan: 'Pakistani counterparts point to India's interest and investment in missile defense, even if it will take many years to field a capable system. They believe this indicates that India is not interested in a balance of power, but intends to degrade the value of Pakistan's nuclear deterrent.'[5] But, given the near impossibility of defense in a situation where missile flight times are a mere 4–6 minutes, this cannot be a genuine concern. It also appears that Pakistan, quite wisely, is not worried by U.S. plans to sell the Patriot Advanced Capability 3 missile defense system to India. According to General Musharraf, the Patriot system also has a response time of up to eighteen minutes, while Pakistani missiles could begin landing within six minutes. Further, 'to top it all, our capability, which we have tested and is no secret, goes in the atmosphere. And when it drops down, it sheds its body in the air. The remaining part is the warhead, which is as small as 10 feet, and hard to hit.'[6]

'Cold Start' is of greater significance. This is an operation conceived by the Indian military in response to more Mumbai-type attacks. Pakistan has now made it known that the response to an invasion by Indian conventional forces could result in a nuclear riposte on the battlefield. But battlefield weapons are very uneconomical in terms of their fissile material requirements, and hence it has still greater need for fissile materials.

WHAT ELSE DRIVES THE EXPANSION?

United Nations Secretary-General Ban Ki-Moon is said to be a calm man. But Moon could not hide his frustration at Pakistan's determined opposition to a treaty that would limit fissile material production for use in nuclear weapons.[7] For three years, Pakistan has single-handedly—and successfully—blocked the Conference on Disarmament (CD) in Geneva from discussing an effort that would put a cap on fissile materials. Consequently, within diplomatic circles, Pakistan has acquired the reputation of an obstructionist that opposes all efforts towards this end.

Pakistan, in defending itself against these charges at the Conference on Disarmament in Geneva, cites the U.S.–India nuclear deal,[8,9] along with older issues related to verification problems and existing stocks, as its principal objection to the FMCT (Fissile Material Cut-off Treaty). Indeed, the Deal was a powerful blow against international arms control. The United States, while pursuing its perceived national interests, had chosen to commit itself to nuclear cooperation with India—a state that had not signed the NPT, and one that made nuclear weapons surreptitiously using technology given to it for exclusively peaceful purposes. America now had to choose between supporting the integrity of the NPT, which it had initiated and pushed for in the 1960s, against its more recent desire to achieve a new strategic balance in Asia in the post-Cold War world. After some initial hesitation, it chose the latter.

Mainstream India was delighted at the Deal, although the Indian Left noisily protested. The sanctions imposed after the 1998 tests had been lifted after India's vehement protestations but now, under the Deal, India wanted much more—such as importing advanced nuclear reactor technology, as well as natural uranium ore from diverse sources including Australia.[10] Although imported ore cannot legally be used for bomb-making, India can in principle divert more of its scarce domestic ore towards military reactors. Joseph Cirincione of the Centre for American Progress, and a critic of the Deal, remarked:

The deal endorses and assists India's nuclear-weapons program. United States supplied uranium fuel would free up India's limited uranium reserves for fuel that otherwise would be burned in these reactors to make nuclear weapons. This would allow India to increase its production from the estimated six to 10 additional nuclear bombs per year to several dozen a year.[11]

The Deal is inimical to the objective of a world with fewer nuclear weapons. But this may not be the full story; another powerful incentive now lies behind Pakistan's forceful rejection of the FMCT, one having to do with America rather than India. Whereas formally the U.S. and Pakistan are still allies in the War Against Terror announced by President G.W. Bush after the 9/11 attacks on U.S. soil, they have long loitered at the brink of open hostility. *The Washington Post* columnist David Ignatius writes that, 'United States and Pakistan have the most neurotic, mutually destructive "friendly" relationship in the world.'[12]

Today, in the Pakistan military's mind, the threat posed by the U.S. competes with that from India. Although TTP (Tehreek-e-Taliban Pakistan) jihadists have killed thousands of Pakistani troops and civilians over the last four–five years, the Americans are considered still more of an adversary. Smarting after U.S. troops intruded into Pakistan and killing Osama bin Laden, General Ashfaq Pervez Kayani reminded the Americans that Pakistan was a nuclear power and should not be compared with Iraq or Afghanistan and to 'think 10 times' before moving into the North Waziristan region from Afghanistan.[13]

Conflict with the U.S. is a possibility that Pakistanis frequently wonder about. Pakistan's former ambassador to the U.N., Munir Akram, hints that this may not be far away:

Today, the relationship has passed into the zone of hostility at the popular and official level. It is entirely uncertain where the American insults, collaboration with our regional adversaries and talk of 'losing patience' with Pakistan will lead. The history of the nuclear era reveals how often states have come, through blunder and miscalculation, to the brink of nuclear catastrophe.[14]

A major reason for the Pakistan Army's growing hostility towards
the U.S. is the increasing conviction that its nuclear weapons are
threatened by America. This perception is reinforced by the decade-
long attention given to the issue in the U.S. mainstream press, and
by war-gaming exercises in U.S. military institutes. Pakistani fears
about a weapon-snatch skyrocketed after the bin Laden raid in
Abbotabad in May 2011. Two weeks later Senator John Kerry,
Chairman of the Senate Foreign Relations Committee, came to
Islamabad. His visit was reported to be a tense one:

> Kayani was still seething. He used a private session with Kerry and
> Pakistan's president and prime minister to demand a written assurance
> that, under no circumstances—even chaos in Pakistan—would the
> United States enter the country to grab or secure the country's nuclear
> treasure. Kerry, thinking he was using a figure of speech, said he was
> prepared to 'write in blood' that the United States had no intention to
> go after the arsenal.[15]

Of course, an American attack on Pakistan's nuclear facilities is very
improbable. It is difficult to imagine any circumstances—except
possibly the most extreme—in which the U.S. would risk going to
war against another nuclear state. Even if Pakistan had just a handful
of weapons, no outside power could accurately know the coordinates
of the mobile units on which they are located. Immediately after the
bin Laden killing, Americans detected that elements of the arsenal
had been moved around.[16] According to *The Atlantic*:

> Nuclear-weapons components are sometimes moved by helicopter and
> sometimes moved over roads. And instead of moving nuclear material
> in armoured, well-defended convoys, the SPD prefers to move material
> by subterfuge, in civilian-style vehicles without noticeable defenses, in
> the regular flow of traffic. According to both Pakistani and American
> sources, vans with a modest security profile are sometimes the preferred
> conveyance. And according to a senior U.S. intelligence official, the
> Pakistanis have begun using this low-security method to transfer not
> merely the 'de-mated' component nuclear parts but 'mated' nuclear
> weapons.[17]

For any attacker, mobile dummies and decoys hugely compound difficulties. Additionally, General Musharraf revealed to American journalist Seymour Hersh that an extensive network of underground tunnels exists: 'The tunnels are so deep that a nuclear attack will not touch them.[18] Within these warheads and missile launchers can be freely moved. Moreover, even if a nuclear location was exactly known, it would surely be heavily guarded. This implies many casualties if intruding troops are engaged, thus making a secret Osama bin Laden type operation impossible.

Although Pakistan's preparations make for a formidable defense and an American attack is unlikely, all armies prepare for contingencies. Post-Osama bin Laden, the Pakistan Army's deepest nightmare is to be stripped of its nuclear weapons. Thus, redundancy is considered desirable—an American attempt to seize or destroy all warheads would have smaller chances of success if Pakistan had more. Hence the impetus for expanding the arsenal increases.

NUCLEAR WARHEADS

Let us take a look at the available information on Pakistan's warhead production, beginning with some general facts. Two types of fission bombs exist. For a Hiroshima sized effect, uranium-based weapons typically need 15–25 kg of HEU with 90 per cent purity or better which, if solidly packed, is about the size of a grapefruit. Plutonium-based weapons can achieve the same power with just 3–5 kg, which is golf-ball sized, and can therefore have more explosive yield in smaller, lighter, packages. Pakistan wants warheads small enough to fit on the cruise missiles it is currently developing.

The maximum number of uranium-based warhead cores that can be produced by Pakistan depends on the quantity of HEU produced in centrifuges at the Kahuta enrichment facility, and perhaps at other undeclared facilities elsewhere in Pakistan. The initial HEU production was achieved using replicas of the aluminium P-1 centrifuge, brought from Europe by A.Q. Khan in the mid-1970s. This had a capacity of less than one 'Separative Work Unit (SWU)' but was initially the mainstay of the centrifuge program. It was supplemented in the late 1980s by the P-2 model which had a throughput of up to 5 SWU's. Typically, centrifuges are cascaded together in groups of approximately 164; in turn one group feeds into another until the desired enrichment is obtained. It takes roughly 5000 SWU to make 25 kg of 90 per cent HEU, which is ·enough for a bomb.

More advanced centrifuges with faster rotor speeds, made possible by using stronger (maraging) steels, were subsequently made at the Kahuta Research Laboratory (KRL).[19] The P-3 was the first of the two later centrifuges. It is a four-tube model with a throughput of just under 10 SWU/yr. According to the reference just cited, the P-4, which is still more advanced, may have a throughput of about 20 SWU/yr. Although there is information about the types of these centrifuges in operation, their numbers are not known but are almost certainly in the few thousands by now. One therefore expects that the yearly production rate of HEU is currently several times larger than in the mid 1980s and that it will keep expanding.

To feed the centrifuges one needs uranium in gaseous form (or, more accurately, uranium hexafluoride UF_6). The amount of natural uranium mined from presently known deposits, principally in the district of Dera Ghazi Khan, is currently enough to sustain the bomb program. But that is because the civilian use is low—the Chashma reactors have fuel supplied by China. Pakistan has declared to the IAEA that it mines 40 tons of uranium ore yearly.[20] This is distributed between fuel fabrication for the Karachi Nuclear Power Plant (KANUPP) and for fissile material production in military reactors; much more mining will be needed if Pakistan's civilian nuclear program ever takes off.[21]

Pakistan almost certainly has a handful of plutonium-based warheads whose smaller weight makes them more suitable for delivery by missiles over longer ranges. Plutonium-rich spent reactor fuel was first produced by the un-safeguarded 50 MW (thermal) reactor in Khushab, which has been functioning since 1998. It produces an estimated 10 kg/year of plutonium, which is roughly two-bombs-worth. Satellite imagery in 2007 showed that there were two similar units that are currently under construction, with the latest unit's construction having been activated in 2007.[22] In 2011, new satellite images showed that a fourth Khushab reactor was under construction.[23] An assessment of fissile stocks in South Asia has been attempted using publicly available information.[24]

The extraction of plutonium from spent fuel (reprocessing) is a difficult and dangerous chemical process. This is done at the New Labs, a part of PINSTECH (Pakistan Institute of Nuclear Science & Technology) near Islamabad, and now possibly at the Chashma nuclear complex too. Earlier, defense analysts in the U.S. had pointed out that a series of commercial satellite images from February 2002 through September 2006 revealed the construction of what appeared then to be a second plutonium separation plant adjacent to the original one, suggesting that Pakistan was planning on increasing its plutonium stock.

According to Albright and Brannan, Pakistan is doubling the rate of making nuclear weapons:

> Pakistan's construction of these new reactors at the Khushab site will result in a dramatic increase in its plutonium production capability. Combined, the three new reactors will be able to produce enough plutonium for over 12 nuclear weapons per year, depending on the reactors' size and operating efficiencies. This compares with Pakistan's current estimated production of enough weapon-grade uranium and plutonium for about 7–14 weapons per year. These three new reactors will roughly double Pakistan's annual ability to build nuclear weapons to about 19–26 nuclear weapons per year.[25]

The authors further state that:

> In total, through 2010, Pakistan has produced enough weapon-grade uranium and plutonium for roughly 100–170 nuclear weapons. Based on available information, the number of deployed weapons is probably less. Assuming that about 30 per cent of its stock of weapon-grade uranium and plutonium is located in its weapons production pipeline, stored, or otherwise unused in weapons, Pakistan has an estimated total of 70–120 nuclear weapons. It can currently add to that stock at the rate

of about 7–14 warheads per year and that value will go up to 19–26 warheads per year when all four Khushab reactors are operational.

It is a mistake to think that the number of uranium and plutonium warheads actually constructed is equal to the amount of uranium/plutonium available divided by the amount needed per bomb. Even if a country should want to convert its entire stock into weapons, inputs other than fissile material are needed. These include available capacities for converting UF6 gas into metal, explosives, electronics, mechanical component construction, etc. A nuclear weapon has typically about 2000 parts and is a highly complex piece of equipment. In Pakistan, much of the metallization and weapon fabrication work is done in and around the Heavy Mechanical Complex in Taxila, and the adjoining military city of Wah.[26] Many stages of fabrication are involved, the first of which involves conversion of the fissile material in gaseous form into pure metal, then machining it to precise dimensions to make the core. None of this is trivial. But, once a design has been standardized, it becomes easily possible to produce many copies. At the current production rate of a few fissile cores annually, warhead production would most likely follow the same rate and further expansion of warhead production facilities is unlikely to be a major constraint.

Nuclear weapon countries generally go from less powerful to more powerful weapons. Boosted nuclear weapons are the easiest next step. They use the same fissile materials but a few tens of grams of deuterium or tritium gas are inserted inside the bomb.[27] The additional neutrons released result in more complete fission and can increase the explosive power several times over.

Tritium is a by-product of the Khushab reactors. Earlier, the PAEC had attempted to produce it by irradiating lithium.[28] By 1987, the PAEC was able to acquire from West Germany parts for a tritium purification facility. Later, Pakistan attempted to procure from Germany 30 tons of aluminium tubing, used to 'clad lithium for irradiation in a reactor.'[29] In a congressional record of May 1989, Pakistan is said to have 'acquired from West Germany United States-origin tritium—originally destined for H-bombs—as well as tritium recovery equipment. It also obtained a United States-origin high-power laser, the latter as part of a package of equipment for making nuclear fuel'.[30]

Another step towards more powerful bombs is the fabrication of composite cores. This idea is over sixty years old. By combining two materials—a smaller plutonium sphere encased in a shell of highly enriched uranium—Pakistan could make more bombs than if the cores were made of plutonium and uranium separately.

What of the fusion (or hydrogen) bomb? Many times more powerful, this requires a qualitatively different science and needs a plutonium fission bomb to trigger it. India claims to have already developed a fusion weapon—one of the devices tested on 11 May 1998 was announced to be of this type. There is little doubt that Pakistan is seeking to make such a weapon. A plasma physics group in the PAEC, established over twenty years ago, has long looked into fusion weapon matters. The current status of its efforts is unknown, but there appears to have been little progress.

MISSILE CAPABILITY

The groundwork for Pakistan's missile program was laid in the early 1960s with the launch of the *Rahbar*-1 and *Rahbar*-2 weather sounding rockets from Sonmiani beach near Karachi, a project assisted by the United States after it had been approached by Abdus Salam, Pakistan's premier physicist. The first surface-to-surface missile was the *Hatf-1*, with a range of 80 km and a payload of 400 kg. The accuracy was said to be low as they did not have terminal guidance. General Zia-ul-Haq had taken the initiative of setting missile development into motion in response to Indian efforts.[31] A quantum jump in range and accuracy followed the induction of Chinese M-11 missiles, the acquisition of which was denied for a number of years.

The Pakistani missile series can be categorized into two distinct sets. The *Ghauri* missile series, based on a template provided by the North Korean Nodong missile, was developed at the Kahuta Research Laboratories (KRL) while the Shaheen series, based on the Chinese

M-9 and M-11 missiles, was developed at the National Defense Complex (NDC).

Table 1
Pakistani Missile Force

Missile Type	Range (km)	Deployment	Fuel
Abdali (Hatf-2)	180	2012	Solid
Ghaznavi (Hatf-3)	400	2004	Solid
Shaheen-I (Hatf-4)	450	2003	Solid
Ghauri (Hatf-5)	1200	2003	Liquid
Shaheen-II (Hatf-6)	2000	2011	Solid
Babur (Hatf-7)	700	2014	Cruise
Ra'ad (Hatf-8)	350	2014	Cruise
Nasr (Hatf-9)	60	2014	Solid

Data from ISPR bulletins, *Bulletin of the Atomic Scientists* 2011 67: 91–99 by Hans M. Kristensen and Robert S. Norris in: *Pakistan's Nuclear Forces, 2011*, and Mahmud Ali Durrani, 'Pakistan's Strategic Thinking and the Role of Nuclear Weapons', *Cooperative Monitoring Center Occasional Paper 37*, Sandia National Laboratory.

A 2007 report says that fewer than fifty four-axled Transporter-Erector Launcher (TEL) vehicles, needed for deploying the solid-fuelled *Ghaznavi* (*Hatf-III*) have been sighted.[32] Most are apparently stored at the Sargodha Weapons Storage Complex adjoining the PAF base. The same report refers to roughly fifty four-axled TELs existing for the *Shaheen-I* missile. About fifteen six-axled TELs, suitable for the *Shaheen-II*, have been seen in satellite imagery.

Pakistan is also developing a 500 km range, nuclear-capable, cruise missile named as *Babur*. A Pakistani government supported website[33] states that its design capabilities are comparable to the American BGM-109 Tomahawk cruise missile, and that a 1000 km version is also being developed. The *Babur* is advertised as a 'subsonic, low-level terrain-mapping, terrain-hugging missile that can avoid radar detection and strike with pinpoint accuracy.' Rather than being GPS guided—which depends crucially on the integrity of satellite systems being preserved in times of conflict—it is said to use inertial guidance (and possibly laser gyroscopes). Launched from a TEL, it was first test-flown on 21 March 2006 with President Gen. Pervez Musharraf in the audience. The ISPR also states that, 'Pakistan is looking into modification that will enable the missile to be launched from its F-16s, Mirage and A-5 air platforms and naval platform such as Agosta 90B attack submarines and its Tariq Class frigates.' A test of the *Babur* on 26 July 2007 was declared successful with a range stated to have been enhanced to 700 km.[34] In June 2012 it was described, again in an ISPR release, as having: 'radar avoidance features that can carry both nuclear and conventional warheads and has stealth capabilities. It also incorporates the most modern cruise missile technology of Terrain Contour Matching (TERCOM) and Digital Scene Matching and Area Co-relation (DSMAC), which enhances its precision and effectiveness manifolds.'[35]

A relatively new development, first reported in 2011, is that of low-yield, mobile nuclear delivery systems—called 'shoot and scoot' tactical nuclear weapons. According to an ISPR statement said the *Nasr* (*Hatf-9*) 'Victory' missile could be tipped with 'nuclear warheads of appropriate yield with high accuracy.' It is reportedly a short-range (60 km) surface-to-surface multi-tube ballistic missile system designed for battlefield use.[36]

In July 2011, *The Express Tribune* reported twenty-four more missiles, with ranges between 700–1000 km, would be added to the arsenal. The addition would be the highest production in a single year.[37]

Pakistan has been surprisingly successful in creating a fairly large and diverse intermediate range missile force in a very short time. How is it possible for any developing country with a weak industrial and scientific infrastructure to do so? Making missiles that can fly over long distances is a complex technical task; even today 'rocket science' is sometimes used as a synonym for the most difficult, cutting edge in science.

Missile-making requires acquisition of a broad range of technologies. Some of the key ones are:

- Chemical technology for liquid or solid fuel propellant manufacture, handling, and testing.
- Mechanical technology for rocket motor design, construction, and testing.
- Aerodynamic and structural engineering for design of structures such as missile body, fins, and re-entry cones.
- Special materials manufacturing and moulding capability for high-temperature applications as well as for plastics and polymers. Heat shields for re-entry are essential for protecting the warhead from being rendered useless.
- Computational capability and specialized software for various applications including ballistics, navigation, flow rates, dynamic payload balancing, etc.
- Electronics for missile guidance and control, telemetry, and terminal guidance.

What conclusions can we draw from this apparently phenomenal progress in missile making?

The sophistication of the *Babur's* propulsion system, a lightweight turbo-fan engine, as well as the complex control systems, electronics, sensors, aerodynamics, etc., places it well outside of any comparable achievements by Pakistani industry or other parts of its technological sector. Much the same can be said of the ballistic missiles in the *Hatf* series. There can be no doubt that Pakistan received substantial help from China, as well as components smuggled from Europe. North Korean help is an established fact for the *Ghauri* series, and may well be important for the *Babur* as well.

The details of missile development remain well under wraps but friction between the two main Pakistani organizations, the Kahuta Research Laboratory and the National Defense Complex, which were at one time headed (respectively) by Dr A.Q. Khan and Dr Samar Mubarakmand, has occasionally led each organization to leak information to the press in order to get a greater share of the glory. An Urdu newspaper gave a rare account in 1999 in a planted article entitled: 'How the *Shaheen* was Developed', pours scorn on the KRL group alleging that the *Ghauri* was an imported item whereas the achievements of the NDC group are extolled.[38] Another Pakistani author, evidently commissioned by the PAEC to denigrate A.Q. Khan and the rival KRL organization, wrote the following in a Pakistani defense journal:

> When the PAEC concluded an agreement with China to acquire the solid fuelled M-11 ballistic missiles from China in 1989, A.Q. Khan soon after managed to get the liquid fuelled *Ghauri*, from North Korea, and again hit the public imagination as the man who also gave Pakistan the delivery system for the [B]omb. The fact was that with the foundations of NDC having being laid in 1990, the PAEC was already on its way to start work on the solid fuelled *Shaheen* ballistic missile, before the *Ghauris* or the Taepodongs and Nodongs became operational.'[39]

While Pakistan officially maintains that its missile fleet comes from indigenous development alone, 'indigenous' can be variously defined. In attempting to bring credit to his parent institution, the PAEC, the author accidentally blows away the year-after-year denials by Pakistan of having obtained M-11 missiles from China, as well as of the *Ghauri* being indigenous and not of North Korean pedigree.

In 2009, it became known that Pakistan would collaborate with Selex Galileo of Italy to manufacture unmanned aerial vehicles (UAVs, commonly known as drones) for reconnaissance purposes.[40] The march of technology, spread by the global commercial interests, has profound consequences for the spread of nuclear and missile technologies as well.

Nevertheless, to conclude that Pakistan's missiles are mere foreign imports would be wrong. Pakistan has moved on a two-track missile policy. The first track was acquisition of complete missile systems as CKD (Completely Knocked Down) kits. These are said to have been brought as commercial cargo, mostly by sea but also through the Khunjarab Pass and down the Silk Route from China (this route was closed in 2010 after an earthquake that created the Attabad Lake).

The second track was to understand the systems, then reverse engineer the systems, section by section. Solutions to issues such as vibrations, stability, overheating etc., may be found in specialized textbooks and monographs that are used as texts in graduate level, university level courses taught in many countries including the U.S. and China. Pakistan sends many students to China for studying rocket propulsion and guidance systems. Services from experts in European countries have been purchased for specific tasks such as fin design and theoretical vibration studies.

Once a successful overall system design—say, that of the Tomahawk—is taken as the basic template, the associated sub-systems must be built or acquired. System integration is an exacting requirement and good engineering expertise is essential, but the design challenges are well understood. For designers and manu-facturers in advanced, as well as developing countries, the modular nature of modern technology allows for separate units to be transported and then joined together to form highly complex and effective systems. Component level design is no longer essential— the availability of ballistic missile technology, complete sub-systems, navigational gyroscopes and GPS equipment, and powerful computers has allowed many third world countries, including Pakistan and India, to leapfrog across major developmental issues. Systems engineering—which deals with how units behave after being assembled is important, and it is of less importance to know the principle by which individual elements work.

Consider, for example, that 30–40 years ago an electronics engineer working on a missile guidance system had to spend years learning how to design extremely intricate circuits using transistors, capacitors, and other components. But now the engineer only needs to be able to follow the manufacturer's instructions for programming a tiny microprocessor chip, available from almost any commercial electronics supplier. Modular technology applies also to rocketry, including engine design and aerodynamic construction. Computer controlled NC machines have made reverse engineering of mechanical parts easy. In this way even North Korea has been able to create rather advanced missile programs.

Missile development is now part of a burgeoning, increasingly export-oriented, Pakistani arms industry that turns out a large range of weapons: from grenades to tanks, night vision devices to laser guided weapons, and small submarines to training aircraft. Dozens of industrial sized units in and around the cities of Taxila and Wah, with subsidiaries elsewhere in the Islamabad–Rawalpindi region, are producing armaments worth hundreds of millions of dollars with export earnings of roughly 300 million dollars yearly in 2008.[41] Much of the production is under license from foreign countries, some from CKD kits, and most machinery for the arms factories is imported from the West or China.

AIRCRAFT CAPABILITY

Fighter-bomber aircraft were once Pakistan's preferred means of delivering nuclear weapons to India, but they have certain definite limitations. First, their ranges do not permit many parts of India to be covered. Moreover, they would have to run the gauntlet of an increasingly sophisticated Indian air-defense system. Nevertheless, they have the distinct advantage of being reliable, recallable, and reusable.

Pakistan had a deliverable nuclear weapon by 1987, and plans for aircraft delivery long preceded those for missile delivery. According to an officially inspired account, during the 1983–1990 period, the Wah Group [of the PAEC] went on to design and develop an atomic bomb small enough to be carried on the wing of a small fighter such as the F-16. It worked alongside the PAF to evolve and perfect delivery techniques of the nuclear bomb including 'conventional free-fall', 'loft bombing', 'toss bombing' and 'low-level lay-down' attack techniques using combat aircraft. Today, the PAF has perfected all four techniques of nuclear weapons delivery using F-16 and Mirage-V combat aircraft indigenously configured to carry nuclear weapons.[42]

The first F-16's purchased by Pakistan from the U.S. in 1981 arrived in 1983. They were intended to protect KRL, the uranium enrichment facility, as well as to mount retaliatory attacks on Indian nuclear facilities.[43] The U.S. had agreed to the sale of forty aircraft, requested by General Zia-ul-Haq. Pakistan was then a close U.S. ally, fighting against the Soviets in Afghanistan. Another sixty aircraft were ordered in 1989 and paid for but were embargoed; Pakistan's utility as an ally had come to an end.

Pakistan started receiving the first of a batch of F-16 C/D block 50/52 fighter aircraft in July 2007, the most modern version then flown by the U.S. Air Force.[44] It also received assistance for modernizing the existing F-16 fleet to the same standard. F-16s are still said to be the mainstay for aerial delivery up to a range of about 1600 km, but two squadrons of A-5 Chinese built fighter-bombers are also suitable vehicles. There is, however, a caveat that has been added by the United States: the F-16's sold under this deal will be specifically disallowed from carrying nuclear weapons. According to a U.S. official, if Pakistan tried to do so then, 'we have this extraordinary security plan with United States personnel, we have monitoring, we have leverage to convince them not to do this.'[45] The modernized F-16's, however, were presumably unaffected by this restriction.

With the expansion of the army-controlled mobile missile force, demands came from the air force for expansion of its capability. . Chief of Air Staff, Air Chief Marshal Tanvir Mehmood Ahmed, announced in March 2009 that $9 billion would be spent on upgrading its 'nuclear status.'[46] What this meant, however, was unclear. Investing in aircraft is no longer an efficient way of increasing nuclear offensive forces.

Today, Pakistan Air Force's technical capabilities remain rather limited and centre around aircraft maintenance. The largest units are the Mirage and F-6 rebuilding factories, an avionics and radar maintenance factory at Kamra, and a factory for manufacturing small training aircraft. There is an Air Weapons Complex located near Wah that manufactures a variety of air-delivered weapons. The JF-17

Thunder, of which 150 will eventually be inducted and become the air force's mainstay, is formally a joint China–Pakistan venture but Pakistani technical input into its design is said to be small so far.

In 2009 PAF air chief stated that an Airborne Warning and Control System (AWACS) was being obtained from Sweden and China, and agreements had been reached with the U.S. to provide electronic warfare system, smart bombs and long-range missile system. He said air-to-air refuelers were being modified. The PAF had almost 550 aircraft, including helicopters and transport aircraft. The number of fighter planes was around 350, he added. At the moment, he said, there were 46 F-16 aircraft in the PAF, including 14 F-16's obtained from the U.S. 'almost free of cost.'[47]

SKILLS: A CRITICAL CONSTRAINT

It would be too easy to ascribe Pakistan's success in bomb and missile-making to merely having allocated a large enough amount of money and resources. However, much wealthier Middle Eastern countries—Iraq, Saudi Arabia and Iran in particular—have been less successful. The difference comes from the few hundred scientists and engineers working under the direction of effective managers, an effective international buying network, as well as the strong will to do it all. Much of the work was reverse engineering, and there are no original applications, devices, or processes of commercial value that have been claimed. Nonetheless, Pakistani weaponeers understood developments in the literature and industry in sufficient detail and with clarity. Most were trained almost entirely in the U.S., Canada, and Britain under a program initiated in the early 1960s by the Pakistan Atomic Energy Commission. By now, many have retired, or are close to retirement.

The burgeoning demand from the principal defense R&D organizations PAEC, NDC, and KRL has resulted in a skill deficit that is perhaps the most serious constraint in the further development of Pakistan's nuclear and missile programs. Public universities are in poor shape, and their graduates are generally ill equipped to understand modern engineering and technical problems. Manpower is being drawn principally from:

Engineering institutes run by the defense organizations. Examples include the Pakistan Institute of Engineering and Applied Sciences (PIEAS), as well as the Centre for Nuclear Studies (CNS). Located on the premises of the Pakistan Institute of Nuclear Science and Technology (PINSTECH) near Islamabad, these institutes offer graduate studies in nuclear engineering, chemical and materials engineering, process engineering, systems engineering, electrical engineering, mechanical engineering, applied mathematics, information technology, etc. The NDC is also in the process of creating various institutes and centres at the Quaid-e-Azam University campus.

- A handful of engineering colleges of relatively better quality such as the army-run National University of Science and Technology (NUST), Ghulam Ishaq Khan Institute of Engineering Sciences and Technology (GIKI), University of Engineering Technology (UET), etc.
- Training of Pakistani missile and weapon designers in Chinese universities and institutes where they undergo short, highly focused, courses on rocket dynamics, navigational techniques, telemetry, etc. These are offered only to employees of government organizations and not general members of the Pakistani public.
- Using the 12-fold increase in its budget over the past five years, the Higher Education Commission of the Government of Pakistan has awarded a number of scholarships to Pakistanis for studying in Europe, Australia, and the United States. Among the beneficiaries are the employees, or former employees, of various defense organizations.
- Academics and engineers in advanced countries can occasionally be interested into solving difficult technical problems for a fee. This follows the widespread global problem of outsourcing technical problems.

- Through better pay and living conditions, the Pakistani weapons complex has managed to get the pick of the crop. But their small number, and the lack of a strict meritocratic system that can get the most out of them, means that skill shortage is likely to remain a serious constraint.

HOW MUCH DO NUKES COST?

The secrecy that surrounds any emerging nuclear program in any country means that, at best, there can only be guess-estimates of the cost involved. Even if items could be freely purchased in the open international market, a country that seeks nuclear weapons would have to put in billions of dollars. But for a program that must be kept under wraps from international watchdogs, one can imagine that the cost would be many times higher. Because imported items are on a list that is carefully watched, circuitous routes must to be found. This entails the use of many middlemen, each with small or large commissions, as well as vendors jacking up their rates.

Neither Pakistan nor India have ever declared their nuclear weapons budgets, treating them as high-level secrets. In fact, an undeclared reason for the Pakistan Army's objection to the Kerry-Lugar Bill, which would have resulted in $1.5bn annually in civilian aid, was its insistence upon financial transparency of the economy. This would have made it easier for outsiders to estimate Pakistan's nuclear budget. The KL program never fully took off.

It has therefore been left up to outsiders to make educated guesses. One such guess is contained in the following table. Figures are in billions of U.S. dollars. Core costs refer to researching, developing, procuring, operating, maintaining, and upgrading the nuclear arsenal (weapons and their delivery vehicles) and its key nuclear command-control-communications and early warning.

Table 2
Total Military and Nuclear Weapons Spending 2010–2011

	Total Military Spending*	Nuclear Weapons		Nuclear Weapons	
		Core Cost	Full Cost	Core Cost	Full Cost
US	687	30.9	55.6	34	61.3
Russia	53–86	6.8	9.7	9.8	14.8
China	129	5.7	6.8	6.4	7.6
France	61	4.6	5.9	4.7	6.0
United Kingdom	57	3.5	4.5	4.5	5.5
India	35	3.4	4.1	3.8	4.9
Israel	13	1.5	1.9	1.5	1.9
Pakistan	7.9	.8	1.8	1.8	2.2
North Korea	8.8	.5	.7	.5	.7
Total:	1052–1085	57.7	91.0	67	104.9

From Bruce G. Blair, Global Zero Technical Report, June 2011

Another estimate, with similar assumptions, arrives at a similar conclusion: Assuming that Pakistan spends on the order of 0.5 per cent of GDP on its nuclear weapons, and using purchasing power parity rather than market exchange rates to convert Pakistani rupees to US dollar equivalents, suggests that in 2009 nuclear weapons program spending amounted to about $2.2 billion a year (the GDP was about $441 billion in purchasing power parity, and $162 billion in nominal terms). For 2011, the nominal GDP was $211 billion, about $484 billion in purchasing power.[48]

FUTURE DIRECTIONS

Looking at the next 5–10 years, one can make reasonable guesses for where Pakistani nuclear forces are likely to be, and the direction of its nuclear policy.

Unless a global fissile material cut-off is somehow agreed upon and implemented, Pakistani production of fissile materials and bombs, as well as intermediate-range ballistic missiles, will continue at the maximum possible rate permitted by technological and resource limitations. A shift towards smaller plutonium weapons, or composite warheads, will accelerate as all Khushab military reactors come on line. The warhead design for the *Nasr* missile suggests that small boosted devices may have been perfected.

The increasing number of warheads will demand an increase in the number of delivery vehicles. In spite of the substantial induction of JF-17 aircraft, as well as newly purchased F-16's, missiles will steadily replace aircraft as delivery vehicles for nuclear weapons. Flight tests and command post exercises will continue to be periodically conducted. Although Pakistan will make efforts to match India's efforts in using outer space for reconnaissance and early-warning systems, it will not be able to do so. An attempt to match India's *Agni-V* ICBM, successfully tested in 2012, is unlikely. But if India is successful in acquiring and installing an anti-ballistic missile system, MIRV, or in deploying submarine launched nuclear-tipped missiles, Pakistan will counter by lowering the strike-threshold and wider dispersion of its mobile launchers, as well as employing decoys and moving towards SLBMs (Submarine-Launched Ballistic Missile).

In the past, Pakistan had felt that hitching its nuclear policy to India's would deflect criticism. The world would understand that its nuclear program was no more than a reaction to a larger, hostile, neighbour's rapid armament. But the 'de-hyphenation' of Pakistan from India—a word that gained particular currency after the visit to India and Pakistan by President George W. Bush in 2006—ultimately drove Pakistan in a different direction; its nuclear policy would henceforth be more than a mirror image of India's.

As for the immediate future: unless India resumes nuclear testing, Pakistan is unlikely to test further. There is little chance that Pakistan will agree to the Fissile Material Cut-off Treaty or to on-site inspections for verification purposes. India will drive the arms race and Pakistan will follow.

REFERENCES

1. 'New estimates put Pakistan's nuclear arsenal at more than 100', *The Washington Post*, 31 January 2011.
2. Pakistani Nuclear Forces 2011, Hans M. Kristensen and Robert S. Norris, http://www.fas.org/blog/ssp/2011/07/pakistannotebook.php
3. http://www.thebulletin.org/web-edition/features/nuclear-notebook-pakistans-nuclear-forces-2011
4. Norris, Roberts and Kristens, Hans, Nuclear Notebook: Pakistani nuclear forces, 2009, *Bulletin of the Atomic Scientists*, Sept.–Oct.
5. Amb. Anne Patterson, 24 November 2009.
6. 'Pakistan Unconcerned About Planned U.S. Patriot Missile Sales to India, Musharraf Says', *Global Security Newswire*, 27 July 2005.
7. 'UN's nuclear disarmament conference may sink over Pakistan's reluctance: Ban-ki Moon', *Express Tribune*, 25 January 2012.
8. 'New estimates put Pakistan's nuclear arsenal at more than 100', *The Washington Post*, 31 January 2011.
9. 'The U.S.–India Nuclear Deal (backgrounder)', Jayshree Bajoria and Esther Pan, Conference on Foreign Relations, November 2010.
10. 'Uranium: now for a deal with India', theage.com.au, 5 December 2011.
11. Joseph Cirincione, 'Nuclear Cave In', *PacNet*, no. 8A, Pacific Forum CSIS, 2 March 2006.
12. 'Our high-maintenance relationship with Pakistan', David Ignatius, *The Washington Post*, 13 July 2012.
13. 'Kayani warns U.S. against anti-Pakistan offensive', *Deccan Herald*, 19 October 2011.
14. 'Nuclear Terror', Munir Akram, *Dawn*, 25 June 2012.
15. 'Confront and Conceal: Obama's Secret War and Surprising Use of American Power', David E. Sanger, Random House, 2012, p. 109.
16. Ibid, Sanger, p. 108.
17. 'The Ally From Hell', Jeffrey Goldberg and Marc Ambinder, *The Atlantic*, December 2011.
18. 'Defending the Arsenal', Seymour Hersh, *The New Yorker*, 16 November 2009.
19. Mark Hibbs, *Nuclear Fuel*, Volume 32, Number 3, 29 January 2007.
20. OECD/IAEA, Uranium Resources, Production, and Demand, 1990, 1997, 1999, 2005, and 2007.
21. See nuclear electricity article in this volume.
22. The second Khushab reactor was reported in July 2006, see e.g. Joby Warrick, 'Pakistan Expanding Nuclear Program', *The Washington Post*, 24 July 2006; and 'U.S. Disputes Report on New Pakistan Reactor', *The New York Times*, 3 August 2006. See also, Thomas Cochran, 'What is the Size of Khushab II?', NRDC, 8 September 2006, and David Albright and Paul Brannan, 'Update on the Construction of the New Large Khushab Reactor,' ISIS, 4 October 2006.

Pictures of the third reactor were released in June 2007; David Albright and Paul Brannan, 'Pakistan Appears to be Building a Third Plutonium Production Reactor at Khushab Nuclear Site,' ISIS, 21 June 2007.

23. http://www.newsweek.com/2011/05/15/fourth-nuclear-reactor-at-pakistan-s-khushab-site.html

24. Zia Mian, A.H. Nayyar, R. Rajaraman, and M.V. Ramana, 'Fissile Materials in South Asia: The Implications of the U.S.–India Nuclear Deal', Research Report No. 1 International Panel on Fissile Materials, Princeton University. See also, Zia Mian, A. H. Nayyar, and R. Rajaraman, 'Uranium Constraint on Pakistan's Fissile Material Production', Science and Global Security, Taylor and Francis, U.S.A., in press.

25. Pakistan Doubling Rate of Making Nuclear Weapons: Time for Pakistan to Reverse Course, David Albright, and Paul Brannan, 16 May 2011, http://isis-online.org/isis-reports/detail/pakistan-doubling-rate-of-making-nuclear-weapons-time-for-pakistan-to-rever/

26. The Heavy Mechanical Complex (HMC), together with the Heavy Forge Factory (HFF) is the biggest undertaking of its type in Pakistan and was established in 1979 with Chinese assistance. HMC has CAD (Computer Aided Designing facilities) and also manufactures equipment for hydro-electric power plants, thermal power plants, sulphuric acid plants, industrial alcohol plants, oil & gas processing plants, and chemical & petro-chemical plants, etc.

27. In fact Pakistan had claimed the weapons tested in 1998 were of the boosted fission genre. See interview of Dr Samar Mubarakmand's on Geo TV. 3 May 2004. http://www.pakdef.info/forum/showthread.php?t=9214

28. Chaudhri, M.A., (2006), Pakistan's Nuclear History: Separating Myth From Reality, *Defense Journal* (Karachi).

29. Ibid.

30. Nuclear and missile proliferation (U.S. Senate—16 May 1989), http://www.fas.org/spp/starwars/congress/1989/890516-cr.htm

31. *The Nuclearization of South Asia*, Kamal Matinuddin, Oxford University Press (2002).

32. Norris, Robert K. and Kristensen, Hans M., (2007), Natural Resources Defense Council, Pakistan's *Nuclear Forces*, 2007, Vol. 63, No. 3, pp. 71–4.

33. http://www.pakistanidefense.com/

34. http://www.pakistanidefense.com/

35. 'Pakistan test-fires Hatf-VII Babur missile 5', *Dawn*, June 2012.

36. 'Pakistan Tests 'Nuke-Capable' Short-Range Missile', http://www.defensenews.com/story.php?i=6282326

37. 'Arms race: 24 more missiles to be added to arsenal', *The Express Tribune*, 25 July 2011.

38. Rawalpindi, *Jang*, p. 10, 19 April 1999.

39. Pakistan's Nuclear History, op. cit.

40. 'Complex at Kamra to manufacture drones', Dawn, Friday, 21 Aug. 2009.

41. 'Official claims big rise in arms exports', *Dawn*, 18 July 2008.
42. Chaudhri, M.A., 'Pakistan's Nuclear History: Separating Myth from Reality', M.A. Chaudhri, *Defense Journal*, (2006), Karachi.
43. 'Cutting Edge PAF: A Former Air Chief's Reminiscences of a Developing Air Force', Air Chief Marshal Anwar Shamim, Vanguard Books, Lahore, (2010).
44. 'US starts delivering F-16 aircraft', *Dawn*, 11 July 2007.
45. Proposed sale of F–16 aircraft and weapons systems to Pakistan, Hearing before the Committee on International Relations, House of Representatives, 20 July 2006, Serial no. 109–220.
46. *The News*, 18 March 2009
47. Ibid.
48. 'Pakistan', by Zia Mian in: *Assuring Destruction Forever: Nuclear Weapon Modernization Around the World*, edited by Ray Acheson, (Reaching Critical Will, New York, March 2012).

CHAPTER 5

KASHMIR: FROM NUCLEAR FLASHPOINT TO SOUTH ASIA'S BRIDGE OF PEACE?*

Pervez Hoodbhoy

One of the twentieth century's most difficult and bloodiest conflicts has been that of Kashmir. Its roots lie in the partition of the British Indian Empire into the Union of India and the Dominion of Pakistan. Muslim-majority areas were to go to Pakistan, Hindu-majority ones to India. Had India abided by the rules of Partition—whatever one might think of them—Kashmir would likely have become part of Pakistan because, according to the British census of India of 1941, Kashmir had a Muslim majority population of 77 per cent and Hindus were just about 20 per cent.[1] But when British rule ended on 14–15 August 1947 the Hindu ruler of this Himalayan kingdom, Maharaja Hari Singh, opted to accede to India instead of Pakistan.

India's refusal to hold a plebiscite—a solution proposed in 1947 to this conflict by the United Nations—was to bedevil relations between the two newly independent countries and led to one war after another. A secret invasion by Pakistan in 1965, 'Operation Gibraltar', erupted into a full-scale war that ended inconclusively. Although the 1971 Pakistan–India war was about the secession of East Pakistan and unrelated to Kashmir, some in India felt that Pakistan's defeat should have been used by Indira Gandhi at Shimla to make it renounce its claim on Kashmir once and for all. Then, in 1999, Pakistan secretly invaded the Indian controlled Kargil area of Kashmir but was eventually forced out. A status quo prevails today: Pakistan-controlled Kashmir comprises of the Northern Areas and

---

* The title of this essay is inspired by the remarks of peace activist Karamat Ali contained in the video-documentary 'Crossing the Lines—Kashmir, Pakistan, India', http://www.youtube.com/watch?v=EeBRVFxe5oQ

Azad Kashmir; India controls the central and southern portion (Jammu and Kashmir) and Ladakh; while China has the north-eastern portion (Aksai Chin and the Trans-Karakoram Tract).

The Kashmir question is among the most vexing ones in the world because it involves both religion and regionalism. Kashmiris are nationalists who subscribe to an eclectic form of Kashmiri nationalism—*Kashmiriyat*. They would prefer independence to being a party of either claimant or, at the very least, greater autonomy. But for India, holding on to Kashmir is more than just a matter about land or even about people having their own way; secession is seen as undoing India's fabric as a secular, pluralistic nation-state.

UNDERSTANDING KASHMIR

How should one analyze a dispute that has consumed so many Kashmiri lives and has brought two nuclear-armed countries repeatedly to the brink of war? What might be some minimum truths to which fair-minded people are likely to agree?

A first, obvious fact is that Pakistan lacks the muscle to wrest Kashmir from unpopular Indian rule. Reciprocally, India cannot win decisively over Pakistan in the difficult, mountainous terrains. India thus remains the status quo power in Kashmir while Pakistan is the insurrectionary one. Pakistan's efforts, spread over many decades, have failed to change ground realities and are likely to fail in the future. Kashmir simply does not have any military solution. Only jihadists, blind to reason and to the value of human life, can think that Kashmir can be wrested from Indian rule.

A second manifest truth is that New Delhi's unconscionable manipulation of Kashmiri politics, and monumental administrative incompetence, is responsible for its progressive alienation from the Muslims of Kashmir. A popular uprising, one that refuses to die down nearly a quarter century later, can be directly traced to the rigging of the 1987 elections by India with the aim of promoting its own candidates. Thereafter, Kashmir was in full-scale rebellion and large numbers of Kashmiri refugees had flowed into Azad Kashmir.

Pakistan could not be blamed for this. India is considered an occupier in the eyes of nationalist eyes, and thus to be resisted.

In 2011 an Indian government human rights commission report corroborated suspicions that thousands of bodies, which may or may not have been those of militants, had been dumped by the security forces into unmarked graves.[2] Using evidence cited in a report by India's government-appointed State Human Rights Commission, an article in the New York Review of Books says:[3] Corpses were brought in by the truckload and buried on an industrial scale. The report catalogued 2156 bullet-riddled bodies found in mountain graves and called for an inquiry to identify them. Many were men described as 'unidentified militants' killed in fighting with soldiers during the armed rebellion against Indian rule during the 1990s, but according to the report, more than 500 were local residents. 'There is every probability,' the report concluded, that the graves might 'contain the dead bodies of enforced disappearances,' a euphemism for people who have been detained, abducted, taken away by armed forces or the police, often without charge or conviction, and never seen again.

The iron fist can work—at least for some time. Indeed, Kashmir was peaceful in 2012. Schools were open; tourists were back; and European countries had removed their travel advisories for visiting the Valley. Just two years earlier it had been up in flames, as in earlier years, after Indian security forces had shot dead dozens of young stone pelters. Even seasoned commentators had then predicted that India was on the verge of losing Kashmir to those seeking independence or accession to Pakistan. They were, of course, wrong. But, as in earlier decades, normalcy can be easily confused for peace; the present may be no more than just another low point in repeated cycles of violence.

The present calm encourages some Indian analysts to deny the need for making any basic changes. Reflecting Delhi's current mood of triumphalism, Vikram Sood, former chief of RAW (Research and Analysis Wing), writes:

> We need to do a few things to bring normalcy in Kashmir that go beyond tourism statistics. We need to go beyond the tokenism of nomenclature.

> We need to keep Pakistan out of the equation . . . we need to ignore this group called the Hurriyat that represents at best themselves but usually Pakistani interests or periodic threats that political space grows from the barrel of a gun. . . . We also make it clear that there is no question of independence to ten districts in the Kashmir Valley on any basis and specially on the basis of religion. So *Azadi* is out.[4]

But New Delhi is fully aware of the tenuous nature of peace in Kashmir and has no intentions of withdrawing the bulk of its troops.

A third truth is that India's unpopularity in Muslim-majority Kashmir has always encouraged Pakistan to translate India's losses into Pakistan's gains. There was not much success in the earlier decades: 'Operation Gibraltar' in 1965, which involved a secret invasion by Pakistani commandos, fell flat because it excited no resonance among Kashmiris. But things suddenly began to look good for Pakistan in 1987. The rigging of Kashmir's elections by Delhi had angered millions, and to quell their protests the Indian Army had responded with extraordinary force. Fortuitously for Pakistan, the Soviets had just been defeated in Afghanistan and mujahideen fighters were aplenty.

Angry and desperate refugees from the Indian side brought local knowledge while the mujahideen were battle hardened and ideologically committed. This situation enabled Pakistan to implement a bleed-India-through-jihad policy. While officially denying involvement, logistical and financial support could be given to militants fighting Indian rule in Kashmir. The military establishment imagined that this low-cost strategy would lead to eventual victory; it was seen as the only practical means to change the status-quo.

COVERT WAR

Pakistan's covert war had two-fold goals. The first was to weaken India by raising the human and economic costs. At some point, Pakistan's military reasoned, it would be too much trouble for the Indians to hang on to Kashmir. The second objective was to internationalize a local dispute by advertising the region's nuclear instability. This would hopefully draw in western negotiators and force India to the table.

There were some initial successes. The economic costs of Indian occupation, which required maintaining large army contingents, paramilitary troops, and police shot up. The total number of security personnel reached a staggering 600,000 (although this figure is disputed) for a land of only 10 million people. Indian forces, both regular and paramilitary, took punishingly high losses of men and material.

Another success for Pakistan was the creation of a world-wide fear that border clashes would escalate into a nuclear conflagration. Indeed, intense artillery duels across the Line of Control had become commonplace in the mid 1990s, and nuclear threats had been bellowed often enough by both sides to make this a possibility. The term 'nuclear flashpoint' for Kashmir soon became commonplace in the international press, particularly after the 1998 tests.

But Pakistan's strategy was doomed to fail. On the one hand it brought a backlash from Indian forces. There was fierce military action against local Kashmiris, leading to thousands of innocent deaths. Anti-Pakistan feelings rose across India. In particular, the 1999 secret Kargil invasion led to a huge swell in Indian chauvinistic national pride and a determination to hang on to 'Bharat ka atoot ung' (a vital part of India's body). Hindutva forces benefited, with leaders like Praveen Togadia threatening to wipe Pakistan off the map.[5]

Still more disappointing for Pakistan's military was that cross border infiltrations failed to dent India's economy, which simply absorbed the losses and kept booming. Buttressed by its huge reservoir of scientific and high-tech manpower, India continued on its path towards becoming one of the world's largest economies. Indian foreign exchange reserves[6] stood at over $289 billion in 2012, and its exports to the U.S. and China have steadily risen. India has penetrated into America's industrial core, providing it with scientists and engineers, and draws work away from U.S. companies into India. Income from just one source—outsourcing and IT services—swelled to nearly $60 billion in 2011. Pharmaceuticals added in another $12 billion. A U.S.–India strategic partnership has emerged, with the agreement on space and nuclear cooperation being one indication of things to come. It is clear that the U.S. no longer regards India as being in the same league as Pakistan, where educational and scientific institutions continue their decline.

The covert war, whatever hurt it might have caused India, had enormously damaging consequences for Muslim Kashmiris. What had earlier been seen as a genuine, indigenous struggle was now seen as Pakistan's war by proxy, leading to a steady loss of international legitimacy for nationalists. Thus, the crimes committed by India's occupation forces in Kashmir, amply documented by various human rights groups, became eclipsed by lesser, but more widely publicized, crimes committed by the Pakistan-based mujahideen. These groups attacked Hindu Pundits and forced them to flee, targeted civilians accused of collaborating with India, assassinated Kashmiri political leaders, destroyed cinema houses and liquor shops, forced women into the veil, and ignited numerous sectarian disputes. The moral high ground held by those fighting occupation was sharply eroded. Attempts to blame many killings on Indian security forces did not always wash. India could thereafter successfully portray itself as a victim of terror exported from Pakistani soil.

Denials by Pakistan that it was not backing the mujahideen fell flat. In an age of television cameras and instant communication, aiding and arming militants came into full public view. In fact, it was hard to see how anyone could accept Pakistan's denials because prior to 9/11, jihadist organizations operated openly. Sometimes visible support was provided by the government. In every city and town of Punjab the Hizb-ul-Mujahideen (HuM), Lashkar-e-Tayyaba (LeT), Jaish-e-Muhammad, and various other jihadist organizations had placed donation boxes in shops and work places, and went around after the Baqr-Eid festival collecting sacrificial hides. Although they suddenly vanished for some years following 9/11, they resurfaced after Musharraf was forced out in 2008 and are to be seen openly once again.** So, for example, in July 2012 the Al-Badr Mujahideen, a breakaway faction of Hizb-ul-Mujahideen group, organised a two-day 'Shuhada Conference' in the Swan Adda area of Rawalpindi to seek recruits and raise funds. The group's chief Bakht Zameen Khan told a thousand-plus supporters at the conference that his commanders want resources to keep the 'jihad' going in Kashmir and Afghanistan.[7]

The 'nuclear flashpoint' strategy also failed. This phrase eventually became jaded and faded from use in the international media. It buys little for Pakistan even when it does appear because once the world in general, and the U.S. in particular, had fully assessed the Kashmir situation, the reaction was not at all what Pakistan had in mind. To have Kashmir associated with nuclear Pakistan does not work well any more.

Jihadi leaders feel differently and some call for having a nuclear war over Kashmir. Speaking before 20,000 people on 5 February 2011 (Kashmir Day), Hafiz Saeed of LeT, who is wanted in India for masterminding the Mumbai attack, demanded nuclear jihad against India: 'I want to give a message to (Prime Minister) Manmohan Singh—quit Kashmir or get ready to face a war. . . . The jihad should continue as long as Kashmir remains under Indian occupation.' He went on to say that there would be 'no problem if the fighting leads to nuclear war between Pakistan and India.'[8]

The idea of jihadists active in a nuclear-armed state is deeply alarming all around. It certainly gets no sympathy in Washington, which has declared the largest mujahideen group fighting Indian rule in Kashmir, the Hizb-ul-Mujahideen, to be a terrorist group. After the Mumbai attacks, the Lashkar-e-Tayyaba and Jaish-e-Muhammad also made it to that list.

** Like other campuses, the Quaid-e-Azam University campus was also plastered with posters and banners from various jihadist groups inviting students to drop their studies and join the jihad, and some of our students. did that. But after 9/11 the walls were wiped clean and banners disappeared.

NUCLEARIZING KASHMIR

India's nuclear test in 1974 introduced a new level of complexity in Kashmir. This certainly encouraged Pakistan to acquire the bomb, which it subsequently used in an attempt to change the status quo. Contrary to what is widely believed, it was India and not Pakistan that first made overt references to nuclear weapons in the Kashmir conflict.

Let us wind the tape back to May 1998. A week had passed since India's second Pokharan test. Uncertain of whether it should respond or not, Pakistan had been vacillating. Then, on 18 May 1998, BJP party member and Home Minister, Lal Krishan Advani, made the first ever direct connection between nuclear weapons and the future of Jammu and Kashmir. He declared that India's, 'decisive step to become a nuclear weapon state has brought about a qualitative new state in India–Pakistan relations, particularly in finding a lasting solution to the Kashmir problem. Islamabad has to realize the change in the geo-strategic situation in the region and the world.'[9] Advani went to add that although, 'we adhere to the no-first-strike principle,' India would deal firmly with Pakistan's hostile activities. Other BJP leaders echoed him: the former Union Minister Madan Lal Khurana inviting Pakistan to join battle 'at a place and time of its choosing' and warned of a fourth war with Pakistan.[10] When Pakistan successfully tested on 28 May 1998, the Indian machismo evaporated.

On Pakistan's side, bringing nuclear weapons out into the open were to provide opportunity for a new strategy in Kashmir. Earlier, throughout the 1980s and even more so in the 1990s, the bomb had been lurking in the background, providing a diffused threat. Pakistani strategy had sought to keep the world alarmed about Kashmir by frequent allusions to a nuclear conflict. This, Pakistani generals calculated, would keep the pot boiling. Fostering a constant high level of tension between two nuclear-armed states would surely alarm the international community—most particularly the United States—and force a recalcitrant India to see reason.

And so a strategy evolved over time: even before the 1998 tests, numerous military and civil leaders deliberately cultivated an image of Pakistan as a defiant, nuclear-armed state ready to go to war over Kashmir. For example, in 1995 General Asad Durrani, a former director of the Inter-Services Intelligence (ISI), who was later Pakistan's ambassador to Germany, put it this way: 'If we were to make it clear that whatever nuclear deterrence we might have is primarily meant to deter the use of nuclear weapons from the other side, then by so saying we will fail to deter a conventional attack.'[11] Therefore, he argued, the other side must be led to believe that, 'we are primed, almost desperate to use our nuclear capabilities when our national objectives are threatened, [as] for example, a major crackdown on [the] freedom movement in Kashmir. . . .'[12] It was understood, of course, that a nuclear exchange would be devastating for Pakistan.

The threat of nuclear apocalypse was sufficiently real to keep a steady stream of Western leaders coming to Islamabad and Delhi at the peak of the tensions in 1987 and 1990, and then, after the nuclear tests, again in 1999 and 2001. Pakistan felt pleased that it had forced international attention on Kashmir, and expectations rose that a frightened world would now rush to solve the dispute. That, of course, did not happen. Aggressive diplomatic intervention by the U.S. and UK was perhaps why war did not happen. But it came at a price: Pakistan was seen as reckless and irresponsible, willing to put an entire subcontinent's people at the edge.

The projection of a 'madman' image alternated with Pakistan's other posture, which was that of a calm, assured, and responsible nuclear power. Both Pakistan and India felt they needed to present this impression of responsibility and so, together and separately, diplomats from both countries developed common goals in the background of their nuclear tests. They had been tasked by their respective military-civil establishments with projecting an image of their state as one fully aware of its new status and completely in control of itself. Both countries wanted to show that their weapons were in responsible hands and could be handled by them just as well as by anyone else, that they sternly opposed proliferation, and that they were victims rather than supporters of terrorism.

The Indian strategic analyst C. Raja Mohan had friendly advice for his Pakistani colleagues:

> New Delhi and Islamabad should know that the willingness of the rest of the world to accept them as part of the official nuclear club depends on the ability of India and Pakistan to responsibly manage their own nuclear relationship. . . . If India and Pakistan want to be taken seriously, they must show results from their nuclear talks.[13]

General Jehangir Karamat who was Pervez Musharaf's predecessor as chief of army staff, was particularly keen to show that Pakistan and India are not trigger-happy, while he was ambassador of Pakistan to the United States:

> For those who observe South Asia from the outside it is considered a most dangerous place and a region in which a nuclear exchange could be a reality. It is thought that the India–Pakistan confrontations in 1987, 1990 and 2002, as well as the Kargil conflict in 1999, all had a nuclear dimension of some sort. This is not what most South Asians think.[14]

Nevertheless, Gen. Karamat did admit that during the Kargil crisis— initiated by Pakistan to change the ground realities in Kashmir— various 'statements and signaling through missile tests could have had unintended consequences.'[15] Indeed, velvet gloves can be rapidly discarded once the going gets rough.

The adversaries, joined in common cause to justify their respective country's nuclear weapons, would even have a nice word or two to say about the other. Officials and experts from both countries frequently meet at arms control workshops and seminars, behave civilly (if not cordially) towards each other, and appear to be rational actors. CBMs (Confidence Building Measures), NRRs (Nuclear Risk Reduction Measures), etc., are part of the standard jargon. The underlying mistrust slips below the surface.

Although they often skate on thin ice, the ploys and stratagems of diplomats can, when combined with immediate needs of other nations, bring success. Over time, Indian strategists and lobbyists in Washington guided it towards fundamentally changing U.S.–India nuclear relations. Thus the sanctions imposed in 1998 were gradually withdrawn, criticism became inaudible, and a grudging acceptance of India's nuclear status followed.

Pakistan, while not faring quite so well and not being privileged by a similar deal, has also been accepted as a de-facto nuclear power. Thanks to its able diplomats, the safety and security of its nuclear arsenal was reduced to the level of a nagging, low-level worry. However, events have led to a sharp downturn in Pakistan's relations with the West. If another crisis similar to those seen earlier should occur, it is unclear what diplomatic forces will be able to intervene effectively for staving off confrontation.

RESOLVING KASHMIR

As the late Eqbal Ahmad passionately argued, although India's leaders bear much responsibility for Kashmir's tragedy, Pakistan's defective Kashmir policy had repeatedly 'managed to rescue defeat from the jaws of victory.'

Pakistan needs to urgently reassess its position and policy for multiple reasons. First, anti-India covert groups, funded and supported by the Pakistan Army, have helped to bring chaos and bloodshed to Pakistan. Some groups are overtly sectarian and anti-Shi'a. But these are not the only dividing lines and the Punjabi Taliban, engaged in fighting the army in Waziristan and FATA (Federally Administered Tribal Areas), have recruited profitably from groups that earlier on had enjoyed the army's patronage.

Second, international support for Pakistan's position on Kashmir has been sharply eroded because of its proxy war strategy. Muslim countries and the OIC have turned lukewarm to the Kashmir cause, even at the level of passing supportive resolutions. More importantly, signifying that the Kashmir issue is of marginal interest to them, their trade with India is many times greater than with Pakistan. Today Indian workers, particularly skilled ones, are still welcome in the Middle East while Pakistanis are finding it progressively harder.

Even more significantly, Pakistan's immediate neighbours—Iran and China—show little interest in liberating Kashmir through jihad. Rather, they feel threatened by jihadist groups nurtured by Pakistan to fight in Kashmir. These have a nexus with other groups that fight for a variety of Islamic causes. Chinese authorities, naming Pakistan in particular, have accused East Turkestan Islamic Movement (ETIM), which wants an independent homeland for Xinjiang's Uighurs, of orchestrating attacks in the region on many occasions. The attackers adhered to 'extremist religious ideology' and advocated 'jihad', said the statement. 'The heads of the group had learned skills of making explosives and firearms in overseas camps of the terrorist group ETIM in Pakistan before entering Xinjiang.'[16]

Groups that have been active in Kashmir: the Sipah-e-Sahaba and Lashkar-e-Jhangvi are also virulently anti-Shi'a. Together with the Jundullah group, they have targeted Shi'as and Iranian interests in Pakistan. Over 350 Shi'as were targeted and killed in the first eight months of 2012 by these groups. Signalling its displeasure with Pakistan, Iran has held joint military exercises with India. India–Iran defense and military-to-military collaboration in 2005, including energy deals, amounted to over $25 billion.[17] With India's new alignment with America, there has been steady pressure to cut Indian oil imports from Iran. But, as if to prove their independence, the Indians have only grudgingly acquiesced to small reductions.

While acknowledging that India is winning the propaganda war, Pakistani hardliners continue to insist that Pakistan's isolation on Kashmir is merely the failure of its diplomatic missions. This is untrue. Pakistani diplomats representing the official position in the world's capitals, as well as in Muslim countries, belong to the world's best. But they must fight with one hand tied behind, especially after the 11 September 2001 attacks on the World Trade Centre and the Pentagon in the U.S., when jihad became a notorious word in the political lexicon. Their efforts cannot compensate for the military establishment's failed 'bleed-India' policy.

The Kashmiri leadership, once a source of hope to Pakistan, is also proving less and less capable of delivering anything. The

Hurriyat Conference, originally set up with Pakistani help to mediate disputes between different anti-Indian Kashmiri organizations, has essentially fallen apart and sharply reduced Pakistan's influence on the Kashmiri freedom movement. Kashmiris have realized that although they are more favourably inclined towards Muslim Pakistan than Hindu India, their interests are by no means identical to Pakistan's. This elementary fact has been finally recognized by the Indian establishment. In a belated move, after having stubbornly resisted talking to the Kashmiri leaders for years, the hawkish L.K. Advani and N.N. Vohra—went in for direct talks with Maulana Abbas Ansari's majority faction of the Hurriyat. Pakistan's sole supporter is the smaller hard-line Geelani faction that seeks Shar'ia for Kashmir. Pakistani influence in Kashmiri domestic politics has been further diminished by fencing the LoC, acquiring high-tech surveillance and night-vision equipment from Israel, and increasing pressure on Pakistan to limit infiltration.

KASHMIR—A BRIDGE OF PEACE?

Can the Kashmir dispute ever be resolved? Can it, as peace activists suggest, ever become a link connecting Pakistan to India instead of being a territory disputed between two nuclear rivals?

Plebiscite was indeed the solution mutually agreed upon in 1948. Although it has given various reasons, it is fairly clear that India reneged on a solemn commitment. Still, even if it had been so earlier, plebiscite may not the best solution today. Changed geo-political circumstances now demand a reappraisal; plebiscite is now no longer the obvious way of determining the wishes of the people of Jammu and Kashmir. For example, it clearly excludes a major section of Kashmiris that would opt for independence today but which, in 1948, may not have wanted it. More frightening is the likelihood of a plebiscite igniting communal passions leading to Gujarat-style bloodbaths across the subcontinent. Moreover, at a practical level there is no agency, including the United Nations, that is equipped and willing to implement a task that all nations (except Pakistan) see as impossibly difficult. Therefore, insisting on plebiscite is the surest way of guaranteeing that a bloody stand-off continues indefinitely.

Moving away from this insistence, in 2003 General Pervez Musharraf brought a whole set of other proposals on to the negotiating table. It was an extraordinary departure from earlier stands taken by Pakistan. Certainly, the General can be faulted on much else during his nine years of rule, including his haughty dismissal of Chief Justice Iftikhar Chaudhry; poor judgment shown in the Lal Masjid crisis; and the double game played in Afghanistan. But on Kashmir, the general deserves an 'A'—this in spite of having played a double game there as well.***

By declaring that, 'we have left aside' the United Nations Security Council resolutions for a solution to Kashmir, Musharraf shattered a long-held taboo.[18] Earlier he had given some confusing hints during his 2001 visit to India and spoken of the need 'to move away from stated positions.' But never before had a Pakistani head of state made an explicit public admission that Pakistan cannot realistically hope for a plebiscite to end the Kashmir dispute and, therefore, is willing to explore other ways. Subsequent attempts by Foreign Minister Khurshid Kasuri to dilute Musharraf's remarks turned out to be insufficient to control outrage. Accusations of treason were made against him by the Pakistani political and jihadist establishments and whispers of unhappiness in the army were also heard. Interestingly, although the press did report Musharraf's Kashmir speech that day, it was not covered by Pakistan Television which is tasked with following the leaders of the country all over Pakistan. Pakistan's hard-liners still believe that Kashmir can someday be liberated by force.

*** On a personal note: The author twice encountered Musharraf in the Aiwan-e-Sadar (President's House): once in 2003 and then in 2005. Each time the topic was Kashmir. The author gave his observations of a high level of jihadist activity in Kashmir which clearly appeared to have the government's backing. Faced by the clear contradiction with his public position, Musharraf flared up on both occasions. Subsequently, as ex-officio chancellor of Quaid-e-Azam University, he endorsed all other routine time-bound promotions but refused to endorse the author's promotion to the next higher academic post.

Among the proposals offered by Musharraf was one that envisioned two Kashmiri regions, each with its own government and constitution. These two neighbouring entities: one associated with Pakistan and the other with India, would have soft borders allowing for easy transit of people and goods. Musharraf also favoured demilitarization, which was quite at odds with simultaneously maintaining jihadist power and influence in Punjab. But then, politics is never a linear game.

Minus the two obvious ones, Kashmir watchers have counted over thirty possibilities for solving the Kashmir issue. For example, in 1999 the Pakistani and Indian prime ministers, in secret negotiations, had privately agreed to the Chenab river as a natural boundary that could potentially become the international border.[19] The 'Chenab Formula' suddenly became the talk of the town although the plan was first suggested in the 1960s. It envisaged a division of Kashmir along the line of the River Chenab. Pakistan and India both officially rejected it, but India had more reason. The plan would have been difficult for any Indian leader to sell because it would have required giving up much land to Pakistan. It would also have been an agreement for another division on the basis of religion.

A more feasible plan envisages two reconstituted Kashmiri entities, possibly straddling the Line of Control, with their own respective governments and constitutions. These two non-hostile entities, one associated with Pakistan and the other India, would have soft borders allowing for easy transit of people and goods. This calls for a preparatory stage in which inflamed nerves are soothed and the high-pitched decades-old rhetoric is toned down. Subsequently, the Pakistani side of Kashmir and the Northern Areas could be formally absorbed into Pakistan. Negotiations could be conducted with India on an LoC-plus solution that allows for some territorial adjustments and soft borders, and possibly a 10-mile deep demilitarized zone. While the division of Kashmir will be resisted by some Kashmiri nationalists, it is better to accept this reality rather than live with the endless suffering that has consumed over 90,000 lives since 1987.

Post-Musharraf, as yet there is little to suggest that Pakistan has any new game plan. Resistance to change comes from many quarters—a possible backlash from the religious parties and extreme elements within the military, as well as a large standing army that needs an enemy. Inertia and default continue to dominate military planning and design. On the other hand, compared to 20–30 years ago, Kashmir is no longer such an immediate or emotional matter. Trade with India, which accelerated after Pakistan granted India the 'Most Favoured Nation' status in late 2011, could bring home the virtues of peace to a large number of people on both sides.

India also needs to reassess its policy on Kashmir. The undeniable fact is that India is morally isolated from the Kashmiri people and incurs the very considerable costs of an occupying power. Its industry, capable of double-digit growth, needs stability to grow. Kashmir remains a thorn in its side, with the prospect of a disruptive conflict breaking out at some point. And—of no small importance— Indian soldiers do not want to die in Kashmir. India, by formally acknowledging Kashmir as a problem that needs a solution; punishing security forces for excesses; releasing political prisoners from Kashmiri jails; and agreeing to a mutual reduction of hostile state-sponsored propaganda, could appropriately acknowledge its part of the deal.

So is there hope for an eventual solution of Kashmir? Yes, but it shall require a spirit of compromise and an emphasis on economic prosperity, social stability, and peace. Logic and pragmatism require India and Pakistan to explore non-maximalist long-term solutions. Positions fixed half a century ago must change. The 'your loss is my gain' mentality must be abandoned.

REFERENCES

1. Bose, Sumantra, 'Kashmir: Roots of Conflict, Paths to Peace, Harvard University Press, (2005), pp. 15–17.
2. 'Kashmir unmarked graves hold thousands of bodies', Jason Burke, Guardian, 21 August 2011.
3. 'India's Blood-Stained Democracy', New York Review of Books, 6 July 2012.

4. 'Jammu and Kashmir—Moving On', Vikram Sood, *Indian Review of Global Affairs*, June 2012.
5. 'Crossing the Lines—Kashmir, Pakistan, India', http://www.youtube.com/watch?v=EeBRVFxe5oQ
6. 'India's forex reserves grow to $289bn, *The Economic Times*, 23 June 2012.
7. 'Jihadists' recruit and raise funds openly in Rawalpindi', *The Express Tribune*, 9 July 2012.
8. 'Would not mind Indo–Pak N-war: JuD Chief', Pakistan Defense, 6 February 2011.
9. '17 Days in May—Chronology of Indian nuclear weapons tests', http://www.fas.org/nuke/guide/india/nuke/chron.htm
10. 'Felled by the fallout', http://archives.digitaltoday.in/businesstoday/22081998/peco.html
11. Lt. Gen. Asad Durrani in: 'Pakistan's Security and the Nuclear Option', p. 92, Institute of Policy Studies, Islamabad, 1995.
12. Ibid.
13. C. Raja Mohan, 'Beyond Nuclear Stability: Towards Military Peace and Tranquillity on the Indo–Pak Border', *The Indian Express*, 14 December 2004.
14. General (retd.) Jehangir Karamat, 'Nuclear Risk Reduction Centres in South Asia', SASSU Research Report, 2005.
15. Karamat, ibid.
16. 'China blames terrorists trained in Pakistan for violence', *Dawn*, 2 August 2011.
17. 'India–Iran Defense Cooperation', Pakistan Defense, http://www.defense.pk/forums/world-affairs/161845-india-iran-defense-cooperation.html#ixzz1z2CHrKiO
18. 'U.S. hails Musharraf offer to drop Kashmir plebiscite', *Asian Tribune*, 19 December 2003.
19. 'Analysis: Dividing Kashmir by religion', Zaffar Abbas, *BBC News*, 21 May 2003.

CHAPTER 6

NATIONALISM AND THE BOMB
Pervez Hoodbhoy

Nation-building is the process of creating, or reinforcing a national identity using the power of the state. The goal is to unify the disparate peoples within an emerging state, reduce internal conflict, and create the conditions for effective governance. Nation-building can involve the use of propaganda, myth building, and the creation of national paraphernalia such as sports teams, national holidays, anthems, flag carrying airlines, and, of course, the display of military might. In much the same way, a few states see nuclear weapons as an instrument for building or consolidating a national spirit.

One can readily understand why this is so because the bomb can level mountains, cause seas to boil when exploded underwater, or snuff out a living city in a flash. Post-Hiroshima, the bomb became the symbol of ultimate power. Even countries allied to the U.S. felt at a disadvantage and rushed to make their own. Ernie Bevin, the foreign secretary in UK's Prime Minister Clement Attlee's post-war government, found the condescending attitude of the nuclear-armed Americans insufferable. In 1946 he remarked:

> I don't want any other foreign secretary of this country to be talked to or at by a secretary of state in the United States as I have just had in my discussions with Mr Byrnes. We've got to have this thing [a nuclear bomb] over here whatever it costs. We've got to have the bloody Union Jack on top of it.[1]

Six years later cash-strapped Britain, though devastated by six years of total war, became the world's third nuclear power. The notion that it would otherwise be considered a second-rank nation was simply intolerable.

France, under Charles de Gaulle, thought similarly. It developed its own deterrent while thumbing its nose at NATO and the U.S. All entreaties made to de Gaulle failed; the *force de frappe* had to be uniquely French. After the first French nuclear test on 13 February 1960, he exclaimed—'Hurray for France! From this morning she is stronger and prouder.'[2]

While democratic governments have used the strong feelings generated by the possession of nuclear weapons, unpopular and illegitimate regimes know this fact still better.

This was evident in India when Indira Gandhi, extremely unpopular in 1974, tested India's bomb for the first time, releasing a burst of nationalist excitement that led to her popularity briefly shooting upward. India glowed again after its 1998 tests, with the BJP and Congress parties setting aside their difference to exult in 'Indian greatness'. Massive celebrations followed, sweets were distributed, and citizens danced on the streets of Delhi and Mumbai.

In Iran today, nuclear nationalism unites a polity that is sharply divided on everything else. Mohammed El Baradei, reflecting upon his term as the IAEA's director general says, 'From what we repeatedly observed, a policy of isolation and sanctions only served to stimulate a country's sense of pride; in the worst case, it could make the targeted country's nuclear project a matter of national priority.'[3]

The North Korean regime has also used nuclear weapons to promote nationalism. Its dynastic dictatorship has twice tested nuclear weapons and demonstrated that even dramatically under-developed countries can go nuclear if they want. Unknown for scientific achievement, the country has little electricity or fuel, food and medicine are scarce, corruption is ubiquitous, and its people live in humiliating conditions. In a famine some years ago, North Korea lost nearly 800,000 people. Its enormous prison population of 200,000 has been subjected to systematic torture and abuse. Nevertheless, nuclear weapons are touted as the country's major accomplishment.

In Pakistan, the 1998 nuclear tests were celebrated with even greater fervour than in India. Missiles were paraded in Islamabad, and bomb and missile replicas were installed on major road crossings and public squares. Some still survive, although, several were removed over the last decade. It was generally expected by Pakistanis that nuclear weapons would make their country an object of awe and respect internationally, and that it would acquire the mantle of leadership of the Islamic world. Indeed, in the aftermath of the 1998 tests, Pakistan's stock shot up in several Muslim countries. Iran's foreign minister paid a congratulatory visit to Pakistan days later, and Saudi Arabia sent congratulations. By gifting $5 billion worth of oil, it helped Pakistan avoid an economic breakdown caused by the sanctions imposed by Western powers. A year later tumultuous celebrations were held across the country on *Youm-e-Takbir* to infuse a new sense of national spirit.

Although May 28 has been celebrated with progressively decreasing fervour every year, the bomb remains popular today as well. A poll conducted in 2011 by YouGov, in association with Cambridge University, revealed that a majority supported the expansion of Pakistan's nuclear arsenal with 81 per cent voting in favour of it and just 9 per cent against it.[4]

This essay explores the relationship between the bomb and Pakistani national identity. After examining the circumstances surrounding Pakistan's birth and the difficulties created by the Two-Nation Theory, it argues that the bomb does create a national consensus, but only in a narrow sense. In spite of the fact that most Pakistanis agree on having the bomb, this unity is unlikely to create anything more than an illusory notion of nationhood, or lead toward a more stable and secure state. But, for all its difficulties, Pakistan does have a fighting chance of becoming a nation provided it concentrates upon bolstering human security, improves the economy, and moves towards better governance.

PAKISTAN'S SEARCH FOR NATIONHOOD

The French historian Ernest Renan (1823–1892) had a useful definition of a nation. He says it is a soul, a spiritual principle:

> Two things, which are really one, constitute this soul and spiritual principle. One is in the past, the other, the present. One is the possession in common of a rich trove of memories; the other is actual consent, the desire to live together, the will to continue to value the undivided, shared heritage. . . . To have had glorious moments in common in the past, a common will in the present, to have done great things together and to wish to do more, those are the essential conditions for a people. We love the nation in proportion to the sacrifices to which we consented, the harms that we suffered.[5]

A more prosaic definition is that a nation is a historically constituted, stable community of people, formed on the basis of a common language, territory, economic life, and psychological make-up manifested in a common culture.

The concept of nation must not be confused with that of nation-state: a modern nation-state refers to a single or multiple nationalities joined together in a formal political union. The nation-state determines an official language(s), a system of law, manages a currency system, uses a bureaucracy to order elements of society, and fosters loyalties to abstract entities like 'Canada', 'the United States' and so on.[6] It is possible to have a nation-state but no nation! For example, Eric Hobsbawm, the influential Marxist British historian, persuasively argues that the state of France under Napoleon made the French nation, not vice-versa.

But Pakistani leaders and governments have failed what Napoleon succeeded at. Although it has been a nation-state since 1947, Pakistan is still not a nation. To be precise: it is the name of a land and people inside a certain geographical boundary. Crucial components needed for nationhood are missing. These include a strong common identity and mental makeup, shared sense of history, and common goals.

The lack of nationhood can be traced to the genesis of Pakistan and the single factor that drove the Pakistan Movement (1930– 1947), namely religious identity. Carved out of Hindu-majority India, Pakistan was the culmination of the competition and conflict between natives who had converted to Islam and those who had not. Converts often identified with Arab invaders of the last millennium. Shah Waliullah (1703–1762), a 'purifier' of Islam on the subcontinent who despised local traditions, famously declared, 'We [Hindustanis] are an Arab people whose fathers have fallen in exile in the country of Hindustan, and Arabic genealogy and the Arabic language are our pride.'[7]

The founder of Pakistan, Mohammed Ali Jinnah, also echoed the separateness of South Asia's Muslims from its Hindus, basing the struggle for Pakistan on the premise that the two peoples could never live together peacefully within one nation-state. This was known as the Two-Nation Theory, first propounded in 1940 by Jinnah while addressing the Muslim League in Lahore.[8]

Walilullah and Jinnah were as different as could be: Waliullah was a bearded religious scholar who knew classical texts and Arabic whereas Jinnah was an impeccably dressed Westernized man with Victorian manners, secular outlook, and a connoisseur of fine foods and wines. Nevertheless, Jinnah effectively articulated the fears and aspirations of an influential section of his co-religionists, insecure at the thought of living in a free Hindu-majority India.[9] Interestingly, he was opposed by a large section of the conservative ulema (Islamic scholars), such as Maulana Maudoodi of the Jamaat-i-Islami, who said that Islam must not be confined to national borders. But Jinnah and his Muslim League won the day by insisting that Muslims constituted a distinct nation which would be overwhelmed in post-British India by a larger and better educated Hindu majority.

EAST PAKISTAN CHALLENGES THE TWO-NATION THEORY

The basis in religious identity soon led to painful paradoxes. Jinnah's Two-Nation Theory, which successfully led to the nascent state, was to receive its first strong challenge in East Pakistan. On 21 March, at a civic reception at Dacca's Racecourse Ground, Jinnah—who could not speak Urdu with any fluency—declared that, 'Urdu, and only Urdu' embodied the spirit of the new Muslim nation and would be its state language. Urdu was the language spoken by the North Indian Muslim elite, many of whom migrated to West Pakistan. Bengalis wanted their language instead, but Jinnah claimed that their protests were designed by a 'fifth column' to divide Pakistani Muslims. He labelled those who disagreed with his views as 'enemies of Pakistan. Before Jinnah left Dacca [Dhaka] on 28 March 1948, he had delivered a speech on Radio Pakistan reasserting his 'Urdu-only' policy.[10]

The Bengali people suffered terribly under West Pakistani rule. They believed their historical destiny was to be a Bengali speaking nation, not the Urdu-speaking East Pakistan which Mr Jinnah wanted. The language riots were just the beginning. Over time, grievances compounded. The East Wing comprised of 54 per cent of Pakistan's population and was the biggest earner of foreign exchange. But West Pakistani generals, bureaucrats, and politicians such Zulfikar Ali Bhutto, feared that a democratic system would transfer power and national resources to East Pakistan.

An overbearing West Pakistan ran roughshod over East Pakistan and became despised as an external imperial power. Pakistanis who grew up when East and West Pakistan were one country knew that we were never one nation. Young people today cannot imagine the rampant anti-Bengali racism among West Pakistanis then. With shame, I must admit that, as a thoughtless young boy, I too felt embarrassed about small and dark people being among our compatriots. Victims of a delusion, we West Pakistanis imagined that good Muslims and Pakistanis were tall, fair, and spoke chaste Urdu. Some of my schoolmates would laugh at the strange sounding Bengali news broadcasts from Radio Pakistan.

Denied of democracy and justice, the Bengalis helplessly watched the cash flow from East to fund government, industry, schools and dams situated in West Pakistan. When the Bhola cyclone killed half-a-million people in 1970, President Yahya Khan and his fellow generals in Rawalpindi's GHQ appeared callously indifferent.

The decisive break came with the 1970 elections. The East Pakistan-based Awami League won a clear majority in Pakistan's parliament. But Bhutto and the generals would not accept the peoples' verdict. The Bengalis finally rose up for independence. When the West Pakistan army was sent in, massacre followed massacre. Political activists, intellectuals, trade unionists, and students were slaughtered. Blood ran in street gutters, and millions fled across the border. After India intervened to support the East, the army surrendered. Bangladesh was born. The enthusiasm of Muslim Bengalis for Bangladesh, and refusal to accept Islam as the basis for their new state, was a deadly blow to the very idea of Pakistan.

Although Pakistani history books attribute the loss of East Pakistan to an Indian conspiracy aimed at misleading Bengalis, the lost territory still shows no desire to reintegrate into Pakistan after over four decades of independence. Bengalis insist upon an apology, one that Pakistan still refuses to give. Reflecting the fact that relations have never normalized between what were once two wings of the same country, Bangladesh's High Commissioner to India, Ahmed Tariq Karim, recently cited 'seven deadly sins' of Pakistan. These were: doctrines of Islamic invincibility over Hindus; West Pakistani superiority over inferior Bengalis (Bangladeshis); its indispensability as a strategic ally of the U.S.; too much emphasis on relations with China and Iran; a belief that majority of Kashmiris want to join Pakistan; and that defense of East Pakistan lay in the plains of Punjab (Pakistan).[11]

COULD THE BOMB HAVE PREVENTED A BREAKUP?

If we had had nuclear capability before 1971, we would not have lost half of our country—present-day Bangladesh—after disgraceful defeat.'
Dr Abdul Qadeer Khan (2011)[12]

Dr Khan and many others who think like him—cling to this dangerous and illogical argument. Given that 30,000 nuclear weapons failed to save the Soviet Union from decay and defeat and collapse, how could the bomb have saved Pakistan in 1971?

Like the Indian Army in Kashmir, or the Americans in Afghanistan, the Pakistan Army was surrounded by a hostile population. When subjected to guerilla attacks, it responded with the iron fist, lashing out with full fury against even unarmed Bengalis. The weakness of West Pakistan's position was fundamental and irreversible: all occupying forces typically exact disproportionate retribution, leading to atrocities which in turn builds up resentment and adds to the insurgency. Moreover, the logistics of supplying 90,000 troops from a thousand miles away, with a hostile India in between, were simply horrendous. India had, of course, refused permission for over-flights, leaving only the sea-route. A long war would have left Pakistan bankrupt.

Could the bomb have been used on the raging pro-independence mobs in Dacca? Or used to incinerate Calcutta and Delhi, and have the favour duly returned to Lahore and Karachi? Threatening India with nuclear attack may have kept it out of the war, but then East Pakistanis would have been killed in still greater numbers. Even without the bomb, estimated civilian deaths numbered in the hundreds of thousands if not a million.

Some West Pakistanis still argue that regardless of the death and destruction, using the bomb to keep Pakistan together would have been a good thing and the people of East Pakistan would have been better off in the long term. But a look at current developmental statistics shows otherwise.

Bangladesh is ranked 96th out of 110 countries in a 2010 prosperity index compiled by an independent London-based think-tank, the Legatum Institute, using governance, education, health, security, personal freedom, and social capital as criteria.[13] Although this is not good, but Pakistan's position is 109 according to the index, rendering it just one notch above Zimbabwe. By this measure the people of the East Wing have actually benefited from independence. Independently, the U.N. Human Development Index ranks Bangladesh at 146 out of 182 countries and Pakistan at 141, which makes Pakistan only marginally better.[14] This suggested that Bengalis would have gained little, if anything at all, by remaining with West Pakistan.

Numerical data does not tell the whole story. Bangladesh is poorer but more hopeful and happier. Culture is thriving, education is improving, and efforts to control population growth are more fruitful than in Pakistan. It is not ravaged by suicide bombings or by daily attacks upon its state institutions and military forces. Some kind of ramshackle democracy has taken hold, and Bangladesh's civil society groups are the envy of some other countries.

PAKISTANI IDENTITY AFTER 1971

Contrary to dire predictions at the time, the Pakistani state survived the split. Its powerful military easily crushed emerging separatist movements in the provinces of Balochistan and Sind. For a while the question of national ideology fell into limbo. Prime Minister Zulfikar Ali Bhutto attempted to create a Pakistani identity around the notion of revenge for the loss of the East Wing, promising a 'war of a thousand years' against India and summoning scientists in 1972 to start Pakistan's quest for the atomic bomb. While anti-Indianism served temporarily as a rallying cry, the military coup of 1977 that sent him off to the gallows revived identity issues.

Soon after he seized power from Bhutto, General Zia-ul-Haq announced his intention to remake Pakistan and, once and for all, end the confusion of Pakistan's purpose and identity. Like Napoleon, he wanted to use the nation-state to create a nation. The word went out that Pakistan was henceforth not to be conceived as a Muslim state. Instead, it had to be re-visualized as an Islamic state, i.e., one where Islamic law would reign supreme. To achieve this new conceptualization, Zia determined that future generations of Pakistanis would have to be purged of liberal and secular values.

Education was pressed into the drive for creating a new national identity based on the 'Ideology of Pakistan' that centred around Islam. Beginning in 1981, major steps were taken: enforcement of *chaadar* (loose outer garment) for girls in educational institutions; organization of congregational *zuhr* (afternoon) prayers during school hours; compulsory teaching of Arabic as a second language from sixth class onwards; introduction of *nazara* Qur'an (reading of

Qur'an) as a matriculation requirement; alteration of the definition of literacy to include religious knowledge; elevation of *maktab* schools to the status of regular schools and the recognition of *maktab* certificates as being equivalent to master's degree; creation of an Islamic university in Islamabad; introduction of religious knowledge as a criterion for selecting teachers of all categories and all levels; and the revision of conventional subjects to emphasize Islamic values.[15]

Notwithstanding the enormous impetus given by Zia-ul-Haq, a new Pakistani identity and a Shar'ia state is nowhere to be seen. Why?

Ethno-nationalism is part of the answer. Historically constituted groups seek to preserve their distinctiveness, expressed in terms of language, dress, food, folklore, and shared history. They reflexively respond against melding into some larger entity. Assimilation of Pakistan's diverse people into a homogenized national culture is opposed by this force which, like the force of gravity, always acts in one direction.

Ethno-nationalism is, of course, vulnerable. It can be overcome by integrative forces, which arise from the natural advantage of being part of a larger economy with correspondingly greater opportunities. For these forces to be effective it is essential that the state machinery provide effective governance, demonstrate fairness, and be indifferent to ethnic origins if not supportive of minorities. But Pakistan's ruling elite is both incompetent as well as ethnically partisan, drawing its roots from the powerful landed and feudal class. The army leadership and the economic elite had joined forces after Partition to claim authority, but they were transparently self-serving and therefore lacked legitimacy.

The prospect of an Islamic state based on justice and equity raised expectations but did little else. A cacophony of voices from different religious groups insisted on their own versions of the Shar'ia; the Shi'a and Hanafi sects were adamant that they would not accept zakat (fixed portion of wealth to charity) to be deducted from their bank accounts. To the chagrin of the establishment, the attempt to have Islamic law replace secular law ultimately backfired and became the cause of infinite division. The post-Zia generation—brought up to believe that 'every issue will be solved if we go back to the fundamentals of Islam'—founders in contradiction and confusion because the so-called 'fundamentals of Islam' turn out to have multiple interpretations. Some interpretations fuel violent political forces, each convinced that they alone understand God's will. Murderous wars between Sunni and Shi'a militias started in the late 1980s. Today, many utopians favouring the vision of an ideal Islamic state are frightened by the Pakistani Taliban who seek to impose their version of Shar'ia through the Kalashnikov and suicide bombings.

THE BOMB FAILS TO UNITE

In spite of a consensus that Pakistan must have the bomb, the hope that it would weld disparate peoples together turned out to be incorrect. Most Punjabis indeed think of themselves as Pakistani first and Punjabi second. But not the Baloch or Sindhis. Sindhis accuse Punjabis of stealing their water, the MQM runs Karachi on strictly ethnic grounds, Pakhtoons had the NWFP renamed Khyber Pakhtunkhwa against the wishes of other residents, caste and sect matter more than competence in getting a job, and ethnic student's groups wage pitched battles against each other on campuses.

While Punjabis are generally more favourable to the bomb, angry Sindhis see this is as far less relevant. Instead, they want water and jobs—and they blame Punjab for taking these away. Karachi staggers along with multiple ethnically motivated killings; Muhajirs and Pakhtuns are locked in a deadly battle. Karachi explodes into killings periodically as the MQM and ANP battle out their Muhajir and Pakhtun identity politics. Pakhtun refugees from Swat and Buner, hapless victims of a war between the Taliban and the Pakistani Army in 2009, were tragically turned away by both Muhajirs and Sindhis, who are mutual adversaries, from entering Sindh. This rejection struck deeply against the concept of a single nation united in adversity.

Balochistan is the strongest evidence of how the bomb has failed to unify. Schools refuse to fly the Pakistani flag, the national anthem is not sung, and black flags celebrate Pakistan's Independence Day. Angry at being governed from Islamabad, some have taken up arms. In stark contrast with Punjab, the Baloch are resolutely anti-bomb. They resent that the two nuclear test sites—now radioactive and out of bounds—are on their soil. Balochistan University teems with the icons of Baloch separatism: posters of Akbar Bugti, Balach Marri, Brahamdagh Bugti, and 'General Sheroff' decorate the campus. The ultra-nationalist Baloch kill the non-Baloch: Punjabis, Muhajirs, and even Sindhis. Poor labourers, school teachers, and professors are also not spared. The Army and the Frontier Constabulary respond with excessive violence against nationalists—even those who believe in using peaceful means only—using a simple principle: abduct, kill, dump. Tortured and disfigured bodies of Baloch nationalists are frequently found dumped in the bushes; Pakistan's top judges fruitlessly instruct law enforcement authorities responsible for enforced disappearances in Balochistan to produce the remaining 'missing persons'.[16]

With a country in deep crisis, beating the nuclear drum does little to soothe such basic anger and resentment. Expressions of despair and frustration abound across the country. An irate citizen, fed-up with electricity load-shedding, circulated the following:

In a span of the last one-month, Pakistan has test-fired 5 hi-tech, ultra-sophisticated, stealth-featured, nuclear-capable, long-range ballistic missiles. Even superpowers at the height of the cold war were unable to afford so many tests of their nuclear arsenal in just one month alone. On the other hand Pakistan's 'rocket science' cannot produce a single mega-watt of electricity, construct new dams, provide regular supply of gas to starving industries, CNG stations, consumers etc., through new LNG terminals or pipelines, develop basic infrastructure for the masses, repair stranded locomotive engines of Pakistan Railways, overhaul grounded engines of PIA aircraft, complete the Lowari Tunnel since last 40 years, exploit Thar Coal and other untapped mineral resources etc.[17]

The hubris following the 1998 tests, together with the promise that the bomb would transform Pakistan into a technologically and scientifically advanced country, is now nowhere in evidence. On the contrary, apart from relatively minor exports of computer software and light armaments, science and technology remain peripheral to process of production. Pakistan's current exports are principally textiles, cotton, leather, footballs, fish and fruit. The value-added component of Pakistani manufacturing somewhat exceeds that of Bangladesh and Sudan, but is far below that of India, Turkey and Indonesia. Nor is the quality of science taught in Pakistani educational institutions satisfactory. It remains at the level that existed before Pakistan embarked on its quest for the bomb. This is not surprising because making a bomb in present times requires technical skills rather than scientific ones.

CAN PAKISTAN BECOME A NATION?

This bleak picture notwithstanding, there is excellent reason why Pakistan should continue to exist as a nation-state even if it has so far failed to evolve into a nation. Unlike the disintegration of the Soviet Union, the shattering of the Pakistani state would be enormously painful all around. As the failed state of Somalia has recently demonstrated, anarchy and local warlords are extremely destructive to any large body of people.

The collective experience of humankind over four centuries has led to the emergence of independent nation-states. They are now the bedrock of the international system and play critical roles in development, management of shared and scarce global resources, and human and collective security. At a minimum, states have legal and normative responsibilities for assuring the security of their citizens, protecting property rights and providing public goods to enable the functioning of the market. Many states do far more than this, providing social services, particularly education, health and sanitation.[18]

Pakistan can, over time, go beyond being just a nation-state and actually become a nation—one that is at peace with itself and the world. Nations are inevitably formed when people experience a common environment and live together for long enough. But how long is long? In Pakistan's case the time scale could be fairly short. Its people are diverse but almost all understand Urdu. They watch the same television programs, listen to the same radio stations, deal with the same irritating and inefficient bureaucracy, use the same badly written textbooks, buy similar products, and despise the same set of rulers. One can see the outlines of an emergent Pakistani culture. Just as rain and snow eventually grind stark stony mountains into fertile soil, adherence to a few basic principles could cause a viable Pakistani culture to emerge.

What might be a suitable manifesto of change?

First, Pakistan needs peace. This means that it must turn inwards and devote its fullest attention to ending its raging internal wars. The sixty-year long conflict with India has achieved little beyond creating a militarized Pakistani security state which uses force as its first resort even when dealing its own people. Attempts to solve Kashmir militarily have bled the country dry and left it dependent on foreign aid. The army's role must be limited to defending the people of Pakistan, and to ensuring that their constitutional and civil rights are protected.

Second, Pakistan needs economic justice. This demands a social infrastructure providing decent employment, minimum incomes, and rewards according to ability and hard work. In rural areas, where old structures of land ownership remain intact, sweeping land reforms are urgent. India abolished feudalism upon attaining independence but the enormous pre-Partition land holdings of Pakistan's feudal lords were protected by the authority of the state. The land reforms announced by Ayub Khan and Zulfikar Ali Bhutto were hardly serious. No agricultural tax is paid to the government because many in parliament own vast tracts of land. On the other hand, even in the urban areas there is gross inequality—mothers commit suicide in the shadow of five-star hotels because they cannot feed their children. The military is landlord and capitalist, owning vast assets that have no relation to national defense. Most countries have armies but, as many have dryly noted, only in Pakistan does an army have a country.

Third, Pakistan must shed its colonial structure of governance. Different historically constituted peoples must want to live together voluntarily, and see the benefits of doing so. A giant centralized government machine sitting in Islamabad cannot effectively manage such a diverse country. The passage in 2010 of the Eighteenth Amendment to the Constitution, which enhanced provincial autonomy, was a positive step. As in India, Pakistan has to be reorganized as a federation where provinces and local governments hold the critical economic and social powers, with defense and foreign affairs held in common. In particular, Islamabad's conflict with Balochistan urgently needs resolution using political sagacity rather than military force. Blaming India cannot change reality—the Baloch are angry for good reasons. At a recent lecture that I gave to senior Pakistan civil service officers in Peshawar, I was taken back at the intensity of those from Balochistan who said that wounds were too deep and the time for reconciliation had passed. A decade ago one would have expected this language from student radicals only—now it is the mainstream Baloch who articulates this sentiment.

Fourth, Pakistan needs a social contract. This is a commitment that citizens shall be treated fairly and equally by the state and, in turn, shall willingly fulfil basic civic responsibilities. But today Pakistanis are denied even the most fundamental protections specified in the Constitution. The poor suffer outright denial of their rights while the rich are compelled to buy them. Rich and poor alike feel no obligation to fulfil their civic duties. Most do not pay their fair share of income tax, leading to one of the lowest tax-to-GDP ratios in the world.

Fifth, the country's education needs drastic revision in the means of delivery and content. Money goes some way towards the first— better school infrastructure, books, teacher salaries, etc. But this is not enough. Schools teach children to mindlessly obey authority, to look to the past for solutions to today's problems, and to be intolerant of the religion, culture and language of others. Instead, we need to teach them to be enquiring, open-minded, creative, logical, socially responsible and appreciative of diversity.

To conclude, Pakistan's security problems cannot be solved by better weapons. If Pakistan is to chart a path to viable nationhood, there must be a national dialogue on its most pressing problems. The way forward lies in building a normal nation held together by mutual interests. Wherever this condition lies unfulfilled for too long, there can be major changes: both the Soviet Union and Yugoslavia broke apart after seventy years.

This means Pakistan must aim towards creating a sustainable and active democracy; an economy for peace rather than war; a federation in which provincial grievances can be effectively resolved; elimination of the feudal order and creating a tolerant society that respects the rule of law. Although religion will certainly remain an important part of its social reality for the foreseeable future, Pakistan must seek new roots that lie beyond religion. This is the only way to deal with the surge of insurgencies in the country. They need to urgently to be brought under control through appropriate use of force, as well as major changes in governance, education, and the political structure.

REFERENCES

1. 'Britain's nuclear weapons—Accounting and the Bomb', *Blighty Britain*, 30 July 2010.
2. Cited in Jacques C. Hymans, *'The Psychology of Nuclear Proliferation: Identity, Emotions and Foreign Policy'*, Cambridge University Press, 2006, p. 86.
3. *The Age of Deception—Nuclear Diplomacy in Troubled Times*, Mohammed ElBaradei, Metropolitan Books, p. 113, 2011.
4. YouGov Siraj Survey Results, Pakistan Poll, May 2011, http://cdn.yougov.com/today_uk_import/yg-archives-pakistan-poll_0.pdf
5. Renan, Ernest. 'What is a Nation?' in Eley, Geoff and Suny, Ronald Grigor (ed.) 1996, *Becoming National: A Reader*, New York and Oxford: Oxford University Press, 1996.
6. 'What is a Nation', http://www.towson.edu/polsci/ppp/sp97/realism/whatisns.htm
7. *Jinnah, Pakistan and Islamic Identity: The Search for Saladin*, Akbar S. Ahmed, Routledge, 1997.

8. *The Sole Spokesman: Jinnah, the Muslim League and the Demand for Pakistan*, Ayesha Jalal, Cambridge University Press, 1985.
9. *Jinnah of Pakistan*, Stanley Wolpert, Oxford.
10. Sayeed, Khalid Bin, 'Federalism and Pakistan'. *Far Eastern Survey 23* (9): pp. 139–43, Sept. 1954.
11. 'Selfish Pakistan army may spark nuclear war with India: Bangladesh envoy', *Times of India*, 25 June 2012.
12. 'I Saved My Country From Nuclear Blackmail', Abdul Qadeer Khan, *Newsweek*, 16 May 2011.
13. Legatum Prosperity Index, 2011.
14. United Nations Human Development Report, 2011.
15. 'Rewriting the history of Pakistan', Pervez Hoodbhoy and A.H. Nayyar in: *Islam, Politics, and the State*, Asghar Khan, Zed Books, 1985.
16. 'Agencies told to produce Balochistan's "missing" in next hearing', 20 June 2012.
17. Note circulated by Irfan Zafar, 24 June 2012.
18. 'Concepts and Dilemmas of State Building in Fragile Situations, Organization for Economic Cooperation and Development', *Journal on Development*, Vol. 9, No. 3, 2008.

CHAPTER 7

IRAN, SAUDI ARABIA, PAKISTAN AND THE 'ISLAMIC BOMB'

Pervez Hoodbhoy

The concept of the Islamic Bomb was first introduced in 1977 by the prime minister of Pakistan, Zulfikar Ali Bhutto. Bhutto, the architect of Pakistan's nuclear program, had just been deposed and convicted of murdering a political opponent. Addressing posterity from his death cell in Rawalpindi Jail he wrote: 'We know that Israel and South Africa have full nuclear capability. The Christian, Jewish, and Hindu civilizations have this capability. The communist powers also possess it. Only the Islamic civilization was without it, but that position was about to change.'[1] Although appending 'Islamic' to 'bomb'—and thus associating destruction with a religion—did cause some Muslims to take umbrage, most welcomed the bomb as a sign of Muslim prowess and power.

Fifteen years later, another Muslim leader stressed the need for a bomb belonging collectively to Islam, meaning one that could be used for protecting all Muslims rather than be limited to serving just one country. Addressing an Islamic conference in Teheran in 1992, the Iranian vice-president, Sayed Ayatollah Mohajerani said, 'Since Israel continues to possess nuclear weapons, we, the Muslims, must cooperate to produce an atomic bomb, regardless of U.N. efforts to prevent proliferation.'[2]

In the celebrations following the 1998 nuclear tests, Pakistan's Jamaat-i-Islami paraded bomb and missile replicas through city streets. It saw in the bomb a sure sign of a reversal of fortunes and a panacea for the ills that have plagued Muslims since the end of the Golden Age of Islam. In 2000, I captured on video the statements of several leaders of religious and jihadist political parties in

Pakistan—Maulana Khalil-ur-Rahman and Maulana Sami-ul-Haq—
who also demanded a bomb for Islam.[3]

A staunch supporter of Al Qaeda and the Taliban, Pakistan's
General Hameed Gul—an influential Islamist leader and former
head of ISI, the country's powerful intelligence agency—made clear
his feelings. In a widely watched nationally televised debate with me,
General Hameed Gul snarled: 'Your masters (that is, the Americans)
will bomb us Muslims just as they bombed Hiroshima; people like
you want to denuclearize and disarm us in the face of a savage beast
set to devour the world.'

Still more recently Hafiz Saeed, head of the Lashkar-e-Tayyaba
and alleged mastermind of the Mumbai attack in November 2008,
has demanded that Pakistan should use its nuclear capability to
'secure the Holy Cities "Harmain" (Makkah and Madina) against any
possible threat especially after exposed USZ design to carry out
destruction of Kaaba and Masjid-e-Nabvi (s.a.w.w.), the most sacred
places for Muslims around the world.'[4]

The Islamic Bomb is indeed a popular concept in Pakistan, and
for different reasons in other Muslim countries. It is seen as a means
of defense against invasions from the West. The blind support given
by the U.S. for the Israeli occupation of Arab lands has certainly
contributed to the idea of a permanent Islam-West divide. This was
reinforced after the invasion and occupation of Iraq in 2003. After
the devastation of Gaza in 2008 by Israeli attacks, many newspapers
in Muslim countries, including Pakistan contained letters from their
readers wishing that Muslims too had nuclear weapons.

But the mythical 'Islamic Bomb' does not exist and may never
will. Bhutto's claim was, in fact, deeply misleading. It was intended
to elicit Arab support to save his life and restore him to power.
Indeed, nothing in the history of Pakistan shows substantial
commitment to any pan-Islamic cause; its bomb was motivated
solely with India in mind. It is therefore difficult, if not impossible,
to conceive of Pakistan—or any other Muslim state—providing a
nuclear umbrella for defending the *ummah* against the United
States or Israel (but it is worth recalling that this kind of 'extended

deterrence', as it was called, had been practiced aggressively by both superpowers in the Cold War, including during the Cuban Missile Crisis.

Looking at the deep fragmentation in Muslim world today, as well as in the past, should put to rest the notion that a bomb made in one Muslim country could be used for defending Muslims belonging to another country. In spite of the Prophet of Islam's teachings, rivalries between Arab tribes could never be overcome and a fierce battle for succession immediately followed his death. Although the subsequent 'Golden Age of Islam', extending from about AD 750 till the sack of Baghdad in AD 1258, saw brilliant Muslim scientific and intellectual achievements; it also witnessed extreme brutalities in the wars between the Umayyads and Abbasid—the majority of caliphs during this five hundred year period were murdered by other Muslims. The only situation where Muslims have behaved as an *ummah* is when facing an external enemy, but this unity has been fragile.

No Muslim state would put itself at nuclear risk. Still, individual engineers and scientists may well be responsive to a 'higher calling'. For example, it is widely known that two highly placed nuclear engineers, Syed Bashiruddin Mahmood and Chaudhry Majid, both well known to espouse radical Islamic views, had journeyed several times into Afghanistan in 2000 and had met with Osama bin Laden. Some months earlier, Mahmood had resigned from his position as director of the Khushab reactor in angry protest at the government's apparent willingness to sign the CTBT. While Osama bin Laden did discuss with Mahmood and Majid the possibility of making nuclear weapons, no further steps appear to have been taken.

IRAN AND THE BOMB

If the 'Islamic Bomb' had been a real concept and Bhutto's claims were actually correct, Pakistan would have been fully supportive of other Muslim countries getting the bomb. But Pakistan's enthusiasm for Iran's bomb, if any, is certainly subdued. Pakistan's local media has been remarkably lacking in sympathy as the U.S. and Israel threaten Iran for attempting to make the bomb. In a country that is today even more anti-American than Iran, one might have expected the exact opposite.

It is fairly clear that Iran does seek the bomb even though the goal is not the "Islamic" one in the sense described above. Iran has, in fact, stood at the threshold to making the bomb at least since 2010, when it had more than enough Low Enriched Uranium (LEU), some 2152 kilograms, to make its first bomb's worth of weapons-grade uranium. Enhancement to the required quality could have been done in a few months if this LEU had been fed into the 4186 centrifuges that it was then operating.[5] Thousands of other centrifuges are also known to be operating at the Natanz nuclear facility. Quite probably, Iran now awaits only a political decision to weaponize; it almost certainly has the capacity. But Iran furiously rejects allegations that it seeks the bomb, and cites *fatwas* (religious edicts) given against it by Ayatollah's Khomeini and Khameini. It says the LEU is only for generating nuclear electricity.[6]

Iran's nuclear program was initiated by Reza Shah Pahlavi with American help in 1959.[7] Initial plans called for producing 23,000 MW of nuclear electricity; these would create the spent fuel from which bomb-grade materials could be extracted. The U.S., which firmly backed the Shah and considered Iran an outpost representing American interests in the Gulf, was pleased with the benefits this would bring to its corporations such as Bechtel and Westinghouse.

Why would Iran, a major exporter of gas and oil—but with very limited natural uranium resources—be investing in nuclear electricity given that it had no expertise in this complex technology? There was then, as now, only one plausible answer—nuclear weapons. But the U.S. was quite indifferent to the Shah's undeclared but obvious pursuit of the bomb. The Atomic Energy Organization of Iran (AEOI) became the most heavily funded program in the country, sending large numbers of students to the U.S. and Europe for nuclear studies. The Massachusetts Institute of Technology (MIT) received a $20 million endowment from the Shah and softened entrance requirements for Iranian students into the nuclear engineering department.[8] The U.S. State Department not only favoured the sale of reactors to Iran but even encouraged the Bechtel Corporation to convince the Shah to invest up to $300 million in a jointly owned uranium enrichment facility in the United States. According to Defense and Energy department memos from the time, the United States was aware that, 'the annual plutonium production from the planned 23,000 MW Iranian nuclear power program will be equivalent to 600–700 warheads.'[9]

The Iranian revolution of 1979 replaced friends with foes. Ayatollah Khomenei ordered Iran's nuclear program to be stopped but it was resumed after Saddam Hussain invaded Iran and started the 'war of cities'. Seared into Iran's consciousness is the Iran–Iraq war, in which an estimated 200,000 Iranians were killed. 'If we had possessed nuclear weapons then, Saddam would not have dared to attack us,' wrote Amir Mohabian, editor of the influential conservative Iranian daily *Reselaat*.[10]

Iran immediately expressed pleasure at Pakistan's successful nuclear tests. Just five days later, Iranian Foreign Minister Kamal Kharrazi arrived in Islamabad to congratulate Pakistan on its achievement. 'From all over the world, Muslims are happy that Pakistan has this capability,' he said.[11] Iran had clearly hoped at that time to benefit from Pakistan's expertise.

There was good reason for expecting nuclear help. Iran was once Pakistan's close ally—probably its closest one—although a generation of Pakistanis is unaware of this fact because Iran–Pakistan relations have been on the rocks for so long. In 1947, Iran was the first to recognize the newly independent Pakistan. In the 1965 war with India, Pakistani fighter jets flew to Iranian bases in Zahidan and Mehrabad for protection and refueling. Both countries were members of the U.S.-led SEATO and CENTO defense pacts, Iran had opened wide its universities to Pakistani students. Although it is 80 per cent Sunni with only a 15–20 per cent Shi'a minority, Pakistan nevertheless considered Iran as a brother Muslim country and the Shah of Iran was considered Pakistan's great friend and benefactor. Sometime around 1960, thousands of flag-waving school children lined the streets of Karachi to greet him. I was one of them.

But Ayatollah Khomenei's Islamic revolution in 1979, and the Soviet invasion of Afghanistan in the same year, set major realignments into motion. As Iran exited the U.S. orbit, Pakistan moved close to the Americans to fight the Soviets. With financial assistance from Saudi Arabia, Pakistan and the U.S. created and armed the mujahideen. The CIA placed advertisements in journals and newspapers across the world, inviting the most hardened of Islamic fighters to participate in holy war against communist infidels. With full backing from the U.S. General Zia-ul-Haq proceeded to create a hyper-religious fighting force and to drive Pakistani society down the road of Islamization. Although this worked brilliantly and eventually drove the Soviets out of Afghanistan, the dynamics that eventually led to 9/11 had been put in place.

Iran too supported the mujahideen. But it supported the Tajik Northern Alliance while Pakistan supported the Pashtun Taliban. As religion assumed centrality in matters of state in both Pakistan and Iran, rifts appeared and then steadily widened. In the wake of the Soviet pullout from Afghanistan, the Taliban took over Kabul in 1996. An initial selective killing of Shi'as was followed by a massacre of more than 5000 in Bamiyan province. Iran soon amassed 300,000 troops at the Afghan border and threatened to attack the Pakistan-supported Taliban government. Today Iran accuses Pakistan of harbouring terrorist anti-Iran groups such as the Jundullah on its soil and of freely allowing the Lashkar-e-Jhangvi and its associates to ravage Pakistan's Shi'a minority. Farsi is no longer taught in Pakistani schools. As religion assumed centrality in matters of state in both Pakistan and Iran, doctrinal rifts widened.

AN UNCOMFORTABLE RELATIONSHIP

When the Iranian nuclear program eventually revived after the Iran–Iraq war, help was sought from its neighbour, Pakistan. At that time, relations were reasonably good—the Taliban had yet to take over Afghanistan. Clandestine nuclear cooperation with Iran, initiated by Dr Abdul Qadeer Khan and his network, began sometime in the late 1980s and lasted until the mid-1990s. This was followed by similar sales to Libya that continued till 2003 and the exposure of the network, leading to a public confession by A.Q. Khan in January 2004. On 31 August 2009, Dr Khan—who had earlier admitted to supplying centrifuges to Iran—told a television interviewer in Karachi that, at the time, the thinking had been that if Iran succeeds in 'acquiring nuclear technology, we will be a strong bloc in the region to counter international pressure. Iran's nuclear capability will neutralize Israel's power.'[12] According to *The Washington Post*, Khan's assistance, 'allowed Iran to leapfrog over several major technological hurdles to make its own enriched uranium.'[13]

But making money, not promoting ideological goals, lay behind Dr Khan's help to Iran. As a nuclear entrepreneur, who has launched his own political party and now aspires towards becoming the president of Pakistan, he was not inclined towards needless discrimination. Those who could pay got his wares. [In 2011, Khan made available documents that he says support his claim that he personally transferred more than $3 million in payments by North Korea to senior officers in the Pakistani military who, he says, subsequently approved his sharing of technical know-how and equipment with Pyongyang.[14] If the released letter is genuine, then this episode demonstrates a remarkable instance of corruption rather than ideological resonance with godless North Korea.]

The official position taken by Pakistan on the matter is that it defends Iran's right to nuclear technology as a 'responsible' nation and therefore 'doesn't expect Iran to pursue nuclear-weapons capability.'[15] The secret help provided by the A.Q. Khan network appears to be a matter of the past. But, even at that time, subterranean voices within the Pakistani establishment were speaking against giving nuclear support to Iran. Pressure from the United States was certainly partly the reason. The discomfort of dealing with a Shi'ite state, however, was intense.

These suspicions were confirmed by confidential American cables revealed by Wikileaks and highlighted by the Pakistani English daily *Dawn*.[16] The cables detail Pakistan's efforts to dissuade Iran from pursuing its weapons program. Gen. Pervez Musharraf, Prime Minister Shaukat Aziz and Foreign Minister Khurshid Kasuri held at least seven meetings, whether face-to-face or by telephone, with the Iranians. There were eleven meetings with the Americans in 2006 alone. Pakistani officials also served as interlocutors between Iran and the United States.

In a May 2006 cable about Gen. Musharraf's meeting with Iranian First Vice President Parviz Davoodi it is reported that, 'according to Kasuri, Musharraf told the visitors that Iran should stop all efforts to enrich uranium now, adding that Tehran was making life difficult for its neighbour, Pakistan'.[17] Later that year, Kasuri would tell the Americans that over the past three years he had 'made it his mission to persuade Tehran not to provoke a conflict over Iran's nuclear program thus endangering regional—and Pakistan's domestic security.' In an April 2006 meeting with U.S. Senator Chuck Hagel, Kasuri provided a list of other reasons why Pakistan was so keen to prevent Iran from acquiring nuclear weapons. 'We are the only Muslim country [with such weapons],' he said, 'and don't want anyone else to get it.'

Later that month, when the U.S. announced its willingness to join the EU-3 (France, Germany, United Kingdom) in talks with Iran, the American ambassador informed Kasuri that 'the U.S. expects Pakistan to vigorously support the U.S. action. Kasuri agreed, saying that he would ensure that the MFA (Ministry of Foreign Affairs) issued a statement of support immediately. 'By 11pm that night a statement had been issued, and Kasuri followed this up with a call to the Iranian foreign minister urging Iran 'to announce an immediate suspension of its enrichment program in order to give dialogue a chance.' This phone call was, again, promptly reported to the American ambassador, who commented that, 'Kasuri may be wildly worried that he has gone out on a limb by endorsing the Secretary [of State's] statement so vigorously.'

To conclude, while revolutionary Iran supported the notion of an Islamic bomb, it did not benefit much from the concept. Even if Iran had not received a Chinese-origin bomb design from A.Q. Khan, the six-decade-old physics of implosion devices would be no mystery to Tehran's sophisticated nuclear scientists who are superior in skill and knowledge relative to their Pakistani counterparts. The transfer of centrifuges from Pakistan was strictly on a cash basis, and limited to the older P-1 types. The main sectarian division within Islam—between Sunni and Shi'a—had proved too big a hurdle for effective nuclear cooperation.

IRAN-SAUDI RIVALRY

Pakistan's thinking on the Iranian bomb issue is primarily influenced by Saudi concerns rather than American desires. It knows that if Iran chooses to cross the nuclear threshold, the Saudis would seek to follow suit. Pakistan would then have to choose sides between a Shi'a neighbour and a Sunni state that has been its benefactor.

From the other side of the Persian Gulf, several countries had watched Iran's nuclear progress with trepidation and hostility. Israel and Saudi Arabia are among them. Sunni Saudi Arabia sees Shi'a Iran as its primary enemy. Since the Iranian Revolution in 1979, both the Saudis and the Iranians have vied for influence in the Muslim world. Saudi Arabia has the world's largest petroleum reserves; Iran the second largest. Saudi Arabia is the biggest buyer of advanced U.S. weapons and is run by expatriates. It is America's golden goose, protected by U.S. military might. But fiercely nationalist Iran expelled Western oil companies in 1951 and built up its own scientific base.

As theocracies, Saudi Arabia and Iran are protectors and promoters of their respective theologies, and locked in an irresolvable conflict that began with the death of the Prophet of Islam some fifteen centuries ago. Saudi Arabia is Custodian of the two most sacred holy sites, the Haram Sharif in Makkah, the birth place of the Prophet of Islam, and where the Holy Kaaba is located—and the Masjid-e-Nabvi in Madina. It is the leader of the Sunni world, culturally conservative, and Arab. On the other hand, after the Khomeini revolution, Iran asserted itself as a Persian, Shi'a-majority state that sought to be the leader of all Muslim revolutionaries, both Shi'a and Sunni, who aspired to confront the West. Saudi Arabia has a long way to go before it can shed tribal customs, but Iran posseses a large segment of educated and forward-looking young people who enjoy more cultural freedom than most Arab countries allow. It is run, however, by a backward-looking Guardian Council of clerics who, in spite of having lost their initial revolutionary ardour, still seek to project Iranian power in Iraq, Lebanon, and Palestine.

Thanks to Wikileaks, it is now well known that that King Abdullah of Saudi Arabia had repeatedly urged the U.S. to destroy Iran's nuclear program and 'cut off the head of the snake' by launching military strikes.[18] More recently, on 8 June 2011, the influential former head of Saudi intelligence and ambassador in London and Washington, Prince Turki bin Faisal, spoke to an audience from the British and American military and security community at Molesworth Air Force base in England. It was a long speech that covered all aspects of Saudi security doctrine. Only a part of his speech was reported in the international press. Some other parts are worth a careful listen.[19]

Faisal begins by reminding his audience of why the Kingdom feels so confident today:

> She is the cradle of Islam, a religion that has today an estimated 1.2 billion adherents. Saudi Arabia represents over 20% of the combined GDP of the Middle East-North Africa (MENA) region . . . the stock market represents about 50% of the entire stock market capitalization of the MENA region. . . . Saudi Aramco, the Kingdom's national oil company, is the world's largest producer and exporter of petroleum and has by far the world's largest sustained production capacity infrastructure at about 12.5 million barrels-per-day, and also has the world's largest spare capacity currently estimated at over 4 million barrels-per-day or about 70% of global unused capacity.

Describing 'Iran as a paper tiger with steel claws,' Faisal accuses Iran of using these claws for its 'meddling and destabilizing efforts in countries with Shi'ite majorities.' After saying that, 'In a certain sense, Saudi Arabia and Iran are uniquely positioned to be at odds,' Faisal then goes on to express his country's position on nuclear weapons:

> First, it is in our interest that Iran does not develop a nuclear weapon, for their doing so would compel Saudi Arabia, whose foreign relations are now so fully measured and well assessed, to pursue policies that could lead to untold and possibly dramatic consequences. This is why, through various initiatives, we are sending messages to Iran that it is their right, as it is any nation's right, and as we ourselves are doing, to develop a civilian nuclear program, but that trying to parlay that program into nuclear weapons is a dead end.

The Saudi opposition to Israeli nuclear weapons at this meeting was characteristically mild and ritualistic:

> A Zone Free of Weapons of Mass Destruction is the best means to get Iran and Israel to give up nuclear weapons. Such a Zone must be accompanied by a rewards regime that provides economic and technical support for countries that join; plus a nuclear security umbrella guaranteed by the permanent members of the Security Council.[20]

WHAT IF IRAN GOES NUCLEAR?

Iran may someday choose to cross the threshold. Among other likely consequences, an Iranian bomb would be a powerful stimulus pushing the Kingdom of Saudi Arabia to follow and seek its own bomb. But for all its wealth, the Kingdom does not have the technical and scientific base to create a nuclear infrastructure. Too weak to defend itself and too rich to be left alone, the country has always been surrounded by those who eye its wealth. It has many universities staffed by highly paid expatriates. Tens of thousands of Saudi students have been sent to universities overseas. However, an ideological attitude unsuited to the acquisition of modern scientific skills means that there has been little success in producing a significant number of accomplished Saudi engineers and scientists.

Perforce, Saudi Arabia shall turn to Pakistan where its footprint has grown steadily since the early 1970s. Pakistan has received more aid from Saudi Arabia than any country outside the Arab world since the 1960s. A large scale migration of Pakistani workers to newly rich Arab countries, especially Saudi Arabia, brought them into contact with a conservative brand of Islam that was different from the one they knew back home. Many came back transformed. Some became vigorous proselytizers, aided by generous grants for creating madrassas (religious seminaries).

Former Saudi intelligence chief Prince Turki bin Sultan was on the mark when, speaking about Pakistan and Saudi Arabia, he said: 'It's probably one of the closest relationships in the world between any two countries.' Both countries are Sunni and conservative; both have ruling oligarchies (though one is dynastic and the other military). They were the first to recognize and support the Taliban regime in Afghanistan. Their relationship to the U.S. had a strong similarity: their populations strongly resented what they saw as a master-client relationship.

Major funding for Pakistan's nuclear program came from Saudi Arabia; it is said that suitcases of cash were brought into Pakistan from Saudi Arabia (as well as Libya). In gratitude, Bhutto renamed the city of Lyallpur as Faisalabad (after King Faisal of Saudi Arabia). The Pak–Saudi–U.S. jihad in Afghanistan was to further cement Pak–Saudi relations. Madrassas belonging to the Wahabi–Salafi school of thought exploded in numbers and enrolment. After India had tested its bomb in May 1998 and Pakistan was mulling over the appropriate response, the Kingdom's grant of 50,000 barrels of free oil a day helped Pakistan decide in favour of a tit-for-tat response and cushioned the impact of sanctions subsequently imposed by the U.S. and Europe.[21] The Saudi Defense Minister, Prince Sultan, was a VIP guest at Kahuta, where he toured its nuclear and missile facilities just before the tests. Years earlier Benazir Bhutto, the then serving prime minister, had been denied entry. Pakistani leaders, political and military, frequently travel to the Kingdom to pay homage.

The quid pro quo for the Kingdom's oil largesse has been soldiers, airmen, and military expertise. Saudi officers are trained at Pakistan's national defense colleges and the Pakistan Air Force, with its high degree of professional training, helped create the Royal Saudi Air Force. Pakistani pilots flew combat missions using Saudi jets against South Yemen in the 1970s. Saudi Arabia is said to have purchased ballistic missiles produced in Pakistan.

Should Iran actually make the bomb, Saudi Arabia, which has received missile help from Pakistan, could turn to it again for nuclear help. This does not mean outright transfer of nuclear weapons by Pakistan to Saudi Arabia. One cannot put credence on rumours that Saudis have purchased nuclear warheads stocked at Kamra Air Force Base, to be flown out at the opportune time. Surely this would certainly lead to extreme reaction from the U.S. and Europe, with no support offered by China or Russia. Moreover, even if a few weapons were smuggled out, Saudi Arabia could not claim to have these weapons. Thus their value as a nuclear deterrent would be uncertain.

Instead, the Kingdom's route to nuclear weapons is likely to be circuitous, beginning with the acquisition of nuclear reactors for electricity generation. The spent fuel from reactors reprocessed for plutonium and uranium enrichment can be pursued under cover of making fuel. Like Iran, it will have to find creative ways by which to skirt around the Nuclear Non-Proliferation Treaty—which forbids reprocessing spent fuel for military purposes. But it doubtless takes heart from the fact that the U.S. forgave India for its nuclear testing in 1998, removed sanctions, and eventually ended rewarding it with a nuclear deal. Saudi Arabia had unwillingly signed on to the NPT in 1988. Its position then was that it would be happy to sign up but only if Israel did the same. That, of course, never happened. But Saudi Arabia had no option but to follow the U.S. diktat.

The Kingdom's first steps on this path are being contemplated. In June 2011, Saudi Arabia said that sixteen nuclear reactors were to be built over the next twenty years at a cost of more than $300 billion, each reactor costing around $7 billion.[22] Arrangements are being made to offer the project for international bidding and the winning company should 'satisfy the Kingdom's needs for modern technology.' To create, run and maintain the resulting nuclear infrastructure will require importing large numbers of technical workers. Some will be brought over from western countries, as well as Russia and former Soviet Union countries. But Saudi Arabia will likely find engineering and scientific skills from Pakistan particularly desirable. As Sunni Muslims, Pakistanis would presumably be sympathetic with the kingdom's larger goals. Having been in the business of producing nuclear weapons for nearly thirty years under difficult circumstances, they would also be familiar with supplier chains for hard-to-get items needed in a weapons program. And because salaries in Saudi Arabia far exceed those in Pakistan, many qualified people could well ask for leave from their parent institutions within Pakistan's nuclear complex—PAEC, KRL, and NDC.

WHAT TO DO ABOUT NUCLEAR IRAN?

As nuclear weapons become easier to make, pre-existing conflicts are also finding a nuclear expression more easily. Iran and Saudi Arabia's present direction suggests that the historical clash between Sunni and Shi'a brands of Islam could move into the nuclear arena. Can anything be done to prevent this?

In a more reasonable world, Iran could be dissuaded from its path by using the force of argument alone. However, the world's pre-eminent power, the United States, lacks the moral authority to act effectively in the domain of nuclear proliferation. Whereas it harshly threatens Iran for trying to develop nuclear weapons it has rewarded, to various degrees, other countries—Israel, India, Pakistan, and North Korea—that have developed such weapons surreptitiously. Also not readily forgotten is the fact that initial nuclear capability was provided to Iran by the U.S. during the Shah's rule.

It is well known that the U.S. gave the green light to Israel's campaign of secret assassination of Iranian nuclear scientists, injection of the Stuxnet virus, and periodically threatens to bomb Iran. While Iran has not attacked any other country in centuries, the United States overthrew Iran's democracy in 1953 and installed a dictator who ensured that American corporations would have a near monopoly over Iranian oil. It supplied weapons to Saddam Hussein in his war against Iran, put Iran on the 'axis of evil', falsely blamed it for 9/11, flies drones over Iran, imposed sanctions, and provocatively sends its aircraft carriers up and down the Persian Gulf. In 2012 President Obama announced new financial and commercial sanctions on companies dealing with Iran. The EU also decided to cooperate with the U.S. and ban Iran's oil exports. But nuclear nationalism and Persian pride could still override the pain of sanctions.

Irans' quest for the bomb does it—and the world—no service. The world certainly needs fewer nuclear weapons, not more. So then what are the alternatives?

One is that of war. An Israeli attack—whether aided or not by the U.S.—could certainly stop Iran's nuclear efforts for a few years, or perhaps a decade or two. But it would have catastrophic consequences and transform the Middle East into a war-zone for the foreseeable future. Dynamics would be unleashed over which the U.S. and Israel will have little control. Sunni–Shi'a divisions would be temporarily pushed aside (Muslims tend to unite against a common enemy). While the third Gulf War would surely devastate Iran, today it is in a position to inflict much greater damage on the U.S. than were Iraq or Libya. The U.S. could plunge into an economic crisis the likes of which it has not seen before. The last bits of its post-withdrawal strategy from Afghanistan would be shredded to pieces.

A second alternative is to vigorously pursue nuclear negotiations. The U.S. has tried threats and coercion with Iran, but never the power of humility. Had American leaders acknowledged having wronged Iran in 1953 by engineering the coup that brought back the Shah, Iranian nuclear nationalism might have been significantly weakened. It remains to be seen whether diplomacy can now succeed.

On the pessimistic side, the Iranian regime could become obstinate and defiant, and become totally insensitive to sanctions or any other kind of punishment. In that case Iran could become the world's 10th nuclear state in a few years. Unwelcome as having yet another set of nuclear issues would be, it would not necessarily be catastrophic. In all likelihood nuclear Iran would moderate its dangerous rhetoric and, like other existing global nuclear rivalries, this one too could be managed. One observes that Iranians have steadily become more pragmatic and less revolutionary since 1997. Quite possibly, in time their nuclear weapons will become like everybody else's.

However unwelcome Iran's bomb (and the Sunni bomb that could someday follow), it is far better to live with potential dangers than to knowingly create a holocaust through military action. Tel Aviv and Washington must never even contemplate an attack; to do so would set the world on fire.

REFERENCES

1. Zulfikar Ali Bhutto, *If I Am Assassinated*, 1979.
2. Brassey's Defense Yearbook 1995, p. 276, Centre for Defense Studies, London.
3. 'Pakistan and India under the Nuclear Shadow', http://www.youtube.com/watch?v=EeBRVFxe5oQ
4. 'Pakistani Nuclear Shield for Makkah & Madina: Hafiz Saeed', Pak Defense Unit, 28 May 2012.
5. 'Bombshell—Obama has run out of time to negotiate with Iran', New Republic, Henry Sokolski and Greg Jones, 7 December 2010.
6. 'An Iran option the U.S. prefers to ignore'. *Asia Times Online*, 17 March 2006.
7. 'The Shah's Atomic Dreams', Abbas Milani, *Foreign Policy*, 29 December 2010.
8. This generated a major controversy at MIT *c.*1975 and eventually a faculty referendum was held which vetoed the MIT administration insistence on this point.
9. Milani, op. cit.
10. Quoted in 'Sanctions Won't Stop Iran', by Selig Harrison, *The Washington Post*, 2 October 2007.
11. 'Pakistan Claims It Has New Missile', *The Washington Post*, 2 June 1998.

12. 'A.Q. Khan boasts of helping Iran's nuclear programprogram', *The Telegraph*, 10 September 2009.
13. 'Nuclear Program in Iran Tied To Pakistan—Complex Network Acquired Technology and Blueprints', *The Washington Post*, 21 December 2003.
14. 'Pakistan's nuclear-bomb maker says North Korea paid bribes for know-how', R. Jeffrey Smith, *The Washington Post*, 6 July 2011.
15. 'Iran Sanctions: Why Pakistan Won't Help', *Time*, 14 September 2009.
16. 'Musharraf govt pushed Iran to abandon N-weapons programprogram', Madiha Sattar, *Dawn*, 9 July 2011.
17. All quotes in this section refer to Wikileaked documents: *Dawn*, 9 July 2011.
18. 'Saudi king urged U.S. to attack Iran', WikiLeaks, Arshad Mohammed and Ross Colvin, http://www.reuters.com/article/2010/11/29/us-wikileaks-usa-idUSTRE6AP06Z20101129
19. 'A Saudi National Security Doctrine for the Next Decade', speech by Prince Turki Al-Faisal, Royal Air Force Base, Molesworth, UK. Date: 8 June 2011. Obtained through private circulation.
20. Ibid
21. 'Saudi Arabia: Nervously Watching Pakistan', Brookings Report, 28 January 2008. This was confirmed to me in private conversation with Sartaj Aziz, finance minister of Pakistan in 1988 at the time of the nuclear tests.
22. '16 Saudi nuclear reactors to cost $300 billion', *Arab News*, 1 June 2011.

CHAPTER 8

POST BIN LADEN: THE SAFETY AND SECURITY OF PAKISTAN'S NUCLEAR ARSENAL

Pervez Hoodbhoy

There is great concern across the world about the security of Pakistan's nuclear weapons, and Pakistan goes to great lengths to assure the world that its weapons will not fall into the hands of extremist groups. This chapter assesses the threat to Pakistan's nuclear weapons from within the country. In this context it will be important to understand the forces that shape attitudes within the Pakistan military, as well as those which are operative within the general public.

Broadly speaking, Pakistan's nuclear weapons face four categories of potential threats:

- From India and the United States: either independently or together. Israel is a distant possibility but not to be ruled out.
- From outside: Islamic militants attacking a nuclear storage site or facility with the purpose of capturing a nuclear weapon, or a sizeable amount of HEU that could be fashioned into a crude nuclear device.
- From inside: Islamic elements in the army who have responsibility for protecting and operating nuclear sites, facilities, or fissile materials.
- From inside and outside: a collaborative effort.

Before 11 September 2001, there was little urgency to safeguard Pakistan's nuclear weapons. But, faced with George W. Bush's ultimatum, General Pervez Musharraf had to choose between 'are you with us or against us'. Thereupon he made his famous U-turn and abandoned the Taliban. Acceding to U.S. demands was necessary, said Musharraf in his public address to the nation; else Pakistan would have lost its nuclear assets and its Kashmir cause.[1] The weapons that were supposed to defend Pakistan now had to be defended.

The subsequent history is well-known: efforts to persuade Mullah Omar refused to break with Al Qaeda failed, and Pakistan joined the U.S. in its 'war against terror'. Foreseeing opposition to this new alliance, Musharraf removed two of his close former associates. Both were strongly Islamist generals: the head of Pakistan's ISI intelligence agency, Lt. General Mehmood Ahmed, and Deputy Chief of Army Staff, General Muzaffar Hussain Usmani. Multiple new dangers were created. Although the government insisted that its nuclear weapons were safe, it did not take chances. Several weapons were reportedly airlifted to various safer and more isolated locations within the country.

Keeping nuclear weapons away from predators is now an overriding concern for the Pakistan Army, which is the custodian of Pakistan's nuclear weapons. Who could these predators be and why would they want nuclear weapons?

It is likely that those currently fighting the Pakistan Army—Muslim extremists of various persuasions with various levels of sophistication and weaponry—want the bomb. Their motives can only be guessed. Some may want a weapon, perhaps deliverable by truck or ship rather than by aircraft or missile, for use against some U.S. or European city. Targets could also include Western economic interests in the Gulf and neighbouring areas. But other groups may consider attacking an Indian or Pakistani city desirable. This is not implausible: truck bombs have been frequently set off in crowded city locales in Pakistan. There is no obvious taboo against the use of a larger bomb in a South Asian city, perhaps hidden inside a container truck. This would not only be logistically easier but could ignite total war between Pakistan and India. Such a goal would be consistent with the apocalyptic vision of Al Qaeda type groups which have, as a matter of strategy, frequently targeted other Muslims (as well as Shi'as or those considered infidels). In the extremist mindset, it is preferable if only enemies are killed but collateral Muslim deaths are acceptable. On this matter, one notes that Osama bin Laden appears to be a man of peace when compared to his bloody-minded deputy, Aiman Al-Zawahiri.[2]

Recognizing that new concerns had to be addressed, General Pervez Musharraf formally instituted a nuclear command and con-trol mechanism in February 2000. This comprised of the National Command Authority (NCA), Strategic Plans Division (SPD), and Strategic Forces Command. The SPD acts as a secretariat for the National Command Authority (NCA) and has a security division with a counter-intelligence network. Employing at least 12,000 personnel, the SPD has physical custody of the weapons. Through one of its outreach publications, *Pakistan Defense*, it provides the following self-profile:

PAKISTAN'S NUCLEAR CONTROLS*

- 10 member National Command Authority in charge of all Nuclear Facilities.
- The president will be the authority's chairman and the prime minister its vice-chairman. The authority will include ministers of foreign affairs, defense, interior, chairman of the Joint Chiefs of Staff Committee, chiefs of army, navy and air force, and director-general of the Strategic Plans Division. The director-general of the Strategic Plans Division will be the authority's secretary.
- Standard 'Two Man Rule' to authenticate access to nuclear release codes.
- Nuclear Warheads 'de-mated' from missiles or bomb casings, and components are to be put into operation only with the consent of a National Command Authority.
- Pakistan has developed its own version of 'Permissive Action Links', or PALs, a sophisticated type of lock the U.S. uses to prevent unauthorised launching.

---

* http://www.defence.pk/forums/wmd-missiles/

- A comprehensive, intrusive Personnel Reliability System (along the lines of one in the U.S.) that monitors employees, before, during and after employment.
- A ten-thousand-member Security Force, led by a two-star General, dedicated to guarding the Nuclear facilities.
- Possible 'phony bunkers and dummy warheads' to deter raids, by internal and external threats.
- Possibly between 100 to 200 nuclear warheads (Number of Missile Delivery Systems unknown).

Publically, Pakistan has consistently denied that its nuclear weapons have ever been under threat. On many occasions the Foreign Ministry has emphatically stated that, 'our [nuclear] assets are 100 per cent secure, under multiple custody.' In June 2011, Interior Minister Rehman Malik went a step further by declaring them to be '200 per cent safe'.[3]

Trust us, says the SPD. But the crux of the problem lies in the following: whatever the procedures and equipment Pakistan may adopt, they can only be as good as the men who operate them. Mindsets and intentions matter more than anything else. Certainly better weapons—or more personnel deputed to protect him—could not have prevented Governor Salman Taseer from being gunned down by his own security guard.

THE ENEMY WITHIN

At one level every country that possesses nuclear weapons is a feared entity because of the catastrophic destruction that it could unleash against an adversary. This could be by design, and may be initiated by extreme emotions or fears existing in a severe crisis. But some wars in history have happened although neither side wanted it. Human error, misjudgment, and miscalculation are impossible to rule out. This could be catastrophic if countries also have nuclear weapons. During the Cold War it was seen that in spite of every possible precaution, false information can be provided by radar and other detection systems, aircraft carrying nuclear weapons can crash, test missiles can veer off course, and so forth. These are 'normal' fears. But Pakistan must deal with another possibility as well: that of nuclear weapons or fissile material escaping the protective custody of the SPD and the Pakistan Army. The fear of loose weapons comes from the fact that Pakistan's armed forces—army, navy, and air force—harbour a hidden enemy within their ranks. Today all bases, installations, headquarters, and residential colonies are protected by massive barricades and sand-bagged machine gun nests. But this has not been enough. Those wearing the cloak of religion freely walk in and out of top security nuclear installations every day.

The fear of the insider is ubiquitous and well-founded. Pakistan's current crop of generals know they are faced with Islamic militant groups fixated upon attacking both America and India, and a heavily Islamicized rank and file brimming with seditious thoughts. Some want to kill their superior officers; they achieved near success when General Musharraf was targeted twice by air force and army officers in 2003. A military court sentenced the mutineers to death, and a purge of officers and men associated with militants was ordered. But in a spectacular jail break at Bannu in May 2012, Musharraf's would-be assassins escaped a death sentence together with at least 384 other prisoners.[4] It is also reported that prison guards stood aside and then raised slogans in support of the Taliban attackers and imposition of Shar'ia law.

The Pakistani military officer who once strode proudly in uniform in public is now restricted to wearing his uniform in the cantonment areas only. The directive to not wear military uniforms was officially given to personnel following numerous assassinations and assassination attempts on them. Even though the military continues to be the most powerful force in the country, its public profile has had to be substantially lowered.

Islamabad's residents recall the times when the Pakistan Day parades and fly-pasts were held in the capital and a full range of armoured carriers, tanks, and missiles were displayed. The tank treads would damage road surfaces, which were therefore carpeted with stronger and more expensive materials. The armoured columns passed by the presidency where especially constructed viewing arrangements had been made for thousands of spectators. But post-9/11, fearing attack by the Taliban or other extremists, or perhaps an attack of the type that led to the Egyptian President Anwar Sadat's assassination in 1981, such parades suddenly stopped. The implausible excuse offered was austerity and cost.

Recently an army enthusiast wistfully remarked: 'Once remembered for an annual graceful congregation of National Armed Forces marking Pakistan Day with a full-fledged display of armaments, Parade Avenue at D-Chowk in the Red Zone area adjacent to the President House on Jinnah Avenue in Islamabad presented a deserted look with a few policemen around heavy barricades and barbed wires.'[5]

Quite naturally, the army has sought to downplay the high level of radicalization within the ranks. But some insider attacks have been impossible to hide. Extremists led by Dr Usman, formerly of the Army Medical Corps, demonstrated their strength with a brazen attack in October 2009 on the General Headquarters of the Pakistan Army in Rawalpindi.[6] This was followed by a gruesome massacre on 4 December 2009 of forty-two army personnel and their family members at the Parade Ground mosque adjacent to the General Head Quarters (GHQ).[7] Those eventually traced to have masterminded the attack turned out to have links within the Army.**

There have been devastating attacks on ISI regional headquarters in Rawalpindi, Multan, Peshawar, and Faisalabad. The suicide bombers had apparently been informed by insiders.

Yet another dramatic exhibition of extremist penetration was provided by the attack on Karachi's Mehran naval base. Three weeks after the U.S. raid on Osama bin Laden's house in Abbottabad on

---

**Among those picked up for this and other bombings by the intelligence agencies was my former colleague at Quaid-e-Azam University, Raja Ehsan Aziz. Known for his close links with the Jamaat-i-Islami, Aziz often bragged that he had fought along with the mujahideen in Afghanistan against the Soviets. His wife ran a *dars* school for women and is a well-known journalist. See, 'The curious case of Amira Ehsan', *The Friday Times*, 24–30 June 2011.

2 May 2011, which resulted in his killing, the Tehrik-e-Taliban Pakistan (TTP) claimed the Mehran naval base attack as revenge for the loss of a great *mujahid* (it also claimed responsibility for an attack upon the Saudi Arabian embassy in Karachi a few days later as revenge).[8] As millions of Pakistanis watched on their TV sets, flames devoured one of the two $36 million aircraft bought by the Pakistan Navy, an anti-submarine P3C Orion. The number of attackers remains disputed but is said to be between six and twenty. However, they had successfully battled hundreds of security forces for eighteen hours, a fact that pointed to both the ineptness of the defenders and the hidden hand inside which replenished the attacker's ammunition supplies. Subsequently, the military authorities arrested from Lahore a former Special Services Group commando of the Pakistan Navy, Kamran Ahmed, and his younger brother Zaman Ahmed.[9] Attempting to disprove that this was a mutiny, a hurriedly convened official inquiry claimed that DNA tests 'proved' the attackers at Mehran Base were *not* Pakistanis. To quote: 'The DNA test result revealed that four terrorists who attacked PNS Mehran Base in Karachi were foreigners, officials said on Saturday. . . . Those terrorists were Anglo-Indians and have blood relations, could be cousins.'[10] But, naval officials told the Standing Committee on Defense of the National Assembly during an in-camera briefing that 'insiders' were involved in the attack.[11]

It is difficult to find another example where the defense apparatus of a modern state has been rendered so vulnerable by the threat posed by military insiders. Following repeated attacks on naval personnel and facilities, fear of a terrorist attack caused Pakistan's fleet of modern warships to flee their home base in Karachi in June 2011.[12] The Navy did not deny this; for months the ships did not return. When asked to comment on this, retired Vice Admiral Tanvir Ahmed said that one of the golden rules in warfare, especially when facing a threat from an unknown enemy, is to disperse your assets in as many bases as you can. 'Never put all your eggs in one basket,' he said.[13] Wise words, perhaps, but surely a fighting force unsafe and insecure in its own home is certainly not well equipped to fight wars hundreds of miles out to sea.

In spite of the fact that most radicalized officers are often quietly discharged and do not come into public view, it is hard to stop information from leaking out. Some senior military officials have proven ties to religious extremists. For example, motivated by a cleric, Qari Saifullah, a coup attempt was initiated against Benazir Bhutto in 1995 and the Chief of Army Staff, General Waheed Kakar. The plotters, Major General Zahirul Islam Abbasi and Brigadier Mustansir Billa, were arrested together with thirty-six other army officers. More recently, in June 2011, the army investigated Brigadier Ali Khan for his ties to militants of the Hizb-ut-Tahrir, a radical organization that seeks to establish a global caliphate and believes its mission should begin from nuclear Pakistan. The highest ranking officer so far arrested, Ali Khan belongs to a family with three generations of military service and is said to have a strong professional record. Reportedly, General Kayani feared a backlash and was initially reluctant to take this step. Four army majors were also investigated.

Although no nuclear facility has yet been attacked by extremists, recent developments suggest that this could be just a matter of time. A high ranking military officer currently serving at the Khushab nuclear complex was quoted in a Pakistani newspaper as saying that 'D.G. Khan houses one of the largest nuclear facilities in the country, and has faced the first-ever serious security threat from the Tehreek-e-Taliban Pakistan (TTP).' The police is said to have recovered bodies of three suicide bombers who accidentally detonated themselves in a building about 30 km away from the Khushab site. When the TTP attacked the Kamra Air Base in August 2012, they had also announced their intent to attack nuclear installations in as revenge for the killing of their South Punjab head, Abdul Ghaffar Qaisrani. Newspapers that take a strong anti-American and pro-bomb position, and which generally promote conspiracy theories, were quick to suggest that the TTP had been infiltrated by 'outside elements'. But this ostrich-like act is merely yet another futile effort to deny reality.

PAKISTAN'S CULTURAL REVOLUTION

The emergence of violent Islamist groups, both pro- and anti-establishment, is a product of the steady radicalization of Pakistan's society and military. Almost invariably this is blamed on to General Zia-ul-Haq and his impositions of orthodox Islam. While there is little doubt that he had accelerated this process, the roots actually lie deeper.

Islam created Pakistan but religion now divides Pakistan. Fuelled by ideological passions, diverse social and religious formations inhabit different parts of the country. This tension within Pakistani society and the military owes fundamentally to an underlying confusion about national purpose and identity. Six decades after Partition, key questions stand unresolved. Are we Arabs or South Asians? Is there a Pakistani culture? Should the country be run by Islamic law? Can Hindus, Christians, and Ahmadis be proper Pakistanis? In a bid to definitively resolve these existential questions, for decades Pakistani school children have learned a linguistically flawed (but catchy) rhetorical question. The question is chanted together with its answer: *Pakistan ka matlab kya? La illaha illala*! (What is the meaning of Pakistan? There is no god but Allah!). But the problem remains unresolved.

The migration of Pakistani workers to the Middle East in the early 1970s was a first major impetus for change. It brought millions into contact with a kind of Islam different from the one they had known. Piety was redefined, and religious practices changed. Mosque preachers received grants from the Saudis to supplement or establish madrassas. Thus, Wahabi and Salafi ideology, with the help of petro-dollars, was imported into a culture that had been carried on from pre-Partition and was a fusion of subcontinental, Sufi and Barelvi influence.

Wahabism, which originated in the eighteenth century in Arabia, is as a revivalist movement initiated by Muhammad ibn Abd al-

Wahhab (1703–1792). Wahabis are ultra conservative in their outlook and believe in a strictly formal and ritualistic religion, promoting a view of Islam that is diametrically opposite to the Sufi view—which considers religion largely a matter between Man and Maker. In its early years, Wahabism succeeded in destroying almost all shrines, together with historical monuments and relics dating to the early days of Islam for fear that they might take the status of shrine worship.

Also influential are the Salafis—who seek the 'purification' of Islam by returning to the pure form practiced in the time of Prophet Muhammad [PBUH] and his Companions. Among the most extreme manifestation of Salafism is Takfir-wal-Hijra. In 1996 the group is said to have plotted to assassinate Osama bin Laden for being too lax a Muslim. Pakistani Deobandis, who were the closest ideologically to the Wahabis and Salafis, generally take a harder line than Indian Deobandis. They do not condemn suicide bombings; are strongly pro-Taliban; and many hard-core ones are heavily armed. Muslims of the Deobandi-Salafi-Wahabi persuasion decry the syncretism of popular Islam, claiming that it arises from innovation (*bidat*) and ignorance of Qura'nic teachings.

Inspired by hard-line groups and the search for Islamic roots, many young Pakistanis have adopted a pseudo Arab identity: the 'abaya' (coat like outer garment) for women did not belong to the South Asian wardrobe nor to the Urdu lexicon but is now ubiquitous on campuses; the Arabic 'Allah' has replaced the Persian 'Khuda' in ordinary discourse; music and dancing at weddings are discouraged; and religious rituals are given disproportionate importance.

Drawing conclusions from a 2009 British Council survey conducted on the role of religion in Pakistani society, *The Daily Telegraph,* a British newspaper, says:

One-third of Pakistanis aged 18 to 29 who were surveyed believe in Shar'ia, or Islamic law; half have 'a great deal of confidence' in religious-based education; and more than 60 per cent have faith in the army—the only widely trusted institution of the state. They believe they do not have adequate skills for the workplace and little anticipation of being able to compete fairly for jobs. The report found that three-quarters of respondents identified themselves foremost as Muslims, with just 14 per cent describing themselves primarily as a citizen of Pakistan. Only 10 per cent have a great deal of confidence in national or local government, the courts or the police and just one third advocate democracy for the country.[14]

Corroborating the above survey, a survey conducted by *The Express Tribune*[15] found that a majority of Pakistan's internet users say that they consider themselves as 'Muslims first' (49%), 'Pakistani' second (28%), while 23% voted as 'other'.

In the Pakistan military, the Tablighi Jamaat religious movement, which formally abjures politics,[16] has made big inroads and may well be the most influential of all religious organizations. Headquartered in Raiwind near Lahore, it has grown enormously. Annual congregations rank in size second only to that of the Haj pilgrimage. With an estimated following of 70–80 million people of Deobandi persuasion, it is spread across Southwest Asia, Southeast Asia, Africa, Europe, and North America. In France it has about 100,000 followers and by 2007, Tabligh members were situated at 600 of Britain's 1350 mosques. Tablighis also despise mystical Islam, which they equate with idolatry and ancestral worship.

The Tablighi Jamaat represents only the tip of the religious iceberg. Attendance at mosques has skyrocketed, as has adherence to prayers, fasting, and other rituals. In Pakistan, an observer who grew up in a military family notes that, 'until the late 1970s, the mosques located at the armed forces bases (military, air force and navy) were 90 per cent Ahle Sunnat Wal Jamaa't (Sufi), 8 per cent Deobandi, and 0 per cent Salafi. Currently 85 per cent of the mosques are Deobandi or Salafi, and less than 10 per cent are Ahle Sunnat Wal Jama'at.[17] This is an enormous transition, and has strong implications for what Pakistan's military will become in the future. Steadily, the culture of the mosque is defeating the culture of the shrine.

MILITANT GROUPS

Pakistan's Army is confronted today by a multitude of hostile Islamist militant groups, each with its own agenda. Their genesis can most often be traced back to the early 1980s U.S.-backed crusade against Soviet Russia. Pakistan thereafter became a central hub attracting a multitude of Islamists from Europe to West and Central Asia to Indonesia. Since there were multiple agendas, Pakistan morphed from the bastion of anti-communism and anti-atheism that it once was into something far less coherent. It would be a mistake to think that today's militant groups only draw upon madrassa graduates—there are large numbers of school and college graduates who fill their ranks.***

All groups target the 'U.S. Empire', which explains why Pakistan was the refuge of choice for Osama bin Laden and the ones that received the greatest backing from Pakistan's establishment, such as the Hizb-ul-Mujahideen (HuM), Lashkar-e-Tayyaba (LeT), and Jaish-e-Muhammad (JeM) focus on freeing Kashmir from India. They have not openly challenged the state and appear to be dependent on it for financial and logistical support. Still other groups, like the Lashkar-i-Jhangvi and Sipah-e-Sahaba, are sectarian warriors seeking to purge Islam of the Shi'a and other minorities, while the fighters of Khatm-e-Nabuwat desire to exterminate 'Qadianis', the slur they use to denigrate the Ahmadiyya sect, whose nineteenth-century founder was born in the town of Qadian. Sectarian outfits dispatch suicide bombers to target mosques, shrines and markets, murdering religious leaders and prominent figures in the various minority communities. They are united only in support of the killing of such 'blasphemers' and those who seek to protect them. Pakistan's Christian, Hindu, and other religious

---

***Over the years, I came to know many students in my physics classes at Quaid-e-Azam University who had received military training from jihadist groups before coming to the university. These were the ones who had decided not to go further with militancy and become general job-seekers; others presumably put their training into practice.

minorities cower in fear. The rich among them have mostly fled the country.

The army's fiercest enemy today is the Tehrik-e-Taliban Pakistan (TTP). It has killed thousands of Pakistani soldiers and policemen. Displaced by an army operation from the Swat valley, it has found refuge in Afghanistan. The TTP does not appear to fully accept Mullah Omar's authority, having refused to release Colonel Imam and Brigadier Khalid Khwaja after kidnapping them from Waziristan. Colonel Imam, whose real name was Brigadier Sultan Amir Tarar, was a Pakistan army officer who served in the ISI and was responsible for training the Afghan mujahideen during the anti-Soviet jihad. Khwaja was also an ISI officer and had direct liaison with Mullah Omar. Both officers, who had retired but continued to help the militants, were killed in captivity after being accused of being Qadianis and American agents. This was a dramatic example of the virulent sectarianism that prevails within the various militant groups.

Why has Islamic radicalism become such a powerful force with the masses as well as in the Pakistan military? In part, it is due to the anger that has been generated among the Muslim populace of the Western military invasions of Muslim countries such as Palestine, Iraq, Afghanistan. Greed for natural resources has imposed U.S. hegemony in much of the Arab world and stunted their natural growth. But anger at oil-hungry imperialism cannot be the entire story. Surveys show that the U.S. is disliked more in Muslim countries than in Cuba, Iraq, and Afghanistan—all countries that have been attacked by America. A private survey carried out by a European embassy based in Islamabad found that only 4 per cent of Pakistanis polled speak well of America; 96 per cent against them. While this depends on several imponderables, the U.S. can potentially displace India as Pakistan's principal adversary.

ONE ARMY OR TWO?

In parallel with the profound social changes discussed above, the Pakistan Army's character and ethos have also changed. Post-independence, it was a tightly disciplined, modern force fashioned along British lines that could boast of non-Muslim heroes in the 1965 and 1971 wars with India. But its secular culture steadily dissipated as Gen. Zia-ul-Haq turned the army into 'a defender of Pakistan's ideological frontiers'. This oft-repeated phrase was to portend a major transformation. The culture of the army messes changed, alcohol was forbidden in the 1980s, officer's wives could no longer accompany them to official parties, and prayers were encouraged. It began to matter whether you were Shi'a or Sunni, Barelvi or Wahabi, Ahl-e-Hadith or Ahl-e-Sunnat. The last of the Ahmadis left the military, and today there are few, if any, Christians serving in the military. Recruiting stations across the country were festooned with big banners with '*Iman, Taqwa, Jihad fi Sabilillah*' (Faith, Piety and Fight for Allah) on them. Jihad, rather than defense of national borders, became a way to manage morale and draw recruits. If military personnel were questioned today whether they considered themselves primarily as soldiers of Islam or of Pakistan, one can almost guess what their answer would be. This is why such a dangerous question cannot (and perhaps should not!) be asked.

Currently, it might be more accurate to consider the Pakistan Army to be consisting of two armies. The first is headed by Gen. Kayani; let us call it Army–A/ISI–A. This army considers the protection of national borders its primary goal. It also seeks to maintain the status quo, giving the army extraordinary powers in national decision-making and financial privileges. The second, Army–B/ISI–B—is Allah's army. It is silent, subterranean, currently leaderless but inspired by the philosophy of Abul Ala Maudoodi and Syed Qutb. Possessed by radical dreams, it seeks to turn Pakistan into a state run according to the Shari'a.

The B-types are inspired by groups like the Hizb-ut-Tahrir (HuT), which claims an estimated global following of about one million. It believes that the Pakistani state must be sufficiently weakened, after which its final blitzkrieg will follow and a global caliphate will spring into being. Hizb-ut-Tahrir has been engaged in penetrating the military although the extent of penetration is unclear. In 2009, former commanding officer of Shamsi Air Force Base Colonel Shahid Bashir, a retired PAF Squadron Leader and lawyer Nadeem Ahmad Shah and U.S.-educated mechanical engineer Awais Ali Khan were arrested for their HuT connections and for leaking 'sensitive' information to this organization. As remarked earlier, the Mehran base attackers are also said to have been HuT inspired.

The B-types were unknown before Musharraf's 9/11 U-turn and were not apparent in the first year or two. But simmering tensions exploded into view in the tribal areas in the years after 9/11 when soldiers were ordered to fight a war in Waziristan, which had effectively turned into an Islamic emirate under the control of the Taliban who had fled Afghanistan after Tora Bora. Fighting co-religionists, who claimed to be engaged in jihad for Islam, was a non-starter. Morale sank, with junior army men openly wondering why they were being asked to attack their ideological comrades. Local clerics refused to conduct funeral prayers for soldiers killed in action. The 'peace accord' in North Waziristan of September 2006, where the Pakistan Army was to show its 'iron fist' softened into a pulpy handshake. In fact it turned out to be a surrender because many soldiers refused to go into battle. The reported reluctance of some military units to confront the Taliban during the 2010 South Waziristan operation is said to have shocked senior officers and limits the range of battle options in North Waziristan.

There is, of course, a strong commonality between Army–A/ISI–A and Army–B/ISI–B. Both were reared on the Two-Nation Theory, the belief of Mohammed Ali Jinnah that Hindus and Muslims could never live together in peace. Both absorb anti-Indianism during their early days in army cadet colleges at Petaro and Hasan Abdal. They also share contempt for Pakistani civilians. This attitude has resulted in Pakistan spending half its history under direct military rule.

But the differences are also significant. Most A–type officers are 'soft Islamists' who are satisfied with a fuzzy belief that Islam provides solutions to everything, that occasional prayers and ritual fasting in Ramzan is sufficient, and that Sufis and Shi'as are bonafide Muslims rather than *mushriks* (idolators) or apostates. They take the position that fundamentalism is okay, but extremism is not. For A–types, defending the Sunni states of Saudi Arabia, Bahrain, or the GCC (Gulf Cooperation Council) is not considered a priority. But, should a well-paying overseas posting in any of these countries be offered, it would be welcomed. While harbouring a dislike for U.S. policies, they are not militantly anti-American.

On the other hand, B–type officers are soldier ideologues who have travelled further down the road of Islamism. They have ensured that the preachers of Tablighi Jamaat, a supposedly non-political religious organization which has a global proselytizing mission, are allowed open access into the army. More severe in matters of religious rituals than their A–colleagues, they insist that officers and their wives be segregated at army functions. An eye is kept out for officers who secretly drink alcohol, and do not pray often enough. Their political philosophy is that Islam and the state should be inseparable. Inspired by Maulana Abul Ala Maudoodi, who preached that 7th century Arab Islam provides a complete blueprint for society and politics, they see capturing state power as a means towards creating the ideal society along the lines of the medieval Medina state. Some B–types are beardless, hence harder to detect. Even if they are fundamentally anti-science, they could be computer savvy. For them, modern technology is a tool of battle, not a triumph of the human imagination.

Generally, A–type officers trivialize the dangers posed by the other side. Mutineers are considered as isolated individuals. Thus, Mumtaz Qadri, the renegade bodyguard who murdered Punjab's Governor Salman Taseer out of religious passion, is seen as an inconvenient aberration rather than a representative of a larger subterranean force. In general, religious terrorism is seen as a passing, relatively inconsequential threat. This is in spite of the fact that such terrorism has claimed more Pakistani lives than were lost in all wars with India, and that captured soldiers are subject to extreme torture followed by a video-taped decapitation. A Taliban video showing seventeen beheaded Pakistani soldiers received scant public media coverage, and disappeared from the news coverage after a day or two.[18] It has subsequently been followed by other mass beheadings of soldiers, none of which have drawn strong reaction either in the army or the public.

The fact that the military stands divided, while obvious, is nevertheless one that must never be publically articulated. Saleem Shahzad, an investigative journalist, paid for his outspokenness with his life for revealing the existence of Al Qaeda groupings within the Pakistan Navy after the Mehran Base attack.[19] That was the first part of a two-part *Asia Times* article series. Part-two, which promised to reveal similar cells in the army and air force, was never published. Shahzad was tortured and kicked to death after being abducted from one of the most secure parts of Islamabad. His mobile phone records are said to be untraceable, and tapes of closed circuit cameras around the abduction area went mysteriously missing. If true, then his murder could not be the work of hunted organizations like the Pakistani Taliban or Al Qaeda. But then was it the ISI–A or ISI–B? Either could have been responsible but the truth may never be known. Admiral Mullen, who was the first top U.S. leader to publicly link the killing to Pakistan's government, stopped short of blaming the ISI for Saleem Shahzad's murder.[20]

THE ARMY—POPULAR BUT WEAKER

The army is far more popular in Pakistan than the country's political parties and its elected leaders. When asked whether they would prefer civilian or military control over nuclear weapons, the preference is towards the military. *The Express Tribune* columnist Aakar Patel expresses puzzlement on the army's continuing popularity:

Why is an army that imposed dictatorship on Pakistanis four times (1958, 1969, 1978 and 1999), displaced governments Pakistanis elected another three times (1990, 1993, 1996) and hanged a prime minister still popular? Why do Pakistanis love the ISI, an institution whose former chief Lt. General Asad Durrani says on oath that it meddles in elections and spent $1.6 million to see the PPP defeated? Why do

Pakistanis hold their politicians responsible for the nation's problems when Pakistan's budget, its foreign policy, its security policy and its Balochistan policy are run by the army? Why do Pakistanis like an army whose chiefs arbitrarily grant themselves extensions (since 1947, India has had 26 army chiefs, while Pakistan has had only 14) because they can?

The answer to the puzzle has two parts. First, the unapologetic theft of public assets by political leaders has seriously damaged Pakistani democracy. But surely this cannot be the whole story. The corruption of Indian politicians like Jayalalitha, Mulayam Singh Yadav, and Mayawati is legendary. They can strongly compete with Benazir Bhutto, Nawaz Sharif, or Asif Ali Zardari. Yet, their actions have not ever led to the threat of an army coup in India.

The difference is to be found elsewhere: a big majority has internalized the belief that Pakistan's enemy is purely external—India. A Pew poll[21] in 2012 found that nearly three-quarters of Pakistanis have an unfavourable view of their neighbour. Little changed from 2011 but this view was significantly up from 2006, when only 50 per cent expressed negative feelings. Only 19 per cent of Pakistanis thought the enemy was internal. Fear of religious extremists and support for army action against the Taliban, which reached a peak after the TTP briefly captured power in Swat in 2009, declined in 2011. The currently rising star of Pakistani politics, Imran Khan, has hitched his popularity to anti-Indian and anti-West attitudes.

The consequence of such views has been to encourage militarism. Therefore as of 2012—and likely to continue until something cracks—a score of Islamic militant outfits remain based in Muridke, Bahawalpur, Mansehra and elsewhere. Hafiz Saeed storms across the country making fiery speeches, while Fazlur Rahman Khalil who heads the banned Harkat-ul-Mujahidin, lives comfortably in Islamabad. Malik Ishaq, the self-professed Shi'a-killer continues his business. The mullahs of the Red Mosque (Lal Masjid), who had declared open war upon the state and engaged the Pakistan Army in

full-scale battle, have been reinstated and rewarded with the choicest
land in Islamabad for a new madrassa.

Only a razor's edge separates the Pakistan Army from the ones
they fight. By official doctrine the army supports fundamentalism
and expression of Islamic symbols. However, it is also in mortal
combat with religious extremists who have taken their faith still
more seriously and are convinced into that the army represents the
forces of *kaafir* (infidels). Thus an uncomfortable equilibrium exists
between the Pakistan Army and the various *armies of God*.

The delicate equilibrium slips, as may be expected, from time to
time. Pakistan has joined a list of countries that have suffered
blowbacks after recruiting non-state actors for accomplishing
foreign or domestic policy goals. Examples are aplenty: Contras
promoted by Ronald Reagan in Nicaragua; Tamil Tigers supported
by Rajiv Gandhi; and Bhindranwale's Khalistanis supported by Indira
Gandhi.

The attacks from within have diminished the military's moral
power and authority. Although still powerful and popular, its
authority and ability to control events have steadily slipped. Absence
of charismatic leadership, the privileges enjoyed by family members,
and the evident accumulation of property and wealth has led to overt
criticism that earlier on would have been unthinkable. In the public
perception the army lacks commitment to the values it espouses,
and has sought to double-deal both the Americans as well as the
Islamists. In September 2012, while confirming that Al Qaeda's
deputy Abu Yahya al-Libi had been killed by a drone in North
Waziristan on 4 June, Aiman Al-Zawahiri, declared that Pakistan had
a 'government for sale and an army for rent'. Many in Pakistan,
particularly among those who oppose the U.S., would agree strongly.
The army's policy of strategic duplicity has been unwittingly
unmasked time and time again. In this regard, the drone attacks
stand out.

DRONE DECEPTIONS

Officially, the army condemns drone attacks in Pakistan's tribal areas, which became no-go areas shortly after 9/11 when there was a massive cross-border influx of Mullah Omar's Talibans. But American drones have also removed some of the most ferocious of the army's enemies, such as Baitullah Mehsud who headed the TTP. Although attacks against its allies, such as the Haqqani group in North Waziristan is certainly resented, there is little question that the army sees the utility of drones when they are used against its enemies. This led the media to question the sincerity of the army's routine condemnations. WikiLeak'ed documents obtained by the English daily *Dawn*, confirmed that these suspicions were well-grounded.[22]

These secret cables, accidentally revealed, include internal American government documents showing that the drone strikes program within Pakistan had more than just tacit acceptance of the country's top military brass. In fact, as far back as January 2008, Pakistan's military was requesting the U.S. for greater drone back-up for its own military operations. In a meeting on 22 January 2008 with United States' CENTCOM (Central Command) Commander Admiral William J. Fallon, Pakistan's Army Chief General Ashfaq Kayani requested the Americans to provide 'continuous Predator coverage of the conflict area'[23] in South Waziristan where the army was conducting operations against militants. The request is detailed in a cable marked 'secret', sent by the then U.S. Ambassador Anne Patterson on 11 February 2008. Around 3–4 March, in a meeting with U.S. Chairman Joint Chiefs of Staff Admiral Mike Mullen, Kayani was asked for his help 'in approving a third Restricted Operating Zone for U.S. aircraft over the FATA.' The request—detailed in a cable sent from the U.S. Embassy in Islamabad on 24 March clearly indicates that two 'corridors' for U.S. drones had already been approved earlier. Instead of acclaiming that drones were an effective weapon against a common enemy, it instead chose safety by hiding its role and criticizing the Americans instead.

Until finally ordered to be closed down in December 2011, drone bases had been located at several places inside Pakistan, such as Jacobabad and the Shamsi Air Base in Balochistan.[24] Unmanned Aerial Vehicles (UAV's) are slow moving targets, easily destroyed by Pakistan's supersonic fighter aircraft, or perhaps by ground-to-air missiles if supplied secretly to the Taliban (this possibility was hinted at by Dr A.Q. Khan in September 2012 while speaking at a rally organized by his newly-formed party's supporters). Their unhindered operation over Pakistani skies would have been impossible without the army's consent.

Other confidential American diplomatic cables, also obtained by *Dawn*, revealed that collaboration with the U.S., strenuously denied by the army, was in fact true and that U.S. special operation forces had been embedded with Pakistani troops for intelligence gathering by the summer of 2009. They were subsequently deployed for joint operations in Pakistani territory by September 2009. Ambassador Anne Patterson reported to the State Department in May 2009 that, 'We have created Intelligence Fusion cells with embedded U.S. Special Forces with both SSG and Frontier Corps (Bala Hisar, Peshawar) with the Rover equipment ready to deploy.'

But cooperation with the Americans was sharply limited. It was confined to the top tiers, was uncertain, had to be deniable, and often some in the military leadership were unaware of what position had to be taken. The tenuous nature of the alliance became acutely obvious once Osama bin Laden came into American cross hairs.

BIN LADEN AT KAKUL

On the midnight of 2 May 2011 an elite squad of helicopter-borne American Navy SEALs quietly slipped into Pakistan from Afghanistan a little past midnight. They found Osama bin Laden inside his house in Abbotabad near the Pakistan Military Academy at Kakul, killed him and then dispatched him to his watery grave hours later. It was only when the Americans had exited Pakistan's airspace that air defenses were scrambled.

As the story broke on Pakistani news channels, the elected government shuddered. Too weak, corrupt and inept to take initiatives, it awaited instructions. The Foreign Office and government officials appeared tongue-tied for many hours after U.S. President Obama had announced the success of the U.S. mission. The silence was finally broken when the Foreign Office declared that, 'Osama bin Laden's death illustrates the resolve of the international community including Pakistan to fight and eliminate terrorism.'[25] Hours later, Prime Minister Yousuf Raza Gilani described the killing as a 'great victory'. Thereupon, Pakistan's High Commissioner to the UK, Wajid Shamsul Hasan, rushed to claim credit: 'Pakistan's government was cooperating with American intelligence throughout and they had been monitoring [bin Laden's] activities with the Americans, and they kept track of him from Afghanistan, Waziristan to Afghanistan and again to North Waziristan.'[26]

But this welcoming stance was reversed hours later once the Pakistan Army had decided to condemn the raid. Praising bin Laden's killing was now out of the question—rapid somersaults followed as officials ate words uttered hours earlier. Official spokespersons became inchoate and contradictory. Without referring to the statement he had made that very morning of 3 May, Wajid Shamsul Hasan abruptly reversed his public position, now saying: 'Nobody knew that Osama bin Laden was there—no security agency, no Pakistani authorities knew about it. Had we known it, we would have done it ourselves.'[27] For thirty-six hours, Pakistan's president and prime minister awaited pointers from the army. But they knew simple obedience was not enough.

Desperate to seek help from the Obama administration and avert a military takeover, the Pakistani government, represented by Ambassador Hussain Haqqani, allegedly approached the Americans by using the services of a Washington insider, Mansoor Ijaz, and sent a secret memo to Admiral Mike Mullen. The memo, whose existence had initially been doubted, was published in November 2011, leading to the resignation of Ambassador Haqqani and the ongoing Supreme Court investigation. The case became known as

'Memogate' and stirred strong emotions. After many months, with the Zardari government's support, and evading the intelligence agencies, Haqqani somehow successfully made it back to the U.S. and resumed his teaching position at Boston University.

Faced with a disaster, the military had opted to raise anti-U.S. sentiment for having violated Pakistan's sovereignty, the question of how Osama bin Laden had found refuge was side-lined. Gen. Kayani announced his unhappiness with Zardari's government: 'Incomplete information and lack of technical details have resulted in speculations and mis-reporting. Public dismay and despondency has also been aggravated due to an insufficient formal response.'[28] The threat was thinly veiled. The government must proactively defend the army and intelligence agencies, else be warned.

A full eight days after the Osama's killing, Prime Minister Gilani broke his silence. He absolved the Inter-Services Intelligence (ISI) and army of 'either complicity or incompetence'. Before an incredulous world, he claimed in a statement that both suggestions were 'absurd'. Attempting to spread the blame, he declared in Paris, before his meeting with French President Sarkozy: 'This is an intelligence failure of the whole world, not Pakistan alone.'[29]

With criticism all around, in the days that followed, Gen. Pervez Ashfaq Kayani toured the garrisons to raise morale. He was asked why the invaders had not been challenged and destroyed, as well as who might have sheltered bin Laden who, together with Al Qaeda, were Pakistan's declared enemies. *The Express Tribune* quotes an un-named young military officer who told the army chief: 'Sir, I am ashamed of what happened in Abbottabad.' Replied General Kayani, 'So am I.'[30] He promptly went on to hold Zardari's government responsible for allowing Pakistan to get such bad press.

The bin Laden operation revealed the distrust the U.S. had in the Pakistan Army. Earlier instances had been tense as well. Leon Panetta, chief of the Central Intelligence Agency, left Islamabad fuming after an apparently fruitless meeting with Generals Kayani and Pasha.[31] According to U.S. media reports, Panetta shared with the military leadership some video and satellite imagery of militants hastily leaving two IED (Improvised Explosive Device) factories in Waziristan. It wanted Pakistan to take action against the two sites. But Panetta alleged at the meeting that the information was leaked within 24 hours of sharing and by the time the raiding teams reached those places, the militants had melted away.

In principle the bin Laden episode could have been used by the military high command to fully investigate and crack down upon the B–types within the military in Abbottabad and elsewhere. The cost would, however, have been high and the establishment preferred to remain in its comfort zone. But, it seemed, that a delicate balancing act—the doctrine of strategic duplicity—was over. Would the A–types now join up with the B–types in wanting to quit the alliance with the United States?

This almost—but not quite—happened just a few months later. On 26 November 2011, twenty-four Pakistani soldiers had been killed by NATO/American forces inside Pakistani territory at Salala, an incident which the U.S. said was by error but refused to apologize for. It said their Pakistani counterparts had supplied incorrect coordinates for their forward posts but Pakistan rejected this explanation.

Thereafter the DPC (Difah-e-Pakistan Council), a spontaneous conglomeration of jihadist and other anti-American groups, suddenly emerged and was given permission to take centre-stage in country-wide protests. This umbrella coalition of more than 30 Pakistani quasi-political religious parties included the Jamaat-ud-Dawa, Lashkar-e-Taiba, Jaish-e-Mohammed, while cricketer Imran Khan, now Pakistan's most popular political leader, lent his party's support. The DPC pushed for closing NATO supply routes to Afghanistan and called for revoking the Zardari government's decision to grant India the MFN (Most Favoured Nation) status. Within weeks it held mammoth anti-U.S. and anti-India rallies in Peshawar, Lahore, Karachi, and other cities. Few doubted that the army had agreed to let loose these street-level forces, and once again it appeared that the army was contemplating 'strategic defiance' against the United States. However this time it would be a go-it-alone effort. Changed circumstances meant that it could not be along the lines of a regional Pakistan-Afghanistan-Iran compact as advocated by General Mirza Aslam Beg in the early 1990s.

As the protests grew, in early 2012, Pakistan announced that it would no longer allow NATO supplies to transit the country, causing extra expenditure of about $2.1 billion to the U.S. for the longer route that required passage through Central Asian countries. But, eventually, pressed for release of the Coalition Support Funds (CSF), Pakistan accepted a rather ragged apology from Hilary Clinton. Expectedly, the DPC called for protests gainst this 'treasonous act'. In July 2012, a 'Long March' moved from Lahore to the front of Parliament House in Islamabad taking two days. Tens of thousands moved by truck, bus, car and bicycle. They were led by Sami ul-Haq, who claims to be a father of the Taliban and a friend of Mullah Omar, and retired Gen. Hamid Gul, one-time head of Pakistan's Inter-Services Intelligence agency, and other prominent 'America Haters'.[32] Nevertheless, NATO supplies started trickling through. The DPC disappeared as miraculously as it had appeared.

For now the A–group had prevailed; the B–group would have to bide its time.

GUARDING THE NUCLEAR ARSENAL

Defending nuclear weapons against other nations as well as internal enemies poses a difficult security dilemma. Pakistan would like to keep them hidden from India, the U.S., or Israel. On the other hand, army insiders are already in the know. The fear is that, perhaps in collusion with an external Islamic group, they could be plotting some move unknown to the Nuclear Command Authority (NCA), the Strategic Plans Division (SPD), or the Chief of Army Staff.

The SPD claims that an efficient system of sensitive material control and accounting along U.S. national laboratory standards exists. This is impossible to check. Nor is it possible to verify the claim that Pakistan's nuclear weapons are protected by a two-man or three-man rule that requires simultaneous actions by officers in different places before a weapon can be launched. Similarly, it is impossible to check if weapons have been de-mated from their delivery systems and stored separately. If these claims are true, then there is indeed a higher margin of safety.

On the other hand some public claims made directly by the nuclear authorities, or at their behest, are simply unbelievable. For example,

> Another [precaution] is the training of a wide variety of personnel from all major organizations. The training involves nuclear security, physical protection, emergency preparedness, detection equipment, recovery operations, and border monitoring. The organizations involved in training are the Coast Guard, Frontier Corps, Pakistan Rangers, Customs, Emergency & Rescue Services, National Disaster Management Cell, intelligence services, law enforcement agencies, and all strategic organizations including offices from the SPD.[33]

The organizations mentioned above are well-known to be beset by chronic problems of incompetence, cronyism, and corruption. Performing their regular duties lies beyond the capacity of most, what to say about extraordinary matters such as nuclear security or detection equipment. Even though it is relatively easy to apprehend ordinary smuggling and lawlessness, the arrest rate is extremely small. A thousand gruesome murders in Karachi over three months of 2012 have gone unsolved and unpunished, while air and rail crashes are un-investigated. It is rare for terrorists to be caught, and still rarer to be punished.

Claims relating to the security of nuclear materials, such as the following one, sometimes pose a challenge to the imagination:

> Nuclear security emergency centres and procedures to secure orphan radioactive sources and to secure borders against any illicit trafficking have been put in place. Rigorous inspections are one key element of the PNRA's activities to strengthen controls. Another is the training of a wide variety of personnel from all major organizations. The training involves nuclear security, physical protection, emergency preparedness, detection equipment, recovery operations, and border monitoring.[34]

Pakistan's borders, especially with Afghanistan, are porous as a sieve. Smuggling of goods and weapons has historically been a major occupation for tribes on both sides of the border. No serious person could conceive of installing nuclear detection equipment there.

SAFETY MEASURES—ADEQUATE?

As early as December 1999, Pakistan had requested senior U.S. officials visiting Islamabad for Permissive Action Links (PALs) that are directly integrated into the firing mechanism and electronics of a nuclear weapon, as well as Environment Sensitive Devices (ESDs), in order to enhance protection against unauthorised use or accidental nuclear detonations. At that time, the U.S. had declined. These devices make it possible for the weapons to be maintained at a higher state of alert for the same level of safety, thereby increasing the threat perceived by India. But subsequent to the big improvement in Pakistan's relationship with the U.S. immediately after 9/11, it is possible that the U.S. may have acceded to Pakistan's request without demanding that Pakistan reveal the location or details of its nuclear weapons.

David Albright, a U.S. nuclear security analyst, prescribed the following forms of additional assistance that could be given to Pakistan in the immediate aftermath of 9/11: Generic physical protection and material accounting practices; theoretical exercises; unclassified military handbooks on nuclear weapons safety and security; more sophisticated vaults and access doors; portal control equipment; better surveillance equipment; advanced equipment for materials accounting; personnel reliability programs; and programs to reduce the likelihood of leaking sensitive information. In addition, aid could focus on methods that improve the security of nuclear weapons against unauthorised use through devices not intrinsic to the design of the nuclear weapon or through special operational or administrative restrictions. Excluded assistance would include nuclear weapons design information aimed at making more secure, reliable or safer nuclear weapons or devices, PALs, coded launch control devices, and environmental sensing devices.[35]

According to an ISIS (Institute for Science and International Security) report,[36] after 9/11, U.S. Secretary of State, Colin Powell, had offered nuclear protection assistance to Pakistan. The U.S. knew that Pakistan was determined to stay on its nuclear course and inducements to do otherwise were futile. Thereafter, one initiative originating from Washington was to encourage Pakistan to enhance the safety of its nuclear weapons. This fitted well with the army's needs especially that now it faced an insider threat. Earlier offers to Pakistan were rejected; the offered technology was said to be quite rudimentary. Later there was grudging acceptance of some safety devices under the condition that the end point usage would remain opaque. Other aspects of the assistance included training courses for Pakistani nuclear weapons personnel in U.S. laboratories where they were instructed on nuclear safety and security issues.

After A.Q. Khan's global nuclear entrepreneurship came to light in 2004, Musharraf's government sharply reversed its earlier policy of keeping all nuclear matters under wraps and accelerated its efforts to assure the world that Pakistan's nuclear weapons were in safe hands. With American help, many safety measures were put in place. These improvements had been paid for out of the $100 million dollar fund created by the Bush administration.[37] The measures were praised by various international visitors to Pakistan. Joseph Lieberman, U.S. Senator, and at the time a presidential hopeful, who also chaired a Homeland Security and Governmental Affairs committee, left reassured after a briefing by SPD's head, Lt. Gen. (retd.) Khalid Kidwai. Lieberman declared in a subsequent press conference: 'Overall I felt reassured . . . and I will take that message back to Congress.'[38] Two months after the bin Laden episode, Admiral Mike Mullen gave soothing comments. Mullen, the highest ranking officer in the U.S. military stated that Pakistan's control over its nuclear weapons appears tight enough to protect against the possibility of seizure by extremist sympathizers who might infiltrate the nation's army or intelligence service.[39]

A stream of highly placed Pakistani officials made a beeline for Washington's think-tanks and military colleges across the United

States. A few years earlier this would have been unthinkable. Visits by top SPD officials to the U.S. became routine. Significantly, the Director General of the SPD, Lt. Gen. Khalid Kidwai, was also a visitor to U.S. institutions. In a special guest lecture given in 2006 to the faculty, students, and guests of the Naval Postgraduate School in Monterey, he sought to debunk the notion that Pakistani weapons could fall into the hands of religious extremists, were on hair-trigger alert, or be used irresponsibly.[40] Other Pakistani military officers associated with the nation's nuclear program were paid by U.S. funding sources for writing reports and papers for U.S. think-tanks and research institutes. Still others began writing books claiming to reveal the 'true history of the Pakistani nuclear program'. Cooperation with U.S. agencies on nuclear weapon safety appears to have continued, at least until 2011, in spite of the rocky Pak–U.S. relationship.

A basic question relates to the *extent* that nuclear weapons can be made safe. Some safety mechanisms suggest themselves. Chances of nuclear sabotage and accident decrease if readiness levels are reduced. It certainly helps if the fissile core and bomb mechanisms are stored separately in safely guarded vaults, and if it takes some appreciable amount of time to assemble the pieces together. If command is centralized, rather than delegated to local commanders, there is less likelihood of an individual or group initiating nuclear hostilities. At the same time, this calls for a command and control system that is protected against decapitation or disruption of communication facilities.

But safety inevitably competes against readiness. A perfectly safe nuclear weapon is also one that cannot be used and hence, by definition, is useless. In times of crisis and war, when casualties and passions run high, there will be a strong urge to weaken the safety mechanisms in place. One can easily imagine that PALs (Permissive Action Links) would be weakened by over-riding software instructions or, as an extreme, disabled by some secret switch.

To meet the insider threat, the SPD's claim is that the Personnel Reliability Program (PRP), named after its model in the U.S., provides adequate security. The PRP involves a battery of checks aimed at rooting out human foibles such as lust, greed or depression that might lead one to betray national secrets. Like the security methods of other nuclear powers, the new Pakistani program delves into personal finances, political views, etc. New recruits are required to take a battery of psychological background checks, and can be watched up to a year. Even after retirement they are monitored by intelligence agencies. According to Feroz Khan, former Strategic Plans Division director, 'The system knows how to distinguish who is a "fundo" [fundamentalist] and who is simply pious.'[41]

But this does not really reassure. Those familiar with engineers and scientists working inside the Pakistan's nuclear program know well how things have changed over the decades. Long beards and prayer marks on the forehead are common, and religious zeal is especially apparent during the month of Ramzan. The murder of the U.S. ambassador to Libya, which followed the screening of a blasphemous movie, was greeted with satisfaction by many individuals within the nuclear establishment. Such attitudes make at least some of those in charge occasionally nervous:

> One employee recently was booted from the nuclear program for passing out political pamphlets of an ultraconservative Islamic party and being observed coaxing colleagues into joining him at a local mosque for party rallies, said the security official, a two-star general who declined to be identified, citing the sensitive nature of his job. Even though the employee did nothing illegal, his behaviour was deemed too disturbing.[42]

There is no way of checking whether the SPD's Personnel Reliability Program (PRP) and the Human Reliability Program (HRP) are effective or if its counter intelligence teams have what it takes. In a religion that stresses its completeness, and in which righteousness is given higher value than obedience to temporal authority, there is plenty of room for serious conflict between piety and discipline. It is not possible, even in principle, to devise a questionnaire—or a set of criteria—that can accurately tell the difference between an extremist who believes that preserving the faith calls for violent action and a peaceful fundamentalist who worries only about the hereafter. To detect religious extremism, especially among those who choose to hide it as a matter of strategy, is a difficult task. At a practical level there is the question of which presiding officer will make the distinction.

There are still other questions. These concern the weapons laboratories and production units. Given the generally sloppy work culture and lack of attention to detail, it is hard to imagine that accurate records have been maintained over a quarter century of fissile material production. So, can one be certain that small, but significant quantities of highly enriched uranium have not already made their way out? Given that A.Q. Khan had successfully arranged for the smuggling of entire centrifuges weighing half a ton each, to keep an open mind on the matter would be wise.

UNITED STATES OPTIONS ARE VERY LIMITED

America's fears about Pakistan's nuclear weapons have not been allayed, nor are they likely to be. A book published in 2012 underscored U.S. worries about Pakistan's nuclear weapons.[43] According to its author, David Sanger, who is chief Washington correspondent of *The New York Times*, President Barack Obama told his staff in late 2011 that Pakistan could 'disintegrate' and that Pakistan is his 'biggest single national security concern.' The president is said to have told his senior aides that he had 'the least power to prevent' the potential collapse of Pakistan and that, in the event that Pakistan disintegrates, it would spark a scramble for nuclear weapons, some of which could fall into the hands of Islamic militants.

Obama's remarks were promptly reported in the Pakistani Press[44] together with other claims reported by Sanger that nuclear officials from Pakistan and the U.S. periodically meet surreptitiously in locales like Abu Dhabi or London to discuss nuclear security and the detection and disablement of atomic weapons in Pakistan.

Excerpts from the book were highlighted by the U.S. media but it assumed an added importance when U.S. officials suggested to Pakistani diplomats, visiting officials, lawmakers and even journalists to read the book.

Such concerns in Washington make it logical to assume that the U.S. must have extensively war-gamed the situation. One assumes that contingency plans exist to either disarm or destroy the weapons, to be put into effect once there is actionable intelligence of Pakistan's nukes getting loose or if a radical regime takes over and makes overt threats. What could these plans be, and could they really work?[45]

According to Jeffrey T. Richelson, a U.S. intelligence historian, there exists a U.S. Nuclear Emergency Search Team (NEST) that is tasked to deal with emergencies such as might arise out of the Pakistani situation. He reportedly obtained an unclassified Power Point presentation titled 'Detecting, Identifying and Localizing WMD' by the Office of Assistant Secretary of Defense for Special Operations and Low-Intensity Conflict (SOLIC). In it were slides referring to 'clandestine or low-visibility special operations taken to: locate, seize, destroy, capture, recover or render safe WMD,' either on land or sea. He said such a mission has been a Special Operations Forces priority since 2002.

A *New Yorker* article by Seymour Hersh published in November 2009 made waves in Pakistan. Hersh suggested that U.S. emergency plans exist for taking the sting out of Pakistan's nuclear weapons by seizing their trigger mechanisms.[46] He also claimed that an alarm, apparently related to a missing nuclear bomb component, had caused a U.S. rapid response team to fly to Dubai. The alarm proved false and the team is said to have been recalled before it reached Pakistan. The Pakistan foreign ministry, as well as the U.S. embassy in Islamabad, vigorously denied any such episode.

What should one make of Hersh's claim? Quite likely it is an exaggerated account of some small incident, while it probably had a tiny core of truth it is difficult to believe that the U.S. acted as claimed by Hersh. First, even if the U.S. knows the precise numbers of deployed weapons, it simply cannot know all their position coordinates—especially for mobile ones. Extensive underground tunnels reportedly exist within which they can be freely moved and there are even reports that warheads are moved by unmarked trucks to locations hidden within cities. Moreover, from afar it is difficult to tell look-alike dummies from the real warhead. India would be of little help to the U.S. in locating nuclear weapons; one imagines it would know even less than the United States. Second, even if a location is exactly known, it would be heavily guarded. This implies many casualties on both sides when intruding troops are engaged, thus making a secret operation impossible. Even a massive use of force is unlikely to net all Pakistani nuclear weapons. Third, attacking a Pakistani nuclear site would be an act of war with totally unacceptable consequences for the United States, particularly in view of its Afghan difficulties, which are expected to last well beyond 2014. All of this suggests that Hersh's source of information was unreliable.

How would the U.S. actually react to theft? Ill-informed TV anchors in Pakistan have often alleged that Blackwater and U.S. forces will descend to grab the country's nuclear weapons. But in a hypothetical crisis that has crossed into the extreme and where the U.S. has decided to take on Pakistan, its preferred military option would not be ground forces. Instead it would opt for precision Massive Ordnance Penetrator 30,000-pound bombs dropped by B–2 bombers or fry the circuit boards of the warheads using short, high-energy bursts of microwave energy from low-flying aircraft. But deeply buried warheads, or those with adequate metallic shielding, would still remain safe. Ground forces would also have to be employed in some situations.

A U.S. attack on Pakistan's nuclear weapon storage sites would, however, be a final act of extreme desperation. Even if by some miracle every one of these weapons was destroyed, the capacity to make more would remain. For actual de-nuclearization of Pakistan, all major nuclear weapon facilities, reactors, and uranium enrichment plants would also have to be eliminated. If this is perceived as imminent, whether or not India is involved, Pakistan could decide to attack India as a co-conspirator and ally of the United States. This, together with the retribution that would inevitably follow, would be doomsday.

Hence the bottom line: there is no way for any external power, whether America or India, to destroy or seize Pakistan's nuclear weapons. War against Pakistan is simply not an option as it would likely lead to the use of nuclear weapons following which the subcontinent would cease to exist in its present form.

REFERENCES

1. 'Partial transcript of Pakistan President Musharraf's televised speech asking the people of Pakistan to support his course of action', 19 September 2001. http://www.washingtonpost.com/wp-srv/nation/specials/attacked/transcripts/pakistantext_091901.html
2. 'Jihad, Martyrdom, and the Killing of Innocents', Ayman Al Zawahiri. Osama bin Laden is said to have disagreed with this point of view because such operations had greatly decreased Al Qaida's popularity in Iraq.
3. 'Pakistan's nuclear weapons 200% safe: Rehman Malik', *The Express Tribune*, 5 June 2011.
4. 'Taliban release Bannu jailbreak video, vow to free more prisoners', *Dawn*, 16 May 2012.
5. 'Parade Avenue presents deserted look on Pakistan Day', Pakistan Today 24 March 2012.
6. 'Security forces arrest close aide of GHQ attack mastermind', *Dawn*, 27 May 2011.
7. Militants kill at least 36 at mosque, *Tribune* newspaper, 4 December 2009.
8. 'Gunmen kill Saudi diplomat in Karachi', *Dawn*, 16 May 2011.
9. 'Strike on Mehran base: Pakistan Navy's sacked commando, brother arrested', *Dawn*, 31 May 2011.
10. 'DNA report of PNS Mehran terrorists', *Aaj News*, 18 June 2011.
11. 'Mehran base attack carried out with insider support', Maritime Security Asia, http://maritimesecurity.asia/free-2/maritime-security-asia/mehran-base-attack-carried-out-with-inside-support/
12. 'Security concerns: Navy battleships moved away from Karachi', *The Express Tribune*, 5 August 2011.
13. Ibid.
14. 'British Council: Pakistan facing "frightening" demographic disaster', *The Telegraph*, 20 November 2009.

15. 'Tribune Survey: Online Pakistanis "Muslims" first, "Pakistani" second', The *Express Tribune*, 16 February 2012.
16. Wahabization–Salafization of Pakistan and Muslim Ummah: Fighting the Terrorists but Supporting their Ideology, Abul Hassaan, http://www.islamicsupremecouncil.com/bothways.htm
17. 'Hiz-but-Tahrir in Pakistan', Ayesha Umar, *Newsline*, 5 August 2011.
18. 'Taliban video shows 17 beheaded Pakistani soldiers', CNN wire staff, 28 June 2012.
19. 'Missing Pakistan journalist Saleem Shahzad found dead near Islamabad', Declan Walsh, *The Guardian*, 31 May 2011.
20. 'Mullen: Pakistan Government Sanctioned Death of Saleem Shahzad', *Huffington Post*, 7 July 2011.
21. 'Pakistani Public Opinion Ever More Critical of U.S.', Pew Poll, 27 June 2012.
22. 'Army chief wanted more drone support', Hasan Zaidi, *Dawn*, 20 May 2011.
23. Ibid.
24. 'U.S. personnel begin to vacate Pakistan's Shamsi Air Base: report', Bill Roggio, *Long War Journal*, 4 December 2011.
25. 'In Pakistani Statements, an Awkward Acceptance', Carlotta Gall, *The New York Times*, 2 May 2011.
26. Interview of High Commissioner Wajid Shamsul Hasan, http://www.youtube.com/watch?v=HI6FNNezJpQ
27. 'How could they not have known he was there? Bin Laden hideout and Pakistan's Sandhurst only 800 yards apart', The *Daily Mail*, 3 May 2011.
28. 'Insufficient response aggravated despondency: COAS', *The News*, 10 May 2011.
29. 'Intelligence failure was global, not just ours: PM', *The Express Tribune*, 5 May 2011.
30. 'Lead up to Abbottabad: Spy chiefs had extensive talks on Osama', *The Express Tribune*, 13 May 2011.
31. Compromised intelligence: Tip-off suspected in Waziristan evacuations, *The Express Tribune*, 12 June 2011.
32. DPC protests outside parliament over Nato supply routes, *Dawn*, 10 July 2012.
33. 'Nuclear Security in Pakistan: Separating Myth From Reality', Feroz Hassan Khan, *Arms Control Today*, July/August 2009.
34. Ibid.
35. David Albright, 'Securing Pakistan's Nuclear Weapons Complex', paper commissioned and sponsored by the Stanley Foundation for the 42nd Strategy for Peace Conference, Strategies for Regional Security, (South Asia Working Group), Airlie Conference Center, Warrenton, Virginia, October 25–27, 2001.
36. Nuclear Black Markets, Pakistan, A.Q. Khan and the rise of proliferation networks. A net assessment. The Institute for Science and International Security, London, 2 May 2007.

37. 'U.S. Secretly Aids Pakistan in Guarding Nuclear Arms', by David E Sanger and William J. Board, *The New York Times*, 18 November 2007.
38. 'U.S. Senator "reassured" on Pakistan nukes', (AFP)—9 January 2008.
39. 'Mullen: Pakistani Nuclear Controls Should Avert Any Insider Threat', *Global Security Newswire*, 8 July 2011.
40. 'Pakistan's Evolution as a Nuclear Weapons State', Lt. Gen. Khalid Kidwai, lecture delivered at the U.S. Naval Postgraduate School, Monterey, California, 1 November 2006.
41. *Daily Times*, Lahore, 29 July 2007 reports that the SPD has confirmed helping two researchers from an American think-tank in California, Dr Peter R. Lavoy and former Pakistan Army Brigadier Feroz Khan, to write a comprehensive account of the country's nuclear program. As of July 2011 the book has not appeared.
42. 'Inside Pakistan's Drive to Guard its A-Bombs', Peter Wonacott, *The Wall Street Journal*, 29 November 2007.
43. *Confront and Conceal: Obama's Secret War and Surprising Use of American Power*, David E. Sanger, Random House, 2012.
44. 'Obama fears Pakistan's disintegration: book', *Dawn*, 25 June 2012, http://dawn.com/2012/06/26/obama-fears-pakistans-disintegration-book/
45. 'U.S. prepares for worst-case scenario with Pakistan nukes', quoted in Robert Windrem, *NBC News* Investigative Producer for Special Projects, 2011.
46. 'Defending the Arsenal; In an unstable Pakistan, can nuclear warheads be kept safe?', Seymour M. Hersh, *The New Yorker*, 16 November 2009.

CHAPTER 9

COMMANDING AND CONTROLLING NUCLEAR WEAPONS

Zia Mian

Nuclear weapons are unrelenting. Managing them has been a hard and costly task for the major nuclear weapons states. It has made building the bomb appear easy in comparison. History may show that managing the bomb is impossible in the political, military, institutional and technological environment that prevails in South Asia.

Efforts to manage nuclear arsenals have typically assumed that a government and its armed forces behave as if they were a single, coherent entity. Decision making powers are seen as concentrated in the hands of a few individuals who exercise their authority through a command and control system that extends down to the nuclear armed military unit, be it an aircraft or a silo-based, submarine-launched or mobile ballistic missile or cruise missile. This command and control system is often treated as an arrangement of human levers or cogs that will engage in an efficient, infallible, effectively mechanical activity guided by clear and precise rules and where everything will function as intended.

At a practical level, the problem of managing nuclear weapons in the real world can involve hundreds if not thousands of people at all levels, many acting under orders and in diverse settings with different powers, interacting with each other and with a variety of technical systems, with nuclear weapons only being a small part of this. What actually happens in any given situation will depend on all the elements of this system. A major study of nuclear weapons operations concluded that the viability of nuclear command and control depends on 'the unpredictability of circumstances and human behaviour' where 'the smallest details can assume central importance' and 'even the most advanced experts and the most experienced practitioners are narrowly and incompletely informed,' and where 'no one understands the whole.'[1]

According to General Lee Butler, who was Commander-in-Chief of the United States Strategic Air Command, and its successor the United States Strategic Command which had responsibility for all U.S. Air Force and Navy nuclear weapons, the people that run the nuclear enterprise have 'a sense of infallibility', even though in day to day reality, 'the capacity for human and mechanical failure, and for human misunderstandings, was limitless.'[2] As examples, General Butler narrates that, 'I have seen bombers crash during exercises designed to replicate, but which were inevitably far less stressful than, the actual conditions of nuclear war. I have seen human error lead to missiles exploding in their silos. I have read the circumstances of submarines going to the bottom of the sea laden with nuclear missiles and warheads because of mechanical flaws and human errors.'[3] Clearly, nuclear weapons are not immune to the rule that sooner or later everything will go wrong that can go wrong.

This chapter looks at the challenges of commanding and controlling nuclear weapons and what these challenges mean for India and Pakistan. It highlights the problems with the technologies and procedures for making sure that weapons are used only when such use is intended, and the difficulties of maintaining such control during a crisis and in case of a war.

POSITIVE AND NEGATIVE CONTROL

It is a normal requirement of every deployed military weapon that it should only be used when authorised by the appropriate authority and that the weapon will function as and when required (i.e., it should be both reliable and safe). With nuclear weapons these demands become especially important since unlike ordinary weapons, nuclear weapons have acquired an important diplomatic and political utility short of their use as an explosive. Only the highest political authorities should be able to authorise the use of nuclear weapons. Thus it is important to assure that possession of a nuclear weapon by a military unit should not equal the ability to use it: the unit that holds, moves, and fires the system cannot (as opposed to may not) use it without approval from higher authority.

One way to formulate this problem is in terms of positive control and negative control, or use-oriented command and control and restraint-oriented command and control.[4] Positive or use-oriented control describes a situation where weapons are used when authorised, while negative or restraint-oriented control reflects the requirement that weapons cannot be used unless authorised. Positive control can be seen as defining how the system should behave in wartime, while negative control is the more powerful constraint on command and control in peacetime.

Positive control involves a set of interlocked technological and administrative systems, with associated procedures and plans to ensure nuclear weapons can be used by a national authority when it decides to do so. These systems include the:[5] (a) early warning system; (b) procedures to assess the nature and extent of an attack that may be taking place; (c) command and decision centres; (d) communications between leaders and nuclear armed units; and (e) military units equipped with nuclear armed missiles or other delivery systems.

The operational viability of each component and the system as a whole is supported by training exercises and drills that work through the steps of the plans that have been developed for the possible use of nuclear weapons. But it is a commonplace in the design and execution of plans and exercises involving complex systems to assume that things will go as expected and that there will be no surprises. This confidence is based more on the lack of any alternative than on actual experience. It is hard if not impossible to foresee every eventuality. There is no way to prepare for every possible combination of events, including all the equipment malfunctions, human errors and misperceptions that may come into play.

Even where detailed procedures are put in place, there are problems. For instance, the U.S. found that for its SAGE (Semi-Automatic Ground Environment) warning and control system 'it was impossible to specify in advance all of the contingencies that could be faced in the course of actual operations. Reliance on formal written procedures proved impractical and unwritten work-arounds soon developed among the human operators.'[6] The larger lesson drawn in a study of this and other systems is that 'any nuclear command organization circumvents official procedures in order to carry out its assigned mission. Such rule short-cutting is likely to be oral and informal, and therefore invisible to outside observation except under the high-stress conditions of actual war or crisis.'[7]

The need for caution about the differences between the way command and control systems are supposed to work and the way they actually work is supported by growing evidence that demonstrates how complex systems that tightly integrate administrative procedures and technologies can fail unpredictably and catastrophically in the real world.[8] This has included major failures of systems involved in managing nuclear weapons.[9] These failures have all been in situations far more subdued than the crisis and chaos that would be associated with imminent nuclear war.

Military planners have traditionally ignored these acute, effectively insoluble problems. For them, the main threat to positive control is decapitation—a successful attack by an adversary that renders a nuclear arsenal unusable because the command and control system is destroyed. Their concern is that the orders to use nuclear weapons need to be communicated to the military units with custody of the weapons through the command and control system, and if this does not take place the order may become undeliverable. Among the specific issues that are raised include the need for early warning of an impending attack that may threaten the command and control system, protection of nuclear decision-makers, reliable communications systems and nuclear weapons that can survive an attack by a determined adversary.

There are a number of steps that have been taken by the nuclear weapon states to mitigate the possible loss of command. These include multiple early warning systems including ground based radar, and in the case of the United States and the Soviet Union the use of satellites; plans to preserve national leadership, including secure command posts, alternative command centres, alternative mobile command centres; multiple, hardened communications between leaders and the nuclear arsenal which are able to, for instance, withstand the electromagnetic pulse from detonation of nuclear weapons;[10] large nuclear arsenals and mobile ballistic missiles and submarines as the survivable core of such an arsenal.

These measures have all proved to be extraordinarily complex and costly. The United States spent approximately $400 billion on building and maintaining its nuclear arsenal between 1940 and 1990.[11] The planes, submarines and land-based missiles systems for these weapons cost in excess of a staggering $3000 billion.[12] It spent almost 200 billion dollars on its strategic command, control and communications system.[13] A cheaper way to overcome the possibility of decapitation is to disperse and delegate the authority and ability to use nuclear weapons in advance. This, however, increases the likelihood of unauthorised nuclear use.

The nuclear armed unit raises command and control issues of its own; it needs to be appropriately trained and should be in possession of weapons systems that are serviceable, reliable, and survivable.[14] Nuclear units assigned responsibility for assembling, maintaining, transporting, or storing nuclear weapons, their components and related equipment need to have adequate knowledge of the unique characteristics of nuclear weapons, and the safety and control features associated with these weapons. They need appropriate training and inspection to determine they are able to perform their assigned mission. Along with their specific technical skills, the individual members of the unit also need to be evaluated for their reliability, and their qualifications to have custody of, control access to, or have access to nuclear weapons. These Personnel Reliability Programs involve investigative and administrative checks of military personnel—between 1975 and 1990 the U.S. disqualified annually between 3–5 per cent of the military personnel it had previously cleared for working with nuclear weapons on the grounds of drug or alcohol problems, conviction for a serious crime, negligence, unreliability or aberrant behaviour, poor attitude, and behaviour suggesting problems with due law and authority, etc.[15]

Some requirements for positive control also figure in establishing negative control, i.e., in making sure that nuclear weapons are not used without authorisation. Negative control involves how nuclear weapons are deployed, military procedures associated with them, and the design of the weapons and their delivery systems. Among the most significant concerns about negative control are possible unauthorised access to the weapons and the safety of the weapons should there be an accident. More specifically, the weapons should be secure against efforts by people to gain unauthorised access to them or to detonate them, and the weapons should not detonate accidentally because of problems with maintenance or the malfunction of the delivery system, including severe situations such as a missile or plane crash.

There are several technical and procedural solutions that have been developed to deal with these concerns, including:

- combination or coded locks (Permissive Action Links, or PALs) which can block unauthorised use of a nuclear weapon.[16]
- safety design features of warheads, e.g., one-point-safe designs and insensitive high explosive that will reduce the risk of a warhead detonating if it catches fire or is otherwise damaged.[17]

The procedural components encompass:

- physical protection of the weapons (in manufacturing, storage, and transport) as well as the codes for unlocking nuclear weapons.
- the requirement that at every stage in the maintenance, deployment, and use of nuclear weapons at least two people

participate, each being capable of detecting incorrect or unauthorised procedures (the two-man rule).

NUCLEAR COMMAND AND CONTROL IN INDIA AND PAKISTAN

In the wake of their nuclear tests, India and Pakistan have begun to create command and control systems for their respective arsenals. From the earlier general discussion of such systems, it is possible to identify at least five important constraints that may be of significance in the effort by leaders in India and Pakistan to make sure they can use their nuclear weapons when their leaders want while ensuring the weapons remain safe in the meantime. First, there are nuclear arsenals and the pressures created by the limited numbers of weapons that are available and the characteristics of the delivery systems. Second, there are specific problems of early warning created by geography and technology in South Asia. Third, there are a number of strategic constraints that stem from a perceived need to be prepared to use nuclear weapons in a conflict and the kinds of military scenarios that are deemed plausible in South Asia. Fourth, ensuring proper safeguarding of the weapons raises important technical and institutional questions. And finally, there is the safety of the weapons and delivery systems India and Pakistan may be capable of fielding.

The creation of a formal command and control structure in India following the 1998 nuclear tests was initially slow and troubled.[18] Lacking a single dominant institution like the Pakistan Army to shape the process, India's efforts in this direction have been shaped by political, bureaucratic and military rivalries. In January 2003, the Indian Government's cabinet committee on national security published a brief official statement on nuclear doctrine and set up a command structure.[19] The doctrine commits India to 'building and maintaining a credible minimum deterrent,' capable of 'nuclear retaliation to a first strike [that] will be massive and designed to inflict unacceptable damage.'

Nuclear decision making was entrusted to a two-layered structure called the Nuclear Command Authority, which includes a Political

Council, chaired by the Prime Minister, and an Executive Council, chaired by the national security adviser to the Prime Minister. The Political Council is empowered to authorise the use of nuclear weapons, although 'arrangements for alternate chains of command for retaliatory nuclear strikes in all eventualities' are mentioned. This means that in some circumstances someone other than the prime minister may be able to order the use of nuclear weapons. The 2003 nuclear doctrine created a Strategic Forces Command to manage and administer India's nuclear weapons. As of 2011, it is headed by Air Marshal K.J. Mathews.[20]

The 2003 statement formalized a more detailed 1999 draft nuclear doctrine.[21] The draft doctrine declared that India would seek to establish: (a) sufficient, survivable and operationally prepared nuclear forces; (b) a robust command and control system; (c) effective intelligence and early-warning capabilities; (d) planning and training for nuclear operations; and (e) the will to employ nuclear weapons. The nuclear forces are to be deployed on a triad of delivery vehicles of 'aircraft, mobile land-based missiles and sea-based assets' that are structured for 'punitive retaliation' so as to 'inflict damage unacceptable to the aggressor'. The doctrine called for an 'assured capability to shift from peacetime deployment to fully employable forces in the shortest possible time.'

Along with the aircraft that can carry nuclear bombs, India has built and tested a range of missiles. These include the 700 km *Agni-I* missile, the 2000 km range *Agni-II* missile and the 3500 km range *Agni-III* missile, which have been approved for deployment with the army.[22] India also has carried out an underwater launch of its 700 km range submarine-launched ballistic missile, *Sagarika*.[23] In 2009 India launched its first nuclear powered submarine.[24] It plans a fleet of three to five, each armed with 12 *Sagarika* ballistic missiles.[25] India also is working on a 5000-km range *Agni-V* missile, which it plans to test in late 2010 or early 2011, and may be developing multiple independently targetable re-entry vehicles for this missile.[26]

There are a few signs of early Indian thinking about a nuclear command and control system.[27] The system is envisaged to include a command post designed to withstand a direct nuclear strike, with the authority to order use of nuclear weapons conveyed by separate coded messages sent over independent communication systems, with all the messages required for authorisation. The physical control over the nuclear weapons was to be divided with the nuclear warhead stored separately and under a separate organization from the military unit in charge of the delivery system.

In Pakistan, a history of military coups and weak elected governments that abdicated national security policy to the military has ensured that the armed forces, in particular the army, have authority over the nuclear weapons program. After its 1998 nuclear tests carried out at the behest of Prime Minister Nawaz Sharif, Pakistan announced that, 'The final authority to use nuclear weapons will remain with the prime minister, but the CJCSC (Chairman of the Joint Chiefs of Staff Committee) will be the strategic commander of the nuclear force.'[28] The first person to hold this responsibility was General Pervez Musharraf, who staged a military coup in October 1999 overthrowing Nawaz Sharif.

In February 2000, General Musharraf established a National Command Authority (NCA) with responsibility for formulating policy and exercising control over the development and employment of Pakistan's strategic nuclear forces and associated organizations.[29] The NCA held its nineteenth meeting in July 2011.[30] The NCA comprises of three components: an Employment Control Committee, Development Control Committee, and the Strategic Plans Division. The Employment Control Committee is chaired by the head of the government and includes the ministers of foreign affairs, defense and interior, chairman of the CJCSC, military service chiefs, director-general of Strategic Plans Division (secretary) and technical advisors. This committee presumably is charged with making nuclear weapons policy, including the decision to use nuclear weapons.

The second part of the NCA, the Development Control Committee, manages the nuclear weapons complex and the development of nuclear weapons systems. It has the same military and technical members as the Employment Committee but lacks the cabinet ministers that represent the other parts of government. The Development Control Committee is chaired by the head of the government and includes the Chairman of the Joint Chiefs of Staff Committee (as deputy chairman of the Committee), military service chiefs, director-general of the Strategic Plans Division, and representatives of the weapons research, development and production organizations. These organizations include the A.Q. Khan Research Laboratory (Kahuta), National Development Complex, and the Pakistan Atomic Energy Commission.[31] It also includes the National Engineering and Scientific Commission, which was initially headed by Samar Mubarikmand (who was formerly the head of technical development at the Pakistan Atomic Energy Commission and led the team that conducted the nuclear weapons tests).[32]

The third arm of the NCA is the Strategic Plans Division (SPD). It was established in the Joint Services Headquarters under the CJCSC and since its creation has been headed by Lieutenant General Khalid Ahmed Kidwai, who continued in the past even after retiring from the army in 2007. This division acts as the secretariat for the NCA and has responsibility for planning and coordination and in particular, for establishing the lower tiers of the command and control system and its physical infrastructure. The SPD is said to have a security division of 9000–10,000 personnel responsible for the security of the nuclear weapons complex.[33]

Pakistan is believed to rely on its air force and its land-based mobile-missiles to deliver its nuclear weapons. Along with jet fighters, such as the U.S. supplied F-16, which can carry nuclear bombs, Pakistan has tested the 350 km range air-launched cruise missile, *Ra'ad*.[34] The Pakistan Army's Strategic Force Command has tested both short- and long-range missiles, including the *Ghaznavi* with a range of 290 km, the *Ghauri* (1300 km), and the *Babur* cruise missile (700 km). In 2008, the Pakistan Army's Strategic Force Command carried out a training launch of a 2000 km range missile, the *Shaheen II* that was said to have 'validated the operational readiness of a strategic missile group equipped with the *Shaheen II* missile.'[35] In 2011, Pakistan tested the 60 km *Nasr* missile that was claimed to be a tactical nuclear weapon delivery system for use on the battlefield and 'to add deterrence value to Pakistan's strategic weapons development program at shorter ranges.'[36] Pakistan has a naval Strategic Force Command, charged with 'exercise technical, training, and administrative control over the strategic delivery systems', but it is not known if this command has yet been issued any nuclear weapons.[37]

If, as seems likely, India and Pakistan continue to increase the size of their respective arsenals and move to increased reliance on mobile missiles and put nuclear weapons at sea, their problems of command and control will grow more complex. There will be more military units with nuclear weapons, some of which may need in a crisis to be dispersed and remain out of communications to become more difficult to detect and so enhance their survivability. With a large number of weapons distributed over many diverse delivery systems, deployed across large areas and in different environments, considerable independent authority over the use of the weapons may need to be handed over to low-level commanders. When to disperse forces and lessen direct central command authority in a crisis becomes an issue in its own right, as does the question of how to ensure central control over the weapons will be regained when a crisis is managed successfully.

THE COURSE OF WAR

The demands on a command and control system that it be appropriate in war-time require looking especially at how war may begin in South Asia. There are many scenarios of how a crisis may develop and escalate into war, perhaps without deliberate intent on either the part of India or Pakistan.[38] Most if not all hinge on Kashmir and the possibility that India may respond to Pakistani action in Kashmir by escalating the conflict and moving it to another area, namely by sending its conventional military forces across the southern desert or central plains into Pakistan.

Pakistan's long narrow geography, paralleling its contiguous border with India, makes all of its military facilities and cities easily within reach of Indian aircraft and missiles. There are few places for Pakistan to hide its nuclear facilities, weapons, or delivery systems. India does not face the same problem, with its southern tip well over a thousand kilometres from the border with Pakistan. Pakistan has also long feared and prepared to counter a pre-emptive attack on its nuclear arsenal and facilities.[39] These date back at least to December 1982—following the example of Israel's destruction of Iraq's Osirak reactor a year earlier—when it was reported that India considered plans for an attack on Pakistan's Kahuta uranium enrichment facility. (That such plans were considered and rejected has been confirmed.)[40] Similar fears were expressed by Pakistani officials again just before Pakistan's 1998 tests, and the air force was put on alert at both the nuclear test site and at Kahuta.[41]

The nature of the border and the pattern of deployment of armed forces close to it, which include frontline strike aircraft, make any significant early warning effectively impossible, especially for Pakistan. The problem will be worsened by the presence of ballistic missiles with ranges of over a thousand kilometres that put major cities, including the respective capital cities and business cities, within a few minutes flight time. (The problems of early warning are addressed separately in this book in the chapter: 'The Infeasibility of Early Warning'). These weapons systems and deployments ensure that policy makers in either country have in effect no time to think. With geography and technology combining to render any solution seemingly impossible, Pakistan may feel it should remain prepared to disperse its nuclear forces early in every crisis rather than risk losing them. But there are other graver risks that would follow.

India has much larger conventional military forces, and it is widely believed they would eventually overwhelm those of Pakistan. India's army chief, General Deepak Kapoor, in 2009 claimed that his forces were developing the ability to mobilize very rapidly and mount a decisive conventional attack on Pakistan. This Indian strategy has been dubbed 'Cold Start',' and has been the subject of extensive war games and military exercises. The 2006 *Sanghe Shakti* (Joint Power) exercise involved aircraft, tanks, and soldiers in a war game whose purpose was described by an Indian commander as 'to test our 2004 war doctrine to dismember a not-so-friendly nation effectively and at the shortest possible time.'[42]

Pakistani civilian and military leaders have repeatedly argued that the conventional forces imbalance is in fact a prime reason for Pakistan's nuclear weapons in the first place.[43] Taking such claims seriously suggests Pakistan may choose to follow the U.S. and NATO strategy in Europe of having three phases of nuclear weapons use. This consisted of a conventional non-nuclear war plan, where nuclear threats are issued once NATO forces were unable to contain a Soviet attack, to be followed by the planned use of nuclear weapons on the battlefield, and finally if the Soviets responded with nuclear forces there was the plan to use strategic nuclear weapons.

Israel apparently had a similar strategy when it prepared to use its nuclear weapons during the 1973 war. According to one description, 'Israeli forces on the Golan Heights were retreating in the face of a massive Syrian tank assault. At 10 p.m. on Oct. 8th, the Israeli Commander on the northern front, Major General Yitzhak Hoffi, told his superior: "I am not sure we can hold out much longer." After midnight, Defense Minister Moshe Dayan solemnly warned Premier Golda Meir: "This is the end of the third temple." Mrs Meir thereupon gave Dayan permission to activate Israel's Doomsday weapons. As each bomb was assembled, it was rushed off to waiting air force units. Before any triggers were set, however, the battle on both fronts turned in Israel's favour.'[44] A slightly different description of these events suggests: 'the nuclear missile launches at Hirbat Zachariah, as many as were ready, would be made operational, along with eight specially marked F-4s that were on twenty-four alert at Tel-Nof, the air force base.'[45]

Pakistan may follow Israel's policy in another way. It has been suggested Israeli strategy during the crisis when it called a nuclear alert and began arming its nuclear arsenal was aimed substantially 'to blackmail Washington into a major policy change . . . to begin an immediate and massive resupply of the Israeli military.'[46] Pakistan may seek to use the threat of nuclear weapons use as a way to incite intervention to terminate the war before it lost more ground. This could be done simply by moving some nuclear armed missiles into the open for U.S. satellites to be able to detect them. Failing appropriate intervention, it is imaginable that Pakistan would consider the battlefield use of nuclear weapons, against advancing Indian tanks for instance, as a way to signal its desperation. (The chapter: 'Pakistan's Battlefield Use of Nuclear Weapons' considers the consequences of Pakistan's use of its nuclear forces against a large-scale Indian conventional military attack.)

Indian military exercises show every indication that India anticipates Pakistan using battlefield nuclear weapons.[47] The *Poorna Vijay* (Complete Victory) exercises were aimed at testing equipment, troops and manoeuvres in a situation where nuclear weapons were used against them, with an Indian official confirming that, 'Drills and procedures to meet the challenges of a nuclear, chemical or biological strike are also being practised.'[48] Among the options worked through were a Pakistani nuclear attack on a bridgehead or bridge, armoured forces and troops.[49]

However, the exercises went further and suggest a more aggressive strategy aimed at putting pressure on, or perhaps even overwhelming, Pakistan's nuclear capability. The Indian Air Force sought to 'test its operational efficacy while underscoring the importance of advanced interception and detection methods in the wake of potential nuclear strikes from adversaries.'[50] The army aimed to rehearse 'deep armoured thrusts'.[51] These were to be combined with attacks by 'deep penetration strike aircraft' and helicopter borne special forces operations.[52]

In turn, Pakistani military planners may well seek to anticipate such Indian attempts to intercept Pakistani aircraft carrying nuclear weapons and perhaps to destroy or degrade Pakistan's nuclear weapons storage sites and delivery systems in the early stages of a conflict. This would pose important constraints on the kind of nuclear command and control system Pakistan may have established and would be a cause of additional possible dangers.

There are many instances of military forces in combat going beyond what had been ordered by senior military or political leaders; where nuclear forces are involved this can lead to what has been dubbed *inadvertent escalation*.[53] This can also result from the simple difficulty of knowing and controlling everything that is happening on a battlefield. The result in either case, and more likely still with both processes working, is the possibility of unforeseen contact between Indian conventional forces and Pakistan's nuclear weapons systems. In such a situation, Indian and Pakistani plans could lead to the use of nuclear weapons without either side having anticipated such an event.

Pakistan's situation is somewhat reminiscent of that faced by U.S. military planners in Europe in the late 1950s and early 1960s who saw themselves confronting overwhelming Soviet conventional forces. To protect their nuclear forces against being destroyed in a surprise attack they placed them on heightened alert. This required that nuclear bombs and warheads were to be loaded on planes and missiles and kept ready for launch within minutes. This option had been made possible by the development of 'sealed pit' weapons, in which a key component no longer needed to be manually or mechanically inserted into the centre of the bomb at the last moment—earlier weapons had been kept disassembled and were only put together as when considered necessary. The pressure for keeping some U.S. nuclear forces in Europe on hair trigger alert raised concerns about access to these weapons by U.S. allies, who were then being trained to operate them; including instances of non-U.S. aircraft loaded with armed U.S. nuclear weapons waiting on airstrips—ready to take off. These problems led to the development of coded arming switches to limit access and possible use of nuclear weapons only to those with the requisite authorisation (i.e., the codes), which have evolved into modern Permissive Action Links.[54]

Permissive Action Links (PALs) are electronic switches that serve to protect a nuclear weapon against all kinds of unauthorised use, and are meant to be effective even when the weapon is assembled, armed and mated to its delivery system and ready for use. They have to be built into the weapon in such a way that it is not accessible for tampering and cannot be bypassed. There are a variety of technical approaches to this, although, for obvious reasons the details are secret.[55] Recent PALs use a set of multiple, six-digit or twelve-digit codes with a limited try capability. Since these are electronic locks, the limited try capability stops any effort to keep trying codes until the correct one is determined.[56]

Both India and Pakistan have sought help with PAL systems. It has been reported that 'India . . . has tried, so far unsuccessfully, to acquire missile safeguards technology from Russia to allay the concerns of Indian political officials that weaponization of missiles could erode tight central control over their use.'[57] Pakistan, for its part, has sought help from the U.S. suggesting that, 'precautions against accidental or unauthorised launch of nuclear weapons are obviously imperative. . . . Cooperation of more experienced states should be solicited.'[58] Other former senior officials are more direct, they highlight the risk of accidental or unauthorised use and approvingly cite U.S. authors on the need for the U.S. to share command and control information with de-facto nuclear weapons states.[59]

In 2006, General Khalid Kidwai, head of the Strategic Plans Division (SPD), stated that Pakistan's nuclear weapons are secured with a system that is analogous to PALs, and Pakistan follows a 'two-man rule' to authenticate these codes for the release of weapons.[60] It is important to appreciate, however, that the efficacy of a technical system depends on the circumstances in which it is to function and the procedures that govern its use. In the case of PALs, there are significant political, military and institutional constraints that need to be kept in mind.

At first sight, by limiting unauthorised access to nuclear weapons PALs may seem as contributing to reducing possible dangers. However, the matter is more complex. The prospect of tight, assured control over nuclear forces that PALs appear to offer may tempt political leaders and military planners to be more forceful in using the alert status and deployment of their nuclear forces as instruments of diplomacy. This was in fact an early argument for PALs. Fred Ikle, described as the 'father' of PALs advocated in the late 1950s that such devices 'could permit substantial gains in readiness by replacing more time consuming operational safeguards and by making higher alert postures politically acceptable.'[61] Control through technology rather than relying on people is presented as making risks seem less daring and thus easier to rationalise.

This temptation may be particularly great in South Asia where both India and Pakistan believe that in a crisis the U.S. would use spy planes, satellites and electronic signals intelligence to closely monitor events, and may be incited into intervening. In the past, Pakistan, in particular, has sought to elicit such intervention through various kinds of military actions, most notably in the Kargil conflict of 1999. It is easy to imagine how in a crisis a perceived increase of control may lead to a greater willingness among Pakistani policy makers to alert their nuclear forces or begin deployment as a signal to the U.S. that they were serious about being prepared to use nuclear weapons unless the U.S. restrained India in some way.

The nature of the conflict between India and Pakistan may be one where nuclear weapons are in the theatre of a conventional conflict. In such a situation, it is recognised that PALs 'do nothing to alleviate the organizational and environmental pressures to decentralise and delegate control of most theatre nuclear weapons . . . if weapons were sent into battle while political authorities retained control of the codes needed to unlock them, there could be no guarantee, not even a likelihood, that all of the codes could be matched with their respective weapons in the confusion of a conventional (war). . . . The political command, or any centralised depository of the codes, could be attacked, thereby paralysing the military's ability to strike back. Practically speaking, a strong pressure exists to release any needed codes at the same time that the weapons are dispersed from their storage sites.'[62] In short, in the circumstances that are likely to prevail in the case of Pakistan, its compulsions to protect its nuclear weapons by dispersing them and to keep them usable could require loosening central authority to such an extent that PALs would be effectively neutralised as a crisis threatened to turn into war.

For PALs to serve as an effective technology of negative control, limiting normal access to nuclear weapons during peacetime, it is the day-to-day procedures of the military as an institution that become important. It is not just that the weapons themselves need to be properly protected; PALs are only effective if the codes for the locks are also kept secure. If anyone can have access to the codes then PALs offer little if any restraint as command and control devices. That this problem is real even where there are decades of experience is evident from the incident in December 1994 when the unlock codes for U.S. strategic forces were reportedly compromised aboard a U.S. Strategic Command airborne command centre.[63]

There are many examples of institutional failure caused by poor planning and procedures on the part of the armed forces, as with other institutions, in India and Pakistan. A useful set of examples to consider is the way that the respective armies have dealt with peacetime storage of their conventional ammunition and look for problems with planning and procedures associated with this.

In March 1988, there was an accidental fire at India's Central Ordnance Depot (claimed to be the largest in Asia), located at the Jabalpur Ordnance Factory and Ammunition Depot, which led to the ammunition stored in underground bunkers exploding over a period of several days and required the evacuation of nearby villages, and the closure of the airport 45 kilometres away.[64] The disaster, involving the destruction of munitions reportedly worth hundreds of millions of dollars, was attributed to 'negligence' on the part of the commandant by both, the workers in the depot and the local member of the state parliament.[65]

Despite warnings about the hazards at other Indian arms depots, the next decade saw more disasters.[66] In 1998, there was a fire at the magazine and ammunition store of the Proof and Experimental Establishment Centre near Balasore.[67] This facility is closely tied to the missile test grounds at the Interim Test Range, Chandipur, and few details were released of the accident. In April 2000, around 12,000 tonnes of ammunition, including surface-to-air missiles, anti-tank guided missiles, tank and artillery shells, were destroyed by a fire at the Bharatpur Field Ammunition Depot—this amounted to 30 to 40 per cent of the operational reserves of India's Southern Army Command.[68] A smaller subsequent fire at a storage site near Pathankot destroyed 400 tons of ammunition. Major General Himmat Singh Gill claimed that at the site residential development habitation had begun to cross the mandatory one kilometre exclusion zone around arms depots, compromising the security of the facility and putting people at risk.[69] Another fire in May 2001, at the Suratgarh Depot in Rajasthan which serves as the Indian Army's forward ammunition stores, consumed 8000 tons of tank and artillery ammunition.[70] The explanation that was offered by Vice Chief of Army Staff was that it was a 'pure accident', an 'act of God'.[71] Other military officials in private spoke of it to be the result of 'a crisis of casualness.'[72]

India is not alone in disasters involving a major weapons storage facility. On 10 April 1988, the Ojhri Ammunition Depot located close to the twin cities of Islamabad and Rawalpindi exploded; the official toll was approximately a hundred people killed and a thousand injured.[73] Other tallies suggested that between 6000 and 7000 people were killed and many thousands injured.[74] The official cause presented to Parliament by the Ministry of Defense was that an accidental fire broke out in an ammunition lorry which spread to the whole site.[75] Prime Minister Mohammad Khan Junejo announced that arms depots were to be shifted from populated areas.[76] Looking back a decade later, a former very senior military officer has claimed that the Ojhri accident case made it clear that, 'orders and instructions were grossly violated,' and noted that despite official claims no lessons had been learned from it about the siting of ammunition stores close to major population centres or establishing a crisis management system bringing together the military services and civilian authorities.[77]

These disasters highlight the effects of poor planning, lax procedures and limited oversight. There have been particular concerns voiced in the *Pakistan Army Journal* about training: 'The Army personnel and organizations (units, formations, institutions) have been overburdened by palpably unrealistic expectations and fruitless activity with the result that nearly all aspects of military life including training itself, discipline, administration, and morals and morale (both) have suffered.'[78] The crisis is traced to a profound mistake: 'To consider that army personnel, however, disciplined they may be, will behave like automatons is absolutely fallacious. Our planners and, with due respect, senior commanders have foundered on this account.' This raises important concerns about any nuclear Personnel Reliability Program that Pakistan may have put in place.

There is limited public information about the nuclear Personnel Reliability Program in Pakistan. The program is reported to examine the 'personal finances, political views and sexual histories' and 'degrees of religious fervour' of people in the weapons complex, with 'recruits . . . subject to a battery of background checks that can take up to a year [and] new employees are monitored for months before moving into sensitive areas. They may also be subjected to periodic psychological exams and reports from fellow workers.'[79] These procedures are however only as effective as the people who are charged with managing and implementing them.

In recent years, Pakistani military officers have been directly implicated in attacks on General Pervez Musharraf while he was Chief of Army Staff and President, and in the 2009 attack on the General Headquarters (GHQ) of the Pakistan Army in Rawalpindi. While insider knowledge may have played a role in the attacks on the offices in several cities of the Inter-Services Intelligence (ISI) Directorate, and in the 2011 attack on the PNS Mehran naval base near Karachi. A number of military officers and soldiers have been arrested and charged for ties to militant Islamist groups. Most recently, in 2011, a Brigadier serving in the GHQ was arrested and four other officers reported to be under investigation for contacts with the radical Islamic group Hizb-ut-Tahrir.[80] Taken together, this history suggests that the Pakistan Army is not reliably able to recognize and pre-empt at an early stage plots by officers and enlisted men with radical Islamist sympathies.

NUCLEAR WEAPONS DESIGN AND SAFETY

India and Pakistan have had limited experience with nuclear weapon design and testing and mating their weapons with delivery systems, both aircraft and missiles. Their armed forces have had even more limited experience with nuclear weapons in the field. One military analyst familiar with the Pakistan Army reports that even more than a decade after the formation (in 1989) of a 'Composite Missile Regiment' and exercises with nuclear missiles, the Pakistan Army's 'procedures are as yet by no means effective.'[81]

The United States began to tackle the risks of accidental detonation of its nuclear weapons in the mid- to late 1950s, once it had deployed nuclear weapons which were stored and placed on aircraft fully assembled. In simple nuclear weapons, a set of detonators are arranged uniformly around a shell of high explosive and set off simultaneously so as to detonate this shell, creating a shock wave that compresses the plutonium or highly enriched uranium until it undergoes a nuclear explosion. Weapons designers assumed that it would be very unlikely for several of the high explosive detonators on a bomb to be triggered simultaneously in an accident and sought to develop weapons that would be one-point safe, i.e., weapons that would not produce a nuclear yield if detonated at any single point. This has become a more or less common standard.

Recognising that an accident could trigger a warhead's electrical arming, fusing, and firing systems and lead to a nuclear explosion, other criteria were introduced that sought to reduce the chance of a weapon prematurely detonating in the normal course of its life (i.e., while in storage, transport, and at any stage in its combat use before it reached its assigned target), including during an accident or in other abnormal situations. As part of this effort, 'Enhanced Nuclear Detonation Safety Systems' were developed. Typically, they rely on a combination of a unique electrical signal and electronic data from sensors that assess whether the movements of the warhead correspond to what would be expected if it was going through its normal, assigned sequence on the way to its target. An unexpected pattern of acceleration, and other measures of the warhead path, should prevent the warhead from being armed and made ready to fire.

To limit the danger of plutonium dispersal from accidents, the U.S. sought to replace the high explosive in nuclear weapons, which was 94 per cent hexamine nitromene (HMX), with new insensitive high explosive (based on 2, 4, 6-tri-nitro-1, 3, 5-benzenetriamine, TATB) resistant to burning and detonation even under extreme conditions, as well as surrounding the uranium or plutonium with a shell of a refractory metal to produce a fire resistant pit that can withstand a jet fuel fire.[82] However, the refractory shell can be punctured or destroyed if the weapon is damaged in an aircraft crash or if the crash leads to a detonation of the high explosive. A fire resistant pit is also unlikely to be very effective if exposed to the much higher temperatures of a missile fuel fire.

The introduction of insensitive high explosive and a fire resistant shell add substantially to the size and weight of the bomb, as well as changing the way it behaves when it is detonated. The U.S. conducted numerous nuclear tests to validate the introduction of insensitive high explosives and fire resistant pits. Full three dimensional simulation of nuclear weapons detonations, which has been made possible by modern computers and use the accumulated data from previous nuclear tests and extensive laboratory experiments, have shown that earlier two-dimensional computer simulations were 'inadequate, and in some cases misleading, . . . in predicting how an actual explosion might be initiated and lead to dispersal of harmful radioactivity or even a nuclear yield.'[83] The U.S. is estimated to have carried out approximately 130 very low yield safety related tests, of which 62 are officially acknowledged as one-point safety tests.[84] For comparison, the USSR conducted about 100 hydronuclear tests, and 25 safety tests involving 42 weapons, between 1949 and 1990.[85] The

ENDS (Enhanced Nuclear Detonation Safety) system requires no additional nuclear tests since it does not affect the high explosive or nuclear fission parts of the weapon.

India conducted its first nuclear explosion in May 1974. By all accounts this was a crude, large, heavy, experimental plutonium-based implosion device, comparable to the first U.S. test in 1945. There are long standing questions about its yield.[86] It was in 1986 that India began to develop a bomb that could more easily and reliably be used from an aircraft, which involved 'a major effort to reduce the size of the bomb by using better quality explosives and lenses, making its detonators fail-safe, producing reliable high voltage capacitors and building in a series of electronic checks to ensure the bomb would go off only when the proper codes were fed in.'[87]

As part of these efforts, the Terminal Ballistic Research Laboratory at Chandigarh attempted to make the bomb lighter and smaller by using HMX as the high explosive (it has a very high detonation velocity).[88] This development in the early- to mid-1990s may been have the basis of the only nuclear weapon that was tested on 11 May 1998; according to a description of the tests by R. Chidambaram, then head of India's Department of Atomic Energy: 'The 15 kiloton device was a weapon which had been in the stockpile for several years. The others were weaponisable configurations.'[89] This would suggest that Indian nuclear weapons do not use insensitive high explosive, and given the compulsion to make the bomb as small and light as possible it may be that they also lack fire resistant pits since these also bring a weight and size penalty.

While Indian weapons scientists have made clear statements about the yields of their nuclear weapons, they have said nothing about safety. There has been no official mention that India's nuclear weapons are one-point safe. There has not even been a claim that nuclear weapons safety tests were conducted. The two small tests on 13 May 1998, claimed as sub-kiloton tests, were said to allow Indian nuclear weapon scientists to improve their computer simulations. There has been no suggestion that either of these were safety tests.

Despite what amounts to only one actual test, and with no evidence for one-point safety, and perhaps lacking modern safety features, India has prepared to deploy nuclear warheads on some of its planes and missiles. It is reported that as part of the 11 April 1999 *Agni-II* flight test, 'the bomb team secretly mounted on its warhead, a nuclear weapon assembly system minus the plutonium core to test whether all the systems including the safety locks would work.'[90] It had been discovered earlier that, 'when the warhead was subject to severe vibrations, a high voltage arching [*sic*] problem occurred that prematurely triggered the device.' *Agni-II* was tested again in January 2001 in what was called 'its final operational configuration.'[91]

Like their Indian peers, Pakistani nuclear weapons scientists have said nothing about the safety of their weapons. In building warheads to be delivered by aircraft and ballistic and cruise missiles and possibly for battlefield use, they face the constraints of minimising the size and weight of the weapons, and a very limited number of tests of both the weapons and the missile systems. This may make it unlikely that they have incorporated either insensitive high explosives or fire resistant pits as safety features. If they are deployed, there may be a risk of accidental detonation.

The experience of the other nuclear weapon states suggests accidents involving a nuclear weapon could be caused by any number of factors, including aircraft crashes, fires and missile explosions. Accidents can also happen in storage and during transport of nuclear weapons. The risks of an accident increase when the weapons are deployed on delivery vehicles (missiles, aeroplanes, etc.) and further increased where the weapons systems are kept on a high state of alert.

The consequences of an accident involving a nuclear weapon in South Asia could be severe. One possibility is if the high explosive detonates and converts the fissile material (the plutonium or highly enriched uranium) into an aerosol, but there is no nuclear yield. If the weapon relies on plutonium, an accidental explosion in a densely populated area (such as a large city) could lead to between 5000 and

20,000 fatalities from cancers caused by inhalation of the radioactive plutonium as it is spread by the wind.[92]

An even more serious possibility is where an accident causes the high explosive to detonate and triggers a nuclear explosion. In principle, the yield could be as large as the design yield of the weapon, i.e., it would have the same effects as the deliberate use of the weapon. It has been estimated that a nuclear explosion with a yield comparable to those claimed for their weapons by India and Pakistan could kill many hundreds of thousands of people.[93] A nuclear weapons accident could be a catastrophe.

CONCLUSION

The development of nuclear weapons by India and Pakistan and the efforts now being made by the respective governments to establish systems of nuclear command and control have created grave risks for the people of both countries. The history of nuclear weapons teaches that the effort to create a robust 'nuclear deterrent' requires creating military forces that are equipped, trained and able to use nuclear weapons. This history also shows how fallible people, institutions and technology can be. The destructive power of nuclear weapons, which has made them so attractive to India, Pakistan and a handful of other states, brings a potential for catastrophe.

The risk of an accident may increase through the action of numerous, often unpredictable factors. There are however some obvious lessons that can be learned from the experience of command and control of nuclear weapons over the past fifty years or so. The most important is that no system for nuclear command and control can be perfect, no matter how carefully it is designed; how carefully selected and well-trained the personnel; how sophisticated the technology; or how much money is spent. There are profound problems built into the task such a system is intended to perform, and these problems leave it open to failure and the possibility of disaster.

Having tested their weapons, both India and Pakistan are now struggling to operationalise their nuclear weapons capability. The nuclear arsenals are growing, delivery systems are under development, and structures of command and control are still in their infancy. There are great pressures on any possible system for nuclear command and control. The size of the arsenal is itself an issue; as arsenals grow and the delivery systems start to include aircraft and missiles, and perhaps eventually even submarines, there will be more bombs and more people in more places under more circumstances that require control, and more opportunities for things to go wrong.

While having fewer nuclear weapons obviously makes exercising control easier, it does not make it easy or simple. There are other factors at work over which there can be no control. The geography of South Asia ensures that for Pakistan in particular there can be no useful early warning of an Indian attack on its nuclear arsenal or facilities, nor are there many places to hide its weapons from such an attack. The history of India–Pakistan relations ensures that these fears shall not pass easily. The failures of the early warning systems of both have been exposed repeatedly. The weapons will always be seen as vulnerable and this fear will make command and control insecure. The temptation will be to disperse the nuclear weapons, and de-centralise control in the hope that some weapons would survive any possible attack. With this step, the risk of accidental or inadvertent use of nuclear weapons is increased, as is the possibility of an accident involving a weapon and its delivery system. Removing this fear will require changing the pattern of military forces on both sides so that no surprise attack is possible.

Even when there are no surprises, war brings pressures of its own. India's conventional military strength is a pressure that is pushing Pakistan to deploy nuclear weapons early in a crisis. Pakistan would seek to protect the weapons against attack, show its determination to escalate a conflict rather than concede, and seek to incite intervention from the international community. Nuclear and conventional forces may clash on the battlefield; India may seek to destroy Pakistan's nuclear weapons and Pakistan may use them for lack of a perceived alternative. With Indian military planners seemingly prepared to include this possibility in their war plans and to keep fighting, Pakistan's generals may feel even more acutely that they must use their nuclear weapons early and hopefully decisively or risk losing the option. Nuclear war in South Asia could result in possibly millions of deaths and injuries. Preventing this apocalypse should become the biggest challenge.

Maintaining command over nuclear weapons produces its own problems. Pakistan and India have both sought technology from other nuclear weapon states to ensure that only the highest political and military authorities are in the position to unleash nuclear weapons. In particular, they have sought to systems such as Permissive Action Links (PALs), the coded switches that seek to prevent unauthorised or accidental use. Unfortunately, experience suggests it is all too common for a simple minded faith in technology to produce a sense of control that slides into over-confidence. Feeling that the bomb is now safely in hand, politicians and generals may all too easily and publicly use the deployment and alert status of nuclear weapons as signals of resolve to adversaries, and to their own people. With time, a growing sense of confidence in control over nuclear weapons may push deployments and alert levels ever closer to the edge of being fully prepared for use at a moments' notice. The United States and the Soviet Union did just this. Nothing should be done, no technology sought, no procedures developed that can help create such dangerous confidence in South Asia.

However, in the fog and friction of war, the decision to unleash nuclear destruction may not be for South Asia's generals or prime ministers to make. Both India and Pakistan will disperse their weapons to protect them in a crisis. The codes to unlock them would also need to be dispersed, otherwise the weapons may become unusable through the countless minor circumstances which cannot properly be illustrated on paper but ensure that things do not turn out as planned. Things have gone dreadfully wrong with far simpler procedures to manage weapons even in peace time. With control of nuclear weapons and their codes in the hands of brigadiers, in the heat of battle, the chances of unauthorised use, misjudgement and accident are great. Again, the consequences would be devastating. There must be a determined search for ways to prevent and manage crises.

The critical first step is for India and Pakistan to not assemble and deploy their nuclear weapons. Even in peace time, assembly and deployment bring increased risk of accidents. There is a long record of accidents and near misses involving aircraft and missiles carrying nuclear weapons belonging to other nuclear weapons states. The safety record of India and Pakistan's military aircraft is poor: accidents are frequent; the causes many. With many of the air bases often located close to major cities, there would always be the risk of an aircraft crash involving a plane carrying a nuclear weapon, or a bomb accidentally falling from a plane. This may be enough to detonate the bomb. South Asian missiles are still at a seminal stage of development; tests have been few and missiles may harbour their own dangers. They may explode and trigger their nuclear warhead. Keeping the weapons disassembled and far from their delivery systems is the only sure protection.

It is not known how safe either India or Pakistan's nuclear weapons would be if they were involved in an accident. Neither state has revealed any information about conducting safety tests, or whether their weapons are safe against detonation if they are in a fire or if subjected to high impact. The limited number of tests they have carried out and the incentive to produce weapons that are as small and light as possible suggests neither country may have adopted either insensitive high explosive or fire resistant pits, both of which add to the size and weight of a weapon.

The consequences of an accident could be devastating. An explosion in which the high explosive is set off and converts the fissile material into an aerosol that can be spread by the wind and inhaled could kill between 5000 and 20,000 people if it involves plutonium and takes place close to a large city. An accident in which the bomb explodes with its full yield could potentially kill hundreds of thousands in a large South Asian city. There would be no warning, and no defense.

REFERENCES

1. Ashton B. Carter, John D. Steinbruner, Charles Z. Zraket, *Managing Nuclear Operations*, (Washington: The Brookings Institution, 1987), p. 3.
2. Lee Butler, 'Zero Tolerance', *The Bulletin of the Atomic Scientists*, Vol. 56, No. 1, January/February 2000, pp. 20–1.
3. Lee Butler, 'Zero Tolerance', *The Bulletin of the Atomic Scientists*, Vol. 56, No. 1, January/February 2000, pp. 20–1.
4. Bruce Blair and Henry Kendall, 'Accidental Nuclear War', *Scientific American* 263, no. 6, December 1990, pp. 53–8.
5. See e.g., Bruce Blair, *Strategic Command and Control*.
6. Paul Bracken, *The Command and Control of Nuclear Forces*, (New Haven: Yale University Press, 1983), p. 12.
7. Paul Bracken, *The Command and Control of Nuclear Forces*, pp. 12–13.
8. Charles Perrow, *Normal Accidents: Living with High-Risk Technologies*, (New York: Basic Books, 1984).
9. Scott Sagan, *The Limits of Safety: Organizations, Accidents, and Nuclear Weapons*, (Princeton: Princeton University Press, 1993).
10. Ashton B. Carter, 'Communications Technologies and Vulnerabilities,' in Ashton B. Carter, John D. Steinbruner, Charles Z. Zraket, *Managing Nuclear Operations*, (Washington: The Brookings Institution, 1987), pp. 217–81.
11. Kevin O'Neill, 'Building the Bomb', in: *Atomic Audit: The Costs and Consequences of U.S. Nuclear Weapons Since 1940*, Stephen I. Schwarz (ed.), (Washington: Brookings Institution Press, 1998), pp. 33–103.
12. Robert S. Norris, Steven M. Kosiak, and Stephen I. Schwarz, 'Deploying the Bomb', in: *Atomic Audit: The Costs and Consequences of U.S. Nuclear Weapons Since 1940*, Stephen I. Schwarz, (ed.), (Washington: Brookings Institution Press, 1998), pp. 95–105.
13. Bruce G. Blair, John E. Pike, and Stephen I, Schwartz, 'Targeting and Controlling the Bomb', in: *Atomic Audit: The Costs and Consequences of U.S. Nuclear Weapons Since 1940*, Stephen I. Schwarz (ed.), (Washington: Brookings Institution Press, 1998), pp. 197–325.
14. Thomas B. Cochran, William M. Arkin, Robert S. Norris and Milton M. Hoenig, *Nuclear Weapons Databook Series Volume I: U.S. Nuclear Forces and Capabilities*, (Cambridge: Ballinger Publishing Company, 1984).
15. Herbert L. Abrams, 'Human Reliability and Safety in the Handling of Nuclear Weapons', *Science and Global Security*, vol. 2, No. 4, 1991, pp. 325–49.
16. Peter Stein and Peter Feaver, *Assuring Control of Nuclear Weapons*, CSIA Occasional Paper No. 2, Center for Science and International Affairs, Harvard University, 1987.
17. Sidney Drell and Bob Peurifoy, 'Technical Issues of A Nuclear Test Ban', *Annual Review of Nuclear and Particle Science* 44, (1994), pp. 285–327.

18. For a history of India's nuclear weapons programs see George Perkovich, *India's Nuclear Bomb*, (Berkeley: University of California Press, 1999); on command and control see P.R. Chari, 'India's Nuclear Doctrine: Confused Ambitions', *The Nonproliferation Review*, Fall-Winter 2000, pp. 123–35.

19. 'Press Release: Cabinet Committee on Security reviews progress in operationalizing India's nuclear doctrine', Prime Minister's Office, Government of India, 2003. The text is at http://pib.nic.in/archieve/lreleng/lyr2003/rjan2003/04012003/r040120033.html

20. *SP's Military Yearbook 2010*, New Delhi, http://www.spsmilitaryyearbook.com/updates.asp

21. Draft Report of National Security Advisory Board on Indian Nuclear Doctrine. New Delhi: National Security Advisory Board, 1999.

22. Sandeep Dikshit, 'Step-up if Agni-II range planned', *The Hindu*, 13 February 2005. Y. Mallikarjun, 'Agni-III gets nod for induction', *The Hindu*, 23 September 2008.

23. T.S. Subramanian, 'Strike Power', *Frontline*, 15–28 March 2008.

24. 'India Launches Nuclear Submarine', *BBC*, 26 July 2009.

25. Sandeep Unnithan, 'The Secret Undersea Weapon', *India Today*, 28 January 2008.

26. Rajat Pandit, 'India Surprised by Chinese Fuss over Agni-V', *Times of India*, 17 October 2009.

27. Raj Chengappa, 'Worrying Over Broken Arrows', *India Today*, 13 July 1998.

28. 'General Musharraf Made Acting CJCSC', *The News*, 10 April 1999.

29. 'National Command Authority Formed', *Dawn*, 3 February 2000.

30. '19th National Command Authority Meeting', Pakistan Ministry of Foreign Affairs, 14 July 2011.

31. Shakil Sheikh, 'Strategic Organisations Put under NCA Control,' *The News*, 28 November 2000.

32. 'Mubarakmand to Chair NESCOM', *Nucleonics Week*, 25 January 2001.

33. Kenneth N. Luong and Naeem Salik, 'Building Confidence in Pakistan's Nuclear Security', *Arms Control Today*, December 2007.

34. 'Pakistan test-fires nuclear-capable cruise missile: military', *AFP*, 8 May 2008.

35. 'Pakistan launches longest-range nuclear-capable missile during exercise', *AP*, 22 April 2008.

36. 'N-capable ballistic missile tested', *Dawn*, 19 April 2011.

37. Kenneth N. Luongo and Naeem Salik, 'Building Confidence in Pakistan's Nuclear Security', *Arms Control Today*, December 2007.

38. For such efforts see Marc Dean Millot, Roger Molander, and Peter A. Wilson, 'The Day After' Study: Nuclear Proliferation in the Post-Cold War World, Volume II, Main Report, (Santa Monica, RAND Corporation, 1993), and Bradd C. Hayes, *International Game '99—Crisis in South Asia*, Decision Support Department Center for Naval Warfare Studies, (Newport: United States Naval War College, 1999).

39. *The Story of the Pakistan Air Force 1988—1998* (Islamabad: Shaheen Foundation, 2000), pp. 132–33.
40. George Perkovich, *India's Nuclear Bomb*.
41. *The Story of the Pakistan Air Force 1988–1998*, p. 133.
42. 'Indian Military Rehearse Pakistan's Dissection in Mock Battles', *Defense News*, 3 May 2006.
43. See Zia Mian, 'Renouncing The Nuclear Option', in: *Pakistan And The Bomb: Public Opinion and Nuclear Options*, Samina Ahmed and David Cortright (eds.), (Notre Dame: University of Notre Dame Press, 1998), pp. 47–68.
44. 'How Israel Got The Bomb', *Time*, Vol. 107, 12 April 1976, cited in Peter Pry, *Israel's Nuclear Arsenal*, (Boulder: Westview Press, 1984), pp. 31–2.
45. Seymour Hersh, *The Samson Option*, (New York: Random House, 1991), p. 225.
46. Seymour Hersh, *The Samson Option*, pp. 223, 227.
47. 'Bracing for a Nuclear Attack, India Plans "Operation Desert Storm" in May', *The Indian Express*, 1 May 2001.
48. 'Unmanned Aerial Spies Used in Wargames', *The Times of India*, 8 May 2001.
49. Harinder Bajewa, 'Readying For Nukes', *India Today*, 28 May 2001.
50. 'Wargame, A Chance to Test Air Force Efficacy', *The Hindu*, 9 May 2001.
51. 'Indian Forces Test Skills Against NBC Background', *The Hindu*, 10 May 2001.
52. 'Bracing for a Nuclear Attack, India Plans "Operation Desert Storm" in May', *The Indian Express*, 1 May 2001.
53. Barry Posen, *Inadvertent Escalation: Conventional War and Nuclear Risks*, (Ithaca: Cornell University Press, 1991).
54. Peter Stein and Peter Feaver, *Assuring Control of Nuclear Weapons*.
55. Dan Caldwell and Peter Zimmerman, 'Reducing The Risk of Nuclear War with Permissive Action Links', in: *Technology and the Limitation of International Conflict*, Barry M. Blechman, (ed.), (Washington: Foreign Policy Institute, School of Advanced International Studies, Johns Hopkins University, 1989), pp. 137–50.
56. See Peter Stein and Peter Feaver, *Assuring Control of Nuclear Weapons*.
57. Bruce G. Blair, *Global Zero Alert for Nuclear Forces*, p. 9.
58. Agha Shahi, Zulfiqar Ali Khan, and Abdul Sattar, 'Securing Nuclear Peace', *The News*, 5 October 1999.
59. Tanvir Ahmad Khan, 'A Command and Control System', *Dawn*, 15 February 2000.
60. Kenneth N. Luongo and Naeem Salik, 'Building Confidence in Pakistan's Nuclear Security', *Arms Control Today*, December 2007.
61. Peter Stein and Peter Feaver, *Assuring Control of Nuclear Weapons*, p. 24.
62. P. Bracken, *The Command and Control of Nuclear Forces*, (New Haven: Yale University Press, 1983), p. 168.
63. Bruce G. Blair, *Global Zero Alert for Nuclear Forces*, p. 60.
64. 'Blast in Jabalpur Ordnance Factory', *The Times of India*, 25 March 1988.

65. Chinu Panchal, 'Army Apathy to Ordnance Fire', *The Times of India*, 29 March 1988.

66. Man Mohan, 'Panel had Warned on Safety at Arms Depots', *The Times of India*, 2 May 2000.

67. 'Fire in Ammo Store Near Balasore', *The Statesman*, 10 November 1998.

68. 'War Reserves Worth Several Hundred Crores Wiped Out', *The Times of India*, 30 April 2000.

69. Sarabjit Pandher, 'Experts Question Army Version on Fire', *The Hindu*, 2 May 2001.

70. 'Fire at Ammunition Depot Put Out', *The Hindu*, 26 May 2001.

71. Vishal Thapar, 'Depot Fire An Act Of God: Army Vice-Chief', *Hindustan Times*, 26 May 2001.

72. Vishal Thapar, 'Depot Fire An Act Of God: Army Vice-Chief'.

73. '80 Killed, 1000 Injured: Army Ammunition Dump Blows Up in Pindi', *Dawn*, 11 April 1998.

74. 'MRD Convenor Seeks Judicial Probe into Ojheri Blasts', *Dawn*, 21 April 1988.

75. '80 Killed, 1000 Injured: Army Ammunition Dump Blows Up in Pindi'.

76. 'Ammunition Depots To Be Shifted: Junejo', *Dawn*, 11 April 1998.

77. Air Marshal (retd.) Ayaz Ahmed Khan, 'Lessons From the Ojri Disaster', *The Nation*, 10 April 2000.

78. Lieutenant Colonel Fazl-e-Ali Naqvi, 'What is Wrong with our Training', *Pakistan Army Journal*, Summer 1995, pp. 7–13.

79. Peter Wonacott, 'Inside Pakistan's Drive to Guard its A-Bombs', *The Wall Street Journal*, 29 November 2007.

80. Imtiaz Gul, 'Reinventing the Army', *Newsline*, 31 July 2011.

81. Brian Cloughley, 'Transition time in Pakistan's Army', *Jane's Intelligence Review*, 1 April 2000.

82. Sidney Drell and Bob Peurifoy, 'Technical Issues of a Nuclear Test Ban'.

83. Ibid.

84. Thomas B. Cochran and Christopher E. Paine, 'Hydronuclear Testing and the Comprehensive Test Ban: Memorandum to Participants JASON 1994 Summer Study' (Washington: Natural Resources Defense Council, 1994).

85. Robert S. Norris and William Arkin, 'Soviet Nuclear Testing, 29 August 1949—24 October 1990', *The Bulletin of The Atomic Scientists*, 54, no. 3, May/June 1998, pp. 69–71.

86. George Perkovich, *India's Nuclear Bomb*, pp. 181–83.

87. Raj Chengappa, *Weapons of Peace: The Secret Story of India's Quest to be a Nuclear Power*, (Delhi: Harper Collins, 2000), p. 304.

88. Raj Chengappa, *Weapons of Peace*, p. 304.

89. 'One N-device at Pokhran was a Weapon', *The Hindu*, 20 June 2000.

90. Raj Chengappa, *Weapons of Peace*, p. 436.

91. 'India Test fires Agni-II, Pakistan Cries Foul', *The Statesman*, 17 January 2001.

92. Zia Mian, M.V. Ramana, and R. Rajaraman, 'Plutonium Dispersal and Health Hazards from Nuclear Weapons Accidents', *Current Science*, vol. 80, No. 10, 25 May 2001, pp. 1275–1283.

93. See Table I; for a detailed study of the effects of a nuclear explosion on a single large South Asian city see, M.V. Ramana, 'Bombing Bombay: Effects of Nuclear Weapons and a Case Study of a Hypothetical Explosion', *International Physicians for the Prevention of Nuclear War Global Health Watch Report*, No. 3, (Cambridge: International Physicians for the Prevention of Nuclear War, 1999).

CHAPTER 10

THE INFEASIBILITY OF EARLY WARNING
Zia Mian, R. Rajaraman, and M.V. Ramana

Since their nuclear weapons tests in 1998, India and Pakistan have been putting in place various elements of their nuclear arsenals, including delivery vehicles and command and control systems. India's 1999 Draft Nuclear Doctrine proposed setting up 'effective intelligence and early warning capabilities,' that would use 'space based and other assets' to provide 'early warning, communications, damage/detonation assessment.'[1] In this context, 'early warning' refers to the means to detect the launch and flight of ballistic missiles fired by an adversary in order to provide time to decision-makers to determine a response.

The notion of early warning is a carry-over from the nuclear confrontation between the U.S. and the Soviet Union. Both countries had plans to launch nuclear armed missiles upon detection of incoming missiles. The purpose of early launch was to prevent missiles from being destroyed on the ground or to prevent the destruction of the leadership at the onset of a nuclear war. This approach was dubbed as 'use it or lose it'. This was widely recognized to pose the risk of inadvertent nuclear war. We argue here that such an approach carries even greater dangers in South Asia. We will not discuss here the feasibility or the desirability of an anti-ballistic missile system. Rather, we focus on the potential use of an early warning system for a launch on warning attack.

This chapter draws on our technical study from 2002–2003 of the prospects for nuclear early warning in South Asia.[2] That study examined the different ingredients that go into setting up early warning systems and assessed their effectiveness. Readers interested in the technical details may refer to our paper in the journal, *Science and Global Security*.[3] In this chapter we present the main results of that study, suppressing the technical details and derivations. Using the insights gained from the study we also drew some policy inferences about the viability and advisability of early warning systems in South Asia.[4]

This chapter considers what may happen in the time that elapses between the launch of a missile by one country and the response by the other. It begins with describing how ballistic missiles work and provides a simple estimate for missile flight times between different locations in India and Pakistan. Then we examine the role of early warning radars and satellites to determine the available missile warning time. Lastly, we analyze what could be done in this available time, using as models the threat assessment and response procedures that have been followed by the U.S. and the USSR (now Russia).

A BALLISTIC MISSILE PRIMER

The flight of a ballistic missile may be broadly divided into three phases. The first is the 'boost phase' when the rocket is powered by its burning fuel. Once all the fuel is exhausted, the missile jettisons the propellant tanks. This 'burnout' altitude is about 30 km for single stage missiles like the *Prithvi* or the Scud, and about 100 km for two stage missiles like the *Agni*. Beyond the burnout point the missile nosecone or re-entry vehicle containing the warhead moves in free fall, i.e., under the influence of only the Earth's gravitational force. This is the 'ballistic phase'. Finally, as the payload falls back towards the earth it re-enters the atmosphere. Motion in this last 're-entry phase', as well as in the launch phase is complicated by air resistance.

If one needs to know the trajectories of missiles to great precision, this can only be done through numerical calculations involving elaborate computer programs that include the boost and re-entry phases and the effects of air resistance. But by employing judicious approximations, one can derive relatively simple formulae to make *back of the envelope* estimates of flight times, missile velocities and so on. The ballistic phase consumes the longest duration in the missile's flight and is also the easiest to calculate since it is free of the complications caused by engine thrust and air resistance. After calculating accurately the time taken in the ballistic phase we added one minute each for the boost and re-entry phases to arrive at our estimates for the total missile flight time. Our estimates are accurate to the nearest minute—which is quite adequate for making strategic and policy judgements.

We estimated the missile flight times for typical pairs of possible launch sites and targets in South Asia, taking as launch-points different military bases (e.g., airbases) and as targets command centres, big cities or national capitals. Examples are a launch from a base near Karachi towards Thiruvananthapuram—the southern headquarters of the Indian Air Force—or from Agra to Karachi, or Sargodha to New Delhi.

Normally, missiles are flown on 'optimal' trajectories, where the goal is to maximize the range (flight distance). But it is also possible to fire a powerful, long-range, missile at a near-by target, along a trajectory designed to minimize the time it would take to cover this distance. For example, Pakistan's *Ghauri* and India's *Agni* missiles, which have ranges in excess of 1000 km, could be used to attack targets only 500–600 km away. Such a 'depressed trajectory' flight of a long-range missile can significantly reduce the flight time compared to that of a short-range missile flown over the same distance and would pose the more significant challenge to an early warning system.

The table provides some typical examples of flight times for both optimal flights and a depressed trajectory flight.

Table 3
Estimated Duration of some Plausible
South Asian Missile Flights

Launch Point	Target	Distance (km)	Est. Total Flight Time (minutes)
Airbase near Karachi	Tiruvananthapuram	2000	13
Sargodha Airbase	Mumbai	1470	11
Agra Airbase	Karachi	1128	10
Agra Airbase	Lahore	608	8
Sargodha Airbase	New Delhi	581	8
Depressed trajectory flight		600	5

The normal (optimal) flight times are around 10–13 minutes for distances between 1000–2000 km, and about 8 minutes for a missile flying the approximately 600 km path from Agra to Lahore, or Sargodha to Delhi. But the estimated depressed trajectory flight time is much shorter; the missile covers a distance of 600 km in about 5 minutes only. For comparison, the U.S. and Soviet land-based intercontinental ballistic missiles, capable of striking the major cities in the other's country, had flight times of over 30 minutes. We have also verified that corrections due to other effects, such as the rotation of the Earth, alter our estimated flight times by only a few per cent.

WARNING FROM RADARS

There are a number of radar systems around the world that are used for early warning or as part of anti-ballistic missile systems. Two examples are the PAVE PAWS (Perimeter Acquisition Vehicle Entry Phased-Array Weapons System) used as part of the U.S. early warning of ICBM (Intercontinental Ballistic Missile) launches from Russia, and the Patriot that was used extensively in the 1991 Gulf War to detect and track incoming Iraqi Scud missiles.

A radar in its essence consists of an antenna that emits electro-magnetic wave pulses, some of which impinge on the potential target. Some fraction of this signal is reflected back by the target towards the radar. Based on this reflected signal, one can calculate the location and speed of the target. The intensity of the radiation reflected from a target decreases rapidly with increasing distance to the target. Thus, beyond a certain distance, depending on the characteristics of the target (its size, geometry, materials used, etc.,) the reflected signal as received by the radar will become indistinguishable from the background 'noise' that radars inevitably pick up. When the target is at this distance or greater, the radar cannot unambiguously detect the target.

In fact, to be reliable, the received radar signal should be many times louder than the background noise. The optimal ratio of signal to noise is set by balancing two competing requirements. To detect all potential targets, the minimum acceptable signal should be as small as possible. At the same time, noise should not be mistaken as a signal from a target. Once a ratio of signal to noise has been decided upon, the characteristics of the radar determine the distance to which a particular target in a given orientation can be detected. This distance is termed the radar range. But, to reiterate, this range is dependent on the target being detected and the target's orientation with respect to the radar beam.

Detection of missiles by radars is not a straightforward or completely reliable process. There are many sources of false, unwanted and unpredictable signals that any radar system must contend with. A flock of birds, for example, can produce significant radar clutter. Rain and clouds may also affect performance, depending on the radar wavelength. In the 2003 U.S. war against Iraq, the advanced version of the Patriot system reportedly generated many false radar signals.[5]

In order to estimate the amount of early warning possible in South Asia, we need to know the kind of radar likely to be used. India has Green Pine radars, and a modified version called Swordfish, that it uses as part of its ballistic missile Interceptor.[6] The technical specifications of these radars are not fully available in the public domain but parameters of other radar systems like the PAVE PAWS and the Patriots are available. From these one can make reasonably educated guesses for the necessary parameters.

Given a radar system with some specific parameters, the range at which it can observe a missile depends on the cross-section the latter presents to the incident radar beam, which in turn depends on the stage of the flight and the tilt angle of the missile. If the missile is in the early boost phase, then the radar signal may be reflected by almost the entire missile's full body (side-on) possibly including its fins as well. Altogether this would offer a cross-section of about 100 m^2. In this situation, we estimate that the Green Pine type of radar may detect the missile as far away as 2000 km. As the missile rises and tilts towards the horizontal, it offers a smaller cross-section. Once the rocket engines have been jettisoned after burn-out, this range may reduce to about 700 km. By the time the warhead has separated and is approaching the radar nose-on (which offers a far smaller cross-section of about 0.01 m^2) the detection range would decrease even further, to about 200 km.

There is one other important factor to keep in mind—the curvature of the earth. A radar cannot see objects located below its horizon, hence, a ground-based radar cannot see the ground-based launch of a missile hundreds of miles away. The missile has to rise above the horizon for it to be visible to the radar. Further, to reduce ground clutter (reflections from objects on the ground and so on) the radar does not scan angles below a certain minimum angle. The PAVE PAWS radar beam, for example, goes only as low as an angle of 3 degrees to the horizon.[7] Thus, if the radar is at a distance of 300 km from the missile, then it can only see missiles that are at an altitude of approximately 20 km or greater.

Keeping all these factors in mind, we examined the hypothetical case of a missile launched from Pakistan's Sargodha Air Force Base towards New Delhi to determine when the missile launched along a depressed trajectory may be detected by a radar kept at India's Ambala Air Force Base. Our calculations show that the earliest that detection can take place is around 87 seconds after launch, i.e., when the missile has travelled for almost one-third of the total time it will take to reach its target. Detection of what may be a missile soon after launch is itself insufficient to serve as useful early warning of a missile attack, for example, countries with missiles frequently conduct flight tests. One needs to track it over a period of time to establish if the missile is in fact heading towards a target within one's own country and to determine the trajectory accurately. We estimate that this could be of the order of about 20 seconds.

All this would imply that a radar system similar to Green Pine could provide a relatively unambiguous detection and warning, at best only about 110 seconds after a missile's launch. Given that the total time of flight along a depressed trajectory over 600 km is about 300 seconds, this would leave less than 200 seconds for all subsequent assessments and responses.

WARNING FROM SATELLITES

As mentioned earlier, India has expressed an interest in setting up satellite-based early warning. Although India already has considerable expertise in launching satellites, any plan of setting up viable early warning satellites can only be considered preliminary. But satellites have been an important component of early warning systems used by the United States and Russia to provide the first detection of missile launches. France is also building an early warning satellite system.[8]

The United States Defense Support Program (DSP) satellites work by detecting the heat of a missile plume against the background radiation emitted by the earth and clouds.[9] These satellites are in geo-synchronous orbit, at an altitude of about 36,000 km, and so seem to stay above one point on the Earth. From that location, the DSP satellites are made to rotate about their own axis six times a minute, sweeping the sensor's field of view around the earth so that it covers almost an entire hemisphere. Any strong source is thus picked up every ten seconds. Multiple observations serve to confirm that it is a missile in flight and to estimate its trajectory, and its impact area. The DSP satellites also carry optical, florescence and X-ray detectors to locate nuclear explosions on the earth's surface, in the atmosphere and in space. India's declared aim in the 1999 Draft Nuclear Doctrine to acquire a space-based capability for early warning and damage and detonation assessment would seem to indicate a goal of a DSP type of system.

The area viewed by a DSP satellite is about 200 million square kilometres, roughly 40 per cent of Earth's surface area. For example, a United States DSP satellite launched in May 1971 into orbit was able to cover much of Europe, almost all of Africa, the Middle East, Russia, Central Asia, South and South East Asia.[10] This coverage is very similar to what India might seek if the aim were to monitor missile launches and nuclear detonations involving Pakistan and China and the Indian Ocean.

There are a number of technical limits on satellite-based missile detection. The infrared radiation from the missile plume is largely absorbed by water vapour and carbon dioxide in the lower atmosphere.[11] The radiation is also scattered by rain, heavy dust and does not penetrate clouds.[12] Thus, a missile can be plausibly detected only when it emerges above the cloud layer. The cloud-top at latitudes of 20–40 N (i.e., covering Pakistan and northern India) is typically at altitudes of 3–4 km, but can be as high as 10 km.[13] Reaching this altitude would require about thirty seconds to one minute after launch.

Once the missile has risen above the clouds, the signal from the plume is still not easily distinguished from the normal background heat radiated from the Earth and solar radiation reflected from the cloud tops. The experience of DSP satellites of the U.S. suggests a number of operational problems. A Congressional study of failures of the U.S. early warning system noted that, 'there are many indications of [missile launch] detections that have to be evaluated but prove not to be associated with a threatening missile launch.'[14] A significant problem has been solar reflection from cloud-tops and the ocean surface, along with ice and snow, including from high mountainous areas, which blinds the DSP satellites.[15] The satellites are reportedly 'frequently put out of commission for several hours by the effects of sun glare.'[16]

Geostationary early warning satellites for the detection of possible missile launches are clearly a very demanding technology. The Soviet Union relied on a system of satellites in very elliptical orbits that did not look directly at the Earth but waited for the missile plume to become visible against the background of space.[17] As of October 2010, Russia had three satellites deployed on such very elliptical orbits.[18] This system has its own set of problems.

Coming to South Asia, India's Geo-synchronous Satellite Launch Vehicle (GSLV) program offers it the capability to launch a satellite comparable in size and weight to a United States DSP satellite.[19] The first developmental flight, GSLV-D1, was launched in April 2001. However, the program has experienced problems: of the seven test launches, four failed for various reasons.[20] Pakistan does not have an equivalent launch capability.[21] The pursuit of this kind of capability will at best give warning of a possible missile launch only 30 to 60 seconds before, by a ground-based radar system, because of the proximity of the two countries.

Because they do not provide round-the-clock coverage optical satellites are of little use as a real-time early warning system. At best these may offer what is described as 'strategic warning'.

In summary, a missile launch may be reliably detected by a geo-synchronous infrared early warning satellite only after it rises above the cloud cover. This means detection of the missile about half-a-minute to a minute after launch. But a radar-like the Green Pine can already detect the missile about 90 seconds after launch. Thus, a geo-synchronous infrared satellite could typically provide only half-a-minute to one minute of additional warning in South Asia. This is to be contrasted with the U.S. –Soviet case where, given the longer flight times, early warning satellites that can detect a missile in the launch phase will provide several minutes of additional warning time.

TIME TO WORRY?

An early warning system is more than the set of detectors and platforms for monitoring missile launches. It includes the procedures for evaluating the information produced by such detectors and assessing the reliability and significance of such data and interpreting it as 'warning'. In the preceeding sections, we arrived at estimates of the maximum time that would be available for this threat assessment and decision-making. To understand the steps needed to translate the initial signal into a meaningful warning and response, we outline the procedures adopted by the United States and the Soviet Union (now Russia) to assess missile warnings. The flight times between the missile fields and targets of those two states are about thirty minutes.[22] We then look at whether analogous procedures could be practical in South Asia, given the much shorter warning times.

U.S. EARLY WARNING PROCEDURES

In the United States, the task of detecting and assessing ballistic missile launches is managed by North American Aerospace Defense Command (NORAD). Though most of the details about its operation are secret, independent analysts have managed to construct a broadly consistent picture of the general procedures that are followed.[23] These are simplified and presented here as sequence of events with their allotted duration:

1. Observation of missile launch by satellites in geo-synchronous orbit and relay of signal to ground stations for processing (half-a-minute after launch).
2. Decision by the ground station staff whether to forward this information to NORAD and other command centres assessing missile warnings (about 15 seconds).
3. Convening of Missile Event Conference at NORAD. Command director would assess the reliability of satellite data, based on telephonic communications with ground station operators, who would re-verify the initial detection and confirm that it was not due to equipment malfunction. Strategic warning analysts, who look at intelligence estimates of the international political and military situation and force deployments are also

consulted. The command director would then forward the level of confidence in the warning to the war rooms at the Pentagon and Strategic Command (3 minutes).

4. About four minutes after a possible missile launch, if the NORAD officer judged there was medium or high confidence in a warning, the information would go up the chain of command, that included the Joint Chiefs of Staff Chairman, and Defense Secretary, ultimately leading up to the President and a Missile Attack Conference would be initiated. By this time, there may or may not have been separate warning from ground-based radars (4–6 minutes).

5. There would now be less than 20 minutes remaining from the initial thirty minute flight time (assuming a Soviet ICBM). This would leave about 10 minutes for discussion, before a decision would have to be made whether U.S. missiles were to be launched.

6. If the decision was made to fire U.S. missiles, it would take 2 minutes to send launch orders, 3 minutes to fire the Minuteman ICBMs (Intercontinental Ballistic Missile), and several more minutes for the missiles to travel to a safe distance from their bases.

This timeline adds up to about 30 minutes, which is comparable to an ICBM flight time from Russia, and would enable the retaliatory missiles to take off and be at safe distance before their silos are destroyed. However, all of this assumes that every procedural and technological element in the early warning system works perfectly.

SOVIET/RUSSIAN EARLY WARNING PROCEDURES

There is less information about Soviet (and now Russian) early warning systems.[24] One description suggests the following expected sequence of events following detection by satellites or ground-based radars of a possible missile launch:[25]

1. Positive attack identification from satellites (about one minute after launch) or radar would lead to warning report by the Centre for the Analysis of Missile and Space Situation, the Russian counterpart of NORAD, to Defense headquarters, general staff, and strategic rocket forces. This centre would send a signal to the president, defense minister and chief of general staff (through the nuclear suitcase).[26]
2. Within 4–6 minutes after a missile launch, political and military leadership along with chief of early warning centre would confer on warning.
3. If the early warning system provides dual sensor (i.e., radar and satellite) warning of attack, then general staff would send a preliminary command activating the communications system to nuclear forces. This communication link is normally kept disconnected.[27]
4. According to Russian procedures, the national command authority (president and defense minister) is allotted three minutes to discuss and authorise (or withhold) permission to launch Russian missiles.
5. To institute and transmit the launch order, with the unlock codes, takes about 2–3 minutes. A total of 12–13 minutes would have elapsed since incoming missile lift-off.
6. Once the order has been received it takes as long as 8 minutes for the Russian missiles to emerge from their silos. A total of about 20 minutes would have elapsed between the time of launch of the enemy attack and the launch of the Russian missiles.

Russian procedures are thus designed to beat the expected arrival time of ICBMs from the continental United States by a margin of ten minutes. But Russia had serious concerns that these procedures may not work as planned. This led them to install in addition a 'dead hand' that would automatically transmit launch orders.[28]

The U.S. and Russian early warning and operating procedures are both fallible and have created false alerts at times.[29] The U.S. for instance had built an elaborate 'early warning system' which would warn them about impending missile attacks, with layers of filters to remove false signals. Yet, from 1977 through 1984, one period for which official information has been released, the early warning systems gave an average of 2598 warnings each year of potential incoming missiles attacks.[30] Of these, about 8 per cent were serious enough for NORAD to convene Missile Event Conferences. In other words, there were about three such serious false alarms every week.[31] More recently, in 1995, a Norwegian scientific rocket launch was interpreted by the Russian early warning system as a possible attack and the matter went all the way up the command chain to President Yeltsin.[32]

CONCLUSION

In South Asia, the estimated total missile flight times range from 8–13 minutes for ranges of 600 km–2000 km respectively for missile flown to their full ranges. These missile flight times encompass paths from plausible missile launch points in both countries to targets such as the national capitals and major military facilities, including possible locations of the nuclear arsenals or their command posts, in the other country. The time could be significantly less if the long range missiles that both countries possess are flown on a depressed trajectory, in which case the missile flight time could be as low as 300 seconds, that is 5 minutes, for a 600 km missile flight. That would clearly offer the greatest challenge to the early warning system, and for this reason it may well be adopted.

The earliest that a missile on a depressed trajectory could be detected and tracked with early warning radars like the Green Pine would be about 110 seconds after launch. That would only be half-a-minute to a minute after what a geo-synchronous satellite with adequate infrared sensors, if available, would take. This is markedly different from the case of the U.S. and USSR/Russia, where satellites provided several additional minutes of warning. In light of the above arguments, it appears that early warning satellites in South Asia will serve little useful purpose.

Regardless, whether missile launch is detected by a satellite or a radar or both, any assessment procedures in India and Pakistan would require that information be processed and evaluated, decision-makers informed, and action taken within at most 4–7 minutes for an attack targeted at the respective capital cities. This is an unprecedented constraint on procedures for evaluation and verification of any warning and for decision-making about retaliatory use of nuclear weapons. In the case of a depressed trajectory missile launched towards a capital city there would be barely enough time for the warning to be communicated to decision-makers. There would be *no time whatsoever* to consult or deliberate after receiving this warning.

Further, any early warning system would inevitably generate both genuine signals of incoming attack as well as false alarms. In the middle of a crisis, such false alarms, combined with the short decision time involved, can raise the prospect of technological and human error leading to inadvertent nuclear war.

REFERENCES

1. 'Draft Report of National Security Advisory Board on Indian Nuclear Doctrine', Available on the internet at http://www.indianembassy.org/policy/CTBT/nuclear_doctrine_aug_17_1999.html
2. Zia Mian, R. Rajaraman, and M.V. Ramana, 'Early Warning in South Asia: Constraints and Implications', *Science and Global Security*, vol. 11, No. 2–3 (2003), pp. 109–50.
3. Our article may be found at: http://www.princeton.edu/sgs/publications/sgs/archive/
4. M.V. Ramana, R. Rajaraman, and Zia Mian, 'Nuclear Warning in South Asia', *Economic and Political Weekly*, 17 January 2004; Zia Mian, R. Rajaraman, and M.V. Ramana, 'When Early Warning is no Warning', *The Hindu*, 2 July 2004.
5. Ross Kerber, 'Military sees Flaws in Patriot Usage', *Boston Globe*, 23 November 2003.
6. 'India closer to deployment of BMD shield', *Times of India*, 6 March 2009, http://articles.timesofindia.indiatimes.com/2009-03-06/india/28019713_1_bmd-system-exo-atmospheric-k-saraswat; See also 'Prithvi Air Defense (PAD)/ Pradyumna Ballistic Missile Interceptor,' at http://www.indian-military.org/strategic-weapons/anti-ballistic-missile-defense/81-prithvi-air-defense--pad---pradyumna-ballistic-missile-interceptor.html. A modified version of the Green

Pine radar called Swordfish has been used in recent missile interception tests. 'Another Ballistic missile defense test next month', *Indian Express*, 23 January 2009, http://www.indianexpress.com/news/another-ballistic-missile-defense-test-next-month/414415/0

7. http://www.fas.org/spp/military/program/track/pavepaws.htm

8. 'France accepts Spirale early warning system demonstrator', *Defense Talk*, 20 May 2009.

9. For the history, technology and capabilities of the US DSP satellites see Jeffrey T. Richelson, *America's Space Sentinels: DSP Satellites and National Security*, (Lawrence, Kansas: University of Kansas Press, 1999).

10. Jeffrey T. Richelson, *America's Space Sentinels: DSP Satellites and National Security*, (Lawrence, Kansas: University of Kansas Press, 1999), fig. 5.1, p. 70.

11. Jeffrey T. Richelson, *America's Space Sentinels: DSP Satellites and National Security*, (Lawrence, Kansas: University of Kansas Press, 1999), pp. 235–40.

12. John C. Toomay, 'Warning and Assessment Sensors', in: *Managing Nuclear Operations*, Ashton B. Carter, John D. Steinbruner, and Charles A. Zraket, (Washington, D.C.: Brookings, 1987), p. 303.

13. K.D. Poore, J. Wang, W.B. Rossow, 'Cloud layer thicknesses from a combination of surface and upper-air observations', *Journal of Climate*, Vol. 8, (1995), pp. 550–68.

14. 'Recent False Alerts from the Nation's Missile Attack Warning System', Report by Senator Hart and Senator Barry Goldwater to Committee on Armed Services United States Senate, 9 October 1980, p. 4.

15. Jeffrey T. Richelson, *America's Space Sentinels: DSP Satellites and National Security*, (Lawrence, Kansas: University of Kansas Press, 1999), p. 96.

16. Bruce G. Blair, *The Logic of Accidental Nuclear War*, (Washington, D.C.: Brookings Institution, 1993), p. 193.

17. Pavel Podvig, 'History and the Current Status of the Russian Early Warning System', *Science and Global Security*, vol. 10, No. 1 (2002), pp. 21–60.

18. Russian Strategic Nuclear Forces website maintained by Pavel Podvig: http://russianforces.org/sprn/

19. http://www.isro.org/gslvd1/gslv05.htm; The DSP satellites weighed 900 kg, were 7m long and 3m wide. The GSLV head-shield is 7.8m long, 3.4 m in diameter and has carried satellites weighing over 1500 kg.

20. T.S. Subramanian, 'GSLV failures fuel disappointment and anxiety', *The Hindu*, 27 December 2010, http://www.hindu.com/2010/12/27/stories/2010122762571200.htm

21. In 2002, reportedly to avoid losing its slot in geostationary orbit, Pakistan leased a geostationary satellite, now named Paksat-I, for five years from the American company Hughes Global Services; Bulbul Singh, 'Pakistan's Paksat 1 begins orbital move', *Aerospace Daily*, 5 December 2002.

22. We note that these procedures would not be applicable to the case of nuclear attacks from off-shore ballistic missile submarines where flight times are about 10 or 15 minutes.

23. Bruce G. Blair, *The Logic of Accidental Nuclear War*, (Washington, D.C.: Brookings Institution, 1993), pp. 188–89. For another reconstruction, see Michael D. Wallace, Brian L. Crissey, Linn I. Sennott, 'Accidental Nuclear War: A Risk Assessment', *Journal of Peace Studies*, vol. 23, No. 1, March 1986, pp. 9–27.

24. See Pavel Podvig, 'The Operational Status of the Russian Space-Based Early Warning System', *Science and Global Security*, vol. 4, No. 3 (1994), pp. 363–84; and Pavel Podvig, 'History and Current Status of the Russian Early Warning System', *Science and Global Security*, vol. 10, No. 1, (2002), pp. 21–60.

25. Bruce G. Blair, *Global Zero Alert for Nuclear Forces*, (Washington, D.C.: Brookings Institution, 1995), pp. 46–50.

26. According to another description, the 'missile attack' signal is sent to the terminals of the Kazbek system, which is accessible to the president, the defense minister, and the chief of General Staff. *Russian Strategic Nuclear Forces*, (Pavel Podvig, ed.), (Cambridge, MA: The MIT Press, 2001), p. 438.

27. The 'missile attack' signal can also be transmitted if there is credible information about two or more launches from only the radar systems, without a signal from the satellites. *Russian Strategic Nuclear Forces*, Pavel Podvig (ed.), (Cambridge, MA: The MIT Press, 2001), p. 438.

28. Bruce G. Blair, *Global Zero Alert for Nuclear Forces*, (Washington, D.C.: Brookings Institution, 1995), pp. 50–1.

29. R. Rajaraman, M.V. Ramana and Zia Mian, 'Possession and Deployment of Nuclear Weapons in South Asia: An Assessment of Some Risks', *Economic and Political Weekly*, 22 June 2002, pp. 2459–2466.

30. Bruce Blair, *The Logic of Accidental Nuclear War* (Washington, D.C.: Brookings Institution Press, 1993), f.n. 46, pp. 342–43. Also see H.L. Abrams, 'Strategic Defense and Inadvertent Nuclear War', in *Inadvertent Nuclear War: The Implications of the Changing Global Order*, H. Wiberg. I.D. Petersen, and P. Smoker (eds.), (Oxford: Pergamon Press, 1993), pp. 39–45.

31. Linn Sennott, 'Overlapping False Alarms: Reason for Concern', in *Breakthrough: Emerging New Thinking*, edited by Anatoli Gromyko and Martin Hellman, (New York: Walker and Company, 1988).

32. Bruce G. Blair, Harold A. Feiveson and Frank von Hippel, 'Taking Nuclear Weapons off Hair-Trigger Alert', *Scientific American*, November 1997.

CHAPTER 11

PAKISTAN'S BATTLEFIELD USE OF NUCLEAR WEAPONS

Zia Mian and A.H. Nayyar

General Deepak Kapoor, India's army chief, claimed in December 2009 that the army had made progress in operationalising a strategy for rapid mobilization of conventional military forces capable of mounting a decisive attack on Pakistan.[1] The strategy, dubbed as 'Cold Start', can be traced to the unexpectedly slow pace of mobilization and deployment of Indian forces to the border with Pakistan after the December 2001 attacks on India's parliament by militants believed to be linked to Pakistan.[2] It involves the creation of eight to ten 'Integrated Battle Groups' (IBGs) of army, air force and special forces intended 'to destroy and not to hold or capture territory.'[3]

As part of this doctrine, India's armed forces have been rehearsing large scale manoeuvres, the most significant of which came in a May 2006 military exercise close to the border with Pakistan.[4] The *Sanghe Shakti* (Joint Power) exercise brought together strike aircraft, tanks, and over 40,000 soldiers from the 2nd Strike Corps in a war game whose purpose was described by an Indian commander as 'to test our 2004 war doctrine to dismember a not-so-friendly nation effectively and at the shortest possible time.'[5]

General Daulat Shekhawat, Commander of the Corps, explained that, 'We firmly believe that there is room for a swift strike even in case of a nuclear attack, and it is to validate this doctrine that we conducted this operation.'[6]

General Parvez Kayani, Pakistan's Chief of Army Staff, responded to General Kapoor's 2009 assessment by declaring that, 'Proponents of conventional application of military forces, in a nuclear overhang, are chartering an adventurous and dangerous path, the consequences of which could be both unintended and uncontrollable.'[7] The implication seemed to be that Pakistan might use nuclear weapons in response to an Indian conventional assault. A former Pakistani brigadier has argued that Pakistan could forestall Cold Start since, 'the Pakistani Army can occupy their wartime locations earlier than the Indian army' and in any case 'failure to do so could lead to firing of low-yield tactical warheads at IBGs as they cross the start line or even earlier.'[8] This implies Pakistan's use of nuclear weapons against Indian conventional forces either before or soon after these forces cross the international border.

While Pakistani leaders have issued no formal nuclear doctrine, it is widely understood that they are prepared to initiate the use of nuclear weapons in a conflict.[9] Pakistan has consistently rejected suggestions that it adopt a policy of no-first use of nuclear weapons, and has instead reinforced the notion that its nuclear weapons are meant in part to counter India's larger conventional military forces.[10] In 2011, Pakistan tested the *Nasr* missile, which has a reported range of 60 km and is intended to deliver nuclear weapons on the battlefield. Pakistan's army claims the missile 'carries nuclear warheads of appropriate yield' and will 'add deterrence value to Pakistan's Strategic Weapons Development program at shorter ranges.'[11] The missile was tested again on 28 May 2012 (the anniversary of the 1998 nuclear weapon tests) using a multi-barrel mobile launcher, which the Pakistan Army described as addressing 'the need to deter evolving threats, specially at shorter ranges.'[12]

India seems to have anticipated the possibility of Pakistani leaders using nuclear weapons against Indian military forces. Since the early 1980s, confronted with the prospect of possible Pakistani use of nuclear weapons on the battlefield, Indian forces have prepared to survive and prevail. Indian Army Chief General K. Sundarji claimed in early 1987: 'We in the armed forces are gearing our organization, training and equipment in such a manner that in the unlikely event of the use of nuclear weapons by the adversary in the combat zone, we will limit the damage, both psychological and physical.'[13] The year-long 'Brasstacks' exercise in 1986 involved Indian tanks and other armoured vehicles practising procedures for moving through an area that had been subject to nuclear attack.[14]

The May 2001 Indian military exercises 'Poorna Vijay' (Complete Victory) gave every indication that Indian planners anticipate Pakistan's battlefield use of nuclear weapons.[15] The exercises were aimed at testing equipment, troops and manoeuvres in a situation where nuclear weapons were used against them, with an Indian official confirming that 'Drills and procedures to meet the challenges of a nuclear, chemical or biological strike are also being practiced.'[16] Among the options worked through were a Pakistani nuclear attack on a bridgehead or bridge, armoured forces and troops.[17] A year later, India's Deputy Chief of Army Staff, Lt. General Raj Kadyan, confirmed that the Indian army was continuing to train to cope with a nuclear strike on the battlefield.[18]

We look below at the conditions under which Pakistan might use its nuclear weapons in response to an Indian conventional military attack, looking in particular at the implications of the battlefield use of nuclear weapons to stem a large-scale incursion by Indian armoured forces. We assess the military consequences of such use given the possible number and yield of nuclear weapons Pakistan might have available. We do not include here the effects of the large-scale use of nuclear weapons on civilian populations or on the ecosystems on or close to the battlefield.

IF PAKISTAN GOES NUCLEAR

There have been some suggestions of where Pakistan may first use its nuclear weapons. They imagine large Indian armoured formations and ground forces threatening to take further territory or inflict further defeat on Pakistani conventional forces. A nuclear strike by Pakistan on Indian forces in Pakistani territory, when there is no conventional response left to Pakistan, might be aimed at preventing imminent conventional defeat rather than fighting and winning a nuclear war. The goal might be to use nuclear weapons to support conventional forces and as the U.S. army manual suggests to 'dramatically increase the possibilities for sudden alterations on the battlefield, which attacks can exploit.'[19]

One analysis argues that Pakistan would initiate the use of nuclear weapons on Pakistan's own soil against Indian attacking forces, and then use them against military targets in India near Pakistan border and finally attack cities.[20] Another historian of Pakistan's army and its wars suggests that, 'If India's two armour-heavy mechanized infantry strike corps managed to penetrate to the line joining Gujranwala-Multan-Sukkur and to the outskirts of Hyderabad in the South, then it is likely Pakistan would have to accept defeat or employ nuclear weapons.'[21] These cities are roughly 50 km, 190 km, 90 km, and 130 km respectively from the nearest points on the border with India.

In the late 1990s, U.S. military war-gaming of a possible conflict between India and Pakistan involved a situation, where after several days of conflict, 'Pakistani forces in the north were defeated and Indian forces moved quickly across the Thar desert toward the Indus river,' and Pakistan responds with 'four nuclear weapons.'[22] The war-game imagined Pakistan using three 20 kiloton nuclear weapons aimed at 'halting invading Indian forces on the border' and the fourth against a rail hub. In the game, India retaliates by launching twelve nuclear weapons at Pakistan's nuclear and command facilities, including near the capital Islamabad.

There is some uncertainty about the type, yield and number of nuclear weapons Pakistan may have available, should it decide to use them. The *Nasr* missile introduced recently is claimed to be nuclear capable, but it is not clear if Pakistan has succeeded in making miniaturized battlefield nuclear weapons. Analysis of photographs of the missile has led to the suggestion that the missile could be as small as 30 cm across, and if so it could in principle carry a very compact nuclear weapon similar to the 20 cm diameter U.S. W33 nuclear artillery shell, which had a yield ranging from less than 1 kiloton to about 10 kilotons.[23] It has not been either demonstrated or otherwise established that Pakistan has such a compact warhead.

It is assumed here that any battlefield use of nuclear weapons would involve warheads of the kind that were tested in 1998. Pakistan's nuclear weapon tests of 28 May 1998 involved as many as five devices and the yield of individual devices is uncertain. Samar Mubarikmand, the scientist who led the nuclear weapon tests, claimed the subsequent nuclear test of 30 May 1998 involved 'only one device and its yield was 15 to 18 kT [kilotons].'[24] An independent estimate by the Federation of American Scientists, the leading non-governmental researchers tracking nuclear arsenals, suggests Pakistan may have between 90–110 nuclear weapons, as of 2011.[25]

We consider in the next section what might be the actual effect of Pakistan's use of such nuclear weapons against Indian land forces. As noted earlier, we do not include the effects of the use of potentially very large numbers of nuclear weapons on the civilian population or ecosystems in the war zone.

BATTLEFIELD USE OF NUCLEAR WEAPONS

Indian military exercises have simulated attacks on Pakistan involving over 1000 tanks and armoured vehicles. The 1986 exercise 'Brasstacks' involved 1300 tanks.[26] The 2001 *Poorna Vijay* military exercise involved 1000 tanks and armoured vehicles.[27] Details of the deployment within the exercise are not available. The Indian Army order of battle has been suggested as comprising regiments of fifty-five tanks, with six tank regiments in an armoured division.[28] This suggests that several divisions were involved in the exercises simulating war with Pakistan.

The United States planned for large tank battles in the early stages of a war with the Soviet Union in Central Europe. It was expected that a heavy division would defend a standard front of 25 km wide.[29] These deployments became much closer when units were attacking, with the operational front for an armoured division being roughly 8–10 km.[30] For the United States an armoured formation for 'deliberate attack or breakthrough' used vehicles spaced 50 meters apart in each row, and the rows were set 200–250 meters apart.[31] This is equivalent to 80 armoured vehicles per km.[2]

The density of 80 armoured vehicles per km² is equivalent to that of a triangular lattice with points spaced about 120 meters apart. Soviet armoured vehicles were typically spaced 100 meters apart.[32] If they were in a triangular formation, they would have an effective density of 115 vehicles per km². Increasing the spacing to 200 meters reduces the density of vehicles to below 30 per km². A density of 3 vehicles per km² is achieved by spacing them about 540 meters apart. This kind of density has been reported for U.S. and Soviet divisions in Europe.[33]

Nuclear weapons produce three important immediate destructive effects: blast, heat and prompt radiation in the form of gamma rays and neutrons. All three effects are expressed equally in all directions and decrease with distance. To estimate how many tanks and crews may be affected by each of these, it is worth noting that for separation of d meters between neighbouring tanks, the number of tanks in a circle of radius r meters is $3.6(r/d)^2$.

BLAST

In actual nuclear weapon tests involving military equipment, a 10 kT explosion at a range of 370 meters produced a peak static overpressure of 33.35 psi (note: 1 atm = 14.7 psi) and a tank oriented on its side towards the explosion was displaced about 2.5 meters with acceleration sufficient to inflict moderate damage to external fittings such as track guards, but the tank was able to be driven off and its gun fired after sand and debris had been removed from the barrel.[34] It seems reasonable to assume that an overpressure of 3 atm (about 45 psi) is sufficient to damage a tank so that it cannot continue to function on a battlefield.

A standard description of the effects of nuclear weapons notes that a 1 kT explosion at a height of about 150 meters produces overpressures of 45 psi at horizontal distances from ground zero as large as about 170 meters. The distance l ratios scale as the 1/3 power of the ratio of yields.[35] This means that a 15 kT burst at a height of about 400 m would generate an overpressure of 3 atm up to a distance of about 420 meters, i.e., over an area of 0.55 km². The number of tanks, N, in this circular area varies as the inverse square of the inter-tank distance d and is approximately given by ($800/d^2$).

For a tank spacing of 100 meters, one 15 kT weapon could destroy about 55 tanks. To destroy this many tanks if they were spaced 300 meters apart would take 8 weapons of 15 kiloton yield each. To destroy by blast alone roughly half of a force of 1000 tanks that were well dispersed would require on the order of 100 nuclear weapons of 15 kiloton yield.

HEAT

A second large effect of nuclear weapons is the intense heat that they generate. The heat flux is instantaneous, lasting only a second. This leads to large firestorms in cities but the effects of this heat on the battlefield, especially on vehicles and their crews, is not as severe.

The Effects of Nuclear Weapons gives standard curves for thermal radiation from a nuclear explosion.[36] Extrapolating this to a 15 kT explosion at a height of 400 meters suggests that at a ground distance of 500 meters from ground zero the thermal flux from such an explosion is about 150 calories per square centimetre. Exposure to a thermal dose of 15 cal/cm^2 is fatal to a person. Anyone in the open on the battlefield up to a distance of 1.3 km would be killed. Those at distances out to 2 km would suffer burns.

The damage to tanks and other armoured vehicles and their crews is more difficult to determine. We assume, as a worst case scenario, that there are no radiative losses, and all the heat received is absorbed by the tank's surface. Because the tank body is made of steel which is a good thermal conductor, all the heat energy received would be rapidly distributed over the entire volume of the tank's steel body. Since at most half the surface area would be exposed to the thermal flux, a tank's body temperature would rise by about 2–3 C.[37]

Thus thermal radiation, while fatal for foot soldiers to a distance of about 1 km from ground zero, will not add significantly to the damage caused by blast on tanks and armoured vehicles.

260 CONFRONTING THE BOMB

RADIATION EFFECTS

In addition to blast and heat, nuclear weapons produce prompt radiation as both neutrons and gamma rays, the latter including direct fission product gammas and secondary gammas from the interaction of the released neutrons with the air. These can be highly destructive of military operations by disabling and killing soldiers, including the crews of armoured vehicles.

The U.S. army assumes that radiation doses of 3000–8000 rads or more would be required to destroy front-line enemy troops.[38] The *US Army Field Manual* reports that radiation doses on this scale cause severe and prolonged vomiting, diarrhoea, fever and prostration within five minutes leading to complete incapacitation, with partial recovery after 45 minutes, and death within five days.[39] Higher doses lead to complete and permanent incapacitation and death within 15–48 hours. Doses down to 800 rads can cause severe and prolonged vomiting, diarrhoea, fever within half-an-hour to an hour and reduced combat effectiveness, with death within fourteen days. Following U.S. practice, we assume a critical dose of 3000 rads as sufficient to incapacitate military personnel inside tanks.

The Effects of Nuclear Weapons gives standard curves for prompt radiation from a nuclear explosion as a function of distance.[40] Only a fraction of the radiation incident on a tank will be transmitted to the crew inside, however. The transmission factors for a tank are 20 per cent of incident prompt gamma rays and 30 per cent for neutrons. The transmission factors are at least two to three times this amount for the much thinner skinned armoured vehicles used to carry infantry.[41]

For a 15 kiloton yield explosion at a height of about 400 meters, and including the effect of transmission factors, the collective neutron and gamma dose is 1500 rads at a slant distance of 1100 meters and nearly 5000 rads at a slant distance of 900 meters. For simplicity, it is assumed that the collective neutron and gamma dose equal to the critical dose of 3000 rads is produced at a slant distance of 1000 meters, which, for an explosion at a height of 400 m would amount to a ground distance of 920 meters from the explosion.

If the attack is organised around tank divisions of 330 tanks, with each division moving forward on a 10 kilometre long front, then the 1000 tanks would occupy a 30 km long front. The depth of the formation would be determined by the spacing of the tanks. As noted earlier, an attacking tank formation following U.S. tactics might have tanks that are 50 meters apart in rows separated by 250 meters (the effective spacing would be 120 meters). A force of tanks prepared for a possible nuclear strike might have larger distances between individual tanks.

The prompt radiation from a 15 kT weapon would kill or incapacitate crews in 75 tanks if the tanks were deployed with an effective spacing of 120 m, but only affect the crews of 35 tanks if they were 300 meters apart. For tanks separated by even greater distances, it would require the use of over 80 nuclear weapons of 15 kT yield each to disable or kill the crews in a force of 1000 tanks.

CONCLUSION

The analysis presented here suggests that while Pakistan has sufficient nuclear weapons to destroy a significant proportion of any invading Indian armoured force, it may exhaust most of its arsenal (as of 2012) of an estimated 100–110 nuclear weapons in such an attempt. If Indian armed forces had prepared for a nuclear attack and were able to rapidly disperse, Pakistan may not have sufficient nuclear weapons to be able to destroy an Indian force.

This conclusion about the limited utility of small numbers of nuclear weapons on a possible South Asian battlefield echoes the experience of the United States and Soviet Union in the European theatre. In their search for ways to counter the large armoured land forces of their adversary, the United States and Soviet Union built up arsenals of tens of thousands of battlefield and tactical weapons. The U.S. for instance had as many as 20,000 tactical nuclear weapons in its arsenal in 1967.[42] It is possible that the Pakistan Army has recognized this problem. It has purchased 5250 TOW wire-guided heavy anti-tank missiles from the United States, of which about 2000 have been delivered as of early 2009.

To build a much larger number of tactical weapons, Pakistan would need a much bigger stockpile of fissile material than it currently possesses. Compact nuclear weapons of the kind that could be used by the *Nasr* missile can in principle be made from Highly Enriched Uranium (HEU), but are usually made from plutonium since a smaller of amount of plutonium is required to create the critical mass that sustains the nuclear explosion. It is significant that Pakistan has been moving to increase its production capacity of weapons plutonium. It is building two new plutonium production reactors at Khushab, where two production reactors are already in operation. It is estimated that by the year 2020, the Khushab reactors could produce enough plutonium for 90 nuclear weapons. Pakistan also has been blocking the start of international negotiations on a treaty to ban the production of plutonium and HEU for weapons.[43]

It is possible to imagine that Pakistan may choose to respond to an Indian conventional attack by using one or a few nuclear weapons as a signal to India to terminate the attack or risk a larger escalation possibly including use of nuclear weapons against Indian cities. Indian policy makers have sought to deter such possible Pakistani use of nuclear weapons on the battlefield. In 2003, India's cabinet announced that as part of India's nuclear doctrine, 'nuclear weapons will only be used in retaliation against a nuclear attack on Indian territory or on Indian forces anywhere.'[44] The explicit mention of 'Indian forces anywhere' suggests that Pakistan's battlefield use of nuclear weapons against Indian conventional forces could trigger an Indian nuclear response, possibly also on the battlefield.

The same logic prevailed between the United States and Soviet Union during the Cold War, which led to the deployment of large numbers of battlefield nuclear weapons by both sides. These large numbers suggest that the United States and Soviet Union had decided that the threat of battlefield use and retaliation was likely to be taken to be more credible than the threat to escalate directly from a conventional conflict to an attack on a major target in the other state. Nonetheless, each side anticipated that a war would escalate to all out nuclear war and the destruction of cities. This will likely be the case in South Asia, and adds to the futility of preparing for the battlefield use of nuclear weapons.

India seems to have largely abandoned the Cold Start doctrine, in part because of a lack of political support along with resource constraints and logistical problems in implementing the doctrine on the battlefield.[45] India's effort to pursue Cold Start has nevertheless contributed to a nuclear arms race that it may not have intended, with Pakistani claims to have introduced tactical nuclear weapons and delivery systems.

Faced with the limited utility of using nuclear weapons in response to large conventional forces on the battlefield and in the larger European theatre, the United States and Soviet Union eventually agreed a series of treaties. The 1987 Intermediate Nuclear Forces Treaty banned ground-launched ballistic and cruise missiles with ranges of between 500 and 5500 kilometres, and required that their launchers and associated support structures and equipment be destroyed.[46] The 1990 Conventional Forces in Europe Treaty aimed to create a 'secure and stable balance of conventional armed forces in Europe at lower levels than heretofore, of eliminating disparities prejudicial to stability and security and of eliminating, as a matter of high priority, the capability for launching surprise attack and for initiating large-scale offensive action in Europe.'[47] It required large reductions in military equipment and obliged an annual exchange of military information and established a system of inspections. In 1991, through unilateral but coordinated presidential initiatives the United States and Soviet Union removed from active service their ground-launched short-range nuclear weapons, tactical nuclear weapons on ships and submarines, and land-based naval aircraft.[48] Pakistan and India might usefully consider such steps in the South Asian context.

REFERENCES

1. Rajat Pandit, 'Army Reworks War Doctrine for Pakistan, China', *The Times of India*, 30 December 2009.

2. For details of the origins of Cold Start and constraints on its operationalisation see Walter C. Ladwig III, 'A Cold Start for Hot Wars? The Indian Army's New Limited War Doctrine', *International Security*, vol. 32, No. 3, (Winter 2007/08), pp. 158–90.
3. 'Army Conducts Largest Ever War Games in Recent Times', *Times of India*, 19 May 2006.
4. Ibid.
5. 'Indian Military Rehearse Pakistan's Dissection in Mock Battles', *Defense News*, 3 May 2006.
6. 'Indian Army Tests its New Cold Start Doctrine', *Indo–Asian News Service*, 19 May 2006.
7. Iftikhar Khan, 'Tough Kayani Warning to Proponents of 'Adventurism', *Dawn*, 9 February 2010.
8. Javed Hussain, 'A Challenging Doctrine', *Dawn,* 8 February 2010.
9. Pervez Hoodbhoy and Zia Mian, *The India–Pakistan Conflict—Towards the Failure of Nuclear Deterrence*, 2002. www.zmag.org/content/showarticle.cfm?ItemID=2659
10. Masood Haider, 'Islamabad Refuses to Accept "No First Strike" Doctrine', *Dawn*, 31 May 2002.
11. Press Release, Inter-Services Public Relations, 19 April 2011.
12. Press Release, Inter-Services Public Relations, 29 May 2012.
13. W.P.S. Sidhu, 'India's Nuclear Use Doctrine', in: *Planning The Unthinkable: How New Powers Will Use Nuclear, Biological and Chemical Weapons*, Peter Lavoy, Scott Sagan and James Witz (eds.), Cornell University Press, Ithaca, 2000, p. 128.
14. Manoj Joshi, 'Atomic Age Warfare,' *India Today*, 20 July 1998.
15. 'Bracing for a Nuclear Attack, India Plans 'Operation Desert Storm' in May', *The Indian Express*, 1 May 2001.
16. 'Unmanned Aerial Spies Used in War-games', *The Times of India*, 8 May 2001.
17. Harinder Bajewa, 'Readying For Nukes', *India Today*, 28 May 2001.
18. 'Army Ready to Face N-strike', *Hindustan Times*, 26 June 2002.
19. 'Operations', *US Army Field Manual FM-100-5*, Department of Army, Washington, D.C., 1982, pp. 6–8.
20. Stephen P. Cohen, *The Pakistan Army*, Oxford University Press, New York, 1998, (edn.), p. 178.
21. Brian Cloughley, *A History of the Pakistan Army: Wars and Insurrections*, Oxford University Press, Karachi, 1999, pp. 340–41.
22. Bradd C. Hayes, 'International Game 99: Crisis in South Asia', Research Report 99–1, Decision Support Department, Center for Naval Warfare Studies, United States Naval War College, 1999, p. 8.
23. http://lewis.armscontrolwonk.com/archive/4866/pakistans-nuclear-artillery
24. Khalid Qayyum, 'Shaheen Missile Awaits Go-ahead for Test Fire', *The Nation*, 1 June 1998.

25. Robert S. Norris and Hans M. Kristensen, 'Pakistan's Nuclear Forces, 2011', *Bulletin of Atomic Scientists*, vol. 67, No. 4, pp. 91–9, 2011.

26. Kanti Bajpai, P.R. Chari, P.I. Cheema, S.P. Cohen. S. Ganguly, *Brasstacks and Beyond: Perception and Management of Crisis in South Asia,* Manohar, Delhi, 1995, p. 30.

27. 'Experts Feel War, if Fought, Will be Across the Desert', *The Statesman*, 16 February 2000.

28. *Indian Army ORBAT,* http://www.bharat-rakshak.com/LAND-FORCES/Army/Orbat.html

29. William P. Mako, 'Demands on Ground Forces in Central Europe in the 1980s', in: The Force Planning Faculty, Naval War College, *Foundations of Force Planning: Concepts and Issues* (eds.), Naval War College Press, Newport, 1986, p. 401.

30. James F. Duncan, *How to Make War: A Comprehensive Guide to Modern Warfare*, William Morrow, New York, 1988, p. 414.

31. 'The Tank and Mechanized Infantry Battalion Taskforce', Field Manual No. 71-2, U.S. Department of the Army, Washington, D.C., 1977, pp. 5–10.

32. S.T. Cohen and W.R. Van Cleave, 'Western European Collateral Damage from Tactical Nuclear Weapons', *RUSI Journal*, June 1976, p. 36.

33. Duncan, *How to Make War*, p. 415.

34. Charles S. Grace, *Nuclear Weapons: Principles, Effects and Survivability*, Brassey's, London, 1994, p. 58.

35. Samuel Glasstone and Philip J. Dolan, *The Effects of Nuclear Weapons*, Third Edition, U.S. Government Printing Office, Washington, D.C., 1977.

36. Glasstone and Dolan, *The Effects of Nuclear Weapons*, p. 371, Fig. 8. 123a.

37. This assumes that the tank body is made of 5 cm thick steel. For steel density of 7850 kg-m-3 and specific heat capacity of 108 cal-kg-1-K-1, each 5 cm3 volume (a hypothetical cylinder in the tank body with a base area of 1 cm2) would experience a rise in temperature of only 4.6 C.

38. 'Tactical Nuclear Operations', *US Army Field Manual FM-100-5*, Washington, D.C., 1982, pp. 10–13.

39. 'Operations', *US Army Field Manual FM-100-5*, pp. 3–4.

40. Glasstone and Dolan, *The Effects of Nuclear Weapons*, p. 371, Fig. 8.123a.

41. Grace, *Nuclear Weapons: Principles, Effects and Survivability*, Table 6.4.

42. Nicholas Zarimpas, 'Tactical Nuclear Weapons', in *SIPRI Year Book 2002: Armaments, Disarmament and International Security*, Oxford University Press, New York, 2002, pp. 568–69.

43. Zia Mian and A.H. Nayyar, 'Playing the Nuclear Game: Pakistan and the Fissile Material Cut-off Treaty', *Arms Control Today*, April 2010.

44. The Cabinet Committee on Security Reviews Operationalization of India's Nuclear Doctrine, Ministry of External Affairs, New Delhi, 4 January 2003. http://meadev.nic.in/news/official/20030104/official.htm

45. Sandeep Unnithan, 'War Strategy: The collapse of Cold Start', *India Today*, 4 December 2010.

46. Treaty Between the United States of America and the Union of Soviet Socialist Republics on the Elimination of Their Intermediate-Range and Shorter-Range Missiles (1987). www.state.gov/www/global/arms/treaties/inf1.html

47. Treaty on Conventional Armed Forces in Europe (1990). www.state.gov/www/global/arms/treaties/cfe.html

48. 'The Presidential Nuclear Initiatives (PNIs) on Tactical Nuclear Weapons at a Glance', Arms Control Association, Washington, D.C., undated. www.armscontrol.org/factsheets/pniglance

CHAPTER 12

WHAT NUCLEAR WAR COULD DO TO SOUTH ASIA

Matthew McKinzie, Zia Mian, A.H. Nayyar, and M.V. Ramana

There is a history of war in South Asia. India and Pakistan fought in 1948, 1965, 1971 and in 1999. But there is good evidence that in no case was there the expectation of a war on the scale and of the kind that ensued. Rather war followed misadventure, driven by profound errors of policy, political and military judgement, and public sentiment. Nuclear weapons do nothing to lessen such possibilities. There is even reason to believe they may make them worse in South Asia.

Pakistan's leaders have made clear they are prepared to use nuclear weapons first in any conflict, they hope by threatening to do so they will prevent war, and in the event of war they fear being overwhelmed by India's conventional military superiority. While India has offered an agreement for no-first use of nuclear weapons, its armed forces seem prepared to try to destroy Pakistan's nuclear capability before it is used, and seek their own capability to launch a nuclear attack if they believe that enemy nuclear missiles are armed and ready for launch. Pakistan, in turn, may seek to pre-empt such a situation by using its nuclear weapons even earlier in a conflict rather than risk losing them.

When it comes to picking targets for nuclear weapons there are really only two options. One option is to indiscriminately destroy cities in the hope of either forcing an end to hostilities or eliciting unconditional surrender. The second option is to try to use nuclear weapons to destroy military command structures and war fighting capabilities. Pakistan cannot hope to prevail in a drawn out war and its leaders have made clear they intend to follow the first option. Should India seek to try the second option and attack only military targets, the results may not be that different from deliberately using nuclear weapons against cities. This is because nearly all of Pakistan's significant military centres are either in or located close to cities. For instance, Karachi, Hyderabad, Bahawalpur, Multan, Lahore, Gujranwala, Rawalpindi, Peshawar and Quetta are all army corps headquarters. Islamabad has the air force and naval headquarters. These are obvious targets. Nuclear weapons cause destruction over such large distances that even if nuclear weapons were targeted specifically at military installations; cities cannot escape.

THE EFFECTS OF NUCLEAR WEAPONS

In 1945 two nuclear weapons were used by the United States to annihilate over 190,000 of the populace of Japan. Agonizing deaths continued to occur for approximately a month after the explosions—indeed deaths continued for weeks after Japan surrendered. The impact of atomic bombings on Japan and other countries has been crushing and ongoing.

Can one predict the effects of the use of nuclear weapons against cities in India or Pakistan today? The answer is: in some ways 'yes' and in other significant ways 'no'.

The effects of a nuclear weapon explosion are so immense and so different from those of conventional weapons that it is useful to present, as a case study, a familiar hypothetical 'target'. The nuclear weapon used by the United States to attack Hiroshima in Japan had a yield equivalent to 15,000 tons of TNT and was detonated at 580 meters above the surface of the earth. This yield is comparable to the yields of the nuclear weapons that India and Pakistan claimed they tested in May 1998. We describe therefore the effects of a single explosion of a Hiroshima-sized nuclear bomb at an elevation of 600 meters over Mumbai, India. The consequences of such an explosion for any other large, densely populated, South Asian city would be similar.

The short-term effects of a nuclear explosion—those that occur within the first few weeks—can be classified as either 'prompt' or 'delayed' effects. In addition there are long term effects that can stem primarily from radiation fallout over years to come.

PROMPT EFFECTS

Any person or object exposed to the explosion would first experience an extremely intense flash of heat and light, brighter than a thousand suns. Even a glance at the flash could result in blindness. Up to 1.6 to 3.2 kilometres around the point of explosion (the epicentre, or ground zero), everything that could burn up: wood, paper, clothes, vegetation, etc. All all other combustible materials would catch fire.

Exposure to neutron and gamma radiation, resulting from the nuclear reactions responsible for the explosion, would occur almost simultaneously. Radiation exposure could lead to a variety of symptoms such as nausea, bloody diarrhoea, and haemorrhages within a few days (other consequences of radiation could appear years later). These health effects are often fatal and include leukaemia, thyroid cancer, breast cancer, and lung cancer, as well as non-fatal diseases such as birth defects, cataracts, mental retardation in young children, keloids, and others.

The third effect is the shock or blast wave, which would result in a forceful blow to any person or object in its path. The winds accompanying the shock wave would reach velocities of more than 110 kilometres per hour to a distance of 2.4 kilometres or more. The shock wave would destroy everything within a circle with a radius of 1.1 kilometres.

Up to 1.7 kilometres from the point of explosion, all houses not built with concrete would be destroyed. Many of the buildings in Mumbai, especially older ones, are either badly designed or constructed with raw materials that are of poor quality (such as adulterated cement or improperly baked bricks). Every year several hundred buildings crumble and collapse, especially during the monsoon season. Faced with the shock wave and these hurricane-force winds, buildings may collapse at significantly greater distances than those estimated here.

DELAYED EFFECTS

A few minutes after the explosion, the delayed effects would begin. The first of these is the firestorm that would result from the coalescing of individual fires started by the initial flash of light and heat. In the case of a Hiroshima-sized explosion over a city like Mumbai, the radius of the region set on fire would be 1.7 to 2 kilometres. Due to the large area of the fire, the fire zone would act as a huge pump, sucking in air from the surrounding areas and driving heated air upwards. This pumping action would create winds with velocities as high as 50–80 kilometres per hour. The temperature in the fire zone would reach several hundred degrees, making it almost certain that there would be no survivors. Furthermore, fire-fighting would be almost impossible due to the combination of hurricane-force winds, thick smoke, the destruction of water-mains and tanks by the shock wave, and the presence of debris from the blast, blocking roads and access routes.

Other factors would lead to a probability of small explosions in the fire region and, therefore, to a greater chance that people would be injured as well as burned. In Mumbai, for example, many houses contain gas cylinders (containing liquid petroleum gas) that are used for cooking. These are known to explode when exposed to fires. In addition, compared to cities in Japan and Germany during World War II, Mumbai and other modern cities have much greater concentrations of motorized vehicles such as cars, scooters and buses that use petroleum-based fuels. The corresponding storage and dispensing facilities for such highly inflammable and explosive fuels would only increase the number of casualties.

The second delayed effect is radioactive fallout. When a nuclear bomb explodes at low altitudes, a large amount of material is vaporized and carried aloft into the mushroom cloud. This material then mixes with the fireball's radioactive materials, which results in a cloud of highly radioactive dust. This radioactive fallout can travel large distances on the winds created by the explosion, as well as in the atmosphere, before ultimately falling back to earth. If, instead of assuming that the weapon is detonated at a height of 600 meters, we assume that the explosion happens at the surface with a wind velocity of 25 kilometres per hour, the area subject to levels of fallout that have a high likelihood of being fatal would be about 25–100 square kilometres. The wind direction during the period that the fallout is aloft (which could be fluctuating) would determine which areas would be subject to these levels of radioactivity. The regions subject to high levels of fallout would have high levels of casualties and radiation sickness. Further, Mumbai, being close to the sea, has high levels of water vapour in the atmosphere. Water droplets would likely condense around radioactive particles and descend as rain, as was the case in Hiroshima and Nagasaki.

Even people who live in areas subject to lower levels of radiation, unless they are immediately evacuated, would be susceptible to radiation sickness. Given the large population of Mumbai, the public panic that would follow a nuclear attack, and the likely damage to all forms of transportation infrastructure, such train stations and railway tracks, roads, petrol stations, dockyards, airports, etc., evacuation of survivors would be nearly impossible.

CASUALTY ESTIMATES

The average population density of Mumbai is about 23,000 people per square kilometre. There are regions, however, where the population density exceeds 100,000 people per square kilometre.

Since a nuclear explosion and its effects are a complicated physical phenomena, with different types of effects occurring almost simultaneously, it is impossible to predict numbers of casualties or injuries accurately. There are three ways to estimate the number of casualties from prompt effects. All of these are based on empirical data from Hiroshima when the casualties were expressed as a function of different variables—radius, overpressure, and thermal fluence, respectively. Using these three models and assuming the above population densities, we can calculate that there will be somewhere between 150,000 and 800,000 deaths in Mumbai within a few weeks of the explosion. These would be the result from just the blast and fire effects of a (Hiroshima-sized) nuclear weapon, and assuming that fallout effects are negligible (assumptions that lead to a very conservative casualty estimate).

For comparison, in the case of a weapon exploding at ground level, the areas damaged by fire and blast are somewhat less but radioactive fallout would be a more significant cause of deaths and sickness. Assuming that all the fallout is deposited in inhabited areas (and assuming they have a population density of 23,000, the average for Mumbai) the number of people dying of all causes could be as high as 350,000 to 400,000 for a 15-kiloton weapon. Many more people would be subject to lower doses of radiation, which in the case of already sick people, old and young, could well be lethal in the absence of medical care.

The above numbers include only the 'prompt' casualties, those who are injured or die right away or within a few weeks of the explosion. Many more will certainly die from long term effects, especially radiation-related causes. Studies involving survivors of the atomic bombing of Hiroshima and Nagasaki reveal that the mortality rates for all diseases, leukaemia, and malignancies other than leukaemia, are all significantly higher than among people not exposed to radiation. Increases in the cancer rates of survivors of an atomic bombing of Mumbai may be comparable to, if not greater than, those among Hiroshima and Nagasaki survivors.

There are a number of other reasons to believe that the casualty numbers cited above would be an underestimate in a city like Mumbai. First, the assumed population densities are lower than the actual densities. Apart from undercounting and variations among regions, a substantial number of people come in every day from places as far away as Pune (four hours by train) to work in Mumbai. The census does not take such commuters into account. Since an attack from the air is quite likely to take place during the day in order to maximize visibility, many commuters will also be killed or injured. Second, casualties from fallout have not been included in the estimates. Since fallout, even if present only in small quantities, can spread out to large regions and cause local hot spots, this is an important omission. Third, conservative figures for blast damage and regions affected by fire have been deliberately chosen. The actual areas are likely to be higher, implying a greater number of casualties.

There is another significant uncertainty in the estimates offered here, one which is likely to increase the casualties. There are a large number of industrial facilities in Mumbai and its vicinity. India's highest concentration of chemical plants is in the Trans-Thane creek area, which has more than 2000 factories. Central Mumbai is home to several mills, which could cause additional fires and explosions, and which could spread toxic substances. The Union Carbide accident in Bhopal is an example of the kinds of effects that are possible due to escape of toxic chemicals. In addition to chemical industries, the largest nuclear laboratory in India—the Bhabha Atomic Research Centre—is in Trombay, just outside Mumbai. A nuclear explosion in the vicinity of either reactor at the Centre (CIRUS and Dhruva) or near the reprocessing plant or the facilities storing radioactive waste and/or spent fuel could lead to the release of large amounts of radioactivity, in addition to the quantities resulting from the explosion itself. This would increase the amounts of fallout significantly.

Hospitals and medical care in an overcrowded city such as Mumbai are limited to begin with, and facilities within the affected area would be destroyed or damaged during the attack. The injured would be unlikely to find medical treatment.

THE EFFECTS OF NUCLEAR WAR

We have illustrated in some detail the effect of the use of one relatively small nuclear weapon on a large South Asian city. It is hard to imagine that if this dreadful event were ever to take place as the result of an attack there would be no response from the other side. Both Pakistan and India have sufficient nuclear weapons, missiles and aircraft to destroy many each others' cities.

To illustrate the terrible consequences of a large scale nuclear war in South Asia, we estimate the numbers of deaths and injuries from nuclear attacks on ten major Indian and Pakistani cities. To arrive at consistent estimates for all of these cities we use a different, simpler methodology than was used earlier for the detailed case study of the consequences of a nuclear attack on Mumbai. We transpose onto each city the characteristics and consequences of the 6 August 1945 Hiroshima bombing with its mass fires, radiation sicknesses, severe burns, deaths in buildings collapsed by the shock wave, hurricane-force winds propelling missiles through the air, and blindness. The graph plots the zones of death and injury experienced at Hiroshima.

Total population and casualty data of the graph for the 6 August 1945 attack on Hiroshima in 500 meter rings around Ground Zero.

This historical data from Hiroshima on the fraction of the population killed and injured in concentric 500 metre wide rings out to a distance of 5 kilometres from the explosion is applied to a

Graph 2: Record of the Hiroshima A-Bomb War Disaster, Hiroshima, 1971, Vol. I.

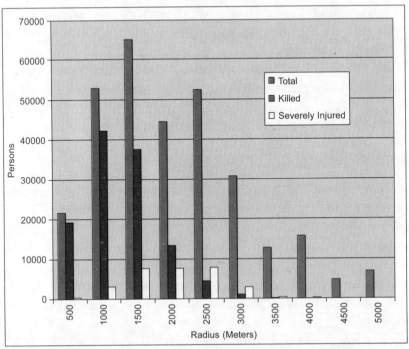

Reference: Hiroshima Shiyakusho [Hiroshima City Office], *Hiroshima Genbaku Sensaishi* [Record of the Hiroshima A-Bomb War Disaster], Hiroshima, 1971, Vol. I.

database that gives population distribution information for each of ten cities in South Asia. The 'LandScan' world population database was used for these calculations. It uses the best available census information and assigns them to grid cells of roughly 1 km×1 km size by creating a probability distribution based on factors such as proximity to roads; environmental characteristics such as climate and terrain slope; and night-time lights as seen by satellites.

The table below shows the numbers of dead, severely injured and slightly injured persons after a nuclear attack on each of ten large South Asian cities. A total of 2.9 million deaths is predicted for these cities·in India and Pakistan, with an additional 1.5 million severely injured.

Table 4
Estimated Nuclear Casualties for each of
10 Large Indian and Pakistani Cities

Total Population within 5 kilometers of Ground Zero	Killed	Severely Injured	Slightly Injured
COUNTRY			
India			
City			
Bangalore 3,077,937		314,978	175,136	411,336
Mumbai 3,143,284		477,713	228,648	476,633
Calcutta 3,520,344		357,202	198,218	466,336
Madras 3,252,628		364,291	196,226	448,948
New Delhi 1,638,744		176,518	94,231	217,853
COUNTRY			
Pakistan			
City			
Faisalabad 2,376,478		336,239	174,351	373,967
Islamabad 798,583		154,067	66,744	129,935
Karachi 1,962,458		239,643	126,810	283,290
Lahore 2,682,092		258,139	149,649	354,095
Rawalpindi 1,589,828		183,791	96,846	220,585

It should be appreciated that this exercise of predicting the casualties from nuclear attacks on cities in India and Pakistan based on the historical record at Hiroshima just scratches the surface of what would play out if nuclear weapons were used. There is also the loss of key social and physical networks that make daily life possible: families and neighbourhoods would be devastated, factories, shops, electricity and water systems demolished, hospitals and schools, and other government offices destroyed. The flood of refugees would carry the physical effects far beyond the cities.

The ultimate impact on both societies would extend well beyond the bombed areas in highly unpredictable ways. Nuclear attacks would provoke profound and enduring responses from citizens of India and Pakistan and of the world. Nothing would ever be the same again.

CHAPTER 13

PAKISTAN'S NUCLEAR DIPLOMACY AND THE FISSILE MATERIAL CUT-OFF TREATY

Zia Mian and A.H. Nayyar

Since May 2009, Pakistan, largely alone, has blocked the start of international talks on a Fissile Material Cut-off Treaty (FMCT) at the 65–country United Nations Conference on Disarmament (CD) in Geneva.[1] The treaty would ban the production of fissile materials for weapons purposes; fissile materials, namely plutonium and Highly Enriched Uranium (HEU), are the key ingredients in nuclear weapons. Pakistan has prevented these negotiations despite having accepted in 2009 a CD program of work that included an FMCT.

Pakistan's ambassador at the CD, Zamir Akram, has indicated that his government may not easily be moved, saying, 'We are not in a position to accept the beginning of negotiations on a cut-off treaty in the foreseeable future.'[2]

At the core of the concerns held by Pakistan's national security managers is a long-running search for strategic parity with India. The most powerful of these managers are from the army, which also runs the nuclear weapons complex. They argue that Pakistan has fallen behind India in producing fissile materials and insist that this fissile material gap be addressed as part of any talks.

Yet, a larger set of issues are at play. These include Pakistan's concerns about the long-term consequences of the U.S.–Indian nuclear deal and the emerging strategic relationship between the two countries; the desire of military planners in Pakistan to move from larger, heavier nuclear weapons based on HEU to lighter, more compact plutonium-based weapons; the interest of nuclear production complex managers in Pakistan in realizing their investment over the past decade in a large expansion of fissile material production facilities and of the nuclear establishment more broadly in expanding its domestic economic and political clout; and, finally, a reluctance in Washington and other key capitals to press Pakistan on an FMCT because of the importance the United States attaches to Pakistan's support for the war against the Taliban and the Al Qaeda in Afghanistan and the FATA (Pakistan's Federally-Administered Tribal Areas) region in Pakistan.

THE EVOLUTION OF PAKISTAN'S POSITION

Pakistan has historically taken an ambivalent position toward a possible FMCT. It supported the December 1993 U.N. General Assembly resolution calling for negotiations on a 'non-discriminatory multilateral and internationally and effectively verifiable treaty banning the production of fissile material for nuclear weapons or other nuclear explosive devices.'[3] Having agreed to talk, Pakistan delayed the start of a negotiating process at the CD by debating the scope of the proposed treaty, insisting that the mandate for negotiating the treaty include constraints on existing stockpiles of fissile materials. The compromise agreed in the March 1995 Shannon mandate for talks at the CD on an FMCT was to finesse the issue by noting that the mandate did not preclude any state from raising the problem of existing stockpiles as part of the negotiations.

Work on an FMCT, however, did not start. In May 1995, the nuclear Non-proliferation Treaty (NPT) was extended indefinitely and without conditions, raising concerns that the nuclear-weapon states might never uphold their obligation to eliminate their nuclear weapons. The following year, the CD pushed through the Comprehensive Test Ban Treaty, despite objections by India, sending the treaty to the General Assembly for approval and opening it for signature. India and Pakistan refused to sign.

In May 1998, India and Pakistan tested nuclear weapons. Within weeks, the U.N. Security Council responded to the tests by unanimously passing Resolution 1172, which called on India and Pakistan to immediately to stop their nuclear weapon development programs; to refrain from weaponization or from the deployment of nuclear weapons; to cease development of ballistic missiles capable of delivering nuclear weapons and any further production of fissile material for nuclear weapons; to confirm their policies not to export equipment, materials or technology that could contribute to weapons of mass destruction or missiles capable of delivering them and to undertake appropriate commitments in that regard.[4]

India and Pakistan ignored the resolution, but under pressure from the United States, Pakistan acquiesced to the fissile material talks.[5] Pakistan agreed to negotiate on the basis of the existing Shannon mandate, but made clear that it intended to 'raise its concerns about and seek a solution to the problem of unequal stockpiles.'[6] Munir Akram, Pakistan's CD ambassador, spelled out in detail Pakistan's concerns by stating: 'We believe that a wide disparity in fissile material stockpiles of India and Pakistan could erode the stability of nuclear deterrence.'[7] In a later statement, he explained that Pakistan assumed 'India will transform its large fissile material stocks into nuclear weapons' and thus Pakistan needed to 'take into account both India's nuclear weapons and fissile material stockpiles.' Pakistan 'cannot therefore agree to freeze inequality,' he said.[8] To make clear its position, Pakistan's ambassador objected even to the term FMCT, arguing that, 'my delegation does not agree to the Treaty being described as a Fissile Material "Cut-off" Treaty, implying only a halt in future production. We cannot endorse the loose abbreviation—FMCT—in any formal description of the Treaty which is to be negotiated by the CD.'[9] He proposed instead the label 'Fissile Material Treaty', or FMT, and a number of other countries and independent analysts adopted this usage.

A CD committee was set up to begin talks on an FMCT in late 1998, but made little progress and could not be re-established in 1999. For the following decade, the CD struggled to agree on a program of work. The United States under the Bush administration shifted priorities to its wars in Afghanistan and Iraq and was ideologically opposed to multilateral arms control. At the CD, it insisted talks be confined to an FMCT, but without verification provisions, and rejected demands for discussions on other long-standing issues, such as nuclear disarmament, measures to prevent an arms race in outer space, and security assurances for non-nuclear-weapon states. Other states, unwilling to concede control of the CD agenda to the United States, tied talks on an FMCT to these other topics.

In the absence of CD negotiations, and taking advantage of the frustration among many non-nuclear-weapon states at Bush administration's policies on nuclear weapons and non-proliferation and disarmament, Pakistan laid out an expansive vision for an FMCT. In 2006, Masood Khan, Pakistan's ambassador to the CD, argued that, '[a] cut-off in the manufacturing of fissile material must be accompanied by a mandatory program for the elimination of asymmetries in the possession of fissile material stockpiles by various states. Such transfer of fissile material to safeguards should be made first by states with huge stockpiles, both in the global and regional context.'[10] He explained what this meant: 'A fissile material treaty must provide a schedule for a progressive transfer of existing stockpiles to civilian use and placing these stockpiles under safeguards so that the unsafeguarded stocks are equalized at the lowest level possible.'[11]

In May 2009, for the first time in 10 years, with Pakistan's assent the CD adopted a program of work organized around four working groups, one of which was tasked with negotiating an FMCT on the basis of the Shannon mandate. The other groups were to manage discussions on nuclear disarmament, preventing an arms race in outer space, and security assurances. In addition, three special coordinators were to be appointed to elicit the views of states on other issues.

Nevertheless, agreement on a program of work was not sufficient to allow FMCT negotiations to begin. Pakistan demanded agreement on procedural issues, including that, '[t]he allocation of time for the four Working Groups should be balanced so that the progress on each issue is ensured,' and that '[t]he appointment of Chairs of the Working Groups should respect the principle of equal geographical representation.'[12] The ensuing dispute over how any talks would be managed, with China, Egypt, and Iran joining Pakistan in expressing concerns, prevented progress. The CD also failed to agree that the 2009 program of work would carry over into 2010.

Pakistan continued to obstruct the start of work at the CD in early 2010. In February, Zamir Akram explained that his country had agreed to the program of work in 2009 in the hope that some of Pakistan's concerns would be addressed with the start of the Obama administration. Pakistan now believed that this would not be the case, he said.[13] Citing a January 2010 decision by Pakistan's National Command Authority (NCA), which is responsible for its nuclear weapons, he said that Pakistan's position at the CD on an FMCT would be based on 'its national security interests and the objectives of strategic stability in South Asia.'[14]

Pakistan rejected the CD plan of work proposed in early March 2010. A number of countries associated with the CD Group of twenty-one, including Egypt, Indonesia, Iran, North Korea, Sri Lanka, and Syria, have joined Pakistan in arguing for a more 'balanced' program of work, highlighting in particular the need for talks on nuclear disarmament.[15] China also did not endorse the CD plan of work. Some states may simply be remaining silent about their opposition to the treaty and taking advantage of Pakistan's refusal to permit talks on an FMCT. Israeli Prime Minister Benjamin Netanyahu told President Bill Clinton in 1999: 'We will never sign the treaty, and do not delude yourselves—no pressure will help. We will not sign the treaty because we will not commit suicide.'[16] For its part, Pakistan is playing a waiting game, arguing that the time is not yet 'ripe' for an FMCT.[17]

THE FISSILE MATERIAL GAP

Pakistan's position clearly is determined by concern about parity with India. On 26 October 1998, Pakistani Foreign Minister Sartaj Aziz was quoted as saying, 'Nuclear scientists have advised the government that there was no harm in signing the CTBT and FMCT at this stage as we had enough enriched nuclear material to maintain the power equilibrium in the region.'[18] This would seem to suggest that a decade ago policy makers in Pakistan believed that its fissile material stockpiles were sufficient to meet perceived needs. Similarly, in 2006, Pakistan's Ambassador to the United States, Jahangir Karamat, a former army chief, seemed to indicate that Pakistan might consider a bilateral moratorium with India, suggesting that, 'if bilaterally, the U.S. can facilitate a moratorium on fissile material production or on testing; we are very happy to be part of that.'[19]

It has been estimated that as of 2010, Pakistan had accumulated a stock of about 2.6 metric tons of HEU for its nuclear weapons (enough for about 100 weapons, assuming 25 kilograms per warhead).[20] Pakistan also has about 100 kilograms of weapons plutonium, enough for about 20 warheads (assuming 5 kilograms per warhead) from its reactor at Khushab.[21] Altogether, Pakistan may have fissile material sufficient for perhaps 120 simple weapons. Advanced weapon designs, including those that use both uranium and plutonium in composite warheads, would allow it to produce significantly more weapons from its HEU. Pakistan also has about 1.2 metric tons of reactor-grade plutonium in the spent fuel from its two nuclear power reactors, but this material is under International Atomic Energy Agency (IAEA) safeguards.

Pakistan is expanding its fissile material production capacity and increasing its reliance on plutonium weapons. A second Khushab reactor was completed in 2010 and may have started operation and an additional production reactor is almost complete.[22] Work started on a fourth Khushab reactor in late 2010.[23] Each of these new reactors could produce about 10 kilograms of plutonium a year, if they are the same size as the existing reactor at the site. Pakistan is expanding its uranium processing operations to fuel these reactors.[24] Satellite imagery from late 2006 shows that Pakistan has also been working on one new reprocessing plant at its New Labs site near Islamabad and another at Chashma, presumably to reprocess the spent fuel from the new production reactors.[25]

India is producing plutonium for weapons in a dedicated production reactor (Dhruva), near Mumbai—a second, older production reactor (CIRUS) that had been operating since 1963 was shut down in December 2010. It is estimated that India may have accumulated about 500 kilograms of plutonium by 2010, sufficient for about 100 weapons.[26] India produces HEU, but this material is believed to be for its nuclear-powered submarine fleet and not for weapons. This would suggest that India and Pakistan today have roughly similar holdings of weapons material.

A large disparity in stocks of the kind emphasized by Pakistan emerges if India's unsafeguarded power-reactor plutonium is included in the accounting. India may have separated about 3.5 metric tons of power-reactor plutonium by 2010, out of a total of 9 tons that have been produced.[27] Assuming that perhaps 10 kilograms of such reactor-grade plutonium may be sufficient for a weapon, this would amount to perhaps 350 weapons. There are reports that at least one Indian nuclear weapon test in 1998 used plutonium that was less than weapons grade.[28]

India claims its stockpile of reactor-grade plutonium is intended for fueling fast breeder reactors, the first of which (the 500–megawatt Prototype Fast Breeder Reactor) is expected to be completed in 2012–2013.[29] This fast breeder reactor will consume reactor-grade plutonium as fuel, but will produce weapons-grade plutonium in the blankets that surround the reactor core. If it operates with a reasonable capacity factor, the reactor would be able to produce 90–140 kilograms of weapons-grade plutonium per year, sufficient for almost 20–30 weapons per year.[30] It is estimated that India may have 1000–1500 kilograms of weapons plutonium by 2020.[31] India would not be the first country to use a breeder reactor for military purposes. France used its Phénix breeder reactor to produce plutonium for weapons.[32] The experience of many other breeder reactors around the world, however, suggests that operating a breeder reactor at such efficiency may not be easy because breeder reactors have proven susceptible to frequent breakdowns and need long repair times.[33]

Pakistan has explicitly raised the issue of reactor-grade plutonium stocks, with its CD ambassador in February 2010 expressing a concern that an FMCT might not 'include other bomb making materials such as reactor grade Plutonium, U233, Neptunium or Americium.'[34]

Pakistan is also concerned about the implications of the U.S.–Indian nuclear deal. Signed into law by President George W. Bush in October 2008, it lifts the thirty-year-old restriction on the sale of nuclear material, equipment, and technology to India. The United States and India convinced the Nuclear Suppliers Group (NSG), which has more than forty members, to exempt India from similar international controls. Responding to the U.S.–Indian deal, Pakistan's NCA declared in August 2007 that the agreement 'would have implications on strategic stability as it would enable India to produce significant quantities of fissile material and nuclear weapons from un-safeguarded nuclear reactors.'[35]

As part of the deal, India is now free to import uranium for its civil program, easing constraints on uranium availability and enabling India to use more of its domestic uranium for its nuclear weapons program. It is estimated that this would enable India to produce up to 200 kilograms a year of weapons-grade plutonium in its unsafeguarded heavy-water power reactors, enough for 40 weapons per year, provided that it can overcome the associated practical problems of increased rates of spent fuel reprocessing and faster refueling.[36]

India has committed that it will declare eight of its indigenously built power reactors as civilian and open them for IAEA safeguarding by 2014 in a phased manner. It is estimated that these eight reactors could produce four metric tons of unsafeguarded plutonium by then.[37] India will keep eight power reactors outside safeguards, which together could produce about 1250 kilograms of plutonium per year, not all of which India can currently separate.[38] All this plutonium is presumably intended for fuelling breeder reactors, but could produce a large number of simple nuclear weapons. The deal allows India to continue to keep outside safeguards its stockpiles of accumulated power reactor spent fuel, and separated power reactor plutonium. Furthermore, India can choose whether any future reactors it builds will be declared as military or civilian.

THE BIG PICTURE

The generals who command Pakistan's army, dominate national security, and control nuclear policy and the nuclear weapon complex through the Strategic Plans Division (SPD), even when there is an elected civilian government, see a troubling future. Their military mind-sets, vested interests, and old habits lead them to find many reasons to continue to seek strategic parity with India and to produce more fissile material to support a larger nuclear arsenal.

One argument Pakistan has raised for building up fissile material stocks is the prospect of a large Indian arsenal. Zamir Akram claimed in February 2010 that India was aiming for an arsenal of 400 weapons. This arsenal would rely on a triad of platforms, the third leg of which is coming into view. In 2009, India launched its first nuclear-powered submarine.[39] It plans a fleet of three to five, each armed with 12 ballistic missiles.[40] There have been suggestions by former Pakistani officials that the country develop its own nuclear submarine and, in the meantime, lease a nuclear submarine from a friendly power, i.e., China, deploy nuclear-armed cruise missiles on its diesel submarines, and continue fissile material production for the 'foreseeable future'.[41]

Another justification being offered for a larger fissile material stockpile is India's pursuit of ballistic missile defenses. (China has raised the same point with regard to U.S. strategic missile defenses.) In 2004 the military officer who serves as director of arms control and disarmament affairs at the Strategic Plans Division argued that India's missile defense program is likely to 'trigger an arms race' and that Pakistan could build more missiles and more warheads, requiring more fissile material; develop decoys and multiple warhead missiles; and move to an alert deployment posture.[42] In 2009, India carried out its third test of a missile interceptor.[43]

More broadly, India's economy and military spending are now so large and growing so rapidly that Pakistan cannot expect to keep pace with it. In January 2010, India's Defense Ministry announced plans to spend more than $10 billion in that year on acquiring new weapons.[44] This was made possible by a 34 per cent increase in India's military budget for 2009–2010, to more than $35 billion; in Pakistan, it went up 15 per cent, to just more than $4 billion. Pakistan has been able to buy major new weapons systems because of the large amounts of U.S. military and economic aid that have flowed since the September 11 attacks in return for Islamabad's support for the U.S. war against Al Qaeda and the Taliban, but President Barack Obama has announced that he intends to begin withdrawing U.S. troops from Afghanistan in 2011. United States military aid to Pakistan will not continue at current levels indefinitely and likely will be increasingly for civilian purposes and more carefully audited. Even if China steps up its assistance, Pakistan's generals believe they cannot keep up with India in a conventional arms race. They may want more nuclear weapons as a counter (see the chapter: 'Pakistan's Battlefield Use of Nuclear Weapons'), while insisting on conventional weapons controls as a condition for progress on an FMCT.

To compound these concerns, Pakistan's generals see an emerging US–Indian strategic relationship. The U.S.–Indian nuclear deal forms part of a broader January 2004 agreement between the United States and India on 'Next Steps in Strategic Partnership', through which the United States committed to help India with its civilian space program, high-technology trade, missile defense, and civilian nuclear activities. The Obama administration seems as committed as its predecessor to pursuing this relationship with a view to maintaining U.S. primacy and containing China.

A HIGH PRICE

Former senior officials in Pakistan have argued that, in exchange for talks on an FMCT, Pakistan should receive a nuclear deal like the one given to India, with a lifting of international restrictions by the NSG.[45] Pakistan's Ambassador to the United States Hussain Haqqani claimed in February 2010 that, '[t]alks between Pakistan and the

U.S. for cooperation on atomic programs are underway and we want the U.S. to have an agreement with us like the one it had with India on civil nuclear technology.'[46] After the U.S.–Indian deal was announced in 2005, U.S. officials repeatedly said the Indian situation was unique and the United States would not extend the same terms to Israel or Pakistan, the other NPT holdouts.[47] However, some U.S. analysts have been urging such a nuclear deal as a way to buy greater cooperation from Pakistan in the war against the Taliban and as a way to assure Pakistan of an enduring U.S. commitment.[48] For their part, U.S. Department of State officials have been cautious in answering questions about the possibility of a nuclear deal with Pakistan. Asked directly in February 2010 if the Obama administration was considering a nuclear deal with Pakistan, State Department spokesman Philip Crowley replied, 'I'm—I don't know.'[49] At a 24 March 2010 press conference with Pakistani Foreign Minister Shah Mahmood Qureshi after what was dubbed a U.S.–Pakistan Strategic Dialogue, Secretary of State Hillary Clinton was asked if the United States would discuss a nuclear deal with Pakistan. She indicated that the U.S. might consider it eventually, arguing 'We have a broad agenda with many complicated issues like the one you referred to . . . this dialogue that we're engaged in is helping us build the kind of partnership that can make progress over time on the most complicated of issues.'[50] In late 2011, Zamir Akram made the connections to the FMCT talks explicit, saying Pakistan was willing to allow the start of talks if the NSG gave Pakistan the same exemption it had granted to India.[51]

A lifting of the current international restrictions on the sale of nuclear reactors and fuel to Pakistan would further strain the non-proliferation regime, already seriously weakened by the U.S.–Indian nuclear deal. With Israel having sought a lifting of NSG restrictions to allow it to import nuclear reactors and fuel, there is a serious danger that the NPT will be rendered largely pointless. Pardoning all three states that chose to remain outside the NPT and develop nuclear weapons would make a mockery of the idea that the treaty offers a platform for moving to nuclear disarmament. Furthermore, by ending the distinction between NPT parties and non-parties with regard to their access to international nuclear trade and technology assistance, it could make countries question the value of being a party to the treaty.

A nuclear deal for Pakistan would carry other costs. It would allow the Pakistan Atomic Energy Commission (PAEC) to become a much more powerful economic, political, and technological force in Pakistan. PAEC today is responsible for everything: from uranium mining to building and operating plutonium-production reactors and reprocessing plants for the nuclear weapons program. It also operates three small power reactors: a 125–megawatt plant bought from Canada in the 1960s and two 300–megawatt plants purchased from China in the 1990s and 2000s. Two more 300–megawatt Chinese reactors have been ordered. Pakistan's plans call for a very large increase in nuclear power capacity: to 2800 megawatts by 2020, reaching 8800 megawatts by 2030.[52] PAEC would become a key gatekeeper for managing the import and operation of the many large and very costly power reactors required to meet these energy targets. A large nuclear energy sector would offer Pakistan a means to mobilize and direct additional financial resources, technologies, material, and manpower to the weapons program. Moreover, Pakistan's current electricity shortage could be addressed much more quickly and more economically by adding natural gas-fueled power plants, which take much less time to construct and require much less capital than comparable nuclear power plants.

The managers of Pakistan's nuclear weapons production complex, the military's Strategic Plans Division, have little incentive to begin talks on an FMCT and even less interest in reaching early agreement or acceding to an eventual treaty. As noted earlier, the complex is in the midst of a very large expansion. An official visit to the Khushab site in 2010 by Prime Minister Yousuf Raza Gilani and senior military and nuclear weapons officials may have marked the completion of work on the second reactor.[53] The prime minister congratulated Khushab engineers for completing important projects and announced one month's bonus pay. Work on the third Khushab reactor seems to have started in 2005–2006 and on the fourth reactor in 2010. These reactors may be completed and pressed into operation later this decade. If FMCT talks begin and seem to go well, there may be international pressure for a production moratorium, which would involve suspending production at existing sites and halting work on new facilities. The large investment made in the new reactors and reprocessing plants would be seen to have been wasted. The Khushab reactors, which do not produce electricity and the associated reprocessing plants would have little if any value for Pakistan's civilian nuclear energy program.

Finally, Pakistan sees itself able to block progress on an FMCT at the CD because it has seen little sign that the United States or other states care about an FMCT or even about nuclear weapons in South Asia beyond wanting to be reassured about the security of Pakistan's weapons. Ambassadors at the CD urge Pakistan to allow talks to start, and foreign ministries may send démarches to Islamabad, but Pakistan sees this as diplomacy as usual and not indicative of an international priority requiring Pakistan to undertake a serious policy review or adjust its position.

The view from Islamabad is that the stream of high-level officials arriving there comes to talk about the Taliban and the Al Qaeda, Afghanistan, and the tribal areas. The key U.S. interlocutors in recent years have been Admiral Michael Mullen, Chairman of the Joint Chiefs of Staff; General David Petraeus, as Head of Central Command and then as Commander of the U.S. war in Afghanistan; and the late Richard Holbrooke, who served as U.S. Special Representative for Afghanistan and Pakistan. It is notable that even during Secretary of State Hillary Rodham Clinton's visits to Pakistan, nuclear weapons issues do not feature on the public agenda except for the security of Pakistan's nuclear weapons and materials. Even Abdul Qadeer Khan seems to have been forgotten. For now, the United States sees the war against the Taliban as more important than the nuclear arms race in South Asia, just as the fight against Soviets in Afghanistan was more important in the 1980s than curtailing Pakistan's nuclear weapons program.

CONCLUSION

When it comes to an FMCT, Pakistan security managers, predominantly the army, have been pursuing business as usual, which for the past five decades has meant trying to maintain strategic parity with India. Blocking talks on an FMCT enables them to continue to build up their fissile material stockpile and to highlight to the international community their concerns about a fissile material gap with India and the consequences of India's current military build-up, especially India's search for missile defenses, and the consequences of the U.S.–Indian nuclear deal. Holding up an FMCT also allows Pakistan's nuclear establishment to keep open the prospect of a nuclear deal of its own, which, if granted, would give it dramatically greater power and influence in the energy sector and civilian economy and the means to channel additional resources to the weapons program.

At the Conference on Disarmament (CD), Zamir Akram has claimed Pakistan has adopted a principled position on an FMCT based on vital national interests and declared that, 'we are ready to stand in splendid isolation if we have to.'[54] So far, this has been possible because it has carried little consequence. The international community, led by the United States, has chosen to focus its relationship with Pakistan on fighting the Taliban and the Al Qaeda. To get started on an FMCT, the United States and other major states, including non-nuclear-weapon states, will need to put it much higher on the agenda. A useful first step might be for Obama and leaders from other countries that want to see an FMCT to put in a call to Islamabad.

Although Pakistan is the most insistent in wanting stocks to be addressed in an FMCT, it is not alone. The group of twenty-one countries such as Brazil, Japan, and New Zealand have raised this issue so that an FMCT can serve both non-proliferation and disarmament. These states and others wishing to begin work on an FMCT should assure Pakistan that they will work together with Islamabad in insisting that the treaty cover fissile material stockpiles in an effective way. One possible way for dealing with such stocks is offered by the draft FMCT developed by the International Panel on Fissile Materials.[55]

It is important for talks on an FMCT to start soon and not be dragged out indefinitely. Among the states still producing fissile material for weapons, Pakistan in particular may seek to delay agreement as a way to add to its fissile material stockpiles. States interested in achieving an FMCT should commit at the CD and as part of the NPT Review Conference to implement the 2000 NPT review conference decision to begin talks on an FMCT and complete them within five years. To create and sustain real momentum for such negotiations and reach quickly a treaty that Pakistan and other potential holdout states will join, however, the nuclear-weapon states will need to put nuclear disarmament on the agenda.

REFERENCES

1. Jonathan Lynn, 'Pakistan Blocks Agenda at U.N. Disarmament Conference', Reuters, 19 January 2010, www.reuters.com/article/idUSTRE60I26U20100119
2. Stephanie Nebehay, 'Pakistan Rules Out Fissile Talks for Now–Diplomats', Reuters, 22 January 2010, www.alertnet.org/thenews/newsdesk/LDE60K2D9.htm
3. U.N. General Assembly, Resolution 48/75L, 16 December 1993, www.un.org/documents/resga.htm
4. U.N. Security Council, Resolution 1172, 6 June 1998, www.un.org/Docs/sc/unsc_resolutions.html
5. 'Ambassador Munir Akram's Statement in the Conference on Disarmament on CTBT, FMCT issues', 30 July 1998, www.fas.org/nuke/control/fmct/docs/980730-cd-pak.htm
6. Ibid.
7. Ibid.
8. 'Fissile Material Treaty, Statement from Munir Akram, Ambassador of Pakistan', 11 August 1998, www.acronym.org.uk/fissban/pak.htm
9. Ibid.
10. Pakistan Permanent Mission to the United Nations, 'Statement by Ambassador Masood Khan, Pakistan's Permanent Representative at the Conference on Disarmament: General Debate: "Fissile Material Treaty"', Geneva, 16 May 2006, www.reachingcriticalwill.org/political/cd/speeches06/statements%2016%20may/16MayPakistan.pdf
11. Ibid.

12. 'Statement by Ambassador Zamir Akram, Pakistan's Permanent Representative to the U.N.: Adoption of CD's ProgramProgram of Work', 29 May 2009, www.reachingcriticalwill.org/political/cd/speeches09/2session/29may_pakistan.html

13. Pakistan Permanent Mission to the United Nations, 'Statement by Ambassador Zamir Akram, Permanent Representative of Pakistan at the Conference on Disarmament (CD)', Geneva, 18 February 2010, www.reachingcriticalwill.org/political/cd/2010/statements/part1/18Feb_Pakistan.pdf (hereinafter Akram February 2010 statement).

14. Ibid.

15. Beatrice Fihn and Ray Acheson, 'The CD Debates the Draft ProgramProgram of Work', 22 March 2010, www.reachingcriticalwill.org/political/cd/2010/reports.html. The Group of 21 at the CD includes Algeria, Bangladesh, Brazil, Cameroon, Chile, Colombia, Cuba, Democratic Republic of Congo, Ecuador, Egypt, Ethiopia, India, Indonesia, Iran, Iraq, Kenya, Malaysia, Mexico, Mongolia, Morocco, Myanmar, Nigeria, North Korea, Pakistan, Peru, Senegal, South Africa, Sri Lanka, Syria, Tunisia, Venezuela, Vietnam, and Zimbabwe.

16. Avner Cohen and Marvin Miller, 'Israel', in: 'Banning the Production of Fissile Materials for Nuclear Weapons: Country Perspectives on the Challenges to a Fissile Material (Cutoff) Treaty', International Panel on Fissile Materials, September 2008, www.fissilematerials.org/ipfm/site_down/gfmr08cv.pdf.

17. Reaching Critical Will, 'Conference on Disarmament: Unofficial Transcript', Geneva, 11 March 2010, www.reachingcriticalwill.org/political/cd/2010/statements/ part1/11March_Pakistan.html (statement by Zamir Akram to the Conference on Disarmament).

18. 'Pakistan Moves Closer to Sign Nuclear Treaty', The Nation, 26 October 1998.

19. 'Pakistan Totally Committed to Non-proliferation, Restraint Regime', Associated Press of Pakistan, April 9, 2006.

20. International Panel on Fissile Materials (IPFM), 'Global Fissile Material Report 2010: Balancing the Books- Production and Stocks', December 2010, http://www.fissilematerials.org/ipfm/site_down/gfmr10.pdf

21. IPFM, 'Global Fissile Material Report 2010', op. cit.

22. Joby Warrick, 'Pakistan Expanding Nuclear Program', The Washington Post, 24 July 2006; 'U.S. Disputes Report on New Pakistan Reactor', The New York Times, 3 August 2006; Paul Brannan, 'Steam Emitted From Second Khushab Reactor Cooling Towers; Pakistan May Be Operating Second Reactor', Institute for Science and International Security (ISIS), 24 March 2010. Pictures of the third reactor were released in June 2007. David Albright and Paul Brannan, 'Pakistan Appears to be Building a Third Plutonium Production Reactor at Khushab Nuclear Site', Institute for Science and International Security (ISIS), 21 June 2007.

23. David Albright and Paul Brannan, 'Pakistan Appears to be Building a Fourth Military Reactor at the Khushab Nuclear Site', Institute for Science and International Security (ISIS), 9 February 2011.

24. David Albright, Paul Brannan, and Robert Kelley, 'Pakistan Expanding Dera Ghazi Khan Nuclear Site: Time for U.S. to Call for Limits', ISIS, 19 May 2009.

25. David Albright and Paul Brannan, 'Chashma Nuclear Site in Pakistan With Possible Reprocessing Plant', ISIS, 18 January 2007; David Albright and Paul Brannan, 'Pakistan Expanding Plutonium Separation Facility Near Rawalpindi', ISIS, 19 May 2009.

26. IPFM, 'Global Fissile Material Report 2010'. op. cit.

27. IPFM, 'Global Fissile Material Report 2010'. op. cit.

28. George Perkovich claims 'knowledgeable Indian sources confirmed' use of non-weapons-grade plutonium in one of the 1998 nuclear tests. George Perkovich, *India's Nuclear Bomb: The Impact on Global Proliferation*, (Berkeley: University of California Press, 1999), pp. 428–30. Similarly, Raj Chengappa claims, 'one of the devices . . . used reactor grade or dirty plutonium.' Raj Chengappa, *Weapons of Peace: The Secret Story of India's Quest to Be a Nuclear Power*, (New Delhi: Harper Collins, 2000), pp. 414–18.

29. 'Further delay for India's breeder reactor', IPFM blog: Fissile Material, 29 November 2010.

30. Alexander Glaser and M.V. Ramana, 'Weapon-Grade Plutonium Production Potential in the Indian Prototype Fast Breeder Reactor', *Science & Global Security*, vol. 15 No.2 (2007), pp. 85–106. The amount of plutonium produced will depend on whether both the radial and axial blanket of the reactor, which contain weapon plutonium, will be reprocessed separately from the spent fuel in the reactor core.

31. R. Rajaraman, 'Estimates of India's Fissile Material Stocks', *Science and Global Security*, vol. 16, No. 3, (2008), pp. 74–87.

32. Mycle Schneider, 'Fast Breeder Reactors in France', in: *Fast Breeder Reactor Programs: History and Status*, February 2010, www.fissilematerials.org/blog/rr08.pdf

33. Thomas B. Cochran et al., *Fast Breeder Reactor Programs: History and Status*, February 2010, www.fissilematerials.org/blog/rr08.pdf

34. Akram, February 2010 statement.

35. 'Press Release by Inter-Services Public Relations, No. 318/2007', 1 August 2007.

36. Zia Mian et al., 'Fissile Materials in South Asia: The Implications of the U.S.–India Nuclear Deal', September 2006, www.fissilematerials.org/ipfm/site_down/rr01.pdf

37. Ibid.

38. Ibid.

39. 'India Launches Nuclear Submarine', BBC, 26 July 2009.

40. Sandeep Unnithan, 'The Secret Undersea Weapon', *India Today*, 28 January 2008.

41. Tariq Osman Hyder, 'Strategic Stability in South Asia', *The News*, 1 August 2009.

42. Khalid Banuri, 'Missile Defenses in South Asia: The Next Challenge', *South Asian Survey*, vol. 11, No. 2 (2004), pp. 193–203.

43. 'India Tests Interceptor Missile', Agence France-Presse, 6 March 2009.

44. 'Armed Forces Modernization on Track: Defense Ministry', *The Hindu*, 1 January 2010. www.hindu.com/2010/01/01/stories/2010010153331800.htm

45. Asif Ezdi, 'US Nuclear Duplicity', *The News*, 25 January 2010, http://thenews. jang.com.pk/print1.asp?id=220571

46. Zulqernain Tahir, 'Talks Under Way for N-deal With U.S.: Haqqani', *Dawn*, 15 February 2010, www.dawn.com/wps/wcm/connect/dawn-content-library/dawn/ the-newspaper/national/12-talks-under-way-for-ndeal-with-us-haqqani-520-- bi-01

47. See, for example, R. Nicholas Burns and Robert G. Joseph, 'The U.S. and India: An Emerging Entente', Remarks as Prepared for the House International Relations Committee, 8 September 2005, www.nti.org/e_research/official_docs/ dos/dos090805.pdf

48. Stephen P. Cohen, 'Addressing the U.S.-Pakistan Strategic Relationship', 12 June 2008, (testimony before the Senate Committee on Homeland Security and Governmental Affairs federal financial management subcommittee); C. Christine Fair, 'Pakistan Needs Its Own Nuclear Deal', *The Wall Street Journal*, 10 February 2010.

49. Bureau of Public Affairs, U.S. Department of State, 'Daily Press Briefing', Washington, D.C., 18 February 2010, www.state.gov/r/pa/prs/dpb/2010/02/136915. htm

50. Hillary Rodham Clinton, 'Remarks With Pakistani Foreign Minister Makhdoom Shah Mahmood Qureshi After Their Meeting', Washington, 24 March 2010, www.state.gov/secretary/rm/2010/03/138996.htm

51. 'The South Asian Nuclear Balance: An interview with Pakistan Ambassador to the CD, Zamir Akram', *Arms Control Today*, December 2011.

52. Zia Mian and A.H. Nayyar, 'Pakistan and the Energy Challenge', in: *International Perspectives on Energy Policy and the Role of Nuclear Power*, Lutz Mez, Mycle Schneider, and Steve Thomas (ed.), (Brentwood, UK: Multi- Science Publishing, 2009), pp. 515–31.

53. 'Pakistan May Have Completed New Plutonium Production Reactor, Khushab- II', IPFM Web log, 28 February 2010, www.fissilematerials.org/blog/2010/02/ pakistan_may_have_complet.html

54. Akram, February 2010 statement.

55. IPFM, 'A Fissile Material (Cut-Off) Treaty: A Treaty Banning the Production of Fissile Materials for Nuclear Weapons or Other Nuclear Explosive Devices', 2 September 2009, www.fissilematerials.org/ipfm/site_down/fmct-ipfm- sep2009.pdf

CHAPTER 14

SPECULATIONS ON THE FUTURE OF NUCLEAR SOUTH ASIA

Pervez Hoodbhoy and Zia Mian

The future of nuclear South Asia is inextricably linked to power and politics in Pakistan and India and to the global nuclear order. The conflict between India and Pakistan may be the most serious and imminent danger to the South Asian region and humanity over the next fifty years. Over this period, India and China will continue their rise as great powers and rivals, even if they do not become peers of the United States. This will ensure that Pakistan remains at the heart of regional and global politics for decades to come.

The dynamics of the still evolving India–Pakistan nuclear relationship will be critical. This relationship is, of course, increasingly a part of a larger set of strategic relationships involving the United States and China. At the same time, Islamist politics in Pakistan, which may gather strength in coming decades, seeks to more directly confront India and the West. We look in particular at the risk of nuclear war and of nuclear terrorism. We consider also how India and Pakistan might respond to the renewed global effort to eliminate nuclear weapons.

NUCLEAR DYNAMICS

The nuclear arms race between Pakistan and India is an expression of a deeper conflict that has shaped the national narratives of the two countries. The wars of 1948 and 1965 over the status of Kashmir and the 1971 war over East Pakistan—which saw India intervene and inflict a decisive defeat on Pakistan—entrenched the idea, especially in Pakistan, of the hostile 'other' across the border. India's first test of a nuclear weapon came soon afterwards, in 1974, and drove Pakistan to press ahead with its own nuclear capability. Six decades of almost unremitting hostility has both limited their economic, political and cultural ties as well as prevented any substantial process of South Asian regional integration from gaining hold.

Nuclear weapon policies seem to have hardened in recent years and the South Asian confrontation seems set to endure, with limited prospects for any kind of long-term restraint or détente. Today these two South Asian countries are locked in an open-ended hostile competition to continuously upgrade and expand their nuclear arsenals.

India clearly seeks to become a major nuclear power. In July 2009, it launched its first nuclear-powered submarine and plans eventually to deploy possibly five of these submarines. In May 2012, the Indian Defense Minister announced that, 'The strategic indigenous submarine . . . would be inducted by the middle of next year.'[1] India is also developing an array of long range missiles that will allow it to project power. In April 2012 India test-launched *Agni-V*, a new 5000-km range missile able to strike the Chinese cities of Beijing and Shanghai.[2] Design work has started for an *Agni-VI* inter-continental ballistic missile with a range of 8000 km to 10,000 km that could carry up to 10 warheads each, to be ready for testing by mid-2014.[3]

With far fewer resources, both technical and economic, Pakistan has been seeking to increase the size of its nuclear arsenal and to maintain some kind of parity with India. It is building new plutonium production reactors and expanding associated fuel and processing facilities. The lifetime of all these facilities may well be of the order of forty years or so.

The nuclear arsenals held by Pakistan and India are widely believed to be around hundred weapons each. It has taken four decades for them to reach this size. It is possible that these arsenals will increase in the next two or three decades to several hundred weapons each, comparable in size to the current arsenals of Britain, China and France.

For both India and Pakistan, as for other countries, making nuclear weapons and their delivery systems is becoming easier with time, and cheaper. Modern technology is highly modular and detailed knowledge of scientific principles is no longer vital. Scientists are only marginally necessary; engineers suffice to make working nuclear weapons.

Computer-controlled precision lathes and other machines have made reverse engineering of mechanical parts easy. No longer is 'rocket science' a correct expression for indicating scientific complexity. This, along with help from China, is why Pakistan has succeeded in building up its nuclear arsenal.

Nuclear weapons have not displaced conventional arms. India is planning to spend as much as $55 billion on weapons over the next five years.[4] As India's economy continues to grow at very high rates, its military spending will continue to increase. India already has the eighth largest military budget in the world.

For Pakistan, defense spending for 2010–2011 was almost $8 billion, a 30 per cent increase over 2009, and amounting to 21 per cent of the total budget.[5] It has signed arms sales agreements worth over $6 billion since 2001, including for new U.S.-built F-16 jet fighters. China, an old ally, is also supplying the country with jet fighters and other weapons.

In both India and Pakistan, which are still very poor countries, the very large commitment of funds to nuclear and conventional arms suggests that the nuclear-military-industrial complex is likely to grow stronger. This will make it more difficult to restrain military competition and associated spending in coming decades in either country.

A continuing India–Pakistan arms race, episodic crises and the nuclear shadow will ensure that South Asia as a whole will remain unstable. For twenty-five years the India–Pakistan conflict has frustrated the hopes underlying the creation of the South Asian Association for Regional Cooperation (SAARC). The SAARC charter declares that, 'the objectives of peace, freedom, social justice and economic prosperity are best achieved in the South Asian region by fostering mutual understanding, good neighbourly relations and meaningful cooperation among the Member States.' Without ending the India–Pakistan conflict, it may prove impossible to build the kind of effective South Asian community required to address the growing political, economic, social and ecological crises expected in the region in the coming decades. Looking forward, one small basis for optimism may be Pakistan's decision in 2012 to finally reciprocate 'Most Favoured Nation' (MFN) status with India.

REGIONAL NUCLEAR POLITICS: CHINA AND INDIA

India's relationship with China is different in some key regards from that between Pakistan and India. It is, on the one hand, less overtly hostile and free from the kind of tension and belligerence that makes a Pakistan–India confrontation an ever present possibility, and at the same time the two Asian giants are bound together by increasing trade and commerce.

India and China have disputes, and although no Kashmir-like dispute exists, regional ambitions create tensions which are exploited by ultra-nationalists. The two countries have had competing territorial claims in Arunachal Pradesh and Aksai Chin, especially since the 1962 India–China border war. This dispute has fuelled intense nationalism in both countries. They are seeking to address these problems. In July 2009 China and India concluded their thirteenth round of border talks with a wide range of agreements including the installation of a hot line between the Chinese and Indian capitals. In March 2012, they agreed on a detailed protocol to deal with border clashes.[6]

India and China also are serious competitors for global markets and global prestige. But this is compensated for by their rapidly growing bilateral trade. In 2011, India–China trade was over $70 billion, a growth of almost 25 per cent since 2010. In comparison, India and Pakistan mutual trade—discounting smuggling and third party trading—was about one to two billion dollars annually in 2011.

Military leaders in India are seeking to make China the centre of their long term strategies, plans and procurements. General Deepak

Kapoor, India's army chief and Chairman of its Chiefs of Staff, created a minor storm in 2010 after declaring that he wanted to be able to fight a two-front war against Pakistan and China.[7] This has involved purchases of over half-a-billion dollars worth of weapons that could be deployed to the mountainous Indian border with China.[8]

The Indian navy for its part wants to be able to project power far beyond the Indian Ocean. In a June 2012 speech, Admiral Nirmal Kumar Verma, Chief of Naval Staff and Chairman of India's Chiefs of Staff, pointed out that the Indian navy is expanding regarding how it deploys ships, observing that with, 'some of our ships are on their way back from a deployment to the South and East China Seas while some others are on their way to the Mediterranean.'[9] Admiral Verma also highlighted India's globe-spanning joint naval exercises, including MALABAR with the United States Navy; VARUNA with the French navy; KONKAN with the British Royal Navy; INDRA with the Russian navy; SIMBEX with the Singapore navy; and IBSAMAR with the South African and Brazilian navies. China is notable by its absence. The launch of the Arihant nuclear submarine was another step in the direction of power projection. Once the Arihant is inducted, India will become the sixth operator of nuclear submarines in the world, after the United States, Russia, France, Britain and China.[10]

China has also been cited by Indian policy makers as a driver for India's nuclear weapons program. In May 1998, Prime Minister Atal Behari Vajpayee wrote a private letter to President Clinton justifying India's nuclear tests that were conducted month, claiming that China was the reason since it was 'an overt nuclear weapon state on our borders, a state which committed armed aggression against India in 1962.'[11] Eleven years later, a controversy erupted when a senior Indian government technical expert, K. Santhanam, claimed that in the May 1998 test the thermonuclear weapon (hydrogen bomb) did not work as designed and that India needed additional nuclear weapons tests to ensure it had a reliable H–bomb, specifically to counter China.[12] Additional nuclear tests could speed India's quest for thermonuclear weapons arsenal comparable to China's.

India's quest for nuclear parity with China also may have played a role in Indian interest in a special strategic relationship with the United States, codified in the January 2004 Statement on the Next Steps in Strategic Partnership, under which the U.S. and India agreed to cooperate on civilian nuclear activities, civilian space programs, high-technology trade and missile defense. The controversial U.S. India nuclear deal, signed into U.S. law in 2008, may serve to boost India's bomb-making capacity, by allowing India to freely import natural uranium and hence can divert its scarce domestic uranium resources to its military reactors.[13]

REGIONAL AND GLOBAL DYNAMICS

The future of nuclear South Asia is increasingly wrapped up in great power politics. For six decades, the United States has sought to have India become part of its strategic and economic plans for Asia especially as a counter to China. In the early years, the U.S. hoped that India could serve as a pro-western capitalist democracy able to compete with communist China, which had its revolution in 1949; two years after India won independence.

In recent years, as China's economy has boomed, it has emerged as a potential great power competitor to the United States. Thus the U.S. has pressed again to recruit India. Indian leaders, for their part, have seen an opportunity to use a new relationship with the U.S. as a way to drive India's rise as a major power. The changed U.S.–India relationship was formalized in the 'Next Steps in Strategic Partnership' agreement of January 2004. A U.S. senior official announced that, 'Its goal is to help India become a major world power in the 21st century. . . . We understand fully the implications, including military implications, of that statement.'[14]

As India builds up its military capacity, with U.S. help, Pakistan will rely even more on China for military assistance. This four-cornered arms race can probably be sustained at a very high level in the decades ahead. The Goldman-Sachs BRICS projections of the future growth of the economies of Brazil, Russia, India and China, suggest that by 2050, India will have a GDP comparable to that expected for the United States (over $37 trillion dollars), and half that expected for China. Pakistan is projected to have a GDP in 2050 that is fourteen-fold greater than in 2010.

An additional regional factor in the nuclear dynamic is the possibility that Iran may decide to turn its search for a nuclear weapon capability into a fully-fledged nuclear weapon program. It is worth recalling that both India and Pakistan acquired the capability many years before they made the decision to build an actual nuclear arsenal.

NUCLEAR RISKS AND CONSEQUENCES

The crises and wars that marked the first fifty years of India and Pakistan have not faded with the coming of nuclear weapons. Major crises and a war followed the 1998 nuclear tests, and crises will continue to recur, and with them will come the risk of war and the possibility of escalation into nuclear war. The new danger is that of nuclear terrorism.

Pakistan's leaders have made it clear they are prepared to use nuclear weapons first in any conflict; they hope this threat will prevent war, because they fear being overwhelmed by India's conventional military might if war should happen. While India has offered an agreement for no-first use of nuclear weapons, its armed forces seem prepared to try to destroy Pakistan's nuclear capability before it is used, and seek their own capability to launch a nuclear attack if they believe that enemy nuclear missiles are armed and ready for launch. Pakistan, in turn, may seek to pre-empt such a situation by using its nuclear weapons even earlier in a conflict rather than risk losing them in a massive, rapid Indian conventional assault that India has war-gamed as part of a strategy it dubs 'Cold Start'.

The experience of Hiroshima and Nagasaki showed that a single nuclear weapon can devastate a modern city. About a hundred thousand people died in each city, but people living a few miles away from these cities were not affected directly and so were able to shelter refugees and provide some assistance to the injured. It is unlikely that nuclear war between India and Pakistan would involve only the use of a single nuclear weapon. Even if each side used only five weapons each, and targeted cities, they would kill on the order of three million people and injure at least as many (see chapter: 'What Nuclear War could do to South Asia'). Relief and recovery from such destruction would be beyond the capacities of either country. The other countries in the region have few resources they could divert. The broader international community would be stretched thin to manage the recovery effort.

A larger India–Pakistan nuclear war would devastate South Asia and much of the world. Recent studies looking at an India–Pakistan nuclear conflict in which they used fifty weapons each found that the smoke produced by burning cities would spread to cover the South Asian region within five days; in nine days it would begin to encircle the world and cover the earth in less than two months. The smoke would darken the sun for as long as a decade, cooling the Earth's surface and causing drought that would devastate global agriculture.[15] This possibility should give new urgency to South Asian regional efforts and broader international efforts to have India and Pakistan restrain their arms race and war plans, and move towards a more cooperative and peaceful relationship.

The other grave nuclear danger facing Pakistan and India is nuclear terrorism. Today, with 90 to110 nuclear weapons spread across Pakistan and fissile materials produced or processed at numerous locations, the threat from religious extremists—both from outside as well as inside the nuclear establishment—is also very real, albeit unquantifiable. It is known that the Al Qaeda leadership met with sympathetic former senior scientists in Pakistan's nuclear weapons program. By engineering a nuclear catastrophe in some Western city, Osama bin Laden and his disciples dream of provoking a nuclear response from the U.S. that would rally new supporters to their cause and unleash a final showdown between the West and the Muslim world.

It is not just the United States but also India—and Pakistan—that need to fear nuclear terrorism. London or New York may be the preferred targets for Al Qaeda militants but Islamabad and Delhi may be much easier. If a retaliatory nuclear response from India on Pakistan's cities is triggered, this would be the fulfillment of a dream to ignite the ultimate conflict that would destroy both *kafirs* (unbelievers) and *munafiqs* (Muslim hypocrites). Along with India and the West, the radical Sunni interpretation of Islam that drives the Islamist militancy in Pakistan treats Shi'a Muslims as an enemy. A radical Islamist takeover in nuclear Pakistan could push Iran to take the decision finally to build a nuclear weapon and create a deadly new nuclear confrontation.

The origin and nature of the Islamist militancy in Pakistan ensures that it will be an inter-generational process and will shape Pakistan and the region's future for at least the next fifty years. In the 1980s, the military regime of General Zia, Pakistan's Islamist parties, Saudi Arabia and the United States created a generation of radical young Afghans and Pakistanis committed to jihad. The madrassas that trained these militants continue to operate and are the only schools for many hundreds of thousands of boys and girls still in their teens. The militant worldview they learn will guide their thinking for decades.

TOWARDS NUCLEAR DISARMAMENT—IMPLICATIONS FOR SOUTH ASIA

Pakistan is at the heart of nuclear fears for much of the international community. The 11 September 2001 attacks on the United States raised fears of nuclear terrorism by Al Qaeda. The beginnings of the 21st century also brought new concerns about the spread of nuclear weapons materials and knowledge on the black market. In 2003, A.Q. Khan was revealed to have trafficked key nuclear weapons technologies and weapon designs from Pakistan's program to Iran, Libya and North Korea, and possibly others. These developments have added new urgency to the long-standing goal of eliminating nuclear weapons.

These concerns are shared by all the great powers. In September
2009 a unanimous United Nations Security Council resolution
declared: 'We are all committed to seeking a safer world for all and
to creating the conditions for a world without nuclear weapons.'[16]
But the abolition of nuclear weapons may not come soon. In his
2009 Prague speech calling for abolishing nuclear weapons,
President Obama stated that the goal of eliminating nuclear weapons
'will not be reached quickly—perhaps not in my lifetime.' Secretary
of State Hillary Clinton has pushed the prospect of disarmament
further back, arguing, 'We might not achieve the ambition of a world
without nuclear weapons in our lifetime or successive lifetimes.'[17]
Even the most ambitious nuclear disarmament effort, led by the
international campaign known as Global Zero, imagines the final
elimination of nuclear weapons only by 2030.

A South Asian Nuclear-Weapons-Free Zone (SANWFZ) offers one
way to pressure Pakistan and India to restrain their nuclear
ambitions and build a stronger South Asian regional community.
Initially such a treaty might include only Sri Lanka, Bangladesh,
Nepal, Afghanistan, the Maldives and Bhutan. A treaty would permit
these countries to exert official and popular pressure on Pakistan
and India to disarm, strengthen nuclear-disarmament movements
in these countries, and offer the two governments a path back from
the nuclear abyss if political circumstances improve. There are
Nuclear-Weapons-Free Zones in Latin America, the South Pacific
and Southeast Asia, Africa and Central Asia, which commit countries
in these regions to not acquire nuclear weapons.

READING A CRACKED CRYSTAL BALL

It is an exercise in grand speculation to imagine in any detail what
South Asia may be like in 2060. Nonetheless, it seems likely that the
struggle between India and Pakistan will continue. Elites in both
countries, for different reasons, seem determined to build-up their
nuclear arsenals and conventional forces and accept the high
economic, political and social costs of their confrontation, and live
with the risk of nuclear war.

The geopolitics will be complex and unstable. United States and India may together seek to balance and contain Chinese power and influence. China may increase its support to Pakistan to help offset India. The United States may be compelled to aid Pakistan to prevent it from being overwhelmed by Islamist forces. The arms race could be fierce, and given rapidly growing economies in China and India, involve massive expenditures, especially in high-tech conventional weapons. Less likely perhaps is that America and Russia move decisively towards abolishing nuclear weapons. Britain, France and China would join them, and India and Pakistan may have no choice but to go along.

The India–China economic rivalry may become the most important concern for India. Knowing that Pakistan, aided by China, will be a thorn in its side, India could make significant concessions to Pakistan on Kashmir and the increasingly charged issue of allocation of the water of the Indus river. If Pakistan is able to end the Islamist militancy, détente could change into the long-awaited rapprochement between Pakistan and India. This could open the door for a process of South Asian regional integration finally to take hold.

It is as likely, however, that the Pakistan army's narrow interests will keep it committed to the struggle against India, regardless of cost and consequence. In a replay of the U.S.–Soviet race, Pakistan could break its back trying to keep up with India. The South Asian region would fester as the two countries wrestle for advantage in every forum. Left unchecked, it would result in the economic, political and social collapse of Pakistan, which would unleash chaos. Under such circumstances, it is possible to imagine that the jihadis may capture a nuclear weapon. A fearful India and United States would intervene, raising concerns in China. The prospect of great power conflict would loom.

The nightmare scenario is that Pakistan's generals, faced with collapse, decide to threaten nuclear war. As the Cuban Missile Crisis showed fifty years ago, in the midst of crisis, there is fear, miscalculation, errors of judgment, flaws in command and control, and simple bad luck, and any of them could trigger a nuclear war. The subcontinent's cities would become radioactive ruins. Tens of millions would die. The pall of smoke would darken the world and become a global calamity.

REFERENCES

1. 'India to get Admiral Gorshkov, nuclear submarine next year, says AK Antony', *The Economic Times*, 8 May 2012.
2. India Nuclear Missile Test: Agni-V Missile Has Capability To Hit Chinese Cities, *The Huffington Post*, 4 April 2012.
3. Hemant Kumar Rout, 'Agni-VI to be ready by mid-2014', IBN Live, 24 May 2012, http://ibnlive.in.com/news/agnivi-to-be-ready-by-mid-2014/260489-60-117.html
4. 'Defense Contractors Target Big Jump in India's Military Spending', Sonya Misquita, *Wall Street Journal*, 17 July 2009, http://online.wsj.com/article/SB124778767144054747.html
5. http://news.bbc.co.uk/2/hi/world/south_asia/10375056.stm
6. 'India, China decide border talks protocol', *Times of India*, 7 March 2012.
7. Rajat Pandit, 'Army reworks war doctrine for Pakistan, China', *Times of India*, 30 December 2009, http://timesofindia.indiatimes.com/india/Army-reworks-war-doctrine-for-Pakistan-China/articleshow/5392683.cms
8. Uttara Choudhury, 'Boom! India in $660 m deal for howitzers aimed at China', First Post, 12 May 2012, http://www.firstpost.com/india/boom-india-in-660-m-deal-for-us-howitzers-aimed-at-china-306994.html
9. Admiral Nirmal Kumar Verma, Address to International Institute for Strategic Studies, London, 25 June 2012, http://www.iiss.org/recent-key-addresses/metamorphosis-of-matters-maritime-an-indian-perspective
10. 'India to Construct Two More Arihant Nuclear Submarines For Navy', *Defense Now*, 28 February 2012.
11. 'Text of a letter sent on Monday to President Clinton from Prime Minister Atal Bihari Vajpayee of India', *The New York Times*, 13 May 1998, http://www.nytimes.com/1998/05/13/world/nuclear-anxiety-indian-s-letter-to-clinton-on-the-nuclear-testing.html
12. K Santhanam and Ashok Parthasarathi, 'Pokhran-II: an H-bomb disaster', Business Standard, 11 December 2009, http://www.business-standard.com/india/news/k-santhanamashok-parthasarathi-pokhran-ii-an-h-bomb-disaster/379156/
13. Zia Mian, A.H. Nayyar, R. Rajaraman, and M.V. Ramana, 'Fissile Materials in South Asia: The Implications of the US-India Nuclear Deal', International Panel on Fissile Materials, Research Report #1, September 2006, Princeton NJ, www.fissilematerials.org/ipfm/site_down/rr01.pdf
14. 'US unveils plans to make India "major world power"', *Reuters*, 26 March 2005.

15. 'Local Nuclear War, Global Suffering', Alan Robock and Owen Toon, *Scientific American*, January 2010.
16. U.N. Security Council Resolution 1887, http://www.un.org/News/Press/docs/2009/sc9746.doc.htm
17. Secretary of State Hillary Rodham Clinton, at the United States Institute of Peace, 21 October 2009, http://www.america.gov/st/texttrans-english/2009/October/20091021180508ihecuor0.8690541.html#ixzz0uAmUOQ7T

CHAPTER 15

AMERICA, GLOBAL DOMINATION, GLOBAL DISARMAMENT

Pervez Hoodbhoy and Zia Mian

If proof is needed that the growth of technology has far outstripped the capacities of the institutions we have to govern human society, we need look no further than the continued existence of nuclear weapons. There are over 25,000 nuclear weapons in the world today. The United States and Russia have almost 20,000 nuclear weapons between them and maintain components and nuclear materials to make many more, while the other seven nuclear-armed countries have at most a few hundred weapons each, and material stockpiled for more.

Throughout the sixty-five years since the first nuclear weapons were created and used there have been efforts to end the nuclear danger. The most visible new international campaign is called Global Zero. Over 400,000 people from around the world have signed on to the Global Zero declaration that:[1] to protect our children, our grandchildren and our civilization from the threat of nuclear catastrophe, we must eliminate all nuclear weapons globally. We therefore commit to working for a legally binding verifiable agreement, including all nations, to eliminate nuclear weapons by a date certain.

Global Zero hopes to move the nuclear-armed states to reduce their arsenals and then to eliminate all nuclear weapons by 2030. At its first meeting in December 2008, Global Zero drew over a hundred political, military, academic, business, and civic leaders from around the world. In February 2010 in Paris, the Second Global Zero Summit convened two-hundred leaders from around the world. United States' President Barack Obama, Russian President Dmitri

Medvedev and the U.N. Secretary General Ban Ki-moon sent strong statements of support. President Obama declared that Global Zero 'will always have a partner in me and my administration.'[2]

Can humanity finally be free of nuclear weapons? It may seem easy given that the President of the United States says he supports this goal. But therein may lie the problem. The United States now has the most powerful military forces in the world and is developing a new generation of highly sophisticated conventional weapons. This means it may not need nuclear weapons to threaten other countries. As a corollary, it is in the American interest that other countries not have nuclear weapons. But it will be difficult to convince countries that fear the United States, or a more powerful neighbour, that nuclear abolition is in their interest. For these countries, the enormous power of nuclear weapons makes them strategic equalizers against more powerful adversaries, including the United States. To abolish nuclear weapons will require addressing these concerns and will entail the United States to give up its overwhelming military superiority and its pursuit of continued global dominance.

THE AMERICAN BOMB

After the American atomic bombing of the Japanese city of Hiroshima on 6 August 1945, President Harry Truman claimed the new weapon as a fundamental breakthrough in military capability and a uniquely American achievement. The Hiroshima bomb, he said, was 'more than two thousand times the blast power of . . . the largest bomb ever yet used in the history of warfare.' The bomb was made possible, Truman announced, only because 'the United States had available the large number of scientists of distinction in the many needed areas of knowledge. It had the tremendous industrial and financial resources necessary for the project. . . . It is doubtful if such another combination could be got together in the world.' Armed with what it believed was a 'winning weapon', America set out to dominate the world.

There were voices of caution, however. Robert Oppenheimer, who had led the American atomic bomb project during World War II, warned in November 1945 that the only hope lay in America giving up its nuclear monopoly otherwise more countries would surely follow and the nuclear danger would worsen:

I think the advent of the atomic bomb and the facts which will get around that they are not too hard to make—that they will be universal if people wish to make them universal, that they will not constitute a real drain on the economy of any strong nation, and that their power of destruction will grow.[3]

The newly formed United Nations embraced the goal of nuclear disarmament as its most urgent priority. The first resolution passed by the U.N. General Assembly in January 1946, was a call for plans 'for the elimination from national armaments of atomic weapons and of all other major weapons adaptable to mass destruction.' But America would not give up its new weapon and Oppenheimer's apprehensions were soon was proven correct. Nuclear weapons programs sprang up in other countries. The Soviet Union tested its first bomb in 1949, Britain in 1952, and France in 1960. The destructive power of weapons increased very soon, as the atom bomb gave way to the hydrogen bomb. In 1954, the U.S. tested a hydrogen bomb with a yield which was about a thousand times larger than the atom bomb dropped on Hiroshima. The Soviet Union soon exploded a bomb that was larger still.

In 1964, China carried out its first nuclear explosion, showing that nuclear weapons were an option even for countries lacking extensive scientific, industrial or financial resources. Since then, other poor developing countries have built nuclear weapons: India, Pakistan and North Korea—overturning a common view that nuclear weapons are expensive. Making the first nuclear weapon is indeed expensive for any country as immense resources are needed to set up a nuclear establishment that prepares fissile materials, to design and fabricate a warhead, create a means of delivery such as a ballistic missile, and set up a system for command and control. But, as in industrial production, once the $n'th$ warhead has been put into place, the $n+1'th$ one costs less.

History shows that not only can poor states afford the cost, but many of their people will support paying for it. Pakistan is perhaps the classic case of how a state successfully used nationalism to convince its people that neither costs nor moral concerns about mass destruction should matter when the country feels its existence, sovereignty, or honour is at stake.

Nuclear nationalism has not carried the day, however. Progressive political movements around the world have struggled for the total elimination of nuclear weapons. They won popular support from time to time because of the fear of nuclear war and moral concerns about countries arming themselves with weapons of mass destruction. The historian of the international nuclear disarmament movement, Lawrence Wittner, has documented the great struggles against the bomb waged in the U.S. and Western Europe, the places where nuclear war was believed to be most likely and where democracy allowed political organizing.

The majority of countries have always supported the goal of nuclear abolition—they have not tried to build nuclear weapons and condemned those that would use them. In 1961 the U.N. General Assembly declared for instance that, 'any state using nuclear and thermo-nuclear weapons is to be considered as violating the Charter of the United Nations, as acting contrary to the laws of humanity and as committing a crime against mankind and civilization.' Similar resolutions continue to be passed each year with overwhelming support.

Faced with domestic and international demands to ban the bomb, from time to time, American leaders and those in other nuclear-armed states have offered a vision of a world without nuclear weapons. Most famously, in October 1986, President Ronald Reagan agreed with the Soviet leader Mikhail Gorbachev on the need to eliminate all nuclear weapons. Each time however these crashed on the rocks of the superpower Cold War.

Hopes for nuclear disarmament and a more peaceful world revived in the 1990s with the end of the Cold War and the collapse of the Soviet Union.

THE END OF THE COLD WAR

With the end of the Cold War and the disintegration of the Soviet Union, United States lost what had been the cornerstone of its foreign policy for almost fifty years. How was the United States going to confront this new world?

A 1992 draft Defense Planning Guidance prepared for U.S. Defense Secretary Dick Cheney by Paul Wolfowitz, then Under-Secretary of Defense for Policy, was leaked to the press. It argued: 'Our first objective is to prevent the re-emergence of a new rival. This is a dominant consideration underlying the new regional defense strategy and requires that we endeavour to prevent any hostile power from dominating a region whose resources would, under consolidated control, be sufficient to generate global power . . . we must maintain the mechanisms for deterring potential competitors from even aspiring to a larger regional or global role.'

In other words, the geopolitical order must be stabilized and the United States must maintain its relative superiority in all the different regions of the world. From the viewpoint of the White House, the Pentagon and the Congress, American military power was a critical asset in winning the Cold War. This force included thousands of bombers, fighter aircraft, missiles, and ships. There was also a global network of military bases, and agreements for basing rights in over forty countries across the world. It was important to maintain and use this power if the U.S. was to stay the world's sole superpower.

But the militarists in the United States establishment could not find a clear focus for the threats that would justify their approach. The Project for the New American Century (PNAC), a Washington-based neo-conservative think-tank founded in 1997 and supported by Dick Cheney, Donald Rumsfeld, and Paul Wolfowitz among others, who went on to serve as senior officials under President George W. Bush, called for unilateral military intervention to protect against threats to America's status as the lone global superpower. In an article in 2000 in the journal *Foreign Affairs*, Condoleezza Rice, soon-to-be Secretary of State for President George Bush, displayed a degree of frustration and uncertainty: 'The United States has found it exceedingly difficult to define its 'national interest' in the absence of Soviet power.'[4] She explained that foreign policy in a future Republican administration would focus the country on 'building a military ready to ensure American power, coping with rogue regimes, and managing Beijing and Moscow.'

The transformative moment for the Bush-Cheney-Rice-Rumsfeld-Wolfowitz team came in September 2001 with Al Qaeda's attack on New York's twin towers of the World Trade Centre and on the Pentagon. America went to war in Afghanistan and then Iraq. These wars however exposed the limits of American military might. The promise of a high-tech war of 'shock and awe' is now all but forgotten. The abiding images of the Iraq war, even in America, are not cruise missiles over Baghdad but torture at Abu Ghraib and the massacre at Fallujah. In Afghanistan, all anyone will remember is a brutal counter-insurgency and a corrupt and inept puppet government led by Hamid Karzai.

Today, America's failure in Iraq and Afghanistan has dampened the ardour for managing and shaping the world. Barack Obama was elected President in 2008 in part because of his opposition to the Iraq war. The blood and treasure expended in the Bush wars has taken a toll on the American economy and on America's standing in the world. A 2011 analysis by researchers at Brown University found that the wars have cost 2.3 to 2.8 trillion dollars so far.[5] Interest payments on the debt incurred for paying for these wars will add another one trillion dollars by 2020. This military spending had helped drive the American economy into its worst recession in eighty years.

In August 2011, as a consequence of the American economic crisis, Standard & Poors downgraded the U.S. credit rating by one notch from 'triple A' to 'double A plus'. This contentious and historic move highlighted the weakened fiscal stature of the world's most powerful country. The manufacturing capacity of the U.S. has also seen a sharp fall. While it remains a top producer of advanced technology, the earlier dominance has eroded. The trade surplus in advanced technology manufactured goods of the previous decade has turned into an $81 billion annual trade deficit. Competition from China, Europe and India—countries that used to make only inexpensive goods at low cost—has caused manufacturing jobs to migrate overseas.

The loss of U.S. economic strength will translate into an ever more costly effort to maintain its military strength. It remains an open question as to whether the United States can learn to fade quietly by reducing its military power or whether U.S. leaders will resist their country's gradual decline and unleash instability and crisis in their effort to stem change in the world order.

For some U.S. leaders, nuclear abolition may offer a way to maintain American power in a changing world. The clearest example of the new logic is the argument laid out by Henry Kissinger, Secretary of State under U.S. President Richard Nixon; former Secretary of State George Shultz; ex-Secretary of Defense William Perry; and Sam Nunn, the former Chairman of the Senate Armed Services Committee (together known as the Four Horsemen), in a 2007 article in the conservative American newspaper, *The Wall Street Journal*. They argued that: 'North Korea's recent nuclear test and Iran's refusal to stop its program to enrich uranium—potentially to weapons grade—highlight the fact that the world is now on the precipice of a new and dangerous nuclear era. Most alarmingly, the likelihood that non-state terrorists will get their hands on nuclear weaponry is increasing. In today's war waged on world order by terrorists, nuclear weapons are the ultimate means of mass devastation . . . unless urgent new actions are taken, the U.S. soon will be compelled to enter a new nuclear era that will be more precarious, psychologically disorienting, and economically even more costly than was the Cold War.'

It was an astonishing turnaround. Kissinger, in particular, is renowned as a realist and arch cold-warrior with hawkish views on nuclear weapons; he had proposed using them in Vietnam. Although he is regarded as a senior statesman in the U.S., in several countries he is wanted for crimes against humanity, engineering U.S.–backed coups and intrigues, and authorizing death squads. He continues to evade legal summons by investigators in France, Chile, and Argentina who seek to question him regarding his role in the disappearances of numerous citizens of the U.S. and other nations.

While advocating the 'the vision of a world without nuclear weapons,' Kissinger, Shultz, Perry, and Nunn urge that significant new investments are needed in the U.S. nuclear weapons complex 'to undo the adverse consequences of deep reductions over the past five years in the laboratories' budgets for the science, technology and engineering programs that support and underwrite the nation's nuclear deterrent.'[6] Rather than use the withering of the U.S. nuclear weapon capability to drive faster toward the goal of abolition, the 'Four Horsemen' want the United States to modernize its nuclear weapons.

Since then, the United States has committed to the modernization of its nuclear weapon complex and arsenal. The Obama administration has announced plans to spend $175 billion on the U.S. nuclear weapon complex in the next two decades, withanother $100 billion to be spent on nuclear weapon delivery systems, including new bombers, ballistic missiles, and submarines.

It should come as no surprise that Russia has launched its own effort to maintain its arsenal for a further fifty years. Britain is considering a plan to replace its nuclear-armed submarines. China is moving to greater reliance on more modern solid-fueled road-mobile missiles and submarine-launched missiles. France has been developing a new ballistic missile and a new nuclear warhead. Israel is believed to have moved to nuclear-armed cruise missiles on its submarines. India, Pakistan, and North Korea are still developing their nuclear forces. Seeing that nuclear weapons may be around for many more decades, other countries may decide it is finally time to build their own.

PREPARING FOR THE NEXT WAR

In many ways, nuclear and conventional weapons policies under Barack Obama have continued the initiatives that emerged under

George Bush. Writing about American military power, Obama, who many hoped would pave the way to a new era in American politics, sounds just like George Bush. In a July 2007 essay, Obama wrote:

> To renew American leadership in the world, we must immediately begin working to revitalize our military. A strong military is, more than anything, necessary to sustain peace. . . . We must retain the capacity to swiftly defeat any conventional threat to our country and our vital interests. . . . I will not hesitate to use force, unilaterally if necessary. . . . We must also consider using military force in circumstances beyond self-defense in order to provide for the common security that underpins global stability.[7]

This approach has been carried forward in policy. In spring 2011, Obama proposed limiting the increase in U.S. military spending over the next decade. At the same time, however, non-military spending especially on issues such as assistance to the poor would be cut. As a result, the military share of the budget will actually increase in coming years.

A similar story can be told about nuclear weapons. In 2002, the Bush administration issued a Nuclear Posture Review that identified the nuclear threats to the U.S. as coming from other nuclear-armed states, 'rogue states', and terrorists armed with weapons of mass destruction. To counter these, they argued that the U.S. needed nuclear weapons and existing conventional weapons, and to develop new conventional weapons that are able to attack a target anywhere in the world in less than 30 minutes. This capability was dubbed 'Prompt Global Strike'.

In his 2009 Prague speech President Obama echoed the language of President George Bush and of Henry Kissinger, George Schultz, William Perry and Sam Nunn in describing the nuclear threat.

In a strange turn of history, the threat of global nuclear war has gone down, but the risk of a nuclear attack has gone up. More nations have acquired these weapons. Testing has continued. Black market trade in nuclear secrets and nuclear materials abound. The technology to build a bomb has spread. Terrorists are determined to buy, build or steal one.

The Obama 2010 Nuclear Posture Review adopted the Bush goal of Prompt Global Strike. Robert Gates, who served as Secretary of Defense both for Bush and Obama observed that Prompt Global Strike really hadn't gone anywhere in the Bush administration but was being embraced by the Obama administration.

For the U.S., Prompt Global Strike is seen as enabling progress in disarmament, since precision guided conventional weapons can destroy some targets that nuclear weapons were previously to be used for. This approach is seen as having the added benefit of avoiding the high political price of using nuclear weapons.

Substituting nuclear arms with precision-guided conventional arms—which may be more useable and perhaps just as effective—carries its own costs, however. In particular, other countries which cannot match U.S. conventional weapons capabilities see them as a new threat. Even major powers like Russia and China see Prompt Global Strike and missile defense capabilities as threatening the strategic balance these countries feel they are currently maintaining with the United States.

According to a Eugene Miasnikov, a Russian defense analyst, Russian military experts see numerous threats to survivability of the strategic forces in future: missile defenses, high precision conventional arms, Anti-Submarine Warfare (ASW), etc. Their concerns grow as the United States are shifting the missions formerly assigned to nuclear weapons to conventional weapons instead of abandoning such missions altogether. Significant U.S. investments in development of conventional counterforce capabilities also do not help diminishing Moscow's concerns.[8]

China also worries about U.S. plans for advanced conventional weapons and how these may threaten its much smaller nuclear arsenal. Lora Saalman has noted that in China, U.S. conventional Prompt Global Strike, along with anti-satellite weapons, and missile defenses 'are all cited by academic, military, and scientific experts as posing long-term challenges . . . [and experts] cite the potential that the goal of a world free of nuclear weapons may open the door to the resumption of a large-scale conventional war.'[9]

Meanwhile, China is advancing its own conventional weapons. It has recently developed a sophisticated anti-ship ballistic missile, is working on an embryonic aircraft carrier program, and made a prototype stealth fighter jet. This may serve only to spur a conventional arms race that adds further instability into the system.

NUCLEAR EQUALIZERS?

United States planners claim Prompt Global Strike is not aimed at Russia or China but to address 'newly emerging regional threats.' This is code for the spread of nuclear weapons to third world countries.

The U.S. has long worried that the spread of nuclear weapons would limit its freedom of action and its power to intervene in key parts of the world. Between 1945 and 2000 the U.S. fought twenty-eight major, and countless minor wars. Korea, Guatemala, Congo, Laos, Peru, Vietnam, Cambodia, El Salvador, Nicaragua, Yugoslavia, Iraq, Afghanistan and Pakistan are only some of the countries which the U.S. has invaded or bombed. The United States would have been more constrained if it had feared that nuclear weapons might be used against invading U.S. forces or against the U.S. bases that were the launch pads of these interventions. In 2003, a Bush administration official summed up this American understanding, declaring that a nuclear weapon 'is a real equalizer if you're a pissant little country with no hope of matching the U.S. militarily.'[10]

To prevent the spread of nuclear weapons, the U.S. drafted and promoted the 1970 Nuclear Non-Proliferation Treaty (NPT). Non-proliferation has had limited success in achieving its goal however. Since 1970, four countries have acquired nuclear weapons—India, Pakistan, North Korea and South Africa (which later gave them up). Several others (Iraq, Libya and perhaps Syria) have tried to acquire them and Iran may be trying to do so. This failure is one of the spurs for the new demand among some American policy makers for nuclear abolition in the United States. For them, abolishing nuclear weapons is the price to be paid for maintaining a capacity to intervene around the world.

But for some states that have developed nuclear weapons, the attraction of these weapons is that they offer a way to balance the greater military capabilities of a foe. North Korea's government believes that its nuclear weapon protect the regime from American attack and give it bargaining power. After the 2003 U.S. invasion of Iraq, North Korea argued that 'disarmament . . . does not help avert a war, but rather sparks it' and only 'a tremendous military deterrent force' can restrain the United States.[11] At the same time, North Korea has agreed to give up its nuclear weapons program in exchange for U.S. diplomatic recognition, a peace treaty and economic aid.

Pakistan offers another example. It argues that nuclear weapons help the country balance both India's nuclear forces and larger conventional forces. This suggests it perceives nuclear weapons in purely defensive terms. In fact, Pakistan has used its nuclear weapons as shield from behind which it can launch attacks against India as hostilities escalate. In 1999, a secret incursion of Pakistani troops across the Line of Control (LoC) in Kashmir near Kargil caused a limited outbreak of hostilities between Pakistan and India. Thousands were killed. India was restrained from an all-out response such as an attack across the international border. It was a war that would not have happened but for nuclear weapons.

But this brief war also exposed the limitations of nuclear weapons. Once the war started, Pakistan had to back off. The cost involved in continuing the conflict was estimated to be far too great. International opinion came down decisively against Pakistan, and Pakistan lacked the economic and military resources to fight an extended war. Pakistan faced the same bitter truth that the United States confronted in Vietnam in the 1960s and 1970s, and the Soviet Union in Afghanistan in the 1980s—nuclear weapons could not prevent defeat.

Some believe that nuclear weapons can protect against the collapse of a regime. Former U.S. Vice-President Dick Cheney has suggested that the downfall of Libya's Colonel Qaddafi offers an example of this. Cheney, who was promoting his memoirs on a television show and justifying the Iraq invasion, claimed that the invasion of Iraq and defeat of Saddam Hussein had frightened Qaddafi into giving up Libya's quest for nuclear weapons. Cheney claimed: 'If Qaddafi still had nuclear weapons last week, do you think he would have fled? I doubt it.'[12]

History tells another story, however. Libya tried to normalize its relations with the West through the 1990s and, according to U.S. officials, in 2002 Libya made clear to the United States that it wanted to settle its 'differences'.[13] In early March 2003, well before the U.S. announced the invasion of Iraq, Libya began secret talks with the West about ending the Libyan nuclear weapons program. Moreover, even if Qaddafi had succeeded in making nuclear weapons, how would he have used them in what was a civil war—would the Libyan regime have dropped a nuclear bomb on one of its own cities? If so, would this not have surely brought down Qaddafi's regime?

Iran now poses the most visible challenge to nuclear non-proliferation. It was encouraged to acquire an expansive nuclear program by the U.S. while the Shah of Iran, Mohammad Raza Pahalavi was ruling Iran in the 1970s. The country now has two facilities for enriching uranium using gas centrifuges. One of these facilities, at Fordo, near Qom, is producing close to 20 per cent enriched uranium; for comparison highly enriched uranium in nuclear weapons is typically over 90 per cent enriched. These facilities are under international inspection since Iran is a signatory of the Non-Proliferation Treaty. The United States has claimed that Iran may have had a nuclear weapons program before 2003, but it may not have made a decision to acquire such weapons. The 2007 U.S. National Intelligence Estimate, a consensus view of its intelligence agencies, said: 'We judge with high confidence that in fall 2003, Tehran halted its nuclear weapons program.'[14] This judgment was upheld in the 2010 National Intelligence Estimate, and as of 2012 remained the consensus view of U.S. intelligence agencies.[15] The International Atomic Energy Agency has raised questions about possible military dimensions of Iran's program and the United Nations Security Council has passed resolutions calling on Iran to suspend its enrichment program until it has resolved the questions from the IAEA (International Atomic Energy Agency). The Security Council has imposed sanctions on Iran for refusing to comply, as has the United States, the European Union and a number of other countries.

In a May 2012 interview, Seyyed Hossein Mousavian, former head of the Foreign Relations Committee of the Supreme National Security Council of Iran, argued that despite Western pressures, 'there is already a consensus that Iran does not need a nuclear weapon and that pursuit or possession of a nuclear weapon will compromise rather than strengthen Iranian national security. This consensus is firmly grounded in numerous *fatwas* (Islamic edicts) issued by the most senior religious authorities in the country, by the ongoing commitment to the NPT framework and numerous other strategic considerations.'[16] The *fatwa*, issued in 2010 by Iran's supreme leader Ayatollah Khamenei, bans the production and use of weapons of mass destruction and was subsequently reaffirmed.[17]

As Mousavian details in his 2012 memoir, efforts by the Iranian government under President Khatami to negotiate with the West after the start of the crisis over Iran's nuclear program in 2002 were frustrated by the U.S. government.[18] Similarly, Ambassador James Dobbins, the Bush administration's special envoy for Afghanistan, Kosovo, Bosnia, Haiti, and Somalia, has observed that:

> The Khatami government had made substantial overtures of cooperation to Washington twice, first after the U.S. victory in Afghanistan, and again after the U.S. invasion of Iraq . . . encompassing offers of cooperation on nuclear technology, Iraq, terrorism, and Middle East peace as well as Afghanistan. This proposal, like its predecessor, was never seriously considered in Washington and once again the Iranians never received a response. . . . U.S. officials have never explained in any detail why they ignored the Iranian overtures of 2002 and 2003.[19]

Nonetheless, in 2012, against a background of tightening sanctions which limit Iran's exports of oil and undermine its domestic economy, Iran continues to negotiate with the five permanent members of the U.N. Security Council plus Germany (known as P5+1) over the status and future of the Iranian nuclear program. As part of these talks, Iran continues to insist on 'its commitments under the NPT and its opposition to nuclear weapons based on the Supreme Leader's *fatwa* against such weapons.'[20] What is less clear is whether the *fatwa* bans research on nuclear weapons, or if it might be revised in case of an attack on Iran by Israel and/or the United States.

NUCLEAR TERRORISM

A new twist to the nuclear danger is the possibility that violent extremists may somehow succeed in making or obtaining nuclear weapons. This is perhaps the most important new argument in favour of eliminating nuclear weapons everywhere, including those in the possession of nation states.

The United States has perhaps the most to fear. *The New York Times* reported that before September 11 the U.S. had intercepted an Al Qaeda message that Osama bin Laden was planning a 'Hiroshima' against America.[21] In a later taped message, released just before the U.S. attack on Afghanistan, bin Laden called up the image of the bombing of Japan, claiming: 'When people at the ends of the earth, Japan, were killed by their hundreds of thousands, young and old, it was not considered a war crime; it is something that has justification. Millions of children in Iraq is something that has justification.'[22]

It is not only Islamist groups that may be a threat. The Norway massacre perpetrated by Anders Behring Breivik in July 2011 is an indication of the fact that terrorism can spring from multiple ideologies. And, it is not only the U.S. that needs to fear the terrorist bomb. Religious extremists often view their co-religionists as deserving of death. Pakistan can bear witness to this. Attacks on mosques and shrines across the country have become all too common.

The technical possibilities for nuclear attack by extremists are many. They are not limited to a bomb stolen from the arsenal of a nuclear state. The making of atomic weapons—especially crude ones—has become vastly simpler than it was at the time of the Manhattan Project. The key challenge is access to the fissile material, the highly enriched uranium or plutonium that is the key ingredient in a nuclear weapon.

Nuclear weapon materials can of course be found in the nuclear weapon states. They are also present in some non-weapon states because highly enriched uranium is used as fuel in some kinds of nuclear research reactors and a few countries produce plutonium for use as fuel in nuclear power reactors.

The risk of nuclear terrorism can be sharply reduced by ending new fissile material production, strong policing of existing stocks, and programs to reduce and eliminate nuclear weapons and fissile material stockpiles.[23] Assuring that the end of nuclear weapons is as irreversible as possible will require the end of nuclear energy.

CONCLUSION

There is great enthusiasm around the world for the goal of abolishing of nuclear weapons, and rightly so. But if the nine nuclear-armed nations are to give up their weapons and others to be dissuaded from building their own arsenals, then there must be powerful reasons which appeal both to universal principles and to narrow self-interest.

The first principle for abolition must be security for all states. Abolition of nuclear weapons cannot be built on a foundation of conventional military dominance by one or even a handful of states over all others. In particular, the United States cannot hope for both: to develop its advanced conventional Prompt Global Strike capabilities to quickly destroy targets anywhere in the world; and to have other nuclear armed states that lack such capabilities agree to eliminate their nuclear weapons.

In the long run, one must recognize that other nations can be prevented from going nuclear only if there is some semblance of equality. Efforts to stop the spread of nuclear weapons must treat all countries alike. There can be special cases, no exemptions.

The only sure way to prevent a terrorist nuclear bomb from becoming a reality is that nation states get rid of nuclear weapons and end their nuclear power programs. Some people say that even with all these measures, nuclear weapons cannot be 'dis-invented'. Hence getting rid of them is no solution because they could always be reinvented. However, in a world where states agree not to commit resources to acquire or maintain nuclear weapons, theoretical knowledge of nuclear weapons would survive but capacities to make them would atrophy. As sociologist Donald MacKenzie has noted: 'Outside of the human, intellectual, and material networks that give them life and force, technologies cease to exist. We cannot reverse the invention of the motorcar, perhaps, but imagine a world in which there were no car factories . . . where no one alive had ever driven, and there was satisfaction with whatever alternative forms of transportation existed. The libraries might still contain pictures of automobiles and texts on motor mechanics, but there would be a sense in which that was a world in which the motor car had been uninvented.'[24]

REFERENCES

1. http://www.globalzero.org/sign-declaration
2. Ibid.
3. J. Robert Oppenheimer, Speech to the Association of Los Alamos Scientists, Los Alamos, 2 November 1945, http://www.plosin.com/BeatBegins/archive/OppenheimerSpeech.htm
4. Condoleeza Rice, 'Campaign 2000: Promoting the National Interest', *Foreign Policy*, Jan./Feb. 2000.
5. Neta C. Crawford and Catherine Lutz, 'Economic and Budgetary Costs of the Wars in Afghanistan, Iraq and Pakistan to the United States: A Summary', 13 June 2011. http://costsofwar.org/sites/default/files/articles/20/attachments/Economic%20Costs%20Summary.pdf
6. George P. Shultz, William J. Perry, Henry A. Kissinger, and Sam Nunn, 'How to Protect Our Nuclear Deterrent—Maintaining Confidence in Our Nuclear

Arsenal is Necessary as the Number of Weapons goes Down', *The Wall Street Journal*, 19 January 2010.

7. Barack Obama, 'Renewing American Leadership', *Foreign Affairs,* July 2007.

8. Eugene Miasnikov, 'Conventional Strategic Arms in the New START Treaty and Prospects for their Control and Limitation', Remarks at the Round-Table 'Nuclear Weapons and Arms Control', FOI, Stockholm, Sweden, 25 January 2011.

9. Lora Saalman, 'China and the U.S. Nuclear Posture Review', *Carnegie Papers*, February 2011.

10. Quoted in Bill Keller, 'The Thinkable', *The New York Times*, 4 May 2003.

11. Quoted in Seamus Milne, 'After Iraq, it's not just North Korea that Wants a Bomb', *The Guardian*, 27 May 2009.

12. 'Cheney: 2003 Nukes Shutdown Helped Pave Way for Qaddafi Ouster', *Fox News*, 30 August 2011.

13. John Hart and Shannon Kile, 'Libya's renunciation of nuclear, biological and chemical weapons and ballistic missiles', in: 'SIPRI Yearbook 2005: Armaments, Disarmament and International Security', Stockholm Peace Research Institute, 2006.

14. U.S. National Intelligence Council, *Iran: Nuclear Intentions and Capabilities*, November 2007, http://www.dni.gov/press_releases/20071203_release.pdf

15. James Risen and Mark Mazzetti, 'U.S. Agencies See No Move by Iran to Build a Bomb', *The New York Times*, 24 February 2012.

16. 'Iran Will Require Assurances', An Interview with Hossein Mousavian by Aslı Bâli, Middle East Research and Information Project, 16 May 2012, http://www. merip.org/mero/mero051612

17. Hossein Mousavian, 'There is an alternative to the Iran impasse', *Financial Times*, 22 May 2012.

18. Seyed Hossein Mousavian, *The Iranian Nuclear Crisis: A Memoir*, Carnegie Endowment for International Peace, Washington, D.C., 2012.

19. James Dobbins, 'Negotiating with Iran: Reflections from Personal Experience', *Washington Quarterly*, 33: 1 January 2010.

20. Government of Iran, 'Some Facts regarding Iran's Nuclear Talks with 5+1', 3 July 2012, http://backchannel.al-monitor.com/wp-content/uploads/2012/07/IranNuclearTalks.pdf

21. James Rosen, Stephen Engelberg, 'Signs of Change in Terror Goals went Unheeded', *The New York Times*, 14 October 2001.

22. Anthony Shadid, 'Bin Laden Warns No Peace for U.S'. *Boston Globe*, 8 October 2001.

23. See for instance the reports of the International Panel on Fissile Materials at www.fissilematerials.org

24. Donald MacKenzie, *Inventing Accuracy,* 1990.

CHAPTER 16

NUCLEAR ELECTRICITY FOR PAKISTAN IS NOT THE ANSWER

Pervez Hoodbhoy

Electricity blackouts are a daily occurrence in Pakistan. This 'load-shedding' has led industries to shut down; markets to close at peak business hours; and have imposed harsh physical conditions in tiny and cramped urban dwellings. In Faisalabad, the centre of Pakistan's textile industry, thousands of power looms are lying idle and workers have been laid off in large numbers. Due to these daily power outages for long hours, riots have frequently broken out, power substations set on fire, and property destroyed by angry mobs. Electric company employees have been attacked and sometimes even killed. Electricity has also become a political weapon: the Punjab government, locked in a confrontation with President Asif Ali Zardari's federal government, has openly encouraged mobs to keep their protests alive.[1]

It seems odd at first sight to understand why this should happen in a country that can make nuclear weapons and ballistic missiles, and which has an Atomic Energy Commission that employs over thirty to forty thousand people. Established in 1956, the PAEC (Pakistan Atomic Energy Commission) promised in the 1970s to meet nearly the *entire* electricity demand for the country. But almost forty years later, a miniscule amount was achieved—less than 2 per cent. Non-nuclear generation dominates: in 2006, ninety-eight billion kWh gross was produced, 37 per cent from gas and 29 per cent from oil. Pakistan's total generating capacity in 2011 stood around 22 GWE (22,000 megawatts of electricity), as shown in the table below.

Table 5
Energy Profile of Pakistan 2011[2]

	Installed (GW)	Available (GW)
TOTAL	21.69	16.3–19.3
Oil/Gas	14.43	12.22
Coal	0.165	0.045
Hydro	6.63	3.68–6.63
Nuclear	0.462	0.390

For the small share of nuclear energy, Pakistani authorities accuse Western countries for denying it nuclear energy; in turn those countries point to Pakistan's refusal to sign the Nuclear Non-Proliferation Treaty (NPT). The NPT expressly forbids transfer of any kind of nuclear technology, including that for power generation, to non-signatories. When Pakistan requests nuclear cooperation on the same basis as India, it is told that the risk of proliferation would be too high or that this could lead to an enhancement of Pakistan's bomb-making capacity. Thus Western nations have shied away from providing it with either nuclear materials or equipment.

In May 2009, President Zardari made a dramatic announcement upon his return from France—a French-Pakistani deal was in the offing. But nothing materialized. It turned out that the French had no intentions of copying the US–India deal and had actually offered to sell technology for safety and monitoring purposes only.[3] Only China sells nuclear reactors to Pakistan. On the other hand, India now enjoys a special deal with the West and may soon become a member of the NSG (Nuclear Suppliers Group).[4]

Unlike India, which has been manufacturing CANDU reactors for decades, Pakistan does not have the option of making its own electricity-producing nuclear reactors. Despite a fifty-year long nuclear history, and a huge nuclear establishment, this requires a technological infrastructure that is presently beyond Pakistan's capability. Power reactors are considerably more complex than nuclear bombs, or even dedicated military reactors.

Political circumstances became even more unfavourable for nuclear power in Pakistan after 11 September 2001, and were further exacerbated by the A.Q. Khan episode in 2004. Nevertheless, in 2010 the PAEC reiterated earlier promises of massive expansion and of achieving a target of 8.8 GW by 2030.[5] This claim was repeated two years later in 2012.[6] Installed nuclear capacity, according to the PAEC, was projected to increase in giant steps after every five year period.[7]

Table 6
PAEC's projections for nuclear electricity generating capacity

2010–2015	0.9GW
2015–2020	1.5GW
2020–2025	2.0GW
2025–2030	4.0GW

But the above projections do not compare well with the facts on the ground. The nuclear input to Pakistan's electricity grid in 2012 was about 0.7 GW. This is a pittance compared to expectations in the 1970s and 1980s.

The history of the nuclear electricity program is well known: a small 100 MW Canadian supplied natural uranium-deuterium reactor of the CANDU type, KANUPP, was Pakistan's first reactor. It was set up in 1972 but, following the Indian nuclear test of 1974, Pakistan refused to sign the NPT. Thereupon Canada withdrew fuel supplies and support. At much cost and effort, the PAEC had KANUPP running again—at least some of the time. Nearly thirty years passed before a second reactor came on line in 2005. This was a Chinese Pressurized Water Reactor (PWR), Chashma-I (or C-1). A similar unit, C-2, started producing electricity in mid-2011. All three reactors are small with design maximum of 0.1 GW, 0.33 GW, and 0.33 GW respectively. Together, they constitute about 2.5 per cent of Pakistan's total installed capacity but the actual amount of electricity produced is around 1.6–1.8 per cent. The next reactor to be connected to the grid may be 6–8 years away, even if some deal is solidified today. The connection between what was projected, and what actually is, is a distant one.

India's record on achieving nuclear targets is also less than stellar. In 1962, India announced that installed nuclear capacity would be 18–20 GW by 1987; but it could reach only 1.48 GW by that year. Vikram Sarabhai, Homi Bhabha's successor, had announced that, 'we have a formidable task to provide a new atomic power station of approximately 500 MW capacity each year after 1972–1973.'[8] Nothing of this sort happened: India's *first* 500 MW reactor—Tarapur 4—went online in 2005 almost thirty-five years later. As noted by Suvrat Raju (this volume) Indian authorities predicted that nuclear energy would provide more than 50 per cent of India's power generating capacity by 2050. Note that this is about 150 times the current nuclear power capacity of 4.12 GW. This amounts to only 2.64 per cent of the country's power generating capacity.[9] Cost overruns and delays are frequent in India. In 1994, an accident during the construction of two reactors at the Kaiga Generating Station pushed up their cost to four times the initial estimate.

COST AND EFFICIENCY

Is nuclear energy cost-efficient, and can nuclear power fulfil the energy needs of countries like Pakistan or India? Keeping for later discussion the issue of safety, we shall focus upon nuclear economics: whether power from uranium can be obtained which is cheaper than which is obtained from oil or gas.

Let us first look at the international context. The United States has the world's largest nuclear industry and generates about 30 per cent of the world's nuclear electricity. But, partly because of stringent safety requirements, it has difficulty in competing with other means (oil, gas, coal, hydroelectric). A 2009 MIT (Massachusetts Institute of Technology) study, which strongly advocates increasing the role of nuclear power globally out of climate concerns, estimates the cost of nuclear electricity in 2010 to be 8.4 cents/kWh and compares it against coal/gas—6.2/6.5 cents/kWh respectively. These costs were arrived at by using standard economic arguments and input costs.[10] One expects that as fossil fuel depletes, the nuclear-fossil price ratio will turn around in favour of nuclear. But this has not happened as yet.

No new nuclear plant has been commissioned in the U.S. over the last twenty years. France on the other hand, generates about 75 per cent of its electricity from nuclear. This may change, however. Whereas Nicolas Sarkozy, France's president, had reaffirmed the country's commitment to nuclear power even after Fukushima, François Hollande, his Socialist rival who won the 2012 presidential election had declared he would reduce nuclear's share of the national energy mix from 75 per cent to 50 per cent by 2025. That would mean shutting roughly 24 reactors. However, it is unclear whether Hollande will stay with his pledge.[11]

In May 2012, both the high capital investment needed for nuclear plants and the fear of Fukushima-type accidents led to Brazil's decision to cancel the building of new plants.[12] The previous government led by former president Luiz Inacio Lula da Silva had planned to construct between four and eight new nuclear plants through 2030.

While countries like France or South Korea do find nuclear energy economical, they may be exceptions to a general rule. Countries that lack engineering capacity, and cannot make their own reactors, will pay more to import and operate the technology.

In the early 1990s the World Bank had labelled nuclear plants 'large white elephants'.[13] Its Environmental Assessment Source Book says: 'Nuclear plants are thus uneconomic because at present and projected costs they are unlikely to be the least-cost alternative. There is also evidence that the cost figures usually cited by suppliers are substantially underestimated and often fail to take adequately into account waste disposal, decommissioning, and other environmental costs.'[14] According to the U.S. Nuclear Regulatory Commission, the cost of permanently shutting down a reactor ranges from $300 million to $400 million.[15] This is a hefty fraction of the reactor's original cost.

There is no evidence that nuclear power is economical for Pakistan. Reliable cost figures do not exist, although the PAEC claims that it is around 8.5 cents per KWh (i.e., about the same as in the U.S.).[16] While this figure may have been derived from the cost of the reactor and fuel, it is difficult to validate. Citing security reasons, the authorities reveal nothing of what has been spent over a period of five decades on creating a vast infrastructure that comprises of hundreds of buildings, fuel processing facilities, local and foreign training, salaries and benefits, security arrangements, etc. There exists zero public data on the funds used for buying smuggled goods such as computers, electronic and electrical machinery, chemical plants and chemicals, lathes and workshop machinery. Apart from the gross amount of the Pak–China reactor deal, nothing else has been made public.

Pakistan's existing reactors have not worked very well, although the performance is improving with added experience. It is perhaps too early to comment on C-2, but there is data on KANUPP and C-1 because all nuclear power reactors that operate under IAEA (International Atomic Energy Agency) rules are required to publish their operating records.

There are two especially important parameters in judging reactor performance: First, the energy availability factor, which is the energy produced after all losses are deducted and divided by total energy produced. Second, the capacity factor, which is the net energy produced divided by the total energy that could have been produced had the plant operated at full capacity all the time. These are computed by the IAEA and reported on an annual and cumulative basis in the Power Reactor Information System (PRIS) database for each commercial nuclear power plant operating in IAEA member countries.[17]

A 2007 Stanford CISAC report based on these reports comments on these two parameters: Inspection of the KANUPP performance data indicates a mediocre plant record with a lifetime energy availability record of less than 28 per cent. . . . Since the 1980s the plant operated at varying performance levels never exceeding 48 per cent and was down for different Pakistani initiated refurbishment campaigns. . . . This is particularly low for a CANDU type reactor, which operates on on-line refuelling principles and is thus expected to demonstrate high availability and capacity factors. In fact, KANUPP performance is lower than even the oldest CANDU reactors operated in Canada and elsewhere except for the Rawatbhata reactors in India. KANUPP represents the oldest CANDU model still refurbished and in commercial operation in the world today. Most other similar model CANDU reactors have already ceased operation and have shut down.[18]

On the other hand, the C-1 data shows significantly higher energy availability levels, in the range of 60 per cent plus, and has improved with time. However QINSHAN-I reactor in China, which is the prototype of the CHASNUPP reactor, does better:

CHASNUPP-1 performance record lags the record of QINSHAN Phase I plant—its reference plant—by ten to twenty annual percentage points over the same operating period. Review of the QINSHAN-I data in the PRIS database indicates that whereas QINSHAN-I has a cumulative (lifetime averaged) energy availability factor of close to 80 per cent over its first five operating cycles, CHASNUPP-1 has reacted a cumulative availability factor of 62 per cent only.[19]

Purely in economic terms, it does not appear that nuclear power has been a good investment for Pakistan. A convincing economic analysis, with reliable data inputs, is essential if the nuclear authorities want to make a strong case.

PAKISTAN–CHINA NUCLEAR COOPERATION

Western apprehensions that Chinese nuclear help to Pakistan's power sector could be used for military applications are frequently articulated at international forums—and promptly rebutted by China.[20] Today China is Pakistan's only nuclear supplier. It has set up the Chashma Nuclear Complex near Kundian along the left bank of the River Indus. The main part of the first nuclear plant was designed by Shanghai Nuclear Engineering Research and Design Institute (SNERDI), based on the Qinshan Nuclear Power Plant.

In February 2010, China agreed to Pakistan's request to build two additional civilian nuclear reactors in Pakistan, each of 330 MW (about one-third the size of most modern nuclear power plants). All four reactors would belong to the same genre, and be identical in essential respects but C-2, C-3, and C-4 would have added safety features. To make this affordable China offered to provide over 80 per cent of the total $1.9 billion cost as a 20-year loan.[21] But, because of cost over-runs across the board on public development projects, the Planning Commission declared that no funds remained for down-payment to meet international obligations for any more nuclear projects, including C-3 and C-4. The PAEC argued that this action 'has jeopardised the contract between the Chinese contractor (CZEC) and Exim Bank.[22]

There is a further stumbling block even if the funds can be found. In 2004 China joined the 46 nation Nuclear Suppliers Group (NSG), whose rules prohibit supply of nuclear materials to non-NPT states. China, which is a member of the NSG, has not yet formally notified this body of its intention to supply the two new reactors. It had earlier explained away the supply of the C-2 reactor under the so-called 'grand-fathering clause', arguing that an agreement had existed prior to China's joining the NSG. For the two new reactors to be supplied to Pakistan, the legality of the clause is unclear. The issue was to come to head in the NSG meeting held in 2010 at Christchurch in New Zealand but China did not bring it up. However, in 2012 it used the grand-father clause to justify the sales of C-3 and C-4.

The U.S. position so far has been to refrain from vocal opposition. Indeed, it has almost no alternative, having strong-armed the NSG in 2008 into agreeing upon a special India-specific exemption. Although the U.S. has a public position on global nuclear trade with non-NPT countries, its geo-political and economic interests sometimes make irrelevant those very restrictions for which it had vigorously worked. The U.S. also worries that any serious effort to block the Chinese sale would further irritate Pakistan, upon which the U.S. relies for helping it fight the Afghan war.

China's interest in pushing the deal with Pakistan is fairly clear. Pakistan is so far China's only client for its small and unattractive reactors of the QINSHAN variety. The sale of two small units is but a step in a larger plan to become a major producer and exporter of nuclear power plants. Although China has an ambitious nuclear power program and is developing new reactor types, it has not made it to the big league yet and must import major components, such as the reactor pressure vessel, from suppliers such as Westinghouse. It is negotiating with western companies to acquire their technology under license for critical components that would enable it to make reactors of 1000 MW and 1400 MW.

In any case, even if the Chinese reactors at Chashma are built, their impact upon Pakistan's energy crisis will be marginal. Because they would also be under full-scope IAEA safeguards, they would not contribute to Pakistan's bomb-making capacity. Moreover, it will take 6–8 years after the contracts are formally signed before their electricity reaches the grid—assuming that there are no unforeseen delays. The small capacity means that they can do little to lessen the severe power deficiency.

There are many implications that a large scale nuclear power program would have for Pakistan, if and when it comes into existence. Fuel is particularly important, so let us briefly consider the issue of nuclear fuel for Pressurized Water Reactors (PWRs).

A 1GW PWR reactor has 200–300 fuel rods containing enriched uranium dioxide (UO2), weighing about 80–100 tons. This is a huge amount, well beyond the capacity of an enrichment plant that is designed to make a few bombs annually. Therefore, in 2007, the PAEC announced its intent to set up its second uranium enrichment facility, which would be placed under international safeguards and geared exclusively for the country's civilian nuclear power program.[23] PAEC sources declared that the new enrichment facility was to be part of the nearly $2 billion Pakistan Nuclear Power Fuel Complex to be built at Kundian in the district of Mianwali in the Punjab

Province.[24] The proposed complex would comprise a fuel fabrication facility, a plant to produce hexaflouride gas (UF6), a zirconium tubing plant, a fuel-testing laboratory, and a uranium enrichment plant that would use thousands of centrifuges. The new facility would be 'much bigger than the controversial Khan Research Laboratory at Kahuta, also in Punjab, where weapons-grade uranium is enriched for use in Pakistan's nuclear weapons program.[25] While the KRL would continue enriching weapons-grade uranium, the new enrichment plant would enrich uranium only to the 3 per cent level needed for use with C-1, C-2, and future such reactors.

As it turned out, nothing came of these plans—there simply was no money to create the fuel complex. Also, the profit-conscious Chinese are keen that Pakistan should buy their UO2 fuel rather than have it prepared locally. Since Pakistan is restricted from purchasing nuclear fuel from any other country, it is far from clear whether it will get a competitive rate from China.

By agreement, and IAEA requirements, Pakistan is obliged to return spent fuel to China. Presumably this means the spent fuel rods rather than the large volume of low-level radioactive wastes. But what has actually happened so far is unknown; the PAEC has divulged no information. One therefore assumes that the spent fuel is stored in pools at, or near the reactor site. One recalls that such pools proved calamitous in the Fukushima disaster. It is not known what, if any, corrective action has been taken by the PAEC in this regard.

REACTORS AND CITIES

Situating reactors close to a city is potentially hazardous. While a nuclear reactor cannot explode like a bomb, after one year of operation even a rather small 200 MW reactor contains more radioactive caesium, strontium, and iodine than the amounts produced in all the nuclear weapons tests ever conducted. These devastatingly deadly materials could be released in nightmarish quantities if the containment vessel of a reactor is somehow breached.

Conscious of the deadly consequences, nuclear designers build redundancy into essential systems, such as those needed for cooling the reactor's super-hot nuclear core. Yet, in spite of all precautions, highly developed countries—Russia, United States, Britain, and Canada—have seen serious reactor accidents. In the country of the *hibakusha* (the surviving victims of the atomic bombings of Hiroshima and Nagasaki), all reactors go through a scrutiny that is more exacting than in any other country.

For a developing country like Pakistan, radiation dangers and reactor safety are yet to enter the domain of public debate. In 2001, the government announced the establishment of the Pakistan Nuclear Regulatory Authority responsible for 'siting, design, manufacturing, operation, QA (Quality Assurance), radiation protection, waste management, emergency preparedness, transportation.'[26] The current strength is 'more than 200 professionals appropriately trained in technical areas, management system and regulatory processes.'

While the PNRA's mandate appears comprehensive, it is important to note that its personnel are totally recruited from the PAEC. Thus, in effect, it is an extension of the PAEC rather than an independent monitoring agency. Citing national security reasons, all regulatory mechanisms are strictly controlled by the authorities. Non-PAEC/ PMRA individuals, or non-government organizations, are forbidden from attempting to monitor radiation levels near any nuclear facility, whether civilian or military. This is typical of how the nuclear authorities in South Asia have created a veil of secrecy. For example, poor and powerless village communities in Pakistan and India that have experienced deleterious health effects from uranium and thorium mining operations, have been forced to withdraw their court cases.[27]

For Pakistan, which sees daily acts of terror directed against its people as well as institutions of the state, the prospect of militants seriously damaging a nuclear plant is a real one. Spent fuel storage, while relatively safe, is potentially vulnerable to theft or attack. As every flood and earthquake that has occurred in the recent past have shown, Pakistan has little capacity to deal with any kind of disaster, either natural or human-caused, such as the one that has left an enduring nuclear legacy at Fukushima.

FUKUSHIMA—A TURNING POINT?

On 11 March 2011, a 30-foot monster wave smashed into Fukushima Daiichi's complex of six nuclear reactors on the northern coast of Japan. Only a handful died from the released radiation but, with the exception of a few countries, everywhere else the dream of a nuclear renaissance suddenly turned nightmarish. Weeks after the disaster, Japan teetered at the knife-edge of a major nuclear disaster. Although heroic reactor operators did their bit—many put their lives on line and absorbed deadly quantities of radiation—the nuclear monster slipped out of their control. Four hydrogen explosions reduced three buildings in the 6-reactor Fukushima nuclear complex to smoking ruins. Radioactive emissions triggered a level-5 emergency which was later upgraded to level-7, and evacuations were ordered up to a 20 km radius.

A heroic effort finally prevented a large-scale melt-down of spent-fuel rods and thus averted catastrophic consequences. But reactor fires were still burning many weeks later. At one point, desperate plans had called for pouring thousands of tons of concrete and turning the reactors into permanent nuclear tombs, although this would not have solved the problem and, in fact, would have created new ones. Radioactive contamination spread far and wide from hydrogen explosions, reaching all the way up to Canada and Europe.[28]

The truth about Fukushima took months to emerge. Although Japanese leaders had spoken soothing words to the public, in fact, they had badly panicked after the tsunami. A 400 page report on the disaster, released in March 2012, quotes the chief cabinet secretary at the time, Yukio Edano, as warning that a 'demonic chain reaction' of plant meltdowns could result in the evacuation of Tokyo a hundred and fifty miles away.[29]

Tokyo escaped, but the damaged plant will take an estimated forty years to be finally closed down. Japan has lost large swathes of its territory to contamination. A 20-kilometre no-go zone surrounds the plants. In spite of much-vaunted Japanese technology and $13 billion so far, decontamination is haphazard and slow. In July 2011, supermarket beef, vegetables, and ocean fish were found to have radioactive caesium in doses several times the safe level.[30] In August 2011, Nameko mushrooms grown in the open air in Soma, a city about 40 kilometers north of the Daiichi plant, were found to contain nine times the legal limit of caesium.[31] Measurements on fields, city streets, and in buildings confirm widespread contamination: with caesium 137, and strontium 90. For the remainder of the twenty-first century, the people living in a wide area will live in contaminated houses, drink contaminated water, and eat contaminated food.

The amount of radioactive caesium ejected by the Fukushima reactor meltdowns is about 168 times higher than that emitted in the atomic bombing of Hiroshima. The Nuclear and Industrial Safety Agency (NISA) stated that the radiation released at Fukushima was about one-sixth of that released during the 1986 Chernobyl disaster, and that the crippled Fukushima No. 1 plant has released 15,000 tera-becquerels of caesium-137, which lingers for decades and can cause cancer.[32] New estimates are that a staggering 40,000 tera-becquerels of radioactive caesium were released. This should be compared with the 89 tera-becquerels released in the U.S. atomic bombing of Hiroshima.

Japan's traumatized population forced the government to shut down all 55 reactors in spite of the fact that nuclear power provided 30 per cent of Japan's energy needs. Germany decided to jump ship; within weeks of the disaster it announced its decision to close its nuclear plants permanently. A third of the country's reactors were decommissioned immediately, others will be wound down by 2022. In the UK, 61 per cent of people said they would be strongly opposed to a new nuclear power station being built near their home. Italy and Switzerland have also voted against nuclear energy, while France is engaged in deep self-reflection.

Fukushima also shook China and India, though much less. Earlier they had been planning 77 and 23 new reactors, respectively. But a normally passive population has begun to speak up in China. For example, the eastern province of China's Anhui province has opposed the Pengze plant in a highly populated area and a formal appeal has been made to Beijing to stop construction.

India's nuclear program, almost a sacred cow until now, is also being increasingly resisted by its citizens. Prime Minister Manmohan Singh angrily denounced protests against the Koodankulam nuclear plant in the Tamil Nadu state, claiming these were being led by foreign-funded NGOs. Mass protests and hunger strikes by social movements have led to deaths, injuries and riots in Maharashtra, Tamil Nadu and Jaitapur. The construction of two nuclear plants has been delayed and West Bengal has dropped plans for six Russian reactors.

Japanese disaster management, though now under severe criticism, was probably better than would be possible elsewhere in the world. Stoic and disciplined, the Japanese behaved wonderfully well. No looting, no panic, and no anti-government demonstrations followed the explosions. People helped each other, relief teams operated unobstructed, and rescuers had full radiation protection gear. Plant operators risked their lives by working in super-high radiation environments, and engineers showed their grasp of emergency reactor dynamics.

On the negative side: even elaborate earthquake-protection and tsunami-protection measures failed badly. The design protection was for a maximum 20 feet tsunami wave. But power sources for emergency cooling pumps were destroyed by the 30-foot high wall of water. Storing thousands of spent-fuel rods on the reactor site turned out to be a terrible mistake.

KARACHI—MORE AT RISK THAN ANY OTHER CITY

Post Fukushima, the science journal *Nature* recently teamed up with the NASA centre based at Columbia University to see which nuclear plants have the largest populations surrounding them and, therefore, could be the most dangerous if something should go wrong. At the top of the list is Karachi, a city of 20 million that has more people than any other in the world who live within 30 km of the plant.[33]

The Karachi Nuclear Power Plant, (KANUPP) located by the seashore, is an aging 40 year reactor that produces only a little electricity but is plagued by plenty of problems—including periodic leakages of heavy water.[34] Supplied by Canada, it went into in operation since December 1972 and completed its 30-year life span in 2002. But lifetime extensions have been routinely sought—and granted since then. According to IAEA statistics, has been unavailable for power production 70.4 per cent of the time. Even if it had operated as per design (120 MW of electrical power), it could supply only 6–7 per cent of Karachi's total electrical power needs, barely enough for the areas of Golimar and Lyari.

Although the gain is small, KANUPP puts much of Karachi's population at risk. Sabotage, terrorist attack, equipment failure, earthquake, or a tsunami could result in large scale radioactive release. The reactor has tons of radioactive material. Deadly radioactivity could be carried by the sea breeze toward the city and the population would need evacuation. The rich and the fortunate might succeed—and then too only if they exceptionally lucky. But the poor would be doomed. In a city that is chaotic even in the best of times, an orderly and disciplined evacuation, as in post-tsunami Fukushima, would be impossible. Looters would strip everything bare, roads would be clogged, and vital services would collapse.

While the safety of nuclear power is under question everywhere, there is—or should be—particular concern wherever a safety culture is absent. Pakistanis are habitual risk-takers looking for shortcuts, choosing to put their faith in God rather than precautions. This could be true for nuclear plant operators who can overlook critical safety procedures; there is simply no way for an outsider to know. Ostensibly for reasons of national security, everything nuclear is kept under wraps. This also covers up for bad practices.

The world may worry about Fukushima, but Pakistani authorities shrugged it off. Even as explosions tore through the nuclear complex, 'experts' summoned on local television channels glibly declared that this could never happen in Pakistan. The PNRA (Pakistan Nuclear Regulatory Authority) issued the following guarantee: 'Due to geographical differences between Pakistan and Japan, the likelihood that similar extreme natural events may occur in the vicinity of the country's nuclear plants is quite small.'

Since no two extreme natural events are likely to be identical in detail, this is technically correct—Pakistan is not located in the Pacific Ocean. But how would one deal with radioactive releases following deliberate sabotage, a terrorist attack, equipment failure, or operator error? Officials and other high-ups in Pakistan have never paid the price for false statements. The aftermath of the recent floods and earthquakes in the country are proof of the fact that our capacity to deal with any kind of disaster, either natural or man-made is minimal.

After dismissing Fukushima as irrelevant, the PAEC announced that it will seek to further extend KANUPP's life.[35] It has further declared that KANUPP-II and KANUPP-III, each more than ten times the power of KANUPP-I, will be built at the same site.[36] Locating nuclear reactors near a megacity that is impossible to evacuate shows poor judgment.

DEALING WITH LOAD-SHEDDING

At 20 GW, Pakistan's installed capacity is in principle roughly adequate for the average power demand of around 17 GW. But a mere 14.3 GW average is actually generated; about 30 per cent of current capacity is not used. The situation with Pakistan's electricity production and distribution system is similar to that of its railways, education, and health systems—they do not deliver, or deliver much below capacity. Mismanagement, rather than lack of installed capacity is the problem.

A key element of the management crisis is 'circular debt'— meaning the non-payment of electricity bills by the military and various government departments to other government departments. This means electricity producers are not paid on time and hence cannot import fuel oil. Their expensive imported plants stand idle; capacity goes waste.

But the problem only partly lies at the production end. The difficulty is enormously compounded by problems at the distribution and consumer ends.

First, an inefficient distribution system wastes about 10 per cent of the electricity as it travels along transmission lines through transformers, and in bad connections. The electricity grid is incapable of effectively distributing electricity from power plants to consumers. Electricity is stolen by rich and poor alike while consumers in the FATA (Federally-Administered Tribal Areas) region have often destroyed substations which have ceased supplying electricity because bills are not paid. Elsewhere, for a small bribe, electric company employees tamper with electricity meters and create unmonitored bypasses called 'kundas'. Electricity producers and distributors thereby lose revenue. The solution lies in rigidly enforcing the rule: you use, you pay. Technology can be pressed into service for this; 'smart meters' that are tamper-proof and remotely read are available and need to be widely installed. Stopping power theft would save far more megawatts than will be generated by Chashma's four nuclear reactors combined, whenever they come on line.

There is much wastage as well: Pakistani factories, offices and homes use machinery and appliances that do much less work with the electricity that is available. A serious energy efficiency and conservation program is needed which is quick to implement and could avoid the need to build additional power plants.

A scientific approach to power planning had indeed been taken in the mid-1980s by the Planning Commission and extensive mathematical modelling was employed using software packages that were used successfully in a number of countries. This is important because, for example, energy demands fluctuate over the year and it is important to be able to predict demand over different seasons and times of the day. But modelling capability requires high-calibre personnel who remain at their jobs for a sizable period of time. A recent report states that this condition was not fulfilled and the maintenance of a reliable repository of data became difficult.[37] Energy plans were hereafter made on mere hunches and influenced by personal factors. The same report predicts a severe energy crisis by 2030 when proven conventional natural gas reserves will be depleted and energy imports will jump from 27 per cent to over 45 per cent.

The opinion is shared by those who have looked at the present system in detail. Wikileaks cables, obtained by the daily *Dawn*, show that energy policy-making in Pakistan's energy sector left U.S. Ambassador Anne Patterson worried. In June 2008, she reported back to Washington that, 'the haphazard mix of horizontally and vertically placed institutions which comprise the energy policy-making sector of Pakistan' has prevented a resolution of the country's power crisis.[38]

Patterson remarks that the situation is enormously complicated by 'the complex maze of GOP policymakers who cannot coordinate Pakistan's energy policy due to overlapping and contradictory authorities. . . . A lack of coordination and absence of any clear line of authority hampers any formulation of policy efforts to address the current energy crisis in Pakistan.'

Indeed, the mess is quite mind-boggling. The water and power ministry with its nineteen subordinate agencies, the ministry of petroleum and natural resources with its sixteen subsidiary agencies, and four other ministries and seven agencies are all involved in setting energy policy and running the power sector. Deprecating the 'insanity that prevails in Pakistan's energy sector', Patterson wrote: 'The lead line agency in government for the electric power sector is the Ministry of Water and Power (MWP). . . . However, the Ministry of Petroleum and Natural Resources (MPNR) controls fuel supplies; the Finance Ministry holds the purse strings; the Planning Commission' manages the investment approval process; and the National Electric Power Regulatory Authority regulates companies operating in the power sector.' Patterson remarked: 'the fact is that not a single megawatt of electricity has been added to Pakistan's national grid since 2000 despite record-breaking economic growth and population expansion.'

CONCLUSION

Climate change gives urgency to finding non-fossil fuel energy alternatives. But a convincing case for nuclear power is hard to make. Neither cheap nor safe, it faces an uphill battle in much of Europe and the United States. Unless there is a radical technical breakthrough—such as a workable reactor fuelled by nuclear fusion rather than nuclear fission—its prospects for growth globally look bleak.

Although nuclear technology has not met any reasonable fraction of Pakistan's energy needs, it remains especially dangerous for multiple reasons—terrorism, sabotage, war, accidents and malfunctions, and natural disasters. Public consciousness and knowledge of waste disposal matters is low, opaque regulatory mechanisms are strictly controlled by the authorities, and disaster management capacity is close to nil. There is little or no public pressure for verifiable safety measures, nor is there an appreciable history of activism on social causes. Hence a hazardous technology becomes still more hazardous. It is therefore time to stop trying to add to Pakistan's nuclear fission power production.

In the public perception, nuclear reactors are conflated with nuclear weapons. But Pakistan's power reactors make no contribution to Pakistan's bomb-making capacity—the fissile material for these is entirely produced in its centrifuges and military reactors.

If nuclear electricity is not the answer then what is? There is no simple quick fix. Until nuclear fusion power becomes available decades from now, Pakistan, like other countries, must rely on a mix of oil, gas, hydro, coal, solar, wind, and other renewable sources.[39] Windmills and photovoltaics must be developed but they are incapable of adding more than a few per cent in the next decade. Pakistan can build gas-fired power plants and fuel them using natural gas imported from Iran. For new electricity generation capacity, Pakistan might use its vast deposits of poor quality Thar coal to meet its energy needs. But this should be done using appropriate technology, such as carbon sequestration, to minimize the negative environmental consequences. At the present time, it is not clear whether investment in Thar coal is viable. A long-term energy strategy is needed that takes into account efficiency, environment, economy, and changing patterns of social life in Pakistan.

REFERENCES

1. 'I shall not tell police to stop power rioters, says CM', *The Express Tribune*, 20 June 2012.
2. 'Nuclear Energy Scenario of Pakistan', Powerpoint slides presented by the Pakistan Nuclear Regulatory Agency at the International Seminar on Nuclear Safety and Security, Islamabad, 21–23 April 2011, available at http://www.pnra.org/seminars.asp
3. 'France offers Pakistan nuclear energy help', AFP, 15 May 2009.
4. 'U.S. works for India's membership in Nuclear Suppliers Group', *Times of India*, 22 June 2011.
5. 'PAEC assigned 8800 nuclear power target by 2030', *Pak-Atom Newsletter*, Nov.–Dec. 2010.
6. 'Pakistan, China mull ambitious nuclear power deal: sources', http://mdn.mainichi.jp/mdnnews/international/news/20120214p2g00m0in116000c.html
7. 'Pakistan's Nuclear Power Needs and Future Options', Parvez Butt, Secretary, Ministry of Science and Technology, and Ahmad Mumtaz, Sr. Director (NEP), PAEC, presentation for South Asian Strategic Stability Institute, at Brussels, 17 November 2006.
8. Vikram Sarabhai, Nuclear Power in Developing Countries, Atomic Energy Commission, 1969.
9. 'For India Nuclear Electricity is not the solution', Suvrat Raju, this volume.
10. 'Update of the MIT 2003 Future of Nuclear Power Study', MIT Energy Initiative, 2009, web.mit.edu/nuclearpower/pdf/nuclearpower-update2009.pdf
11. 'EDF warns Hollande on nuclear plant closure', *Financial Times*, 24 May 2012.

12. 'Brazil shelves plans to build new nuclear plants', *Google News Service*, 9 May 2012.

13. 'The Least Cost Path for Developing Countries: Energy Efficient Investments for the Multilateral Development Banks', M. Phillips, Washington, D.C., IIEC, 1991.

14. World Bank, 'Guidelines for Environmental Assessment of Energy and Industry Projects', World Bank technical paper No. 154/1992. Environmental Assessment Sourcebook, Vol. III, 1992.

15. http://www.nrc.gov/reading-rm/doc-collections/fact-sheets/decommissioning. html

16. 'Nuclear Energy Scenario of Pakistan', ref.1.

17. 'Security Issues Related to Future Pakistani Nuclear Power Program', Chaim Braun, CISAC document 2007.

18. Ibid.

19. Ibid.

20. 'West worried by China–Pakistan atomic deal', Fredrik Dahl, *Reuters*, 27 June 2012.

21. 'Pakistan in civil nuclear deal with China', *The Daily Times*, 30 March 2010.

22. 'Cuts in PSDP led to power, water, crises: govt', *Dawn*, 29 July 2011.

23. 'Pakistan to set up 2nd uranium enrichment plant', *Kyodo News*, 22 August 2007.

24. 'Nuclear Power in Pakistan', April 2011, http://www.world-nuclear.org/info/inf108.html

25. Ibid.

26. 'Nuclear Energy Scenario of Pakistan', ref.1.

27. 'Villagers Pay the Price of Nuclear Ambitions', Zofeen Ebrahim, http://www.ipsnews.net/news.asp?idnews=33437

28. 'New Study: Aerosolized plutonium from Fukushima detected in Europe—Spent fuel indicated', *Energy News*, 2 January 2012.

29. 'Japan Weighed Evacuating Tokyo in Nuclear Crisis', *The New York Times*, 27 February 2012.

30. 'Contaminated beef in Japan', http://www.bbc.co.uk/news/mobile/business-14195987

31. http://www.bloomberg.com/news/2011-07-24/threat-to-japanese-food-chain-multiplies-as-cesium-contamination-spreads.html

32. 'Fukushima caesium leaks equal 168 Hiroshimas', *The Telegraph*, 25 August 2011.

33. Reactors, residents, 'Risks', *Nature*, 21 April 2011.

34. 'KANUPP Leak: PAEC Issues Clarification', *The Express Tribune*, 22 October 2011.

35. 'Rebooting: KANUPP licence expires in Dec, plans afoot for extension', *Dawn*, 20 October 2011.

36. http://www.islamist.com/index.php/world/1210-pakistan-to-build-2-new-nuke-power-plants-with-chinese-help

37. Pakistan Integrated Energy Model (Pak-IEM), ADB TA-4982 PAK, Final Report, Volume I, Model Design Report, prepared by International Resources Group for Asian Development Bank and Ministry of Planning and Development, Government of Pakistan, August 2011.

38. 'Haphazard mix of Pakistan's energy bureaucracy', 6 July 2011, *Dawn*, Idrees Bakhtiar, Cables referenced: WikiLeaks # 151716, 152294, 150573, 150925 and 151070.

39. A strong case is made in: 'Is Nuclear Power Pakistan's Best Energy Investment—Assessing Pakistan's Electricity Situation', John Stephenson and Peter Tynan, in: *Pakistan's Nuclear Future—Reining in the Risk*, edited by Henry Sokolski, Stanford, 2005.

CHAPTER 17

NUCLEAR ELECTRICITY IS NOT THE ANSWER FOR INDIA

Suvrat Raju

Within India's dominant discourse, atomic energy has long been depicted as a ticket to modernity and great power status. While inaugurating India's first nuclear reactor in 1957, Nehru explained that the 'Atomic Revolution' was like the 'Industrial Revolution'; if India did not develop atomic energy, it would lose out once again. 'Either you go ahead with it or you succumb and others go ahead, and you fall back and gradually drag yourself along in the trail.[1]

These two themes were strongly revived in the debate over the U.S.–India nuclear deal. For example, when George W. Bush visited India in 2006, *The Times of India* (TOI) ran a prominent interview with him.[2] About a quarter of the front page was taken up by a single question: *The Times of India* to Bush: 'Do you consider India a responsible nuclear nation?' The reply—'I Do'—was typeset to be about four times as large as the other headlines on the front page![3] Undoubtedly, it also sent the TOI editors and parts of the Indian establishment into paroxysms of pleasure.

However, the Congress leadership recognized that great-power arguments were insufficient to win broad political support. So, it claimed the deal would not only end 'nuclear apartheid' but was necessary for 'development'. While laying the foundation stone for a coal power plant in Jhajjar, Sonia Gandhi explained that electricity was required for development and the nuclear deal was required for electricity. Consequently, opponents of the deal were 'enemies of progress and development.'[4]

This thread was also prominent in the Lok Sabha debates on the nuclear deal. In a major debate (held on 28 November 2007),

Jyotiraditya Scindia, the first speaker from the Congress, said that for growth at the 'grass root level,' the 'civilian nuclear option' was necessary, and claimed that by 2020, India would have a nuclear power-generating capacity of 30,000–40,000 megawatts. For Scindia, though, it was 'far more important [that] the Deal . . . raised the stature of India.'[5] Pranab Mukherjee, opening the debate for the government in the confidence motion (on 21 July 2008), explained that, 'power is needed for everything' and pointed to the grim danger that, by 2050, without nuclear power, 'our energy deficit would be 4,12,000 megawatts.' Nuclear power would 'reduce the deficit . . . to only 7000 megawatts' and hence solve the energy crisis.[6]

These figures originate with the Department of Atomic Energy (DAE), but are they realistic? This question remains important even after the political victory of the Congress. First, the change in the American administration has slowed down nuclear negotiations between India and the U.S.; more than a year after the nuclear deal was actuated, these negotiations have not concluded. In fact, one of the focal points of Manmohan Singh's visit to the U.S. in November 2009 was to resolve differences over the reprocessing of spent fuel of American origin.[7] Separately, the government has already signed nuclear pacts with seven countries. Companies from the U.S., France and Russia have been allocated land for setting up nuclear plants.[8]

It is imperative, in this context, to review the hopes for atomic energy that are projected by the government. What is the history of atomic energy in India and is it likely to play a major role in India's energy-basket in the near future? What is the link between the civilian and military program and how does the nuclear deal bear upon weaponization? If the government does go ahead with massive nuclear expansion, will this necessarily make India dependent on imperialist powers? We discuss some of these questions below.

ATOMIC ENERGY PROJECTIONS

We will begin by discussing the government's argument for atomic energy. As we mentioned above, the DAE has made some very ambitious projections for atomic energy over the next few decades.

These projections underlie the argument that India must divert resources towards nuclear energy.

In 2004, the DAE, surveying various studies, estimated that India would need 8 trillion kilowatt-hours (kWh) of electricity per year by 2050.[9,10] The DAE study mentioned that electricity generation in 2002–2003 was about 0.6 trillion kWh; it projected that this would grow about 13 times. After factoring in the increase in population (which was projected to stabilize at about 1.5 billion) the DAE projected that per capita electricity consumption would rise about nine times—from about 614 kWh to 5305 kWh.

The study argued that it would be very difficult to meet these great demands without nuclear power, and estimated that atomic energy would meet about 25 per cent of the total demand by 2050. This translates to about 2 trillion kWh of electricity per year with an installed capacity of 275 GW.

However, this initial study was published in 2004, before the nuclear agreement between Bush and Manmohan Singh was signed. During the debate on the nuclear deal, these projections were revised upwards. The figures that are quoted today come from these new projections.

Anil Kakodkar, the head of the DAE till November 2009, in a talk given at the Indian Academy of Science[11] (on 4 July 2008, just after the government decided to break with the Left parties and push the nuclear deal) and a similar talk given at the Tata Institute of Fundamental Research (in June 2009) retained the electricity demand projections, but increased the projections for the total installed nuclear capacity by almost 250 per cent. Kakodkar claimed that if the nuclear deal went through and India was allowed to import a specified number of Light-Water Reactors (LWR) and fuel, then the recycling of fuel from these reactors would lead to an installed capacity of 650 GW! These are the figures that were used by Pranab Mukherjee in the parliamentary debate about two weeks later. So, Kakodkar predicted that nuclear energy would provide more than 50 per cent of India's power generating capacity by 2050. Note that this is about 150 times the current nuclear power capacity of 4.12 GW that provides 2.64 per cent of the country's power generating capacity![12]

Similar figures have been repeatedly mentioned at the highest levels of the Indian government. The Prime Minister recently predicted that atomic power could generate 470 GW of electricity by 2050.[13] The exact origins of this figure are unclear, but this might be related to a second possibility, corresponding to a different import-pattern for LWRs, mentioned by Kakodkar in his talk.

A BRIEF HISTORY OF ATOMIC PROJECTIONS

The Department of Atomic Energy (DAE) has made ambitious predictions of this kind several times in the past. Homi Bhabha, the first secretary of the DAE, announced in 1962 that installed capacity would be 18–20 GW by 1987.[14] In actuality, the installed capacity in 1987 was 1.06 GW, which corresponds to about 5 per cent of Bhabha's predictions.[15] Vikram Sarabhai, who succeeded Bhabha, already had to admit, in 1970 that, 'the program has slipped badly in relation to targets.'[16] A little earlier, Sarabhai had concluded that the DAE needed to construct large reactors with a capacity of 500 MW to recoup capital costs. So he announced that, 'we have a formidable task to provide a new atomic power station of approximately 500 MW capacity each year after 1972–73.'[17] In fact, India's *first* 500 MW reactor—Tarapur 4—went online in 2005 almost 35 years later.

This failure is sometimes explained away by noting that foreign cooperation in civilian nuclear energy declined after the 1974 Pokharan explosions. However, in 1984, the DAE announced, through a nuclear power 'profile', that it would set up a power generating capacity of 10,000 MW by 2000. In 1989, a DAE-appointed committee reviewed this, found that the target continued to be feasible, and even increased the projected capacity slightly. This figure was repeatedly quoted publicly. For example, the chairperson of the Atomic Energy Commission wrote in 1989 that, 'while . . . nuclear energy constitutes about 3 per cent of the country's total electrical power generation, work is on hand to increase it to about

10 per cent by the year 2000, by implementing the 10,000 MWe nuclear power program.'[18]

Almost fifteen years after the profile was launched, the Comptroller and Auditor General of India reviewed its progress and concluded that 'the actual additional generation of power under the "Profile" as of March 1998 was *nil* in spite of having incurred an expenditure of Rs5291.48 crore!'[19] [emphasis added]. Moreover, even in 2009, nuclear energy continues to account for only about 3 per cent of India's total electricity generation.

The DAE has been unable to meet targets even over the very short run. For example, in 2003, Kakodkar predicted that, 'in about four years from now, DAE will reach an installed capacity of 6800 MWe.'[20] Six years later, nuclear capacity was only 4120 MW.[21]

THE THREE-STAGE NUCLEAR PROGRAM

It is evident that DAE has been unable to keep its previous promises. In light of this, are the current projections realistic? The first obvious point is that the DAE's figures are very ambitious and quite out of step with international expectations. For example, a large multi-disciplinary Massachusetts Institute of Technology (MIT) study in 2003 projected that *worldwide* nuclear power capacity would increase to 1000 GW by 2050.[22] In contrast, the DAE projects that India alone would have an installed capacity of about 650 GW or 65 per cent of the worldwide figure above!

The DAE's projections are based on a *three-stage nuclear program* first proposed by Bhabha in 1954. Of the three planned stages, only the first stage comprises conventional nuclear reactors that use uranium as a fuel. The second and third stages were to consist of fast breeder reactors and thorium reactors. Of these three stages, only the first stage has been implemented, albeit somewhat unsuccessfully, after more than 50 years.

The second and third stages use technology that is not used commercially, on a large scale, *anywhere* in the world. Fast breeder reactors were tried and abandoned in several countries. Thorium reactors, of the kind envisioned in India, have never been used commercially at all.

However, in the energy projections above, the contribution of the first stage is very insignificant. About 90 per cent of the power-capacity projected is to come from the second and third stages of the nuclear program. So the DAE's energy projections are based overwhelmingly on technology that either does not exist or has been abandoned in favour of more conventional nuclear technology!

This leads to another issue. The three-stage program was envisioned at a time when self-sufficiency was considered exceedingly important. India's uranium resources are very poor both in quantity and quality. Since uranium is what is used in nuclear reactors worldwide, it is impossible for India to sustain a large indigenous atomic energy program. The second stage of the program was designed to squeeze the maximum possible energy from this low-quality fuel while the third stage focused on thorium, which is widely available in India.

However, uranium is available plentifully in the world and so these other technologies were not pursued elsewhere. In fact, it is unlikely that these technologies will come to prominence in the near future. The MIT study cited above emphasized that, 'over at least the next 50 years, the best choice . . . is the open, once-through fuel cycle, i.e., conventional uranium reactors.

Since India has failed to develop the second and third stages indigenously, it is safe to say that the three-stage program has failed. However, what is more important is that the three-stage program is not *relevant* to policy-makers any more. This is because the emphasis on self-sufficiency has been extensively diluted in the past two decades. In fact, one of the major consequences of the nuclear deal was to allow India to participate in international uranium trade and import nuclear reactors from abroad. Since energy produced this way (even though imported) is likely to be cheaper than energy from fast breeder reactors or thorium reactors, it is quite likely that India will quietly abandon the focus on the three-stage program.[23]

Nevertheless, we discuss the three stages of the Indian program below.

The three-stage program was based on the recognition that India's uranium resources are poor. As Kakodkar put it, 'for nuclear energy, there is hardly any uranium in India.'[24] On the other hand, India has one of the largest deposits of thorium in the world. The three-stage process was designed to take advantage of this fact.

An excellent review of the idea behind this program can be found in the book by Venkataraman.[25] Another review may be found at the website of the Bhabha Atomic Research Centre (BARC).[26] We summarize this very briefly here. The first stage of the nuclear program involves the use of Pressurized Heavy-Water Reactors (PHWRs). Naturally occurring uranium contains about 0.7 per cent uranium-235 (U^{235}) with the rest[27] being U^{238}. The fissile fuel is U^{235}, and often naturally occurring uranium is enriched (via centrifuges for example) to separate the U^{238} and increase the percentage of U^{235}. A PHWR can use this fuel directly, without enrichment. This saves some expense, but the disadvantage is that this kind of reactor uses *heavy-water*, which is expensive, as a moderator. Bhabha chose these reactors because some of the U^{238} is transmuted to plutonium-239 (Pu^{239}) in the operation of the reactor.

In the second stage, this Pu^{239} is fed into a *fast breeder* reactor (FBR) together with the waste U^{238} from the first stage. The reaction in the breeder reactor uses the Pu^{239} for energy and converts the U^{238} into Pu^{239}, thus breeding its own fuel. Theoretically, this process squeezes all the energy out of naturally found uranium by using U^{238} also.

The third stage involves another kind of breeding. The core of the FBR can be wrapped with thorium-232 (Th^{232}). In the operation of the FBR, this undergoes transmutation to U^{233} (another isotope of uranium!) which is fissile. This starting stockpile of U^{233} is fed into the third stage. This third-stage U^{233} reactor is also wrapped in a thorium blanket, and so the operation of the reactor produces more U^{233}. Bhabha suggested that this three-stage process would allow the utilization of India's extensive thorium resources.

It is clear, in hindsight, that Bhabha's proposals for the three-stage program were premature and impractical. Fifty-five years after these proposals were made, the program is still stuck at the first stage.

STAGE–I

The first stage was just meant to get the three-stage program started, and it made up only a tiny part of Bhabha's grand scheme. The DAE estimates that the uranium available in India will allow it to build up a power-capacity of only about 10 GW—about 2 per cent of Kakodkar's final prediction for 2050. The DAE plans to supplement this indigenous capacity with imported reactors and fuel. At least publicly, the DAE insists that the imported reactors too will make up a negligible fraction of the nuclear capacity by 2050.

Nevertheless, the first stage of the nuclear program is the only stage to have been commercially implemented. As we described above, and will discuss in more detail below, this is likely to continue being the case. So, in effect, the practical debate on nuclear electricity production in India is confined to the first stage of the nuclear program. Since this stage uses conventional technology (as opposed to the second and third stages), this debate meshes with the worldwide debate on nuclear energy.

We consider the following key questions:

- Why has the idea of nuclear energy seen a worldwide revival?
- What is the economics of nuclear power?
- What about the safety and environmental impact of nuclear installations?
- How do these factors apply to India?

THE NUCLEAR RENAISSANCE

After years of stagnation due to high costs and safety concerns, the nuclear industry has seen something of a revival, especially in the West.[28] Partly, this is because of concerns about climate change and greenhouse gas emissions.[29] A second, often unstated, reason is geopolitical. As the *Economist* put it: 'Western governments are concerned . . . [that] oil and gas is in the hands of hostile . . . governments. Much of the nuclear industry's raw material is . . . located in friendly places such as Australia and Canada.'[30]

While these arguments have been widely discussed over the past few years with concomitant changes in policy, the much-touted nuclear renaissance is fast running into severe problems. Areva, the French company that is supposed to build a reactor in Jaitapur, Maharashtra, is also building a reactor in Finland—the first *generation III* plant in the world. However, this plant is now expected to be three years late and is 60 per cent over the budget.

In Britain, the construction of new plants by Areva and Westinghouse (an American company that is also expected to build a plant in India) has run into regulatory difficulties. The British Health and Safety Executive (HSE) recently issued a report on the construction of proposed plants by these companies. The HSE was dissatisfied with both designs stating, in similar reports that, 'we have identified a significant number of issues with the safety features of the design . . . If these are not progressed satisfactorily then we would not issue a "Design Acceptance Confirmation".'[31,32] (A summary of these reports was carried by *The Guardian*).[33]

The argument that nuclear energy is the best way to fight climate change has also been vigorously challenged. For example, Lovins and Sheikh argue in favour of alternative sources of energy, including wind and small hydro-power projects.[34] In spite of all this, it appears likely that, barring an accident or a technological breakthrough in a different field, the nuclear industry will build several new nuclear reactors in the next few decades.

So it is important to ask, first, whether nuclear energy is cost-effective and safe; and second, how the global debate over nuclear energy applies to India. India's obligations under climate treaties are likely to be different from those of developed countries, at least over the next few decades. Second, given India's poor uranium resources, a large-scale nuclear program would make the country dependent on imperialist countries for fuel; this is evidently not desirable.

INDIA'S NUCLEAR ECONOMICS

India uses slightly non-standard reactors. These reactors have the advantage that they can work with naturally occurring uranium, without the need for enrichment. While this saves some expense, these reactors use heavy-water, which is expensive. The DAE plans to construct more such pressurized heavy-water reactors in the future.

The economics of nuclear power in India is particularly complicated by two factors. First, it is hard to obtain an accurate estimate of the subsidies that go into various aspects of nuclear power, including heavy-water production.[35] Second, the DAE uses a so-called 'closed cycle', where the spent fuel is reprocessed. This reprocessing is very expensive, but is not included in the official estimation of the cost of power. The reasoning behind this is that the reprocessed fuel will eventually be useful in the second stage of the nuclear program; since this second stage has not yet become operational, this is rather specious.

It is sometimes argued that nuclear power is cost-competitive with coal.[36,37] Under reasonable assumptions for the subsidy that goes into heavy-water production, nuclear power is not cost-competitive with coal even for (real) discount rates as low as 3 per cent. This conclusion holds even if the costs involved in reprocessing are completely neglected.[38,39] This is consistent with the international pattern that we describe below.

GLOBAL NUCLEAR ECONOMICS

The extensive MIT study of 2003 referred to above concluded, by studying a range of discount rates, that 'in deregulated markets, nuclear power is not now cost competitive with coal and natural gas.' An extensive study performed at the University of Chicago came to the same conclusion. It noted that, except for France, 'for most other countries, the high capital costs of nuclear power prohibit it from being cost-competitive with coal and natural gas-fired technologies.'[40] Moreover, the study pointed out that even in the 'most favourable case,' the cost of the first new nuclear plants in the U.S. would be above the *highest* coal and gas costs.[41]

As the *Economist* summarized: 'Since the 1970s, far from being "too cheap to meter"—as it proponents once blithely claimed— nuclear power has proved too expensive to matter.'[42] It is as a result of this that no new applications for plant-construction were made in the U.S. for almost three decades.

The other question is whether putting a price on carbon emissions would change these calculations. Here, the *Economist* points out: 'The price of carbon under Europe's emissions-trading scheme is currently around €14 per tonne, far short of the €50 that power-industry bosses think would make nuclear plants attractive.[43]

So, there is a wide consensus internationally that nuclear power is more expensive than coal.[44] India conforms to this pattern. While this has dampened the growth of the nuclear industry, it has not stopped new nuclear plants from being constructed. To the contrary, at times, the fact that nuclear power is more expensive has been seen as a rationale for further policy assistance and subsidies!

SAFETY AND ENVIRONMENT

As we mentioned above, concerns about climate change have partly driven the revival in the nuclear industry in recent times. Atomic energy does have the advantage of not producing greenhouse gases. As a result of this (and other pecuniary reasons), some environmentalists like Patrick Moore, an influential former member of Greenpeace, have become advocates of nuclear energy. However, Greenpeace itself and most other environmental groups still disavow nuclear energy. One of their primary objections is to the waste that is generated.

Nuclear reactors produce radioactive waste, some of which remains hazardous for a very long time. For example, Pu^{239} (which is produced in nuclear reactors) has a half-life of 24,000 years (which means that the radioactivity from a lump of this material decreases by half every 24,000 years).

Unfortunately, there is no established technique of disposing this waste. In the long run, there is some agreement, among nuclear planners, that the waste should be put into a stable *geological repository*. Only one such repository—the Waste Isolation Pilot Plant in the U.S.—exists, but operates only with military waste. The U.S. plans to dispose of some of its radioactive civil waste in the Yucca mountain repository, but this has not yet been constructed. A discussion of the logistics of these programs can be found in the *Nuclear Engineering Handbook*.[45]

In India, the spent fuel from reactors is reprocessed. However, this process still produces dangerous radioactive waste. This volume is currently small. In 2001, it was estimated that about 5000 m^3 of 'high-level-waste' had been generated in India (this is about two Olympic size swimming pools).[46] However, this is likely to go up sharply. In 2004, the DAE estimated that, by 2011, it would produce about 700 m^3 of high-level waste every year. Although the DAE claims that it will finally dispose of this waste in a deep geological repository, it is forced to admit that 'demonstration of feasibility and safety of deep geological disposal is a major challenge ahead.'[47]

Another concern regarding nuclear energy is the safety of nuclear plants. The 1986 accident at Chernobyl (in the Ukraine, then part of the Soviet Union) sent up a huge amount of radioactive material into the atmosphere. This radioactive material carried across the Soviet border into other countries and as far north as Sweden. In 2006, the WHO estimated that there would be 'about 4000 [excess] deaths . . . over the lifetimes of the some 600,000 persons most affected by the accident' due to cancer caused by exposure to radiation. Beyond this, over the lifetime of the population of the more than 6 million people in 'other contaminated areas,' it estimated that there would be about 5000 excess deaths. (Table 12 of the WHO report)[48] However, as Greenpeace pointed out,[49] with a disaster of this magnitude, 'any description which attempts to present the consequences as a single, 'easy to understand' estimation of excess cancer deaths . . . will . . . inevitably provide a gross over-simplification of the breadth of human suffering experienced.'[50]

The accident at Chernobyl probably happened because of poor design and operator error. In particular, the reactor was not enclosed within proper containment. Also, at the time of the accident, it seems to have had a *positive void coefficient*,[51] which meant that the escaping coolant increased the intensity of the reaction which in turn caused more of the coolant to escape, thus leading to catastrophic positive feedback. Newer reactors seem to be better contained and designed. One can only hope that the nuclear industry has learned its engineering lessons well.

As we have described above, nuclear power is inherently hazardous. However, in any discussion about the safety of nuclear plants, there is a point made by proponents of nuclear energy that cannot be overlooked. Nuclear energy is most commonly compared to coal, as we have also done above. However, coal is also hazardous. This is because thousands of people lose their lives in coal-mines every year. China is the most egregious example. According to official statistics, there were 4746 fatalities in China in 2006[52] and 3786 fatalities in 2007.[53]

Coal-mining affects hundreds of people in India also. Statistics on coal-mining in India are somewhat problematic. According to the Ministry of Coal, coal-mining in India is so safe that fatalities per man-shift are considerably lower than in the U.S. and about as low as they are in Australia.[54] This is not entirely believable. However, even taking the ministry's figures[55] at face value, there were 128 fatalities and 966 serious injuries in coal-mining in 2006. In 2007, there were 69 fatalities and 904 serious injuries.[56]

This is partly a result of the tremendous inequality that exists in our society today. A nuclear meltdown would be catastrophic and would affect everyone. So, a great amount of attention is paid to safety in nuclear installations. However, hundreds of people lose their lives in coal-mining around the world each year. Since these people are overwhelmingly poor and dispossessed, this does not attract anywhere near the same level of protest or attention.

INDIA-SPECIFIC FACTORS

There are two factors that modify the debate regarding the desirability of nuclear power in India.

The first has to do with the poor uranium resources of the country. As we have already mentioned, uranium deposits in India are not only rare, they are of poor quality. The report of the Kirit Parikh-led expert committee on energy policy, appointed by the Planning Commission, pointed out that, 'India is poorly endowed with uranium. Available uranium supply can fuel only 10,000 MW of the Pressurised Heavy-Water Reactors (PHWR). Further, India is extracting uranium from extremely low grade ores (as low as 0.1% uranium) compared to ores with up to 1214 per cent uranium in certain resources abroad. This makes Indian nuclear fuel 2–3 times costlier than international supplies.'[57] It is evident then that a large nuclear program can only be sustained on the basis of imported fuel. Of course, this makes nuclear energy more expensive. However, more seriously, importing fuel will make India dependent on imperialist countries for fuel supplies. After the nuclear tests in 1974, the U.S. stopped fuel supplies to the Tarapur plant. Last year, India was given a waiver by the Nuclear Suppliers Group,[58] allowing it to engage in nuclear trade, only because it was strategically allied with the United States. A large-scale nuclear program, relying on imported fuel, would make it difficult for any future government to extricate itself from this relationship.

The second important issue in India is the lack of a strong regulatory framework. Once again, this poor institutional design can be traced to Bhabha and Nehru. In 1948, Bhabha wrote to Nehru stating that, 'the development of atomic energy should be entrusted to a very small and high-powered body, composed of say three people with executive power, and *answerable directly to the Prime Minister without any intervening link* . . . this body may be referred to as the Atomic Energy Commission.'[59] [emphasis added]. Evidently, Bhabha was no great believer in democracy. In this case, as in many others, he used his personal closeness to Nehru to free himself of even the minimal checks and balances that existed in other areas of the government. The AEC (Atomic Energy Commission) was set up in 1954 and fifty-five years later this small opaque clique of bureaucrats continues to oversee all aspects of atomic energy in the country.[60]

In fact, for decades, the atomic energy establishment did not even see the need to have an independent regulatory body. The DAE was in charge of both the construction *and* regulation of nuclear power plants. It was only after the serious nuclear accident at the Three Mile Island (Pennsylvania, U.S.) in 1979 that the DAE started the process of setting up a separate Atomic Energy Regulatory Board (AERB).[61] However, the AERB, which was set up in 1983 with the mission of ensuring the safety of atomic energy, reports directly to the AEC, which is chaired by the head of the DAE! This makes its claim of being independent of the DAE somewhat specious.

In 1995, the AERB, under a proactive chairperson, A. Gopalakrishnan, compiled a report citing 130 safety issues in Indian nuclear installations, with about 95 being top priority. It is unclear what, if any, action was taken on the AERB report.

Later, after leaving the AERB, Gopalakrishnan wrote that, 'the safety status in the DAE's facilities is far below international standards.' Further, he said that, 'the lack of a truly independent nuclear regulatory mechanism and the unprecedented powers and influence of the DAE, coupled with the widespread use of the Official Secrets Act to cover up the realities, are the primary reasons for this grave situation.'[62] In its response, the Nuclear Power Corporation dismissed these concerns as 'alarmist' and expressed its sorrow that Gopalakrishnan was 'tilting at windmills.' Moreover, it stated that, 'we do not consider the AERB . . . as being adversaries. We are all part of a single scientific fraternity that has been mandated by the founding fathers of the nation to develop and deliver the numerous benefits of nuclear energy to the nation in an economical and safe manner.'[63]

While this evocation of fraternal cooperation is undoubtedly touching, it is somewhat problematic for the regulators and builders of a hazardous technology like atomic energy to be so cosy. In fact, as Gopalakrishnan points out, this is in violation of the international convention on nuclear safety that asks every contracting party (including India), to take 'appropriate steps to ensure an effective separation between the . . . regulatory body and . . . any other body . . . concerned with the . . . utilization of nuclear energy.'[64]

Nuclear accidents are a low-probability event. So it is often possible to get away with violations of safety norms, as the DAE has been doing. However, the reason these low probabilities are taken so seriously is that the consequences of a single nuclear accident can be disastrous. The current regulatory framework is clearly broken, and this makes the planned expansion in the atomic energy program particularly alarming.

STAGES II–III

As we mentioned above, the first stage of the nuclear power program is the smallest of the three planned stages. In the proposals by the DAE described above, most of the energy is supposed to come from the second and third stages comprising fast breeder reactors and thorium reactors. Unfortunately, fifty-five years after Bhabha's initial proposal, the technology for both these stages remains nascent. Except for one thirty-year-old fast breeder reactor in Russia,[65] neither of these two technologies is in commercial use *anywhere in the world*.

The technology for the second stage is somewhat more developed than the technology for the third stage. Several countries did build prototype fast-breeder reactors but soon abandoned them. Nevertheless, India is now building its own Prototype Fast-Breeder Reactor (PFBR) at Kalpakkam. No one has even tried to build a thorium reactor of the kind envisaged in the third stage. To implement the thorium fuel cycle commercially would require a massive research effort and, without technological breakthroughs, a thorium reactor would be considerably more expensive than a conventional uranium reactor. Given that uranium is available plentifully in the world (although not in India), there is no worldwide economic impetus for this. India is one of the only countries in the world that has continued to pursue research into a thorium reactor program.

The DAE portrays this state of affairs by stating that the first stage involves 'World Class Performance', the second stage involves 'Globally Advanced Technology', and the third stage is 'Globally Unique'!

Let's look at the second stage more closely. India has been planning to build a PFBR for many years. The 'Profile for the Decade 1970–1980' had as one of its targets the 'Design and Construction of a large 500 MW Prototype Fast-Breeder Test Reactor.' Since the PFBR, at Kalpakkam, is now scheduled to come online in 2010, it is at least thirty years late!

In fact, even this deadline is unlikely to be met since, true to form, this project is delayed and heavily over budget. In March 2009, the Ministry of Program Implementation summarized that the PFBR project was on schedule for completion in September 2010 and within the allocated budget of Rs3492 crores.[66] However, a few months later, the 2009 annual report of Bhavini (the public sector corporation set up to oversee this project) was forced to state[67] that 'the revised project cost is estimated to be of Rs5677 crores.' This is more than 60 per cent above the original budget. Moreover, this annual report also states that, 'as on 31 May 2009 the overall physical progress achieved by the Project is 45% as compared to 35% progress achieved on 31 May 2008.'

It is useful to review the history of fast-breeder reactors in other parts of the world. Several countries have built prototype fast-breeder reactors. The fast reactor database of the IAEA[68] helpfully reviews this history. France, Germany, UK, U.S., Soviet Union and Japan started building commercial size prototype fast-breeder reactors in the eighties. Each of these programs failed. The French reactor was shut down in 1998 after popular protests. The German reactor was completed but, despite the large expense involved in construction, it was never made operational! The Japanese reactor suffered a serious accident in 1995 and has been shut since then. The American program also petered out, and a thirty-year-old

Russian reactor is now the only commercial fast-breeder reactor in existence. The IAEA summary is forced to state that, 'it has to be admitted that there simply was no economic need for fast-breeder reactors.' The PFBR, at Kalpakkam, was not expected to be an economical source of energy, even with the original cost estimates for the project.[69] The revised cost estimates above only serve to exacerbate this state of affairs.

There are very serious issues about the safety of the PFBR. Kumar and Ramana argue that the DAE has designed the PFBR with a weak containment wall to save money.[70] According to their calculations, the containment of the reactor could be breached in the event of a severe accident, releasing radioactivity into the atmosphere. A very serious problem, that these authors discuss, is that the PFBR has a positive void coefficient. As we described above, this was one of the characteristics that led to the Chernobyl explosion. The DAE, in its design statement,[71] claims that, 'voiding of the core is highly improbable,' and states that this 'is of concern only in the case of hypothetical core disruptive accident.' Given that this 'hypothetical' case could be catastrophic, one would expect that great care would be taken in analyzing it. The DAE merely states (citing unspecified 'studies') that the 'positive void coefficient . . . is considered admissible.'

We should emphasize that the second stage of the nuclear program is meant to provide most of the energy-generating capacity projected by the DAE. It is probably clear to the reader, by now, that this should not be taken too seriously. However, even if one were to believe the DAE, Ramana and Suchitra argue that their predictions are simply inconsistent.[72] Briefly, the DAE's estimates for the growth of fast-breeder reactors are based on the notion of a *doubling-time*. As described above, these reactors breed their own fuel; so, after a while a breeder reactor produces plutonium that can be used to fuel another reactor.

However, what is important is that the process above (doubling) involves a *delay*. The plutonium for the first reactor must be set aside some time in advance. Second, only after the reactor has operated for a while can the plutonium from its core be extracted. This must then be reprocessed for use in another reactor. The DAE seems to have neglected this delay, and the paper above points out that if the DAE's projections were to come true, they would 'result in negative balances of plutonium!' Ramana and Suchitra argue that the DAE cannot possibly achieve more than 40 per cent of its projections; of course, the other factors discussed above imply that this too is extremely unlikely.

The fast-breeder reactor program also has an important link with the weaponization program that we will discuss below.

The technology for the use of thorium as a nuclear fuel is even less developed. Thorium is far more abundant than uranium in the Earth's crust. However, the reason that the thorium fuel-cycle has not been developed widely is simple. With uranium, the fissionable U^{235} occurs naturally. So to go from the ore to the fuel requires purification of the naturally occurring ore. The situation with thorium is different. Naturally occurring thorium cannot be used as a nuclear fuel. It is uranium-233 (U^{233}) that is produced when thorium undergoes a *nuclear reaction* that is fissionable. So producing fuel from thorium ore does not require just physical or chemical processes, but rather a nuclear reaction itself.

Moreover, even this process is riddled with complications. There are two reasons for this. The first is that the nuclear reaction that produces U^{233} also produces another isotope of uranium—U^{232}. The decay of this isotope leads to high amounts of gamma radiation. Hence, fuel fabrication and reprocessing has to be handled remotely. Second, the thorium fuel cycle must involve breeding of the kind described above. After an initial batch of (very expensive and remotely prepared) fuel is fed into the reactor, the spent fuel must be reprocessed and fed back in. However, apart from the problems with gamma radiation, thorium dioxide is very inert and hard to dissolve and process chemically.

Given these facts, it is not surprising that *no other* country in the world has an active program to utilize thorium. What is surprising is that India has steadfastly continued to pursue this path. As the

World Nuclear Association points out, 'for many years India has been the only sponsor of major research efforts to use it [thorium].'[73]

The DAE claims that it has made some progress on the issues described above[74] and it is now planning to build an Advanced Heavy-Water Reactor (AHWR) to gain experience with the thorium cycle. Nevertheless, it is clear that surmounting all these difficulties will require a massive and very expensive research effort; the uranium fuel cycle was developed only after the Manhattan project.

It is quite unclear whether, at the end of this research, thorium-based power will ever be economically competitive. Is the massive expense involved in developing the thorium fuel cycle indigenously justified? Unfortunately, given the lack of transparency and democratic debate in India, it seems unlikely that this question will be brought up or debated openly.

WEAPONIZATION

It is very hard to separate the civilian aspect of atomic energy from the military aspect of nuclear bombs. Both Bhabha and Nehru recognized this. As Bhabha himself pointed out, 'the rise of an atomic power industry . . . will put into the hands of many nations quantities of fissile material, from which the making of atomic bombs will be but a relatively easy step.'[75] Nehru, for his part, said at the opening of the Atomic Energy Establishment in Trombay (later renamed the Bhabha Atomic Research Centre) that, 'I should like to say on behalf of my government . . . [and] with some assurance on behalf of any future Government of India . . . [that] we shall never use this atomic energy for evil purposes.' Of course, Nehru also recognized that the civilian and military aspects of nuclear energy could not be separated. Several years earlier, in the Constituent Assembly debates, he conceded: 'I do not know how you are to distinguish between the two [peaceful and military applications of atomic energy].'[76]

Nevertheless, for four decades, successive Indian governments sought to publicly maintain this distinction. In 1974, at the time of the first Pokharan nuclear test, the Indian government argued that it was testing nuclear explosives for possible civilian uses. This is why this explosion was called a 'peaceful nuclear explosion'.[77] 'Absolutely categorically, I can say we do not have a nuclear weapon,' Rajiv Gandhi declared in 1985.[78] This ended with the 1998 Pokharan blasts. Pramod Mahajan, a representative of the 'future government' of the time, clarified that that nuclear weapons were 'not about security;' rather, the significance of the Pokharan blasts was that, 'no Indian has to show his passport [since] the whole world now knows where India is.'[79]

The research for both the 'peaceful nuclear explosion' of 1974 and the later atomic tests of 1998 was largely performed at BARC. In fact, as P.K. Iyengar, a former chairperson of the Atomic Energy Commission, helpfully explains,[80] 'the exercise of detonating a nuclear explosive was . . . a small deviation from the normal work carried out by many scientists and engineers at Trombay. This was the reason . . . the whole project remained a secret.'

Other than the issue of overlapping research, there is the important issue of the buildup of fissile materials. India's nuclear explosions have used plutonium. The plutonium that is most commonly used in nuclear bombs is called *weapons-grade* plutonium and, by definition, this contains more than 93 per cent Pu^{239}.

As we described above, Pu^{239} is produced even in electricity-generating reactors when U^{238} absorbs a neutron. However, when a reactor is meant to generate electricity, the uranium fuel-rods are kept in for a long time to use up as much of the uranium as possible. In this time, other nuclear reactions happen and the spent fuel in reactors ends up also containing other isotopes of plutonium, including Pu^{240}. The presence of these other isotopes makes it difficult to make bombs with this kind of *reactor-grade* plutonium. (See pp. 37–39 of a U.S. Department of Energy declassified document for a discussion on this.)[81]

However, research reactors, in which the fuel-rods are pulled out after *low-burnup*, can be used to produce weapons-grade plutonium. The fissile material for the 1974 Pokharan explosions came from the research reactor, CIRUS. The history of CIRUS is quite interesting. CIRUS stands for 'Canadian Indian Reactor US,' because the design was Canadian, the heavy-water used was American and the fuel was Indian. The Canadian negotiators imposed no explicit conditions on how the fuel from this reactor could be used. In fact, an Indian commitment that the fuel would be used peacefully was placed in a *secret* annex to the treaty! Furthermore, while the initial idea was that the fuel would be supplied by the Canadians, the Indian side pre-empted this and succeeded in fabricated indigenous fuel rods in time for use in the reactor. This allowed India to argue that it could do as it wished with the spent fuel from the reactor because the fuel, after all, was Indian.

This use of the plutonium from CIRUS is often discussed in the context of proliferation[82] caused by the supply of peaceful nuclear technology. Some accounts, such as that of Abraham (cited above), portray this sequence of events by suggesting that the well-intentioned but somewhat injudicious Canadians were out-manoeuvred by the nefarious Indians. This conclusion arises from the axiom that Western countries are always well-intentioned.

These narratives need not be taken seriously. The Canadian technology transfer was undoubtedly done with the full knowledge that it would help India produce weapons-grade fissile material. A more pertinent question to ask is: 'What were the calculations that led the imperialist world to encourage India to arm itself with nuclear weapons?'

In fact, a few years later, the Americans almost directly provided India with a nuclear bomb! Perkovich describes (pp. 90–93) that in 1964, the U.S. defense department conducted a secret study examining the 'possibilities of providing nuclear weapons under U.S. custody' to 'friendly Asian' military forces for use against China. At the same time, the U.S. Atomic Energy Commission was *independently* exploring the possibility of helping India conduct nuclear explosions for 'civilian' purposes. While neither of these two initiatives was brought to fruition, this goes to show that the commonly made assumption that the U.S. ruling elite is uncomfortable with Indian nuclear weapons is incorrect. There are opposing forces within the American establishment and, as we will discuss below, very similar tensions continue to operate today. In 1985, India built a companion to CIRUS called Dhruva. Dhruva adjoins CIRUS but is significantly larger, and can also be used to produce weapons-grade plutonium. A study by Mian et al.[83] estimates that India has built up a stockpile of 500 kg of weapons-grade plutonium from CIRUS and Dhruva. This is enough for more than a hundred nuclear warheads.

As we mentioned above, it is hard to build nuclear weapons with the plutonium that is produced in power-reactors. However, this is not impossible; bombs using reactor-grade plutonium can be built. In fact, there is some evidence that in the 1998 blasts, reactor-grade plutonium was used. If this is true, then the amount of fissile material available to the Indian government is considerably larger than the estimate above, since large stockpiles of spent reactor fuel are available. The fast-breeder program, which constitutes the second stage of the three-stage program, is quite important here. As we mentioned, fast breeder reactors work with a fuel core and also a blanket of uranium. This blanket breeds weapons-grade plutonium. Glaser and Ramana estimate[84] that the PFBR under construction at Kalpakkam might itself allow India to produce 140 kg of plutonium every year. This would allow the Indian government to greatly increase its nuclear arsenal. In this context, it is relevant to note that one of the key initial disagreements between the U.S. and India was over whether the FBR program would come under IAEA safeguards.[85] When asked whether the breeders would be put under safeguards, Kakodkar replied, 'no way, because it hurts our strategic interests,' and suggested that he would rather have the deal sink.[86]

In the final deal, breeder reactors were kept out of IAEA safeguards. Once again, it is somewhat naive to attribute this to India's negotiating skills or American innocence and simple-mindedness. There was evidently disagreement between different sections of the American ruling elite. Stephen Cohen, from the influential Brookings Institution, claimed that, 'we [the U.S.] probably could have put more restraints on the fast-breeder reactor program.' However, 'Bush stopped the negotiations.'[87] Hence, this was a *political decision*. As in the case of CIRUS, a section of the imperialist ruling-class seems to have decided that it was in its interests to allow India to arm itself with nuclear weapons. In both cases, it is quite plausible that this was intended to build India into a nuclear armed regional counterweight to China.

Highly Enriched Uranium (HEU) can also be used for military purposes. India's facilities to enrich uranium are somewhat poor. India has two gas centrifuge enrichment facilities. One is at BARC and the other is at Rattehalli, near Mysore. According to Mian et al. India could have built up a stockpile of about 400–700 kg of 45–30 per cent enriched uranium. Another study estimated that India might have 94 kg of 90 per cent enriched uranium.[88] This enriched uranium was undoubtedly used in India's nuclear submarine project and can also be used to make bombs.

To summarize this section, it is clear that the Indian atomic energy program has had a major weapons component. In some cases, like the fast breeder reactor, the objective of the reactor seems to be, not to produce energy, but rather to use energy as a veneer to cover up a weapons-making factory. More broadly, it is quite possible that, despite the failure to produce electricity, the atomic energy program has received state patronage because of its contribution to India's nuclear bomb. An unconfirmed anecdote might be relevant here. Ashok Parthasarathi an adviser to Indira Gandhi at the time of Sarabhai and Homi Sethna claims that he repeatedly brought up the DAE's failure to produce atomic energy and objected to its plans for future expansion. He claims that he was finally overridden by P.N. Haksar who explained to him that 'there are *larger objectives* to our nuclear program than nuclear power and those objectives cannot be compromised at any cost.'[89] [emphasis in the original]

CONCLUSIONS AND THE POLITICS OF NUCLEAR ENERGY

The analysis above raises an interesting question: 'Why was the nuclear deal so important for the government that it was willing to risk its very survival to ensure its passage?' This is slightly outside the main line of this article but is interesting and important in its own right. This question has also been discussed elsewhere.[90]

We emphasize that this discussion must be placed in its proper context. When the government decided to go ahead with the nuclear deal (in mid-2008), this precipitated a political crisis because the Left parties withdrew their support to the UPA (United Progressive Alliance) government. While the Congress eventually emerged unscathed from this crisis and even returned to power with an enhanced majority, this was not at all clear at the time; the government could well have fallen. Moreover, the time was hardly propitious for elections. Among other issues, inflation was at a 13 year high![91] Surely, it was suicidal for the Congress to destabilize its government in such a scenario? What were the strong forces that impelled it to undertake this bizarre behaviour?

As we saw in Section 1, the government argued that the nuclear deal was necessary for energy security. However, from the analysis above it is quite clear that atomic energy is rather unimportant for India's energy needs and is likely to remain so. The nuclear deal was not even critical for the weapons program. While the availability of international uranium will free domestic resources for use in weapons, the primary build-up in fissile materials is likely to come from indigenous fast breeder reactors.

One argument is that the government was taken in by its own propaganda. However, the data presented above is so public and well known that this seems unlikely. Moreover, even going by the DAE's figures, atomic energy will not contribute significantly to India's energy mix for many years to come. So this argument leads to the conclusion that the Congress was so perspicacious that it was willing to sacrifice its government for a small gain in India's energy-security several decades later. Evidently, the argument is incorrect.

Another argument is that the nuclear deal was pushed by the Indian atomic energy establishment which desperately required a lifeline for its civilian energy program.[92] While this might have been a factor, it seems unlikely that a major political decision of this sort was taken under the influence of technocrats. A far more believable answer was given by Ashley Tellis,[93] an important adviser to the Bush administration. Tellis noted that the deal was 'extremely important.' He went on to say: 'It is the centre piece of everything . . . for the simple reason that it goes fundamentally to the president's and the prime minister's efforts to build a new sense of trust . . . In my view, this is the ultimate reason why it cannot fail, why it must not fail, because both leaders have staked a lot in trying to do something really important—something that implicates issues of credibility, issues of commitment, and finally issues of confidence for the future of the relationship.' However, what do terms like 'credibility' and 'commitment' really mean in the context of an alliance with the United States? The answer is quite clear and forms a cornerstone of American foreign policy.

Credible governments are those that do not allow *domestic political compulsions* to prevent them from adhering to American interests. This is extremely important. The American ruling elite does not enjoy dealing with the vagaries of third world denizens. A 'trustworthy ally' is a country that manages domestic politics well and keeps its 'international commitments.' As Noam Chomsky pointed out,[94] 'attitudes toward democracy were revealed with unusual clarity during the mobilization for [the Iraq] war.' Even old Western allies like France and Germany were pushed off to 'Old Europe' because domestic considerations prevented them from supporting the Iraq war. Chomsky noticed that, 'the governments of Old and New Europe were distinguished by a simple criterion: a government joined Old Europe in its iniquity if and only if it took the same position as the vast majority of its population and refused to follow orders from Washington.'

Influential figures on both the American and Indian side were in agreement on this issue. Ronen Sen, India's ambassador to the U.S., explained[95] that the failure of the deal would leave India with 'zero credibility.' He pointed out that the despite having 'revolving door' governments, 'one thing that distinguishes India . . . is that we have always honoured our commitments . . . not just that it is a democracy.' He regretted that at the state level, this had not always been true and that in 'one instance . . . after an election a state government changed one contract, and that is Enron!' Evidently, according to Sen, elections and the wishes of the people should not come in the way of fulfilling obligations, however onerous or unjustified, to multinational corporations or the U.S. government. Ashton Carter, a member of the Clinton administration, explained[96] to the U.S. Senate that, 'India's bureaucracies and diplomats are fabled for their stubborn adherence to independent positions regarding the world order, economic development, and nuclear security.' He lamented that the fact that 'India . . . is a democracy' meant that 'no government in Delhi can . . . commit . . . to a broad set of actions in support of U.S. interests.'

The Indian ruling elite was very unhappy with this fact also. When the Left parties stalled the nuclear deal, Chidambaram went on record[97] stating that, 'Indian . . . democracy has often paralyzed decision making . . . this approach must change.' Manmohan Singh was so upset that he began to question the efficacy of a multi-party system itself. In a conference on federalism, he asked, 'does a single party state have any advantages' and wondered whether 'a coalition . . . [was] . . . capable of providing the unity of purpose that nation-states have to often demonstrate.'

What is almost conclusive is that, after a long stalemate, the Congress chose to precipitate a showdown with the Left parties exactly a week before Manmohan Singh was to attend a G8 summit in Japan. As *The Times of India* explained, 'the prime minister has consistently cited the possibility of an embarrassing loss of face with the international community to lobby the Congress leadership.'[98] Evidently, the reason that Manmohan Singh was desperate to pass the nuclear deal had nothing to do with electricity, but was related to maintaining his credentials as a reliable imperialist ally. The

Indian parliamentary system, for all its iniquities, is based on the notion that governments privilege their survival over all else. The fact that the Congress was willing to violate this tenet and imperil the existence of its own government to fulfil commitments made to the U.S. is a revealing indicator of the strength of its ties to imperialism.

EPILOGUE

This article was written in December 2009 but almost two years later the question of nuclear energy continues to be extremely important in India. While the Fukushima accident has put paid to the 'nuclear renaissance' in many countries, the Indian Government has continued to forge ahead with its plans for a nuclear expansion. In fact, on 26 April 2011—the twenty-fifth anniversary of the disaster in Chernobyl—the government held a high level press conference to reiterate its commitment to the nuclear expansion and, in particular, to the controversial Jaitapur nuclear power plant.

The events of the past two years have confirmed the analysis that the government's nuclear push has less to do with energy and more to do with building a strategic alliance with the West. For example, the Manmohan Singh Government spent the entire 2010 monsoon session of the parliament in passing a 'nuclear liability law' that was primarily aimed at *taking away* the rights of Indian victims to demand compensation from multinational suppliers in the event of an accident. The controversy over the Liability Bill led to another political crisis but just as in 2008, the government invested a massive amount of political capital to pass the bill before the visit of the U.S. President Barack Obama.

Apart from passing invidious laws, the Indian Government has also shown no hesitation in beating up and arresting its citizens to placate multinational interests. In Jaitapur where the French company Areva is planning to install several 'EPR' reactors, the government has brutally suppressed popular protests. The fact that the EPR is an untested design and that the two EPRs under construction in Olkiluoto (Finland) and Flamanville (France) are years behind schedule and heavily over their already exorbitant budgets has failed to deter the government.

On the other hand, resistance movements have sprung up all over the country against the government's nuclear plans. In Jaitapur, only 114 of the 2375 families eligible for compensation have accepted their cheques. In Mithi Virdi and Kovvada, the sites earmarked for U.S. companies, villagers have barricaded roads and prevented the government from even surveying their land. The planned Russian site in Haripur will probably have to be moved.

The anti-nuclear resistance must keep the political motivations underlying Indian nuclear policy in mind. For example, this is a useful predictor of the government's actions: it has been far more repressive in Jaitapur than in Fatehabad (Haryana)—the site proposed for an indigenous nuclear plant. However, this also means that if peoples' resistance movements are able to stop the Indian nuclear expansion, this will not only be a local victory but also a step towards fulfilling one of the most critical political necessities in both India and Pakistan today—that of purging the influence of imperialism from the subcontinent.

REFERENCES

1. Jawaharlal Nehru, 'Significance of the Atomic Revolution'. Speech at the opening of the Atomic Energy Establishment, 20 January 1957.
2. Chidanand Rajghatta, 'Times Interview with George Bush', Times of India, 24 February 2006.
3. Susan Piver, The Hard Questions: 100 Questions to Ask Before You Say 'I Do'. Tarcher, 2007.
4. Neha Sinha, 'Sonia targets Left: Deal critics are enemies of Cong, progress'. Indian Express, 8 October 2007.
5. 'Discussion regarding Indo–U.S. Nuclear Agreement', Lok Sabha debate on 28 November 2007.
6. 'Motion of confidence in the Council of Ministers', Lok Sabha debate on 21 July 2008.
7. 'N–deal: India says reprocessing talks will take time'. The Hindu, 24 November 2009.
8. 'U.S. welcomes site allocation for nuclear plants'. The Hindu, 18 October 2009.
9. R.B. Grover and Subash Chandra, A strategy for growth of electrical energy in India, Department of Atomic Energy, 2004.

10. R.B. Grover and Subhash Chandra, 'Scenario for growth of electricity in India', *Energy Policy*, vol. 34, no. 17, pp. 2834–2847, 2006.

11. Anil Kakodkar, 'Evolving Indian Nuclear Program: Rationale and Perspectives', Talk at Indian Academy of Sciences, Bangalore, July 2008.

12. 'Monthly Review of Power Sector (Executive Summary)', Ministry of Power, November 2009.

13. Sandeep Dikshit, 'Big scope for rise in nuclear energy', *The Hindu*, 30 September 2009.

14. Lord Penney, 'Homi Jehangir Bhabha 1909–1966', *Biographical Memoirs of Fellows of the Royal Society*, vol. 13, November 1967.

15. International Atomic Energy Agency, 'Power Reactor Information System'.

16. Atomic Energy Commission, Atomic Energy and Space Research: A Profile for *the Decade 1970–80*, 1970.

17. Vikram Sarabhai, Nuclear Power in Developing Countries. Atomic Energy Commission, 1969.

18. M.R. Srinivasan, 'Remembering Pandit Nehru and Dr Bhabha', *Nuclear India*, vol. 26, October 1989.

19. Comptroller and Auditor General of India, Report on the Union Government (Scientific Departments) for the year ended March 1998, Chapter 2: Department of Atomic Energy, 1999.

20. Anil Kakodkar, 'Five Decades of the DAE', *Nuclear India*, vol. 34, September–October 2003.

21. Nuclear Power Corporation of India, 'Plants Under Operation', 2009.

22. Stephen Ansolabehere, John Deutch, Michael Driscoll, et al., 'The future of nuclear power: an interdisciplinary MIT study', tech. rep., Massachusetts Institute of Technology, 2003.

23. Fast breeder reactors (from the second stage) continue to be of importance for India's weapons program, as we describe below. So apart from the prototype reactor, currently under construction, it is possible that a few others will be built. This is not of much relevance to the energy projections above.

24. 'The Heart of the Matter'. *Outlook*, 3 October 2009.

25. G. Venkataraman, *Bhabha and his Magnificent Obsessions*, Universities Press, 2008.

26. Bhabha Atomic Research Center, 'Atomic Energy in India', http://www.barc.ernet.in/about/anu1.htm

27. These are two common isotopes of uranium, i.e., they have identical chemical properties but different physical properties. The number in the superscript gives the total number of protons+neutrons in the nucleus. For the purposes of this article, it is sufficient for the reader to know that U235 is the form that is useful as fissile fuel.

28. Some developing countries like China have also announced ambitious plans for nuclear expansion.

29. Keith Bradsher, 'Nuclear Power Expansion in China Stirs Concerns', *The New York Times*, 15 December 2009.

30. 'Nuclear power's new age', *The Economist*, 6 September 2007.

31. Health and Safety Executive, UK, Generic Design Assessment of New Nuclear Reactor Designs AREVA NP SAS and EDF SA UK EPR Nuclear Reactor, 2009.

32. Health and Safety Executive, UK, Generic Design Assessment of New Nuclear Reactor Designs, Westinghouse Electric Company LLC AP1000 Nuclear Reactor, 2009.

33. 'Nuclear reactors contain safety flaws, watchdog reveals', *The Guardian*, 27 November 2009.

34. Amory B. Lovins and Imran Sheikh, '*The Nuclear Illusion*', tech. rep., Rocky Mountain Institute, 27 May 2008.

35. M.V. Ramana, 'Heavy Subsidies: The Cost of Heavy Water Production', *Economic and Political Weekly*, 25 August 2007.

36. M.R. Srinivasan, R.B. Grover, and S.A. Bharadwaj, 'Nuclear power in India: Winds of change', *Economic and Political Weekly*, vol. 3, p. 5184, 2005.

37. Sudhinder Thakur, 'Economics of Nuclear Power in India: The Real Picture', *Economic and Political Weekly*, vol. 40, no. 49, p. 5209, 2005.

38. M.V. Ramana, A. D'Sa, and A.K.N. Reddy, 'Economics of nuclear power from heavy water reactors', Economic and Political Weekly, vol. 40, no. 17, pp. 1763–73, 2005.

39. M.V. Ramana, 'Economics of Nuclear Power: Subsidies and Competitiveness', *Economic and Political Weekly*, vol. 42, no. 2, p. 169, 2007.

40. George S. Tolley, Donald W. Jones, et al., 'The Economic Future of Nuclear Power', tech. rep., University of Chicago, 2004.

41. The Chicago study used data from an OECD estimate of electricity generation costs from 1998. By 2005, the OECD estimates had changed and its report on projected electricity generating costs found nuclear power to be cheaper in several countries! The OECD bases its conclusions on questionnaires sent to different countries and the data used in the 2005 report is rather suspect. For example, on page 43, the overnight construction cost for a nuclear plant in Finland is taken to be about 2000 USD/kW. The Areva plant current under construction in Finland is expected to cost more than USD 6 billion and provide 1600 MW of power leading to a cost per kW that is almost twice as large as the cost used by the OECD.

42. 'Atomic renaissance', *The Economist*, 6 September 2007.

43. 'Splitting the cost', *The Economist*, 12 November 2009.

44. However nuclear power does continue to be considerably cheaper than some alternative forms of energy, like solar power.

45. Kenneth Kok (ed.), Nuclear Engineering Handbook, CRC Press, 2009.

46. M.V. Ramana, Dennis George Thomas, and Susy Varughese, 'Estimating nuclear waste production in India', Current Science, vol. 81, no. 11, p. 1458, 2001.

47. Department of Atomic Energy, *Our Collective Vision*, August 2004.

48. World Health Organization, Health Effects of the Chernobyl Accident and Special Health Care Programs, 2006. Report of the U.N. Chernobyl Form Expert Group 'Health'.

49. Greenpeace, The Chernobyl Catastrophe: Consequences on Human Health, April 2006.

50. Of course, uranium mining is also hazardous. However, because it is carried out on so much smaller a scale than coal-mining, accidents are fewer.

51. International Atomic Energy Agency, 'The Chernobyl Accident: Updating of INSAG-1', 1992, A report by the International Nuclear Safety Advisory Group. Available from: http://www-pub.iaea.org/MTCD/publications/PDF/Pub913e_web.pdf

52. Ted Plafker, 'Chinese coal industry in need of a helping hand', *The New York Times*, 19 June 2007.

53. Jim Yardley, 'As most of China celebrates New Year, a scramble continues in coal country'. *The New York Times*, 9 February 2008.

54. Ministry of Coal, 'The fatality rates per 3 lakh manshift in the coal mines of India and that of other countries', http://coal.nic.in/weboflife-minessafety/fatality_rates_per_3_lakh_manshi.htm

55. Ministry of Coal, 'Annual Report 2007–08', 2008, http://coal.nic.in/annrep0708.pdf

56. Ministry of Coal, 'Annual Report 2007–08', 2008, http://coal.nic.in/annrep0708.pdf

57. Kirit S. Parikh, T.L. Sankar, Amit Mitra, et al., *Integrated Energy Policy: Report of the Expert Committee*. Planning Commission, August 2006.

58. A cartel, dominated by the U.S. and other imperialist countries, that controls international nuclear trade.

59. Homi Bhabha, 'Note on the Organization of Atomic Research in India', 26 April 1948, reproduced in *Nuclear India*, vol. 26, 1989.

60. The AEC has since been somewhat enlarged. As of December 2009, it had 12 members including the chairperson, who is the head of the DAE, and one MP—Prithviraj Chavan—the Minister of State, in the PMO, for science and technology.

61. Atomic Energy Regulatory Board. 'The Formation of AERB: Down the Memory Lane', http://www.aerb.gov.in/cgi-bin/aboutaerb/AboutAERB.asp

62. A. Gopalakrishnan, 'Issues of nuclear safety', *Frontline*, vol. 16, 13 March 1999.

63. M. Das, 'An alarmist view on nuclear safety: NPC speaks', *Frontline*, vol. 16, 8 May 1999.

64. 'Convention on nuclear safety', INFCIRC/449, 5 July 1994. http://www.iaea.org/Publications/Documents/Infcircs/Others/inf449.shtml

65. World Nuclear Association. 'Fast Neutron Reactors', http://www.world-nuclear.org/info/inf98.html

66. Ministry of Statistics and Program Implementation, Project Implementation Status Report of Central Sector Projects Costing Rs20 Crore and Above, (January–March 2009). http://www.mospi.gov.in/QSR_jan_march_2009.pdf

67. Bharatiya Nabhikiya Vidyut Nigam Limited, 6th Annual Report 2008–2009. http://www.bhavini.nic.in/attachments/Bhavini\%20-\%20Final.pdf

68. International Atomic Energy Agency. 'Brief History of IAEA's Project on Technology Advances in Fast Reactors and Accelerator Driven Systems', http://www-frdb.iaea.org/auxiliary/history.html, Fast Reactor Database, 2006.

69. M.V. Ramana, 'The Indian Nuclear Industry: Status and Prospects', 9 December 2009. Nuclear Energy Futures Paper #9. Available from: http://www.cigionline.org/publications/2009/12/indian-nuclear-industry-status-and-prospects

70. Ashwin Kumar and M.V. Ramana, 'Compromising Safety: Design Choices and Severe Accident Possibilities in India's Prototype Fast Breeder Reactor', *Science and Global Security*, vol. 16, no. 3, pp. 87–114, 2008.

71. S. Raghupathy, Om Pal Singh, S. Govindarajanand, S.C. Chetal, and S.B. Bhoje, 'Design of 500 Mwe Prototype Fast Breeder Reactor', *Nuclear India*, vol. 37, April 2004.

72. M.V. Ramana and J. Y. Suchitra, 'Slow and stunted: Plutonium accounting and the growth of fast breeder reactors in India', *Energy Policy*, 2009.

73. World Nuclear Association, 'Thorium,' http://www.world-nuclear.org/info/inf62.html

74. K. Anantharaman, V. Shivakumar, and D. Saha, 'Utilisation of thorium in reactors', *Journal of Nuclear Materials*, vol. 383, no. 1–2, pp. 119–21, 2008.

75. Homi Bhabha, 'Peaceful Uses of Atomic Energy', Presidential Address to the International Conference on the Peaceful uses of Atomic Energy, 8 August 1955.

76. Itty Abraham, *The Making of the Indian Atomic Bomb: Science, Secrecy and the Postcolonial State*, p. 49, Orient Longman, 1999.

77. Contrary to a widespread belief, this oxymoronic term was not invented by the Indian government. The American government had for long argued for the use of nuclear devices for civilian purposes such as broadening canals. Bhabha simply adopted the terminology from an American study on the Peaceful Uses of Atomic Explosions.

78. George Perkovich, *India's Nuclear Bomb: The Impact on Global Proliferation*, University of California, 2002.

79. Anand Patwardhan, 'War and Peace', Transcript of Chapter 1: 'Non-violence to Nuclear Nationalism'.

80. P.K. Iyengar. 'Briefings on Nuclear Technology in India', May 2009. http://pkiyengar.in/yahoo_site_admin/assets/docs/New_version_book_May_2009.124232514.pdf

81. U.S. Department of Energy, Non-proliferation and Arms Control Assessment of Weapons-Usable Fissile Material Storage and Excess Plutonium Disposition Alternatives, January 1997.

82. The word 'proliferation' is, of course, problematic because it is applied only to the spread of weapons of mass destruction outside the control of imperialist governments.

83. Zia Mian, A.H. Nayyar, R. Rajaraman, and M.V. Ramana, 'Fissile materials in South Asia: The Implications of the U.S.–India Nuclear Deal', tech. rep., International Panel on Fissile Materials, September 2006.

84. Alexander Glaser and M.V. Ramana, 'Weapon-Grade Plutonium Production Potential in the Indian Prototype Fast Breeder Reactor', Science and Global Security, vol. 15, no. 2, p. 85, 2007.

85. Siddharth Varadarajan, 'Safeguards for breeder reactors a key obstacle'. *The Hindu*, 21 January 2006.

86. Pallava Bagla, 'Anil Kakodkar Interview: Breaking Up (a Nuclear Program) is Hard to Do', *Science*, vol. 311, no. 5762, pp. 765–66, 2006.

87. Richard Stone and Pallava Bagla, 'Proliferation: Last-Minute Nuclear Deal Has Long-Term Repercussions', Science, vol. 311, no. 5766, pp. 1356–1357, 2006.

88. Taraknath V.K. Woddi, William S. Charlton, and Paul Nelson, India's Nuclear Fuel Cycle: Unravelling the Impact of the US–India Nuclear Accord, No. 1, in: *Synthesis Lectures on Nuclear Technology and Society*, Morgan & Claypool Publishers, 2009.

89. Ashok Parthasarathi, *Technology at the Core: Science & Technology with Indira Gandhi*, Pearson Longman, 2007.

90. Suvrat Raju, 'The Nuclear Deal and Democracy', *Counter Currents*, 10 July 2008.

91. Andrew Buncombe, 'Fuel costs push India's inflation rate to 13-year high'. *The Independent*, 5 July 2008.

92. Zia Mian and M.V. Ramana, 'Wrong Ends, Means, and Needs: Behind the U.S. Nuclear Deal with India', *Arms Control Today*, vol. 36, January/February 2006.

93. Aziz Haniffa, 'Interview with Ashley J. Tellis', *India Abroad*, 20 July 2007.

94. Noam Chomsky, 'The Iraq War and Contempt for Democracy', *Znet*, 31 October 2003.

95. Aziz Haniffa, 'Ambassador Sen: "We will have zero credibility"'. *Rediff News*, 20 August 2007.

96. Ashton Carter, 'The India Deal: Looking at the Big Picture', Testimony before the Committee on Foreign Relations, U.S. Senate, 2 November 2005.

97. P. Chidambaram, 'Convocation Address, IIM Ahmedabad', 31 March 2007.

98. Manmohan Singh, 'Inaugural address', in: *4th International Conference on Federalism*, 5 November 2007.

ACRONYMS

AEC—(Atomic Energy Commission)
AEOI—(Atomic Energy Organization of Iran)
AHWR—(Advanced Heavy-Water Reactor)
ASW—(Anti-Submarine Warfare)
AWACS—(Airborne Warning and Control System)
BARC—(Bhabha Atomic Research Centre)
BJP—(Bharatiya Janata Party)
CBMs—(Confidence Building Measures)
CD—(Conference on Disarmament)
CENTCOM—(Central Command)
CIRUS—(Canadian Indian Reactor U.S.)
CJCSC—(Chairman of the Joint Chiefs of Staff Committee)
CSIR—(Council of Scientific and Industrial Research)
CTBT—(Comprehensive Test Ban Treaty)
DAE—(Department of Atomic Energy)
DPC—(Difah-e-Pakistan Council)
DRDL—(Defense Research and Development Laboratory)
DRDO—(Defense Research and Development Organization)
DSMAC—(Digital Scene Matching and Area Co-relation)
ENDS (Enhanced Nuclear Detonation Safety)
ESDs—(Environment Sensitive Devices)
ETIM—(East Turkestan Islamic Movement)
FATA—(Federally-Administered Tribal Areas)
FMCT—(Fissile Material Cut-off Treaty)
GCC—(Gulf Cooperation Council)
GHQ—(General Head Quarters)
GIKI—(Ghulam Ishaq Khan Institute of Engineering Sciences and Technology)
HRP—(Human Reliability Program)
HSE—[British] (Health and Safety Executive)
HuM—(Hizb-ul-Mujahideen)
IAEA—(International Atomic Energy Agency)
IBGs—(Integrated Battle Groups)

ICBM—(System Inter-Continental Ballistic Missile)
IDSA—(Institute of Defense and Strategic Analysis)
IED—(Improvised Explosive Device)
IGMDP—(Integrated Guided Missile Development Program)
ISI—(Inter-Services Intelligence)
ISIS—(Institute for Science and International Security)
JeM—(Jaish-e-Muhammad)
KANUPP—(Karachi Nuclear Power Plant)
LeT—(Lashkar-e-Tayyaba)
LEU—(Low Enriched Uranium)
MAD—(Mutually Assured Destruction)
MFA—(Ministry of Foreign Affairs)
MFN—(Most Favoured Nation)
MIT—(Massachusetts Institute of Technology)
MPNR—(Ministry of Petroleum and Natural Resources)
MQM—(Muttahida Qaumi Mahaz, formerly Muhajir Qaumi Movement)
MWP—(Ministry of Water and Power)
NAS—(National Academy of Sciences)
NCA—(National Command Authority)
NEST—(Nuclear Emergency Search Team)
NISA—(Nuclear and Industrial Safety Agency)
NORAD—(North American Aerospace Defense Command)
NPT—(Nuclear Non-Proliferation Treaty)
NRC—(National Research Council)
NRRs—(Nuclear Risk Reduction Measures)
NSG—(Nuclear Suppliers Group)
NUST—(National University of Science and Technology)
NWFP—(North-West Frontier Province)
PAEC—(Pakistan Atomic Energy Commission)
PALs—(Permissive Action Links)
PAVE PAWS—(Perimeter Acquisition Vehicle Entry Phased-Array Weapons
System)
PFBR—(Prototype Fast-Breeder Reactor)
PHWRs—(Pressurized Heavy-Water Reactors)
PINSTECH—(Pakistan Institute of Nuclear Science & Technology)
PNE—(Peaceful Nuclear Explosives)
PNRA—(Pakistan Nuclear Regulatory Authority)
PRIS—(Power Reactor Information System)
PRP—(Personnel Reliability Program)

PWR—(Pressurized Water Reactor)
QA—(Quality Assurance)
RAW—(Research and Analysis Wing)
SAARC—(South Asian Association for Regional Cooperation)
SAGE—(Semi-Automatic Ground Environment)
SAM—(Surface-to-Air Missile)
SANWFZ—(South Asian Nuclear-Weapons-Free Zone)
SDPI—(Sustainable Development Policy Institute)
SLBMs—(Submarine-Launched Ballistic Missile)
SNERDI—(Shanghai Nuclear Engineering Research and Design Institute)
SOLIC (Special Operations and Low-Intensity Conflict)
SPD—(Strategic Plans Division)
TEL—(Transporter-Erector-Launcher)
TERCOM—(Terrain Contour Matching)
TNWs—(Theatre Nuclear Weapons)
TOI—(*Times of India*)
TTP—(Pakistani Tehreek-e-Taliban)
UAVs—(Unmanned Aerial Vehicles, commonly known as drones)
UET—(University of Engineering Technology)
UPA—(United Progressive Alliance)